INSTRUCTOR'S RESOURCE MANUAL

America's History

Volume 2 Since 1865

Bradley T. Gericke

*U.S. Army Command
and General Staff College*

Bedford/St. Martin's

Boston ◆ New York

Manufactured in the United States of America.

7 6 5 4 3
f e d c b a

For information, write: Bedford/St. Martin's, 75 Arlington Street, Boston, MA 02116 (617-399-4000)

ISBN: 0–312–41185–5

Preface

The questions historians pose about the past are often more illuminating than the answers that are revealed. It is the process of inquiry that propels the historical method forward and provides our profession the unique ability to contribute to the human condition. This *Instructor's Resource Manual* should be a valuable tool for every teacher who loves the questions of American history. Designed for use with *America's History*, Fifth Edition, by James Henretta, David Brody, and Lynn Dumenil, it contains a vast array of relevant and informative material for the novice and veteran instructor alike. It has been thoroughly edited and revised to achieve greater clarity and precision of expression while maintaining the essential features of the previous edition that have proven so successful.

Since every instructor teaches history differently, the resources presented can feasibly be used in a variety of ways, giving you many options for designing and redesigning a course to focus on specific topics or areas of interest.

Chapter Resources

Instructional Objectives presented in a question format open each part and chapter. Instructors can use the objectives to organize and refine their delivery, to craft exams, and to aid students' understanding of the reading.

A **Chapter Summary** provides a succinct recap of the text's most essential issues and arguments. This information is fully dissected in the **Chapter Annotated Outline**. As quick surveys of the full reading, these complete outlines reflect the narrative of the text and serve as excellent memory joggers. They should prove quite useful to keep at lectern-side or when preparing speaking notes before class.

The **Lecture Strategies** for each chapter outline key themes that instructors may wish to consider and suggest ways that the text may be presented. To prompt in-class discussion, and particularly effective for new instructors or those coming to the subject material for the first time, there are **Class Discussion Starters**. This feature consists of questions with several possible responses to help students interact with the factual information in the text.

Chapter Writing Assignments provide questions that seek to build upon the text and require a longer, more developed answer to address. This feature may assist instructors to fashion quizzes or exams.

Students can gain practice in working with primary material through the **Document Exercises**. Both **Document Discussion** questions and **Writing Assignments** provoke discussion and encourage student reflection about the American Voices, Voices from Abroad, American Lives, and New Technology features in the textbook. **Skill-Building Map Exercises** highlight key aspects of the text's maps and help students to understand how maps can enhance their comprehension of the written narrative.

Each chapter has a **Topic for Research** that provides direction for further study and can be a starting point for instructors who wish to pursue more fully a particular period or topic.

This manual serves as a keystone for the comprehensive collection of ancillaries available for *America's History*, Fifth Edition. To help instructors utilize this wealth of resources we have added a section on **How to Use the Ancillaries Available with *America's History*** to all chapters in the *Instructor's Resource Manual*. This detailed, chapter-by-chapter guide outlines specific supplementary readings and custom-made online activities that will provide integrated support to the U.S. history survey and allow instructors to customize their course to suit their students' needs. For a full description of all of these ancillaries, please see the Preface to *America's History* (p. vii).

Acknowledgments

This manual was made possible by the combined efforts of many people. While there are far too many to list individually, there are several whom I would particularly like to thank: development editor Corinne McCutchen, whose talented and incisive editorial work elevated this manual with fresh scholarship; editorial assistant Elizabeth Harrison, whose expert guidance directed this project from beginning to end; production editor Tina Lai, whose watchful eye ensured consistency and accuracy in the text; and, most important, my wife Tonya, whose instinctive acumen and steadfast commitment created the opportunity for this project to become a reality.

Perhaps the highest compliment that can be paid to a text is that it spends little time on the shelf. Such is our hope for the *Instructor's Resource Manual*. If we have done our job well, the copy you hold today will soon be dog-eared and tattered. Please let us know how we have done, and best wishes for your journey through *America's History*.

Bradley T. Gericke

Contents

CHAPTER 15

Reconstruction

1865–1877

Chapter Instructional Objectives

After you have taught this chapter, your students should be able to answer the following questions:

1. How did Presidents Lincoln and Johnson envision Reconstruction?

2. How and why did Republicans in Congress take control of Reconstruction?

3. Analyze and explain what African Americans expected and the realities they encountered during Reconstruction.

4. What was the southern response(s) to Reconstruction?

5. Analyze and explain the political crisis of 1877 and the end of Reconstruction.

6. What were the successes and failures of Reconstruction?

Chapter Summary

When the Civil War ended in 1865, the slaves had been emancipated and the South militarily defeated, but there was no consensus about how to integrate the slaves into American society and restore the rebel states into the Union.

Presidents Lincoln and Johnson attempted to install loyal state governments quickly but faced opposition from congressional Republicans who wanted to punish southerners. Johnson foiled his Republican opponents while Congress was not in session by restoring the southern states on generous terms, but Johnson refused to give land on plantations confiscated by Union troops to African Americans who had hoped to keep it.

Johnson's supporters fared poorly in the congressional elections of 1866, so congressional Republicans divided the South into five military districts through the Reconstruction Act of 1867. Congress impeached Johnson, failing to convict him by only one vote, and in 1868 the nation elected Ulysses S. Grant, a supporter of the Radical Republicans, to the presidency.

Southern state governments under Republican control included African Americans, white southerners who hoped to attract northern capital or rid the South of the planter aristocracy, and northerners who moved south to settle. They modernized and democratized state governments and built schools, hospitals, roads, and railroads. African Americans built their own social institutions, creating new communities and founding their own churches.

Former slave owners united in the Democratic Party to regain political control of the South. Appealing to racial solidarity and southern patriotism, they gained the allegiance of poorer whites and terrorized black voters through violent secret societies. Grant's unwillingness to risk reopening the war allowed former Confederates to regain control of all but three southern states by 1877. With diminishing political power and limited land redistribution, freedmen became sharecroppers in debt to the landlords and merchants who provided them with supplies at exorbitant prices and interest.

During his second term, Grant's administration was plagued by scandals and economic depression. In 1876, although Democrat Samuel J. Tilden won the popular vote, electoral votes were contested in the three southern states still under military control. A congressional commission gave the contested electoral votes to Republican Rutherford B. Hayes, a decision congressional Democrats accepted. Reconstruction then ended, leaving African Americans without federal support.

Chapter Annotated Outline

I.   Presidential Reconstruction
   A. Lincoln's Approach
      1. The Constitution did not address the question of secession or any procedure for Reconstruction, so it did not say which branch of government was to handle the readmission of rebellious states.
      2. Lincoln offered general amnesty to all but high-ranking Confederates willing to pledge loyalty to the Union; when 10 percent of a state's voters took this oath — and abolished slavery — the state would be restored to the Union.
      3. Most Confederate states rebuffed the offer, assuring that the war would have to be fought to the bitter end.
      4. As some African Americans began to agitate for political rights, congressional Republicans proposed the Wade-Davis Bill, a stricter substitute for Lincoln's Ten Percent Plan.
      5. The Wade-Davis Bill served notice that congressional Republicans were not going to turn Reconstruction policy over to the president.
      6. Rather than openly challenge Congress, Lincoln executed a pocket veto of the Wade-Davis Bill by not signing it before Congress adjourned.
   B. Johnson's Initiative
      1. Andrew Johnson, a Jacksonian Democrat, championed poor whites. A slave owner himself, he had little sympathy for formerly enslaved blacks.
      2. The Republicans had nominated Johnson for vice president in 1864 in order to promote wartime political unity and to court southern Unionists.
      3. After Lincoln's death, Johnson offered amnesty to all southerners except high-ranking Confederate officials and wealthy property owners who took an oath of allegiance to the Constitution and ratified the Thirteenth Amendment.
      4. Within months, all the former Confederate states had met Johnson's requirements for rejoining the Union and had functioning, elected governments.
      5. Southerners held fast to the antebellum order and enacted Black Codes designed to drive the ex-slaves back to plantations and deny them civil rights.
      6. Southerners perceived Johnson's liberal amnesty policy as tacit approval of the Black Codes; emboldened, the ex-Confederates filled southern congressional delegation with old comrades.
      7. Republicans in both houses refused to admit the southern delegations, and the Joint Committee on Reconstruction began public hearings on conditions in the South.
      8. In response, some Black Codes were replaced with nonracial ordinances whose effect was the same, and across the South a wave of violence erupted against the freedmen.
      9. Congress voted to extend the life of the Freedmen's Bureau and authorized its agents to investigate cases of discrimination against blacks.
      10. Lyman Trumbull, chairman of the Judiciary Committee, proposed a Civil Rights Bill that declared all persons — regardless of race — born in the United States to be citizens and gave them equal rights.
      11. Republicans demanded that the federal government accept responsibility for securing the basic civil rights of the freedmen.
   C. Acting on Freedom
      1. Across the South, ex-slaves held mass meetings and formed organizations; they demanded equality before the law and the right to vote.
      2. In the months before the end of the war, freedmen had seized control of land where they could; General Sherman had reserved tracts of land for liberated blacks in his March to the Sea.
      3. When the war ended, the Freedmen's Bureau was charged with feeding and clothing war refugees, distributing confiscated lands to "loyal refugees and freedmen," and regulating labor contracts between freedmen and planters.
      4. Johnson's amnesty plan entitled pardoned Confederates to recover confiscated property, shattering the freedmen's hopes of keeping the land on which they lived.
      5. To try to hold onto their land, blacks fought pitched battles with plantation owners and bands of ex-Confederate soldiers; generally the whites prevailed.
      6. A struggle took place over the labor system that would replace slavery; because owning land defined true freedom, ex-slaves resisted working for wages, preferring to sharecrop, even though sharecropping was not in their best interest financially.
      7. Many freedpeople abandoned their old plantations in order to seek better lives and more freedom in the cities of the South; those who remained refused to work under the gang-labor system.

8. To help former slaves with their struggle to control their lives, blacks turned to Washington and the federal government.

D. Congress versus President

1. In February 1866, Andrew Johnson vetoed the Freedmen's Bureau Bill and a month later vetoed Trumbull's Civil Rights Bill calling it discriminatory against whites.

2. Galvanized by Johnson's attack on the Civil Rights Bill, Republicans enacted the Civil Rights Act of 1866; Congress had never before overridden a veto on a major piece of legislation.

3. As an angry Congress renewed the Freedmen's Bureau over a second Johnson veto, Republican resolve was reinforced by news of mounting violence in the South.

4. Republicans moved to enshrine black civil rights in the Fourteenth Amendment to the U.S. Constitution.

5. Johnson urged the states not to ratify the amendment and began to maneuver politically against the Republicans; the Fourteenth Amendment became a campaign issue for the Democratic Party.

6. Republicans responded furiously by decrying Democrats as the party responsible for the Civil War, a tactic that came to be known as "waving the bloody shirt."

7. Johnson embarked on a disastrous railroad tour campaign and made matters worse by engaging in shouting matches and exchanging insults with the hostile crowds.

8. Republicans won a three-to-one majority in the 1866 congressional elections, which registered overwhelming support for securing the civil rights of ex-slaves.

9. The Republican Party had a new sense of unity coalescing around the unbending program of the radical minority, which represented the party's abolitionist strain.

10. For the Radicals, Reconstruction was never primarily about restoring the Union but rather remaking southern society, beginning with getting the black man his right to vote.

II. Radical Reconstruction

A. Congress Takes Command

1. The Reconstruction Act of 1867 divided the South into five military districts, each under the command of a Union general.

2. The price for reentering the Union was granting the vote to the freedmen and disenfranchising the South's prewar political class.

3. Congress overrode Johnson's veto of the Reconstruction Act and, in effect, attempted to reconstruct the presidency with the Tenure of Office Act.

4. After Congress adjourned in August 1867, Johnson "suspended" Edwin M. Stanton and replaced him with General Ulysses S. Grant; he then replaced four of the commanding generals governing the South.

5. When the Senate reconvened, it overruled Stanton's suspension, and Grant, now Johnson's enemy, resigned so that Stanton could resume office.

6. On February 21, 1868, Johnson dismissed Stanton; the House Republicans introduced articles of impeachment against Johnson, mainly for violations of the Tenure of Office Act.

7. A vote on impeachment was one vote short of the required two-thirds majority needed, but Johnson was left powerless to alter the course of Reconstruction.

8. Grant was the Republicans' 1868 presidential nominee, and he won out over the Democrats' Horatio Seymour; Republicans retained two-thirds majorities in both houses of Congress.

9. The Fifteenth Amendment forbade either the federal government or the states to deny citizens the right to vote on the basis of race, color, or "previous condition of servitude."

10. States still under federal control were required to ratify the amendment before being readmitted to the Union; the Fifteenth Amendment became part of the Constitution.

11. Women's rights advocates were outraged that the Fifteenth Amendment did not address women's suffrage.

12. At the 1869 annual meeting of the Equal Rights Association, Elizabeth Cady Stanton and Susan B. Anthony spoke out against the amendment.

13. The majority, led by Lucy Stone and Julia Ward Howe of the American Women's Suffrage Association, accepted the priority of black suffrage over women's suffrage.

14. Stanton's new organization, the National Women's Suffrage Association, accepted only women and took up the battle for a federal woman suffrage amendment.

15. Fracturing of the women's movement obscured the common ground of the two sides, until both sides realized that a broader popular constituency had to be built.

B. Republican Rule in the South

1. Southern whites who became Republicans were called "scalawags" by Democratic ex-Confederates; rich white northerners who

moved to the South were called "carpetbaggers."

2. Some scalawags were former slave owners who wanted to attract northern capital, but most were yeoman farmers who wanted to rid the South of its slaveholding aristocracy.

3. Although never proportionate to their size in population, black officeholders were prominent throughout the South.

4. Republicans modernized state constitutions, eliminated property qualifications for voting, got rid of the Black Codes, and expanded the rights of married women.

5. Reconstruction social programs called for hospitals, more humane penitentiaries, and asylums; Reconstruction governments built roads and revived the railroad network.

6. To pay for their programs, Republicans introduced property taxes that applied to personal wealth as well as to real estate, similar to the taxes the Jacksonians had used in the North.

7. In many plantation counties, former slaves served as tax assessors and collectors, administering the taxation of their onetime owners.

8. Reconstruction governments' debts mounted rapidly, and public credit collapsed; much of the spending was wasted or ended up in the pockets of state officials.

9. Republican state governments viewed education as the foundation of a democratic order and had to make up for lost time since the South had virtually no public education.

10. New African American churches served as schools, social centers, and political meeting halls as well as places of worship.

11. Black ministers were community leaders and often political officeholders; they provided a powerful religious underpinning for the Republican politics of their congregations.

C. The Quest for Land

1. The Southern Homestead Act of 1866 was mostly symbolic since the public land it made available to former slaves was in swampy, infertile parts of the lower South.

2. After Johnson's order restoring confiscated lands to the ex-Confederates, the Freedmen's Bureau devoted itself to teaching blacks how to be good agricultural laborers.

3. Sharecropping was a distinctive labor system for cotton agriculture in which the freedmen worked as tenant farmers, exchanging their labor for the use of land.

4. Sharecropping was an unequal relationship, since the sharecropper had no way of making

it through the first growing season without borrowing for food and supplies.

5. Storekeepers "furnished" the sharecropper and took as collateral a lien on the crop; as cotton prices declined during the 1870s, many sharecroppers fell into permanent debt.

6. If the merchant was also the landowner, the debt became a pretext for peonage, or forced labor.

7. Sharecropping did mobilize black husbands and wives in common enterprise and shielded both from personal subordination to whites.

8. By the end of Reconstruction, about one-quarter of sharecropping families saved enough to rent with cash, and eventually many black farmers owned about a third of the land they farmed.

9. Sharecropping committed the South inflexibly to cotton because it was a cash crop; the South lost its self-sufficiency in grains and livestock, and it did not put money into agricultural improvements.

III. The Undoing of Reconstruction

A. Counterrevolution

1. Democrats worked hard to get the vote restored to ex-Confederates, appealing to racial solidarity and southern patriotism and attacking black suffrage as a threat to white supremacy.

2. The Ku Klux Klan first appeared in Tennessee as a social club, but under Nathan Bedford Forrest, it quickly became a paramilitary force used against blacks.

3. By 1870 the Klan was operating almost everywhere in the South as an armed force whose terrorist tactics served the Democratic Party.

4. The Ku Klux Klan Act of 1871 authorized Grant to use federal prosecutions, military force, and martial law to suppress conspiracies that deprived citizens of the right to vote, holding office, serving on juries, and enjoying equal protection of the law.

5. The Grant administration's assault on the Klan illustrates how dependent African Americans and the southern Republicans were on the federal government.

6. But northern Republicans were growing weary of Reconstruction and the bloodshed it seemed to produce, and sympathy for the freedmen also began to wane.

7. Prosecuting Klansmen under the enforcement acts was difficult, and only a small fraction served significant prison terms.

8. Between 1873 and 1875, Democrats overthrew Republican governments in Texas, Alabama, Arkansas, and Mississippi.

9. In Mississippi, local Democrats paraded armed, kept assassination lists of blacks called "dead books," and provoked rioting that killed hundreds of African Americans.

10. By 1876, Republican governments remained in only Louisiana, South Carolina, and Florida; elsewhere the former Confederates were back in control.

B. The Acquiescent North

1. Sympathy for the freedmen began to wane, as the North was flooded with one-sided, often racist reports describing extravagant, corrupt Republican rule and a South in the grip of a "massive black barbarism."

2. The political cynicism that overtook the Civil Rights Act signaled the Republican Party's reversion to the practical politics of earlier days.

3. Some Republicans had little enthusiasm for Reconstruction, except as it benefited their party, and as the party lost headway in the South, they abandoned any interest in the battle for black rights.

4. As Grant's administration lapsed into cronyism, a revolt took shape inside the Republican Party; the dissidents broke away and formed a new party called the Liberal Republicans.

5. The Liberal Republicans nominated Horace Greeley during the 1872 election; the Democratic Party, still in disarray, also nominated Greeley.

6. Grant won the election overwhelmingly, yet the Democrats adopted the Liberal Republicans' agenda of civil service reform, limited government, and reconciliation with the South as they reclaimed their place as a legitimate national party.

7. Charges of Republican corruption came to a head in 1875 with a scandal known as the "Whiskey Ring"; the scandal implicating Grant's cronies and even his private secretary engulfed the White House.

8. The economy fell into a severe depression after 1873; among the casualties was the Freedmen's Savings and Trust Company, and many ex-slaves lost their life savings.

9. In denying the blacks' plea for help with their banking disaster, Congress signaled that Reconstruction had lost its moral claim on the country.

C. The Political Crisis of 1877

1. Republicans nominated Rutherford B. Hayes as their presidential candidate, and his Democratic opponent was Samuel J. Tilden; both favored "home rule" for the South.

2. When Congress met in early 1877, it was faced with both Republican and Democratic electoral votes from Florida, South Carolina, and Louisiana.

3. The Constitution declares that Congress regulates its own elections, so Congress appointed an electoral commission; the commission awarded the disputed votes to Hayes by a vote of 8 to 7.

4. Democrats controlled the House and set about stalling a final count of the electoral votes, but on March 1 they suddenly ended their filibuster, and Hayes was inaugurated. Reconstruction had ended.

5. By 1877, however, three rights-defining amendments had been added to the Constitution, there was room for blacks to advance economically, and they had confidence that they could lift themselves up.

Lecture Strategies

1. Presidential Reconstruction is a complex topic. Discuss why the executive branch preferred lenient plans for the South. Explore Lincoln's early policies toward the South as well as his last speech, which moved toward an endorsement of freedmen's suffrage. Examine Johnson's policies as an attempt to build a coalition to oppose congressional Republicans. Consider Johnson's hope of rooting southern politics in the independent yeomanry as a reflection of his own background and the principles of Jefferson and Jackson. Historians typically rate Johnson as one of our worst presidents and Lincoln as one of the best. Consider how Lincoln might have fared if he had lived. How would he have handled Congress and the South? Consider the degree to which Johnson's problems were of his own making and which were the product of a vengeful Congress.

2. Students often have difficulty keeping track of the changes in the period of 1865 to 1877, from the two presidents' policies, to a Congress torn between moderate and Radical Republicans, to the loss of commitment on the part of the North, and the resulting success of those wishing to deny civil rights to blacks. Stress the reverses in policy caused by these changes and their impact on the South. Emphasize the fact that this wavering in policy was due to the constant struggle for political power both in the South and in Washington, D.C.

3. Explain to students the important precedent set by the Johnson impeachment and hearing. Begin with the reasons for Lincoln's choice of Johnson as his vice president. Explain Johnson's quarrels with congres-

sional Republicans over Reconstruction, including his vetoes of the civil rights bill and extension of the Freedmen's Bureau and his attempt to build an opposition party. Discuss the Tenure of Office Act and review the Supreme Court's conclusion that it was a breach of constitutional separation of powers, referring to Article II of the Constitution. Explore the impeachment hearing and the decisions of the various congressmen. Discuss the precedent set by impeaching Johnson on criminal, not political grounds. Compare Johnson's impeachment to Congress's situation during the presidencies of Richard Nixon and Bill Clinton.

4. Explore the changing historiography of Reconstruction. Discuss the historical interpretation that black suffrage was a disaster for the South. Explain how this interpretation survived for so long because it fit with American prejudices as well as with social and political realities. Discuss the impact of the civil rights movement of the 1950s and 1960s on changing interpretations of Reconstruction. Consider whether the Radical Republicans were cynical, self-serving politicians or idealists. Thaddeus Stevens is a good example of the radical as idealist. Explore whether the Radicals' programs were practical or unrealistically visionary. Discuss the Radicals' linkage of political power for freedmen with economic independence. Explore why land distribution was unacceptable to many people in the North. Relate these issues to the present day, showing how political and economic power are linked today, as well as the extent of the American commitment to protecting private property.

5. The Freedmen's Bureau is an interesting topic for students. Explain who became involved in it and why. Describe the conditions agents found in the South. Discuss what the bureau tried to do in education, employment, housing, and medical care and then explore the bureau's degree of success in those areas. Question whether the Freedmen's Bureau was essentially radical or conservative, and why.

6. Discuss the struggle in the South among former slave owners, independent yeomen, and freedmen. Describe the goals of each group; show where they conflicted and where possible alliances existed between any two groups. Show how these groups struggled over labor control, race relations, and political power and how these three issues were interrelated. Discuss the crucial role played by white small-acreage farmers, and explain how and why the planters courted them. Explain how the resulting systems of sharecropping and segregation represented compromises among the three groups. Compare the situation in the southern states with the end of slavery in other

countries, particularly in the Caribbean. Explain some of the factors that made the United States different, including demographics and the attempt to achieve political equality during Reconstruction.

7. Explore the contributions of the African American community to southern Republican state governments. Use the careers of men such as Blanche K. Bruce to illustrate how African Americans participated in politics. Describe the accomplishments of these governments, including the democratization of southern politics and the development of the southern infrastructure (schools, roads, railroads). Show how African Americans addressed the needs of their community. Explain, however, that this community was not always unified. Compare and contrast the interests and goals of freedmen with those of African Americans who had been free before the Civil War. Discuss how African Americans strengthened their family structures and built their social institutions on the local level.

8. Discuss white resistance to maintaining civil rights for blacks in both the North and South. Explain how the declining social position of blacks was due to the activities of planters in groups such as the Ku Klux Klan and how much it was due to the loss of northerners' commitment to, and interest in, the plight of the freedmen. Discuss planters' attempts to resist Republican state governments and freedmen. Show how the planters' desire for a disciplined labor force led them to organize against freedmen's suffrage. Describe the degree of violence used by groups such as the Klan. Discuss how the North responded, including the effectiveness (or lack thereof) of the Force Acts. Describe President Grant's position and his fear of restarting the war. Discuss the movement by the Liberal Republicans to capitulate to planters' desires by removing troops from the South. Consider the degree of racism in the North and the impact it had on Reconstruction.

9. Historians have attempted to describe the concept of southern honor and explain how it created a particularly violent society. Use Nathan Bedford Forrest's life to illustrate this concept. Discuss how Forrest emphasized family honor and how affronts to his relatives led him to respond with violence. Discuss how the loss of the war was particularly shameful to men such as Forrest, and examine the degree to which that sense of shame played a role in the formation of the Ku Klux Klan. Discuss how this concept of southern honor had to find new bases after the war.

10. Students sometimes become confused by the Thirteenth, Fourteenth, and Fifteenth Amendments to the Constitution. Explain what each one entails and

how it came about. Discuss how the Fourteenth and Fifteenth Amendments substantially changed the relationship between the federal government and state governments. Show how they created a national citizenship for the first time. Explain that these amendments shifted power toward the national government. Discuss how this process was a result of the Civil War as well as of the amendments. Discuss the difference between the pre-Civil War Union and the post-Civil War United States.

11. Women tend to be neglected in most histories of this period. Discuss the differing experiences of white women in the North and South and freedwomen. Note that although the end of war brought men home, it also led to the return of white women to traditional roles. Discuss how the high death rate in both the North and the South left a generation of widows and single women who had to survive without male breadwinners. Describe the experiences of freedwomen who chose to leave field work, drastically reducing the South's labor supply. Explore the activities of freedwomen in creating black communities in the South. End with a discussion of suffrage, and explain why woman suffrage leaders felt betrayed. Explore how the Fifteenth Amendment led the woman suffrage movement to change its strategies.

12. Students need to understand how and why the North failed to support the freedmen in the long run. Describe the North's sense of exhaustion with freedmen's issues in the 1870s. Describe how the North became reconciled with the white South politically, socially, and culturally.

13. Compare and contrast the post-Civil War economic status of the South with that of the North. Show how the Republican Party's commitment of government assistance to industrial capitalism created a dynamic northern economy moving toward the Industrial Revolution. Explain the rationale for this government-business alliance, and show how the Civil War pension plan satisfied many workers and farmers in the North. Describe the state of the southern economy at the end of the war. Show how some southerners attempted to bring industry to the region. Describe how and why the South differed from the North. Describe how the South remained dependent on agriculture and why tenancy and sharecropping came to characterize southern farming. Explain the long-range effect of this situation.

Class Discussion Starters

1. **How might Reconstruction have been different if Lincoln had not been assassinated?**

Possible answers:
- a   Lincoln would have allied himself with the moderate Republicans in support of a program less lenient than what he initially wanted but not as severe as what the Radicals desired.
- b. Reconstruction would have been more consistent, without changes in policy. Southerners would not have been encouraged by battles between the president and Congress, which would not have occurred.
- c. Lincoln would have broken with congressional Republicans and would have had struggles with Congress similar to Johnson's, although with less personal hostility because of Lincoln's more tactful personality.
- d. Lincoln would have remained committed to full citizenship for ex-slaves; he would not have backed down before the Ku Klux Klan and would have used the force necessary to root it out. He could have co-opted Lee and other southerners with genuine honor to help him rebuild the Union.

2. **Lincoln is frequently considered our best president for his handling of the Civil War. How do you rate his early attempts at Reconstruction?**

Possible answers:
- a. Lincoln was too ready to give in to the South on slavery and was too soft toward the Confederates.
- b. Lincoln's moderate approach was exactly what the country needed to recover from the war.
- c. Lincoln had an easy time of it because of patriotic support for the president; after the war he would have had problems similar to Johnson's.

3. **How would American political development have differed if President Johnson had been removed from office?**

Possible answers:
- a. Reconstruction would not have changed much, since Congress took control of policy anyway, and the North was ambivalent.
- b. Impeachment and conviction would have occurred more often in American history because they would have resulted from a lack of political support, not from criminal activity.
- c. Congress's power would have increased even more than it did in the late nineteenth century.

4. **Did Reconstruction go too far, not far enough, or was change impossible to achieve?**

Possible answers:
- a. It went too far. The attempt to give African Americans political equality with white southerners was fruitless. It could not, and did not, last.

b. It did not go far enough. Land redistribution alone would have made a difference in the political and economic relationship between white southerners and freedmen.

c. It was an impossible task. The North was never prepared to support the extent of change that was necessary in the South.

5. Were the Radical Republicans astute when they abandoned woman suffrage to ensure that African American suffrage would be accomplished?

Possible answers:

a. Yes. Woman suffrage was considered so extreme that to insist on it might have led the moderates to abandon the movement to extend suffrage to blacks.

b. No. Woman suffrage might not have passed, but it would not have damaged the movement for African American suffrage.

c. No. Women's efforts in support of the war should have gained them suffrage.

6. Why didn't freedmen and poor whites form an alliance against the planters?

Possible answers:

a. Planters successfully appealed to white racism in order to prevent such an alliance.

b. Freedmen and poor whites were in competition for land in the distressed southern economy after the war.

c. Both groups distrusted each other and could not overcome latent racism.

7. In what ways was the African American community in the South split after the war?

Possible answers:

a. African Americans who had been free before the war were more conservative in their goals for Reconstruction and were more protective of private property.

b. Freedmen often sought the confiscation and redistribution of former Confederate estates.

c. Freedmen enjoyed their new geographical mobility, often seeking out relatives who had been sold away.

8. Why do you think the Fifteenth Amendment's provision for reducing congressional representation in states that denied suffrage to their citizens was never enforced?

Possible answers:

a. Once southern states again had representatives in Congress, southern Democrats blocked political support for enforcement.

b. Northerners and the Republican Party were not sufficiently unified to agree on a plan to enforce the amendment.

c. Presidents after Grant did not want to risk reopening the war.

d. The Republican Party was torn between reformers who wanted to abandon Reconstruction and a scandal-torn administration.

e. Racism prevented northerners from seeing African Americans as citizens whose right to vote had to be protected.

9. How did changes in the North during the war prepare the country for the postwar Republican economic program?

Possible answers:

a. The war accustomed northerners to massive government spending.

b. The war weakened Democrats, who traditionally opposed government expansion.

c. Wartime spending led northerners to look to the federal government as a customer for their products.

Chapter Writing Assignments

1. Contrast the postwar careers of several important military leaders from the North and the South.

2. Explain why, during radical Reconstruction, Congress gave in on issues such as woman suffrage and land redistribution but remained firm on issues such as black suffrage.

3. How similar were the interests of congressional Republicans during Reconstruction and the interests of southern African Americans? How were they different? Explain the reasons for these similarities and differences.

4. How did the Republican economic program in the North appeal to both industrial capitalists and northern farmers?

5. Why do you think so much government corruption occurred in the North and the South in the decade after the Civil War?

Document Exercises

VOICES FROM ABROAD

David Macrae: The Devastated South (p. 432)

Document Discussion

1. According to Macrae, how did the war affect the South?

(The war changed nearly every aspect of antebellum southern society. Not only were lives lost outright, but hundreds of thousands were wounded and maimed, homes had been demolished, and businesses were destroyed. The fact that so much physical damage remained several years after the war suggests that southern society also suffered pains of a more intangible sort. The cotton-based, slave-dependent economic and political structures had been eliminated. However, before the end of the century, whites would reassert their influence. In many respects, the "old South" would not disappear until well into the post-World War II era, when full economic and political integration demanded change in the South.)

2. **What evidence did Macrae include to support the assertion that the Civil War had been a total war?**
   (The fact that so much of the destruction Macrae witnessed was not constrained to the boundaries of the battlefield is the most obvious evidence that the Civil War had been a wide-ranging military contest. The information he provided about the human devastation provides further evidence of the all-encompassing nature of the Civil War. The fact that within several decades many of the former political and cultural power structures that supported whites would reemerge was difficult to imagine in 1865.)

Writing Assignments

1. Compare Macrae's description of the South in 1867 to 1868 with an account prepared before the war. What are the most important differences?

2. Why weren't southerners busily repairing the damages that Macrae witnessed?

3. Did Congress and the Reconstruction presidents miss an opportunity to co-opt the South by repairing the damage done in the war and providing for war widows and orphans, etc.?

AMERICAN VOICES

Jourdon Anderson: Relishing Freedom (p. 433)

Document Discussion

1. **What does Anderson's letter reveal about the lives of young slave women?**
   (Anderson declares that he would rather die than subject his daughters to the predations of young male masters. While Anderson mentions no specific act or event, his letter clearly indicates that young slave women were subject to sexual and physical exploitation. Another matter of concern for Anderson

is the availability of education. He links the development of "virtuous habits" with school attendance and wants this opportunity for his girls.)

2. **In exchange for a return to service, what did Anderson demand from his former master?**
   (Anderson insists upon a secure environment and educational opportunity for his children. He also describes in detail the level of financial remuneration he expects, first for his prior labor while a slave and second what he will charge a free man. Interestingly, Anderson set his wage rate to equate his current income in Ohio.)

Writing Assignments

1. Why would Anderson write a letter to his former owner? What part of his text (if any) is serious, and which is sarcasm?

2. Assess the nature of the relationship between Jourdan and Colonel Anderson. How does Jourdan feel about his master and the life he led while a slave?

AMERICAN LIVES

Nathan Bedford Forrest: Defender of Southern Honor (p. 446)

Document Discussion

1. **What factors led to Forrest's success in the prewar South?**
   (His willingness to use violence and his physical courage fitted with the antebellum southern mentality. He was hardworking. He took advantage of the expansion of cotton agriculture into the Southwest.)

2. **Why do you think that so many whites joined the Klan after the war?**
   (Forrest was known for his physical bravery and spectacular success as a commander, and that attracted many young men whose side had just suffered defeat. Forrest was very entrepreneurial in his ability to attract supporters. Many white men were unwilling to accept the roles given to African Americans during radical Reconstruction.)

Writing Assignments

1. Compare and contrast the postwar career of Forrest with another Confederate general officer such as Robert E. Lee, James Longstreet, or Joseph Wheeler.

2. In what ways did Forrest's life and personality typify southern conceptions of honor? Forrest quit the Klan when it became too violent for him; how does his southern honor explain that? or does it?

AMERICAN VOICES

Harriet Hernandes: The Intimidation of Black Voters (p. 448)

Document Discussion

1. **Why did the Klan terrorize Harriet Hernandes and her daughter?**
    (Hernandes's husband had voted for Republican candidates. The women were vulnerable because Mr. Hernandes was not home. The Klan wanted to punish Mr. Hernandes and his family for his voting. They hoped to change the way he voted, or to get him to stop voting altogether, by terrorizing his wife and daughter.)

2. **What effect do you think this testimony had on the Joint Congressional Select Committee?**
    (They would have been furious at this attempt to intimidate black Republicans, for both compassionate and political reasons. The committee would have been appalled by this treatment of a woman and would want to protect others like her. Many Republicans hoped to create a political base in the South by earning the loyalty of black voters.)

Writing Assignments

1. In what ways did the Klan terrorize Hernandes, her family, and her neighbors? Why were those tactics chosen?

2. Do you think vigorous, long-term enforcement of the 1871 Ku Klux Klan Act eventually would have defeated the Klan? Why or why not?

Skill-Building Map Exercises

Map 15.1: Reconstruction (p. 437)

1. **In what area of the South did states return to the Union earliest? Latest?**
    (The border state of Tennessee returned to the Union in 1866. Arkansas, Louisiana, Florida, Alabama, South Carolina, and North Carolina returned to the Union in 1868. Texas, Mississippi, Georgia, and Virginia did not reenter the Union until 1870.)

2. **Why do you think the Confederate states returned to the Union at different times?**
    (Before being accepted by Congress, the southern states had to construct acceptable governments. The time it took for each state to do this varied. Tennessee had many Union sympathizers and state politicians

who were acceptable to congressional Republicans, so Tennessee was subjected to a military government under the Reconstruction Act of 1867. Other states fell under military control and thus took a few years to organize new state governments that Congress would approve.)

Map 15.2: The Barrow Plantation, 1860 and 1881 (p. 444)

1. **Why did the pattern of African American residence and farming change?**
    (Valuing autonomy, freedmen left their old plantation grounds to establish their own farms independent of former slave owners. They set their farms on good land and near roads and rivers to make it easy to get their crops to market.)

2. **Whose interests did this change serve?**
    (This pattern reflected freedmen's interests as they resisted gang labor and white control.)

Topic for Research

The Overthrow of Radical Reconstruction

One by one, the Reconstruction state governments fell to counterrevolutions. This text has surveyed the general reasons for the victories of the Democratic redeemers over the Republicans, but the timing and particular circumstances differed from state to state. Choose one of the states of the former Confederacy, and investigate how and why Reconstruction came to an end there. You should explore the methods of the redeemers, examining the extent to which they relied on conventional methods of political persuasion and organization as opposed to terrorism and guerrilla warfare. You should also consider the role of divisions among the various groups of Republicans — African Americans, carpetbaggers, and scalawags — in the party's defeat. And, finally, examine the role of the federal government and the Union army. Could greater effort and commitment in Washington have saved the Republicans? General books on Reconstruction, such as Eric Foner's *Reconstruction: America's Unfinished Revolution, 1863–1877* (1988), have bibliographies listing books, articles, and other sources on the individual states. Be alert to the possibility of consulting the documents compiled by Congress as it struggled to understand the problems of Reconstruction. Especially fascinating, for example, are the hearings on the Ku Klux Klan: *Testimony Taken by the Joint Committee to Enquire into the Condition of Affairs in the Late Insurrectionary States*, indexed as 42nd Cong., 2nd sess., H. Rept. 22.

Recent examinations of Reconstruction include Eric Foner, *Reconstruction* (2002, originally published in 1989); John Hope Franklin and Daniel J. Boorstin, eds., *Reconstruction After the Civil War* (1995); David Herbert Donald, et al., *Civil War and Reconstruction* (2000); James McPherson, *Ordeal By Fire* (3rd edition, 2000); and Roger L. Ransom and Richard Sutch, *One Kind of Freedom* (2000).

How to Use the Ancillaries Available with *America's History*

Refer to the Preface to *America's History* at the front of the book for descriptions of instructor resources, including the Instructor's Resource CD-ROM, Computerized Test Bank, transparencies, and *Using the Bedford Series in History and Culture in the U.S. History Survey*. Student resources, also described in the Preface, include the Online Study Guide and *Documents to Accompany* America's History, a primary-source reader.

For Instructors

Using the Bedford Series in History and Culture in the U.S. History Survey
This brief online guide by Scott Hovey provides practical suggestions for incorporating volumes from the highly regarded Bedford Series in History and Culture into your survey course. Titles that complement the material covered in Chapter 15 include *Up From Slavery by Booker T. Washington with Related Documents*, edited with an introduction by W. Fitzhugh Brundage. For a description of this title and how you might use it in your course, visit **bedfordstmartins.com/usingseries**.

For Students

Online Study Guide at bedfordstmartins.com/henretta
Each of the activities listed below includes short-answer questions. After submitting their answers, students can compare them to the model answers provided.

Visual Activity
The visual activity presents an engraving of a lynching (p. 439) and asks students to analyze the image to discern southern attitudes toward Reconstruction.

Reading Historical Documents
The document activity provides a brief introduction to the documents Harriet Hernandes: The Intimidation of Black Voters (p. 448) and Jourdon Anderson: Relishing

Freedom (p. 433) and asks students to analyze their content, thinking critically about the sources.

Documents to Accompany *America's History*
Each of the documents listed is introduced by a headnote, which places the document in context, and is followed by questions, which help students to analyze the piece.

Sources for Chapter 15 are
Carl Shurz, *Report on Conditions in the South* (1865)
The Mississippi Black Codes (1865)
The Civil Rights Act of 1866
Thaddeus Stevens, *Black Suffrage and Land Redistribution* (1867)
The Fourteenth Amendment and Woman Suffrage (1873, 1875)
Richard H. Cain, *An Advocate of Federal Aid for Land Purchase* (1868)
Statistics on Black Ownership (1870–1910)
Thomas Nast, *The Rise and Fall of Northern Support for Reconstruction* (1868, 1874)
Albion W. Tourgee, *A Fool's Errand. By One of the Fools* (1879)
President Grant Refuses to Aid Republicans in Mississippi (1875)
Samuel F. Miller, *The Slaughterhouse Cases* (1873)
Susan Myrick's Interview of Catherine Beale, Former Slave (1929)

Thinking about History: Religion in American Public Life (p. 452)

Discussion Questions

1. How and why did the contradictory traditions of constitutional secularism and religious conviction originate in America?

2. How did the eighteenth-century Enlightenment seek to reconcile rational inquiry with Christian theology? How has the Enlightenment compromise manifested itself during modern times?

3. Imagine that you are a judge or government official and are asked to preside over a contemporary issue of state and religion such as the teaching of evolution, the recital of the Pledge of Allegiance in schools, or references to God on U.S. currency. How would you rule? Why?

PART FOUR

A Maturing Industrial Society
1877–1914

Part Instructional Objectives

After you have taught this part, your students should be able to answer the following questions:

1. Describe the industrialization of the American economy.

2. How did economic consolidation lead to political change and progressive reform movements?

3. What were the causes and consequences of urbanization?

4. Assess and discuss the racial, ethnic, and gender divisions apparent in American society between the end of Reconstruction and World War I.

5. How did America emerge as a world power by 1914?

Thematic Timeline

	ECONOMY	SOCIETY	CULTURE	GOVERNMENT	DIPLOMACY
	The Triumph of Industrialization	**Racial, Ethnic, and Gender Divisions**	**The Rise of the City**	**From Inaction to Progressive Reform**	**An Emerging World Power**
1877	▶ Andrew Carnegie launches modern steel industry Knights of Labor becomes national movement (1878)	▶ Struggle for black equality defeated Nomadic Indian life ends	▶ National League founded (1876) Dwight L. Moody pioneers urban revivalism	▶ Election of Rutherford B. Hayes ends Reconstruction	▶ United States becomes net exporter
1880	▶ Gustavus Swift pioneers vertically integrated firm American Federation of Labor (1886)	▶ Chinese Exclusion Act (1882) Dawes Severalty Act divides tribal lands (1887)	▶ Electrification transforms city life First *Social Register* defines high society (1888)	▶ Ethnocultural issues dominate state and local politics Civil service reform (1883)	▶ Diplomacy of inaction Naval buildup begins
1890	▶ United States surpasses Britain in iron and steel output Economic depression (1893–1897) Era of farm prosperity begins	▶ Black disfranchisement and segregation in the South Immigration from southeastern Europe rises sharply	▶ Settlement houses spread progressive ideas to cities William Randolph Hearst's *New York Journal* pioneers yellow journalism	▶ Populist Party founded (1892) William McKinley wins presidency; defeats Bryan's free-silver crusade (1896)	▶ Social Darwinism and Anglo-Saxonism promote expansion Spanish-American War (1898–1899); conquest of the Philippines
1900	▶ Great Industrial merger movement Immigrants dominate factory work Industrial Workers of the World (1905)	▶ Women lead social reform Struggle for civil rights revived	▶ Muckraking journalism Movies begin to overtake vaudeville	▶ Progressivism in national politics Theodore Roosevelt attacks the trusts Hepburn Act regulates railroads (1906)	▶ Panama cedes Canal Zone to United States (1903) Roosevelt Corollary to Monroe Doctrine (1904)
1910	▶ Henry Ford builds first automobile assembly line	▶ NAACP (1910) Women vote in western states World War I ends European migration	▶ Urban liberalism	▶ Woodrow Wilson elected (1912) New Freedom legislation creates Federal Reserve, FTC	▶ Taft's diplomacy promotes U.S. business Wilson proclaims U.S. neutrality in World War I

While the nation was absorbed by the political drama of Reconstruction, few people noticed an equally momentous watershed in American economic life. For the first time, as the decade of the 1870s passed, farmers no longer constituted a majority of working Americans. Henceforth, America's future would be linked to its development as an industrial society.

Economy   The effects of accelerating industrialization were felt, first of all, in the manufacturing sector. Production became increasingly mechanized and increasingly directed at making the capital goods that undergirded economic growth. As the railroad system was completed, the vertically integrated model began to dominate American enterprise. The labor movement became firmly established, and as immigration surged, the foreign-born and their children became America's workers. What had been partial and limited now became general and widespread; America turned into a land of factories, corporate enterprise, and industrial workers.

Society   The final surge of western settlement across the Great Plains was largely driven by the pressures of this industrializing economy. Cities demanded new sources of food; factories needed the Far West's mineral resources. Defending their way of life, western Indians were ultimately defeated not so much by army rifles as by the unceasing encroachment of railroads, mines, ranches, and proliferating farms. These same forces disrupted the old established Hispanic communities of the Southwest but spurred Asian, Mexican, and European migrations that made for a multiethnic western society.

Culture   Industrialization also transformed the nation's urban life. By 1900, one in five Americans lived in cities. That was where the jobs were — as workers in the factories; as clerks and salespeople; as members of a new salaried middle class of managers, engineers, and professionals; and at the apex as a wealthy elite of investors and entrepreneurs. The city was more than just a place to make a living, however. It provided a setting for an urban lifestyle unlike anything seen before in America.

Government   The unfettered, booming economy of the Gilded Age tended at first to marginalize political life. The major parties remained robust not because they stood for much programmatically but because they exploited a culture of popular participation and embraced the ethnocultural interests of their constituencies. The depression of the 1890s triggered a major challenge to the political status quo by the agrarian Populist Party, with its demand for free silver. The election of 1896 turned back that challenge and established the Republicans as the dominant national party.

Still unresolved was the threat that corporate power posed to the marketplace and democratic politics. How to curb the trusts dominated national debate during the Progressive Era. In those years as well, the country took a critical look at its institutions and began to address its social ills. From different angles, political reformers, women progressives, and urban liberals went about the business of cleaning up machine politics and making life better for America's urban masses. African Americans, victimized by disfranchisement and segregation, found allies among white progressives and launched a new drive for racial equality.

Diplomacy   Finally, the dynamism of America's economic development decisively altered the country's foreign relations. In the decades after the Civil War, America had been inward-looking, neglectful of its navy and inactive diplomatically. The business crisis of the 1890s, however, brought home the need for a more aggressive foreign policy that would advance the nation's overseas economic interests. In short order the United States went to war with Spain, acquired an overseas empire, and became actively engaged in Latin America and Asia. There was no mistaking America's standing as a Great Power and, as World War I approached, no evading the responsibilities and entanglements that came with that status.

CHAPTER 16

The American West

Chapter Instructional Objectives

After you have taught this chapter, your students should be able to answer the following questions:

1. How and why did the economic and social values of white Americans clash with those of Native Americans in the West?

2. How did the Industrial Revolution affect the settlement of the West?

3. How did mining, farming, and ranching shape the development of the West?

4. How did diversity both fundamentally define the West and become the source of conflict in western society?

Chapter Summary

As late as the 1860s, the Great Plains remained the ancestral home of nomadic Indian tribes. In the eastern section lived the Mandans, Arikaras, and Pawnees; in the Southwest, the Kiowas and the Comanches; on the Central Plains, the Arapahos and Cheyennes; to the north, the Blackfeet, Crows, Cheyennes, and the Sioux nation. The Sioux were nomadic people, and once they were on horseback, they claimed the entire Great Plains north of the Arkansas River as their hunting grounds. The Sioux dominated the northern Great Plains by driving out or subjugating longer-settled tribes.

On first encountering the Great Plains, Euro-Americans thought the land "almost wholly unfit for cultivation" and best left to the Indians. In the 1840s, settlers began moving to Oregon and California, and the Indian country became a bridge to the Pacific. In 1861, telegraph lines brought San Francisco into instant communication with the East; the next year the federal government began a transcontinental railroad project. The federal government awarded generous land grants, plus millions of dollars of loans to the Union Pacific and Central Pacific Railroads.

During the next thirty years, the expansion of American society crowded Native Americans onto reservations and forced them to abandon their traditional way of life. A burgeoning, increasingly urbanized population required more food and manufactured goods; factories and smelters needed the raw materials of the Rocky Mountain West and the Pacific slope. The area constituting the forty-eight contiguous states eventually became a single integrated economic unit. New technology — steel plows, barbed wire, and strains of hard-kernel wheat — helped settlers to overcome obstacles presented by the land. By the turn of the century, the Great Plains had fully submitted to agricultural development; agriculture depended on sophisticated dry-farming techniques and modern machinery.

Beyond the Rockies, the arid and often uninhabitable land meant that the progressive settlement along a frontier did not often occur. Rather, occupation took the form of isolated settlements situated at places promising mineral wealth. Remote areas turned into mob scenes of prospectors, traders, gamblers, prostitutes, and saloonkeepers; prospectors made their own mining codes, or laws. Prospecting gave way to entrepreneurial development and large-scale mining as original claim holders quickly sold out to generous bidders. Entrepreneurs raised capital, built rail connections, devised technology for treating lower-grade copper deposits, constructed smelting facilities, and recruited a labor force that went on to organize trade unions.

By population, economy, and geographical location, California dominated the Far West during the final decades of the century. Its Hispanic heritage linked it to the Southwest, and its geography linked it with Washington and Oregon to form the Pacific slope. The discovery of gold prompted a tremendous migration of white settlers that quickly urbanized the state and transformed its culture. Its Hispanic origins were subsumed within a new, distinctive culture that was influenced by Asians who had also emigrated to the West in search of economic opportunity.

The pace of settlement throughout the West was accelerated by the nation's burgeoning economic growth. As the United States became an industrial colossus, most of the North American continent was drawn into the process. The Indians resisted encroachment by fighting and by attempting to flee. Conflict intensified in the mid-1870s, but Indian tribes were forced onto reservations. Whites flooded the newly acquired land, making Indians the minority. American industry needed the West's natural resources; the cities demanded agricultural products; and settlers sought a place to make a new beginning. By the time the nineteenth century came to a close, America's uncivilized western "frontier" ceased to exist.

Chapter Annotated Outline

I.   The Great Plains
   A. Indians of the Great Plains
      1. About a hundred thousand Native Americans lived on the Great Plains at mid-nineteenth century; they were divided into six linguistic families and over thirty tribal groupings.
      2. In the eastern section lived the Mandans, Arikaras, and Pawnees; in the Southwest, the Kiowas and the Comanches; on the Central Plains, the Arapahos and Cheyennes; to the north, the Blackfeet, Crows, Cheyennes, and the Sioux nation.
      3. The Sioux were nomadic people, and once they were on horseback, they claimed the entire Great Plains north of the Arkansas River as their hunting grounds.
      4. The Sioux dominated the northern Great Plains by driving out or subjugating longer-settled tribes.
      5. Sioux women labored on the buffalo skins that the men brought back; the women did not see their unrelenting labor as subordination to men.
      6. The Sioux saw sacred meaning in every manifestation of the natural world; the natural world embodied a "series of powers pervading the universe."
      7. Once white traders appeared on the upper Mississippi River during the eighteenth century, the Teton Sioux traded pelts and buffalo robes for the goods they offered.
   B. Wagon Trains, Railroads, and Ranchers
      1. On first encountering the Great Plains, Euro-Americans thought the land "almost wholly unfit for cultivation" and best left to the Indians.
      2. In 1834, Congress formally designated the Great Plains as permanent Indian country.
      3. In the 1840s, settlers began moving to Oregon and California, and the Indian country became a bridge to the Pacific.
      4. In 1861, telegraph lines brought San Francisco into instant communication with the East; the next year the federal government began a transcontinental railroad project.
      5. The federal government awarded generous land grants, plus millions of dollars of loans to the Union Pacific and Central Pacific Railroads.
      6. The Union Pacific built westward from Omaha, and the Central Pacific built eastward from Sacramento until the tracks met in Promontory Point, Utah, in 1869. Other rail companies laid track in the West, but many went bankrupt in the Panic of 1873.
      7. Railroad tycoons realized that rail transportation was laying the basis for the economic exploitation of the Great Plains; a railroad boom followed economic recovery in 1878.
      8. To make room for cattle, professional buffalo hunters eliminated the buffalo; in the early 1870s, when eastern tanneries learned how to cure buffalo hides, the herds almost vanished within ten years.
      9. Texas ranchers inaugurated the famous Long Drive, hiring cowboys to herd cattle hundreds of miles north to the railroads that pushed west across Kansas.
      10. As soon as railroads reached the Texas range country during the 1870s, ranchers abandoned the Long Drive.
      11. North of Texas, where land was public domain, a custom of "range right" quickly became established.
      12. News of easy money to be made on cattle traveled fast; by the early 1880s the plains overflowed with cattle.
      13. After a hard winter in 1885, followed by severe drought the next summer, cattle died by the hundreds of thousands; ranchers dumped cattle on the market, and beef prices plunged.
      14. An enduring ecological catastrophe occurred: the destruction of native grasses caused by relentless overgrazing during the drought cycle.
      15. Open-range ranching came to an end, and sheep raising became a major enterprise in the sparser high country.

C. Homesteaders
1. Railroads, land speculators, steamship lines, and the western states and territories did all they could to encourage settlement of the Great Plains.
2. The government encouraged settlers with the Homestead Act of 1862, offering 160 acres of public land to all settlers — including widows and single women.
3. For migrants traveling west, prescribed gender roles sometimes broke down as women shouldered men's work and became self-reliant in the face of danger and hardship.
4. By the 1870s, farmers from the older agricultural states looked westward for land.
5. "American fever" took hold in northern Europe as Germans, Russians, Norwegians, Swedes, and Scandinavians emigrated to the United States.
6. The motivation for these new European immigrants was to better themselves economically, but for several thousand southern blacks, Kansas briefly held the promise of racial freedom.
7. Homesteaders' crops were highly susceptible to natural disasters such as fire, hail, and damage caused by grasshoppers.
8. New technology — steel plows, barbed wire, and strains of hard-kernel wheat — helped settlers to overcome obstacles presented by the land.
9. From 1878 to 1886, settlers enjoyed exceptionally wet weather, but then the dry weather typical of the Great Plains returned, and recently settled land emptied out as homesteaders fled.
10. By the turn of the century, the Great Plains had fully submitted to agricultural development; agriculture depended on sophisticated dry-farming techniques and modern machinery.
11. The economic capital of the Great Plains was Chicago, the hub of the nation's rail system.
12. Farming was becoming an industry, and farmers began to understand the disadvantages they faced in dealing with big businesses that supplied them with machinery, arranged their credit, and marketed their products.
13. The National Grange of the Patrons of Husbandry was formed in 1867. Local granges spread across rural America, providing meeting places and entertainment; soon cooperative programs were added.
14. The Grange encouraged independent political parties that ran on antimonopoly platforms. Farmers believed, not always correctly, that they were victims of manufacturers and banks, so they turned to the cooperatives and state regulation to remedy the perceived imbalance.
15. Deflation in the international wheat market had dire consequences for farmers in debt; falling prices forced them to pay back in real terms more than they had borrowed.

D. The Fate of the Indians
1. Incursions by whites into Indian lands increased from the late 1850s onward; the Indians struck back, hoping whites would tire of the struggle.
2. A peace commission was appointed in 1867 to end the fighting and negotiate treaties by which Indians would cede their lands and move to reservations.
3. The southwestern quarter of the Dakota Territory was allocated to the Teton Sioux tribes, and Oklahoma was allocated to the southwestern Plains Indians and the Five Civilized Tribes.
4. The Indians resisted, by fighting and by attempting to flee the army, and fighting intensified in the mid-1870s; Congress appropriated funds for more western troops to control the Indians.
5. A crisis came on the northern plains in 1875 when the Indian Office ordered the Sioux to vacate their Powder River hunting grounds and withdraw to the reservation.
6. On June 25, 1876, George A. Custer and his troops were surrounded and annihilated by Chief Crazy Horse's Sioux and Cheyenne warriors at Little Big Horn.
7. Pursued relentlessly by the army, Sioux bands gradually gave up and moved onto the reservation, only to have part of both the Dakota and Oklahoma Territories taken away in 1877 because whites were looking for gold and still more farmland.
8. During the 1870s the Office of Indian Affairs developed a program to train Indian children for farm work and prepare them for citizenship by sending them to reservation schools or boarding schools.
9. The Indian Rights Association thought that the only way Indians could fit into the white man's world was by radical assimilation.
10. The Dawes Act of 1887 declared that land for the Indians would be allotted in 160-acre lots to heads of households and held in trust by the government for twenty-five years, at which time the Indians would become U.S. citizens; remaining reservations were sold off, with proceeds going toward Indian education.

11. The federal government announced that it had tribal approval to open the Sioux "surplus" land to white settlement in 1890.

12. The Indians had lost their ancestral lands, faced an alien future of farming, and were confronted by a winter of starvation; but at the same time, news of "salvation" came from a holy man called Wovoka, who predicted the disappearance of the whites and encouraged the Ghost Dance as a ritual to prepare for the regeneration.

13. As the frenzy of Wovoka's Ghost Dance swept through the Sioux encampments in 1890, alarmed whites called for army intervention.

14. The bloody battle at Wounded Knee erupted when soldiers attempted to disarm a group of Wovoka's followers; it was the final episode in the long war of suppression of the Plains Indians. Thereafter, the division of tribal lands proceeded without hindrance.

15. As whites flooded the newly acquired land, Indians became the minority.

II. The Far West
A. The Mining Frontier
   1. Fewer than 100,000 Euro-Americans lived in the entire Far West when it became a U.S. territory in 1848; mining spurred its development.
   2. San Francisco became a bustling metropolis overnight and was the hub of a mining empire that stretched to the Rockies.
   3. By the mid-1850s, prospectors began to strike it rich elsewhere, including in the Sierra Nevada, the Colorado Rockies, Montana, and Wyoming.
   4. Remote areas turned into a mob scene of prospectors, traders, gamblers, prostitutes, and saloonkeepers; prospectors made their own mining codes, or laws.
   5. Prospecting gave way to entrepreneurial development and large-scale mining as original claim holders quickly sold out to generous bidders.
   6. At some sites, gold and silver proved less profitable than the more common metals for which there was a huge demand in manufacturing.
   7. Entrepreneurs raised capital, built rail connections, devised technology for treating lower-grade copper deposits, constructed smelting facilities, and recruited a labor force that went on to organize trade unions.
   8. California and its tributary mining country created a market for Oregon's produce and timber.
   9. Portland, Oregon, and Seattle, Washington, became important commercial centers, prospering from farming, ranching, logging, and fishing.
B. Hispanics, Chinese, Anglos
   1. The first Europeans to enter the Far West were Hispanics moving northward out of Mexico.
   2. The economy of the Hispanic Southwest consisted primarily of cattle and sheep ranching, and the social order was highly stratified.
   3. In New Mexico, European and Native American cultures managed a successful, if uneasy, coexistence; but in California, Hispanics treated the Native Americans very poorly.
   4. Anglos were incorporated into the New Mexican society through intermarriage and business partnerships, but by the 1880s, California Hispanics had lost most of their land to Anglos.
   5. New Mexico peasant men began migrating seasonally to pursue wage work on the railway or in the Colorado mines and sugar beet fields, leaving the village economy in the hands of their wives.
   6. Driven by poverty, a worldwide Asian migration began in the mid-nineteenth century; many Chinese came to North America by a "credit-ticket system."
   7. Chinese immigrants normally entered a powerful confederation of Chinese merchants in San Francisco's Chinatown, known as the Six Companies.
   8. Chinese men labored mainly in the California gold fields until the 1860s, then the Central Pacific hired the Chinese to work on the transcontinental railroad.
   9. In California, where there were few blacks, whites targeted the Chinese with racism; the frenzy climaxed in San Francisco in the late 1870s, when anti-Chinese mobs ruled the streets.
   10. Democrats and Republicans in California wrote a new state constitution replete with anti-Chinese provisions, and in 1882, Congress passed the Chinese Exclusion Act.
   11. California was a land of limitless opportunity, boastful of its democratic egalitarianism, yet it simultaneously was a racially torn society that exploited and despised the minorities whose hard labor helped make it what it was.
C. Golden California
   1. Location, environment, and history all helped to set California apart from the rest of the American nation.
   2. California found its cultural traditions in its Spanish past, although much of the cultural celebration was actually commercialism.

3. In the 1880s, the Southern Pacific Railroad was boasting of California's attractions; by 1900, southern California had firmly established itself as the land of sunshine and orange groves.

4. A dizzying real estate boom developed along with the frantic building of resort hotels; California had found a way to translate climate into riches.

5. In 1890, California's national parks — Yosemite, Sequoia, and King's Canyon — were established; the Sierra Club was formed in 1892 as a defender of California's wilderness.

6. In 1913, preservationists were unable to prevent the federal government from approving the damming of Hetch Hetchy to serve the water needs of San Francisco.

7. California's well-being was linked with the preservation of its natural resources; the urge to conquer and exploit was tempered by a sense that nature's bounty was not limitless.

Lecture Strategies

1. Examine the destruction of the way of life of the Plains Indians. Explore the origins of Indian-white conflict. Note the reasons why the Native Americans were subdued with relative ease. Explain the failure of "solutions" to the Indian "problem."

2. Students often believe that settlement occurred in a steady march westward. Explain how the settlement of the American West took place in a very different fashion — with the Pacific slope territory attracting population before the Rocky Mountain West and the Great Plains — and point out the forces that prompted this settlement pattern.

3. Discuss the development of agriculture on the Great Plains. Define and discuss the geography of the region. Note the technological innovations that made farming on the plains possible. Explain the role of plains agriculture in the developing American economy.

4. For much of American history, farming has been seen as a noble vocation; yet farming has been a very difficult way to survive. Farmers have frequently found themselves in desperate straits — whipsawed by nature, impoverished by low commodities prices, and politically friendless. Discuss the plight of American farmers from the end of the Civil War to the turn of the century, being sure to explain that not all American farmers had the same experience.

5. Detail the role of women in the settlement of the Great Plains. Explain why a disproportionate burden fell on women. Note the hardships experienced by women. Explore how gender roles eroded and how that might have benefited women.

6. Explore Hispanic culture in the West beginning with the geographical limits of the Spanish-speaking areas. Consider the different experiences of Hispanics in New Mexico, California, and Texas. Describe the influx of Mexicans and Anglos into the Southwest, and explain its impact on southwestern Hispanics.

7. Historians tend to focus on European immigration to America. The text offers an opportunity to explore immigration from other areas. Using examples from the American West and Southwest, explain immigration from China, Japan, and Mexico. Note the common reasons for immigration. Discuss the experiences and contributions of these non-European immigrants. Finally, explain the imposition of restrictions on Chinese and Japanese immigration.

8. Consider the California mystique. Explain the diverse geography of the "Golden State," and show how it attracted immigrants but divided the state. Explore how California's beauty and immense natural wealth strengthened the American dream. Discuss California as a crossroads between an industrial economy and an economy based on a new desire to limit industrialism.

Class Discussion Starters

1. **Why do you think the federal government's Indian policies rarely met the expectations of either Native Americans or settlers?**

Possible answers:
  a. Politicians who directed Indian policies often had little direct knowledge of, but plenty of contempt for, Native Americans.
  b. The government was controlled by expansionist-minded administrations, and the Indians stood in the way of settlement; they viewed reservations as the best possible solution for the Indian "problem."
  c. Many Indians were slow to recognize the serious threat that settlers posed to their way of life; the tremendous population growth of Europeans and Americans through birthrates and emigration led to inevitable conflict.
  d. Given the fundamentally different basis of American and Indian societies, no policy could have succeeded.

2. **What were the results, both positive and negative, of rapid western settlement?**

Possible answers:
  a. Indian removal and degradation.

b. The brushing aside of Hispanics; disregarding treaties and earlier land grants.

c. Rapid economic expansion and creation of wealth.

d. Unprecedented opportunity for settlers, both to improve their economic position and to fall into crippling debt.

e. Destruction of the native ecology.

3. Why has the West had such a powerful impact on the American imagination?

Possible answers:

a. The West's natural features — great rivers, soaring mountains, magnificent forests, endless stillness — have been a lure.

b. The West was seen as a place where one's personal fortune could be made or enhanced.

c. The federal government made western settlement attractive.

d. The West was considered free — a place where people could begin anew.

4. What forces sparked the astronomical growth of California in the nineteenth century?

Possible answers:

a. The gold rush of the late 1840s and early 1850s.

b. Rail links with the East.

c. The attractiveness, natural and human-built, of San Francisco and Los Angeles.

d. Irrigation.

e. The development of a major agricultural industry, especially in the central valley.

f. A superb climate in some areas.

5. What difficulties did farmers on the Great Plains and in the South face in the late nineteenth century?

Possible answers:

a. International competition.

b. Transportation problems.

c. Weather.

d. Cost-price pressures.

e. Necessity for greater capital investment.

f. Vast expansion of productivity, which increased supply and depressed prices.

Chapter Writing Assignments

1. In what ways was the culture of the Plains Indians dependent on the environment of the Great American Desert? Did the reservation program automatically destroy that culture?

2. Were the policies and practices of the federal government decisive in the loss of the autonomy and freedom of the Plains Indians, or would settlement by non-Indians have taken place anyway?

3. Discuss the roles of Mexican or Chinese immigrants in the development of the West, particularly California.

4. What were the attractions of California that led to a rapid increase in white settlement in the nineteenth century? Compare the development of the San Francisco and Los Angeles regions.

5. Despite the impact of the environment on agriculture in the Great Plains, it quickly became America's biggest supplier of grain and meat. Compare plains agriculture with farming styles in other regions of the United States to explain why.

Document Exercises

AMERICAN LIVES

Buffalo Bill and the Mythic West (p. 462)

Document Discussion

1. In what ways was Buffalo Bill Cody an "authentic hero"?
(Bill actually had done some amazing feats — he had been a scout, fought Indians, ridden for the Pony Express, hunted buffalo, and ridden with royalty.)

2. Why is Cody a figure of enduring appeal?
(He had an adventurous life and represents a seemingly glamorous past, recent chronologically but distant technologically.)

Writing Assignments

1. Compare and contrast the life and work of William F. Cody with the mythic history of Buffalo Bill.

2. In what ways did Buffalo Bill help to create the legend of the Old West that became such an important part of popular culture?

AMERICAN VOICES

Ida Lindgren: Swedish Emigrant in Frontier Kansas (p. 465)

Document Discussion

1. According to Ida Lindgren, what hardships did settlers face?
(Isolation, loneliness, poor transportation, illness, natural enemies.)

2. If conditions were so harsh, why did the settlers remain?

(For many, there was no turning back. They left their homelands in search of a better life. They sold most everything they owned, save the necessities for the journey, and headed to the frontier. Most settlers could not finance a return trip to their homelands, and in any case, the health of some would not have allowed it. Also, there was always hope that circumstances would improve.)

Writing Assignments

1. What were the hardships faced by settlers such as Ida Lindgren, and how were they overcome in the last third of the nineteenth century?

2. White pioneers often spoke of the loneliness they felt amidst the great distances and open spaces of the Great Plains. The Indians, however, were presumably content with their natural setting. Contrast the different responses by assessing the cultural contexts of whites and Indians.

AMERICAN VOICES

Zitkala-Ša (Gertrude Simmons Bonnin): Becoming White (p. 473)

Document Discussion

1. **Why does Zitkala-Ša feel so diminished by having her hair cut?**
   (Zitkala-Ša's cultural beliefs associated short hair with mourners and shingled hair with unskilled warriors captured in battle. To lose her hair was to lose a part of her cultural and personal identity and to have her status as a captive reinforced.)

2. **How does Zitkala-Ša characterize the motivation that inspired the whites to place her in a mission school?**
   (According to Zitkala-Ša, the "civilized" people who passed through the mission, marveling and ogling the Indian children whom they found to be docile and industrious, were motivated by a misplaced sense of charity. While the whites may have felt that they were helping the Indians, Zitkala-Ša raises the question whether life among the whites was "real life or long lasting death.")

Writing Assignments

1. How significant are modes of dress and personal grooming to an individual or a group's identity? How and why do people use such distinctions to communicate with one another?

2. Would you evaluate Zitkala-Ša's school as a success? Why or why not?

VOICES FROM ABROAD

Baron Joseph Alexander von Hübner: A Western Boom Town (p. 475)

Document Discussion

1. **According to Hübner, what were the characteristics of an American "rowdy"?**
   (He identifies a rowdy as an individual possessing raw talent, high energy, and an active sense of adventure who, because of the unstructured nature of daily life in the West, lacks moral perspective and restraint. Within properly established society, rowdies could become well-mannered citizens, but Hübner does not relate in detail how a town like Corinne could make such a transition.)

2. **What was it about the town of Corinne that impressed Hübner the most? Is his assessment of the town's inhabitants convincing?**
   (Hübner first described the geographical setting. He noticed the physical construction and layout of the town but wrote at length not about buildings but rather the effect that the environment had on the character of Corinne's inhabitants. Hübner argued that the "temper of the time and place" conditioned many men to turn their "really fine qualities" to unedifying pursuits. He noted a lack of formal legal systems, "women of bad character," and the propensity to cheat as evidence that the rowdies of Corinne were merely the products of the human struggle to "conquer savage nature." In short, the choices and behavior of the men and women of Corinne were determined by the environment.)

Writing Assignments

1. Assess Hübner's assertion that Corinne represented a "border" existence between civilization and savage men and things. Which elements of Corinne were civilized, and which were savage?

2. Hübner finds reasons to admire the "true rowdy." What does he admire about them and why? Would the urban easterner or the "backwoodsman" have agreed? What would the rowdies have thought about Hübner once they sobered up?

Skill-Building Map Exercises

Map 16.1: The Natural Environment of the West (p. 458)

1. **Explain the significance of the ninety-eighth meridian.**

(West of the line, 20 inches or less of annual rainfall inhibits normal agricultural practices.)

2. **Had European settlers ever faced a situation similar to that experienced by Americans pushing into the western frontier?**
(Yes, the early generation of colonists who settled the eastern seaboard likewise encountered a vast, unfamiliar environment.)

Map 16.6: The Mining Frontier, 1848–1890 (p. 474)

1. **What was the geographical significance of the mining industry in the settlement of the West?**
(Valuable metals were discovered in areas of the West that were unsuitable for agriculture or ranching. This led to the growth of population in sections of the nation that otherwise would have remained unsettled.)

2. **The map illustrates numerous towns in the Far West. What factor(s) determined their locations?**
(The towns associated with the mining boom grew in places in which miners required goods and services. The fortunes of the towns were closely tied to that of the mines. When the mining boom went bust, so did most, but not all, of the mining towns.)

Topic for Research

Women on the Frontier

Until recently, historians paid little attention to the experiences of women in the westward movement. When they did, they relied on a few well-worn stereotypes of the frontier woman as "victim," dragged down by a harsh and lonesome frontier life, or as "heroic civilizer," uplifting by her example a raw frontier society. A number of books provide a more realistic and complex portrait of women on the frontier: Julie Roy Jeffrey, *Frontier Women: The Trans-Mississippi West, 1840–1880* (1979); Sandra L. Myres, *Westering Women and the Frontier Experience, 1800–1915* (1982); Glenda Riley, *Women and Indians on the Frontier, 1825–1915* (1984) and *The Female Frontier: A Comparative View of the Prairie and the Plains* (1988). Sarah Deutsch, *No Separate Refuge: Culture, Class, and Gender on an Anglo-Hispanic Frontier in the American Southwest, 1880–1940* (1987), focuses on Hispanic women. Another kind of frontierswoman — the prostitute — is discussed in Marion S. Goldman, *Gold Diggers and Silver Miners: Prostitution and Social Life on the Comstock Lode* (1981).

Choose one of these books to help you answer some of the questions posed by Sandra L. Myres: What preconceptions did women have about the frontier? How did they view the physical wilderness? What preconceptions did they have about Indians, Mexican Americans, and other groups they would encounter in the West? How, if at all, were these ideas changed by life on the frontier? Did women's ideas about their role in the family and the community change as a result of the westering experience? Did women take on new roles in the West? In what ways did women's reactions and adaptations to the frontier differ from those of men?

Since the books cited above seek to answer these questions through the voices of women, they rely heavily on diaries and other contemporary writings, some of which have been published and may be available in college libraries. For a more ambitious paper, consult one or more of these primary sources in addition to a secondary work. The place to begin is with the notes and bibliographies of the books cited above.

Suggested Themes

1. How did the lives of women on the frontier differ from the lives of men? In what ways did those differences enhance or diminish the quality of life experienced by the women?

2. Imagine you are a woman living on the frontier in the nineteenth century. Write a letter back home (the East? Europe?), indicating the reasons you would encourage or discourage family members from joining you. Use specific historical material from diaries or other sources in formulating your advice.

How to Use the Ancillaries Available with *America's History*

Refer to the Preface to *America's History* at the front of the book for descriptions of instructor resources, including the Instructor's Resource CD-ROM, Computerized Test Bank, transparencies, and *Using the Bedford Series in History and Culture in the U.S. History Survey*. Student resources, also described in the Preface, include the Online Study Guide and *Documents to Accompany* America's History, a primary-source reader.

For Instructors

Using the Bedford Series in History and Culture in the U.S. History Survey
This brief online guide by Scott Hovey provides practical suggestions for incorporating volumes from the highly regarded Bedford Series in History and Culture into your survey course. Titles that complement the material covered in Chapter 16 include *Our Hearts Fell to the Ground: Plains Indian Views of How the West Was Lost*, edited with an introduction by Colin G. Calloway, and *Does the Fron-*

tier Experience Make America Exceptional by Richard W. Etulain. For descriptions of these titles and how you might use them in your course, visit **bedfordstmartins .com/usingseries.**

For Students

Online Study Guide at bedfordstmartins.com/henretta
Each of the activities listed below includes short-answer questions. After submitting their answers, students can compare them to the model answers provided.

Map Activity
The map activity presents Map 16.4: The Indian Frontier, to 1890 (p. 470), and asks students to analyze how the Plains Indians were eventually confined to scattered reservations.

Visual Activity
The visual activity presents an advertisement for Buffalo Bill's Wild West show (p. 463) and asks students to compare the myth represented by Buffalo Bill to the reality of the American West.

Reading Historical Documents
The document activity provides a brief introduction to the documents Ida Lindgren: Swedish Emigrant in Fron-tier Kansas (p. 465) and Zitkala-Ša (Gertrude Simmons Bonnin): Becoming White (p. 473) and asks students to analyze their content, thinking critically about the sources.

Documents to Accompany *America's History*
Each of the documents listed is introduced by a head-note, which places the document in context, and is followed by questions, which help students to analyze the piece.

Sources for Chapter 16 are
Helen Hunt Jackson, *A Century of Dishonor* (1881)
The Dawes Severalty Act (1887)
Buffalo Bird Woman, *Beginning a Garden* (1917)
Howard Ruede, *Letter from a Kansas Homesteader* (1878)
John Wesley Powell, *Report on the Lands of the Arid Region* (1878)
On Chinese Exclusion (1876, 1882)
Nuestra Platforma: Hispanics Protest Anglo Encroachment in New Mexico (1890)
John Muir, *A Perilous Night on Shasta's Summit* (1888)

CHAPTER 17

Capital and Labor in the Age of Enterprise

1877–1900

Chapter Instructional Objectives

After you have taught this chapter, your students should be able to answer the following questions:

1. What factors led to the economic success of industrial capitalism in America after 1877?

2. How were business practices organized and new technologies harnessed in order to maximize profits in American industry?

3. What were the working conditions of American industrial laborers?

4. How and why did American workers seek to improve their working conditions in the late nineteenth century?

Chapter Summary

The United States became a great industrial power in the late nineteenth century. The factories that sprung up in America before the Civil War had been appendages of the agricultural economy. Prices fell after the war, but manufacturing efficiency increased, creating a boom in consumer goods. Meanwhile, a demand for these goods grew steadily. Central to this development were the shift from iron making to the manufacturing of steel, the rapid expansion of coal mining, an efficient railway system to move goods and increase access to markets, and the improvement of technology for generating steam and electrical power. These advances made possible the production of capital goods and energy required by a manufacturing economy. The scale of enterprise increased, and the vertically integrated firm became the predominant form of business organization.

In the largely agrarian South, laborers earned wages that were below average even by the depressed standards of that time. In the North, the enormous demand for labor led to an influx of immigrants, making ethnic diversity a distinctive feature of the American working class. Women joined the labor force in growing numbers but were restricted to work that became sex typed as female. They also earned substantially smaller wages than men.

The mass production of standardized goods improved the productivity of American manufacturing. As technology advanced, American employers needed fewer craftsmen but more unskilled labor. Workers gradually lost the esteem and satisfaction they had derived from independent craft work. A new system of mass production mechanized industry. Employers were attracted to machinery because it increased output. Scientific management promised to get the maximum work from each worker by training him or her to work as mechanically as possible. Employers and managers assumed that the workers' only concern was money.

Poor working conditions and unrelenting pressure for increased productivity led disenchanted workers to form labor organizations. Unionization was only partially successful, however, as the workers' militancy antagonized many citizens and led the government to side with management. As the twentieth century dawned, some radical workers and their leaders turned to socialism or syndicalism to achieve their goals.

Chapter Annotated Outline

I. Industrial Capitalism Triumphant
   A. Growth of the Industrial Base
      1. Early factories produced consumer goods — goods that replaced articles made at home or by individual artisans.

26

2. Gradually, capital goods — goods that added to the productive capacity of the economy — began to drive America's industrial economy.

3. In 1856, British inventor Henry Bessemer designed the Bessemer converter, a furnace that refined raw pig iron into steel, which is harder and more durable than wrought iron.

4. In 1872, Andrew Carnegie erected a massive steel mill that used the Bessemer converter; the Edgar Thompson Works of Pittsburgh became a model for the modern steel industry.

5. The technological breakthrough in steel spurred the intensive mining of some of the country's rich mineral resources: iron ore and coal.

6. The nation's energy revolution was completed with the coupling of the steam turbine with the electric generator; after 1900, American factories began a conversion to electric power.

B. The Railroad Boom

1. Americans were impatient for year-round, on-time transportation service that canal barges and riverboats could not provide; the arrival of locomotives from Britain in the 1830s was the solution.

2. The United States chose to pay for its railroads by free enterprise, but the governments of many states and localities lured railroads with offers of financial aid.

3. The most important boost that government gave the railroads was a legal form of organization — the corporation with limited liability.

4. Railroad promoters ran the railroad construction companies, which raised cash by buying and selling railroads' bonds.

5. The most successful railroad promoters were those with access to capital; John Murray Forbes, Cornelius Vanderbilt, and James J. Hill were the most famous.

6. With the early railroads, gauges of track varied widely, and at terminal points the railroads were not connected.

7. In 1883 the railroads divided the country into the four standard time zones to manage scheduling, and by the end of the 1880s, the track gauge was standardized.

8. The inventor George Westinghouse perfected the automatic coupler, the air brake, and the friction gear; this resulted in a steady drop in freight rates for shippers.

9. For investors, the price of railroad competition was high; when the economy turned bad, as in 1893, a third of the industry went into receivership.

10. After 1893, the investment banks of J. P. Morgan & Co. and Kuhn Loeb & Co. stepped in to court new investors and consolidate old railroad rivals; this reorganization shifted the nerve center of American railroading to Wall Street.

11. By the early twentieth century, a half dozen great regional systems had emerged out of the jumble of rival systems.

C. Mass Markets and Large-Scale Enterprise

1. Until well into the industrial age, most manufacturers operated on a small scale for nearby markets and left distribution to wholesale merchants and commission agents.

2. As America's swelling population flocked to the cities, the railroads brought tightly packed markets within the reach of distant producers.

3. The Union Stock Yard of Chicago opened in 1865; livestock came in by rail from the Great Plains, was auctioned off in Chicago, and then shipped east for processing in "butchertowns."

4. Gustavus F. Swift and his engineers developed an effective cooling system for shipping beef. Swift invested in a fleet of refrigerator cars and built a central beef-processing plant in Chicago as well as a network of branch houses.

5. Swift & Co. was a vertically integrated firm, absorbing the functions of many small, specialized enterprises within a single centralized structure.

6. John D. Rockefeller's Standard Oil Company had a national distribution system for kerosene, and the Singer Sewing Machine Company used retail stores as well as door-to-door salesmen.

7. In the late nineteenth century, modern advertising appeared as big businesses set about creating a national demand for their brand names.

D. The New South

1. After the Civil War, the South remained overwhelmingly agricultural, and wages for farm labor in the South were low.

2. Southern textile mills recruited workers from the surrounding hill farms; mill wages exceeded farm earnings, but not by much.

3. The new southern mills had an advantage over those of the long-established New England industry — southern mills' wages were as much as 40 percent less.

4. A "family system" of mill labor developed, with a labor force that was half female and very young.

5. Blacks sometimes worked as day laborers and janitors but seldom got jobs as operatives in the cotton mills.

6. When cigarettes became fashionable in the 1880s, southerner James B. Duke took advantage of James A. Bonsack's new machine that produced cigarettes automatically.

7. The businesses that developed in the South produced raw materials or engaged in the low-tech processing of coarse products; the South consistently lagged behind the North economically.

8. Many southerners blamed the North for economic disparity, as most of the capital came from the North.

9. Low wages in the South discouraged employers from replacing workers with machinery, attracted labor-intensive industry, and inhibited investment in education.

10. Northerners and immigrants avoided the South and its low wages, and prior to World War I, few southerners left for the higher wages of the North.

II. The World of Work
  A. Labor Recruits
    1. Unlike Europe, the United States did not rely primarily on its own population for a labor supply.
    2. The U.S. demand for labor tripled between 1870 and 1900; white Americans found opportunities in the multiplying white-collar jobs in the cities.
    3. Modest numbers of blacks began to migrate out of the South between 1870 and 1910; most settled in cities but were not given factory work because immigrants provided cheaper labor.
    4. Ethnic origin largely determined the kind of work immigrants took in America: the Welsh were mostly tin-plate workers; the English were miners; and Germans were machinists.
    5. With the advance of technology, fewer European craftsmen were needed, yet the demand for ordinary labor skyrocketed.
    6. By 1895, arrivals from southern and Eastern Europe far outstripped immigrants from Western Europe.
    7. Heavy, low-paid labor became the domain of the immigrants; their relatives and neighbors often followed them to America, and a high degree of clustering resulted.
    8. Immigrants were often peasants displaced by the breakdown of the traditional rural economies of southern and Eastern Europe; many returned home during America's depression years.
    9. In 1900, women made up a quarter of the nonagricultural labor force. Contemporary be-

liefs about womanhood determined which jobs women took and how they were treated at work.

10. In 1890, fewer than 5 percent of white wives had worked outside the home, while more than 30 percent of black wives worked for wages.

11. Women were not permitted to do "men's work" nor were they paid the same wages as men, regardless of their skills. Employers maintained that because women had men to support them, they did not require a "living wage."

12. At the turn of the century, women's work fell into three categories: domestic service; female white-collar jobs; and industry, such as the garment trade.

13. Black women were excluded from all but the most menial jobs, as were black men.

14. The family household could not function without the wife's contribution; therefore, society disapproved of wives taking paying jobs.

15. Working-class families had a hard time getting by on one income; in 1900, one in five children under the age of sixteen worked.

16. By the 1890s, all northern industrial states had passed child labor laws and regulations on work hours for teenagers.

17. Deprived of their children's earnings, yet still needing more than one income, more women in working-class families entered the workplace.

  B. Autonomous Labor
    1. Autonomous male craftsmen flourished in many branches of nineteenth-century industry.
    2. These workers abided by the "stint," an informal system of restricting output that infuriated efficiency-minded engineers.
    3. Many young female workers found a new sense of independence and new social outlets from working.
    4. Women workers rarely wielded the kind of craft power that the skilled male worker commonly enjoyed.
    5. For men, dispersal of authority was characteristic of nineteenth-century industry; the most skilled workers were autonomous — hiring, supervising, and paying their own helpers — but the subordinates were sometimes exploited.

  C. Systems of Control
    1. With mass production, machine tools became more specialized, and the need for skilled operatives disappeared.
    2. Employers were attracted to "dedicated" machinery because it increased output; the impact on workers was not their greatest concern.

3. Frederick W. Taylor's method of scientific management eliminated the brainwork from manual labor and deprived workers of the authority they had previously known.

4. Influenced by Taylor, managers subjected tasks to time-and-motion studies in order to determine the workers' pay; Taylor assumed that workers would automatically respond to the lure of higher earnings.

5. Scientific management did not solve the labor problem as Taylor had thought it would, rather it embittered relationships on the shop floor.

6. Taylor's disciples created the new fields of personnel work and industrial psychology, which they claimed extracted more and better labor from workers.

7. For textile workers, the loss of autonomy came early; for miners and ironworkers, it came more slowly; and construction workers mostly retained their autonomy.

III. The Labor Movement

A. Reformers and Unionists

1. The Knights of Labor was founded in 1869 as a secret society of garment workers in Philadelphia, and by 1878 had emerged as a national movement.

2. To achieve labor "emancipation," the Knights had originally intended to set up factories run by the employees; led by Terence V. Powderly, they instead devoted themselves to "education."

3. The labor reformers expressed the higher aspirations of American workers, but the trade unions tended to the workers' day-to-day needs.

4. The earliest unions were organizations of workers in the same craft and sometimes the same ethnic group.

5. By the 1870s the national union was becoming the dominant organizational form for American trade unionism.

6. Many workers carried membership cards in both the Knights of Labor and a trade union.

7. As did most trade unions, the Knights barred women until 1881, when women shoe workers won the right to form their own local assembly.

8. The Knights of Labor allowed black workers to join out of the need for solidarity and in deference to the Order's egalitarian principles.

B. The Triumph of "Pure and Simple" Unionism

1. In the early 1880s the Knights began to act more like trade unions; as the Knights won more strikes, its membership rapidly increased.

2. As the Knights stood poised as a potential industrial-union movement, the national trade unions insisted on a clear separation of roles, with the Knights confined to labor reform.

3. Samuel Gompers led the ideological assault on the Knights, and he hammered out the philosophical position known as pure and simple unionism.

4. The Knights favored an eight-hour workday because workers had duties to perform as American citizens, and unionists favored it because it spread the work among more people, providing more jobs and protecting them from overwork.

5. Seizing on the antiunion hysteria set off by the Haymarket affair, employers broke strikes violently, compiled blacklists, and forced some workers to sign "yellow-dog contracts" that renounced union membership.

6. In December 1886, the national trade unions formed the American Federation of Labor (AFL); the underlying principle was that workers had to take the world as it was.

7. The Knights of Labor never recovered from the Haymarket affair, and by the mid-1890s, the Knights had faded away while the AFL took firm root.

C. Industrial War

1. American trade unions wanted a larger share for working people; this made employers opposed to collective bargaining.

2. Andrew Carnegie had once stated that workers had the right to organize and that employers should honor workers' jobs during labor disputes.

3. Carnegie decided that collective bargaining had become too expensive and wanted to replace the workers at his steel mill in Homestead, Pennsylvania, with advanced machinery.

4. Carnegie's second-in-command, Henry Clay Frick, announced that Carnegie's mill would no longer deal with the Amalgamated Association of Iron and Steel Workers.

5. The Homestead strike on July 6, 1892, ushered in a decade of strife that pitted working people against the power of corporate industry often backed by the government.

6. George M. Pullman cut wages at his factory but not the rents for employee housing; he denied that there was any connection between his roles as employer and landlord.

7. Pullman workers belonged to the American Railway Union (ARU), and Eugene V. Debs directed all ARU members not to handle Pullman sleeping cars (a secondary labor boycott).

8. The Pullman boycott was crushed by the federal government, which — pressured by the railroad companies — used its power to protect the U.S. mail carried in railcars.

D. American Radicalism in the Making

1. Eugene Debs devoted himself to the American Railway Union, a union that organized all railroad workers irrespective of skill — an industrial union.

2. With the formation of the Socialist Labor Party in 1877, Marxist socialism established itself as a permanent presence in American politics.

3. After being incarcerated after the Pullman strike, Debs gravitated to the socialist camp and helped to launch the Socialist Party of America in 1901.

4. Under Debs, the Socialist Party of America began to attract not only immigrants but farmers and women as well.

5. A different brand of American Marxist radicalism was taking shape as the atmosphere of western mining camps turned violent in the 1890s.

6. The Western Federation of Miners joined with left-wing socialists in 1905 to create the Industrial Workers of the World (Wobblies).

7. The Wobblies supported the Marxist class struggle at the workplace rather than in politics (syndicalism).

8. American radicalism bore witness to what was exploitative and unjust in the new industrial order.

Lecture Strategies

1. Examine the rise of American railroads. This discussion could describe the technological innovations that allowed for rapid expansion, the development of managerial expertise that permitted control of far-flung rail networks, and the men behind the rail companies. Explore the role of the railroads, as the nation's first big business, in transforming the American economy.

2. Discuss the growth of the American mass market. Compare the United States with Europe in terms of growth rates and free trade. Explore the roles of mass production, advertising, new technology (for example, the refrigerator car), and growing purchasing power in preparing Americans to be consumers.

3. Explore the rise of the "New South." Explain the vision of New South apostles; the economic realities of the southern states; and why, two decades after the movement began, the South continued to lag behind

the rest of the country. Be certain to discuss the impact of race on the South and the emergence of southern industrialism.

4. Discuss the development of the American labor movement in the late nineteenth century. Among the topics to cover are the division between craft workers and unskilled workers, the difficulties of organizing labor in gigantic manufacturing facilities, the effect of immigration on the union movement, the negative consequences of strikes and violence, and the role of scientific management in the workplace.

5. The origins of American radicalism make an excellent lecture topic. The social and economic dislocations caused by rapid industrialization should be mentioned, along with Karl Marx's impact on American radicals. Discuss how the government's backing of big business and the failure of strikes were important to the beginnings of American radicalism.

Class Discussion Starters

1. **Why was the year 1877 so significant in American history?**

Possible answers:

a. Reconstruction ended, and the federal government left the South to its own devices.

b. The Panic of 1873 ended.

c. It was a year of violence. Rail strikes swept the nation in July and August, and the ensuing carnage led President Rutherford B. Hayes to call up federal troops to restore order.

2. **What factors influenced the rapid growth of the American steel industry in the late nineteenth century?**

Possible answers:

a. The introduction and ready acceptance of new technologies such as the Bessemer steel furnace.

b. Rapidly expanding markets.

c. An abundance of natural resources.

d. Available labor.

e. Available capital.

f. High profits.

3. **What was the significance of the massive American rail network?**

Possible answers:

a. Railroads linked the various sections of the country together: virtually every American lived fairly close to a rail line.

b. The railroads made possible the rapid movement of large numbers of passengers and vast amounts of freight at a decreasing cost.

c. The railroads spurred the growth of the steel industry because rails were the chief product of American steel mills in the 1870s and 1880s.

d. The tremendous sums needed to finance track construction revolutionized American capital markets as large stock and bond issues were floated to underwrite the building boom.

e. The explosive growth in track mileage made mass marketing possible.

4. What were the keys to large-scale enterprise in late nineteenth-century America?

Possible answers:
   a. A rapidly growing population.
   b. The lack of internal trade barriers.
   c. The protection of domestic manufacturers through high tariffs.
   d. The availability of cheap labor.

5. Explain how Gustavus Swift changed the American meatpacking industry.

Possible answers:
   a. Swift and his engineers designed and manufactured refrigerated railcars, allowing fresh meat to be shipped safely over long distances.
   b. Swift's company pioneered the system of vertical integration, controlling the processing, distribution, and marketing of meat.
   c. Swift's company helped to eliminate smaller competition. Within a few years, an oligopoly dominated the American meat industry.

6. How did American society prepare its citizens to be consumers of standardized goods?

Possible answers:
   a. Geographical mobility broke down local customs and regional distinctions.
   b. Advertising gave products national recognition and a national market.
   c. The blurring of social distinctions meant that citizens ate and dressed similarly.

7. What was the "New South" movement, and how successful was it?

Possible answers:
   a. Its leaders wanted the South to catch up with the North economically; thus they favored a leadership dominated by industrialists.
   b. Ultimately, the New South movement failed. Most southerners continued farming, and those who moved into industry made substantially less than did their northern counterparts.

8. What distinguished craft workers from common laborers in the United States in the nineteenth century?

Possible answers:
   a. Craft workers performed specialized tasks that required a high level of skill.
   b. Craft workers were more or less autonomous employees who needed little or no supervision as they performed their appointed tasks.
   c. Craft workers tended to be independent and less tolerant of poor working conditions.

9. How was immigrant labor beneficial to the United States?

Possible answers:
   a. Immigrant labor was the backbone of basic industries such as steel. Without immigrants, the United States could not have industrialized as it did.
   b. When the American economy was weak, many jobless immigrants returned to their homelands. Immigrants who stayed only temporarily were thus a safety valve for the growing American labor force.

10. Why did American workers become increasingly alienated in the late nineteenth century?

Possible answers:
   a. The new factory jobs required fewer skills ("deskilling").
   b. The emphasis was on increased production; as a result, workers performed the same repetitive tasks.
   c. Management was ever more distant from the factory floor.

11. Explain the weaknesses of the American labor movement late in the nineteenth century.

Possible answers:
   a. The labor movement was divided. Craft workers joined the new American Federation of Labor, which had traditional goals. Other workers joined the Knights of Labor, an amorphous fraternal-like organization that was hurt by being linked to the labor violence of the 1880s.
   b. Racial, ethnic, and gender divisions hindered workers' solidarity.
   c. Incidents of violence alienated the public and damaged the labor movement.

12. Explain the rise of radicalism in the United States.

Possible answers:
   a. Industrial strife, exemplified by the unsuccessful Pullman boycott and Homestead strike, contributed to workers' disillusionment.
   b. Economic downturns, such as the Panic of 1893, caused untold numbers of workers to lose their jobs and turn to radical organizations for redress.

c. Real and perceived social injustices prompted workers to take a more activist stance.

d. Desperation led some workers to seek solutions outside traditional political avenues.

Chapter Writing Assignments

1. Evaluate and rank in terms of importance the advances in industry — railroads, mass marketing, and managerial techniques — that worked together to promote a surge of industrial development in the late nineteenth century.

2. Describe the development of industry in the South during this period. How and why did southern factories and labor conditions differ from those in the Northeast and Midwest?

3. Why did most immigrants choose to work in American factories rather than in the agricultural sector?

4. Which factory and office jobs were open to women? How did prevailing stereotypes affect the sex typing of occupations?

5. Many Americans today assume that the pace of "change" in recent decades has been the most rapid in American history. Contrast economic and technological changes of the late nineteenth century with those of recent years. During which period were Americans' lives more significantly affected, and how?

6. Explain why the labor actions of the late nineteenth century failed to achieve their goals.

Document Exercises

NEW TECHNOLOGY

Iron and Steel (p. 488)

Document Discussion

1. **What advantages did steel have over iron?**
(It was harder and more durable and thus better suited for the products of a demanding industrial economy. Railroad track was a prime example. When made from steel, it could be produced in much greater volume at a considerably lower cost, and it lasted longer.)

2. **How did the revolution in steelmaking change American industrialism?**
(Industrial activity was concentrated geographically, and steel companies became vertically integrated businesses. The scale of steel production was large,

and workers labored under harsh conditions. Steel remained in high demand and enjoyed a multitude of uses in the transportation, manufacturing, and construction industries. The growth of steelmaking resembled what occurred overall in the American economy — the primacy of capital goods.)

Writing Assignments

1. In what ways was the late nineteenth century an age of steel? What were some of its most important uses?

2. The discovery of how to make steel did not alone account for steel's widespread production. Examine the rise of a steelmaking industry in America. What political and economic conditions contributed to its rapid success?

AMERICAN LIVES

Jay Gould: Robber Baron? (p. 492)

Document Discussion

1. **Why is there ambiguity about Jay Gould's reputation as a robber baron?**
(In Gould's time, his reputation as a ruthless businessman who sought to maximize profit captured the attention of observers. Gould's business deals often caused others to lose money, which earned him a degree of notoriety. Only much later was Gould recognized for the positive contributions he made to the development of the railroad industry by making available speculative capital and forcing efficiencies.)

2. **Why was Gould successful as a railroad owner?**
(Gould used novel financing techniques so that his railroad had access to necessary capital. He also understood that railroads operated most effectively when trunk lines were integrated with business centers, industries, and population hubs to ensure that demand for freight transportation remained high.)

Writing Assignments

1. How much of Gould's success was attributable to his personal talent, and how much to other factors? If in fact Gould created his own opportunities, what were his civic obligations?

2. How was Jay Gould similar to other businessmen and entrepreneurs of the late nineteenth century? Were such men necessary to the major industrialization of the period?

VOICES FROM ABROAD

Count Vay de Vaya und Luskod: Pittsburgh Inferno (p. 503)

Document Discussion

1. To what does de Vaya attribute the persistence of poor working conditions in the steel district?
(According to de Vaya, new immigrants who were eager for work would readily accept poor working conditions. Workers had no leverage because if they threatened to quit in protest of the poor conditions, they could be easily replaced. Thus as long as new immigrants continued to arrive, mill owners would not expend effort improving workers' safety).

2. What were de Vaya's feelings in regard to the American steel industry in Pittsburgh and the troubles of the Hungarian workers?
(De Vaya felt distressed at the difficult and dangerous working conditions that he witnessed in the steel mills. He felt that Hungarian immigrants were being exploited because of their economic desperation. De Vaya was pessimistic and saw little hope that the situation would be remedied in the future.)

Writing Assignments

1. What does de Vaya's assessment of the plight of Hungarian immigrants working in the steel mills suggest about the potential success or failure of labor organizers in this industry?

2. Why did Hungarian workers continue to seek employment in the Pittsburgh steel district despite the harsh environment? Were the Hungarians unique in this regard, or was this typical?

AMERICAN VOICES

John Brophy: A Miner's Son (p. 504)

Document Discussion

1. Why did Brophy admire the work of his father as a miner?
(Brophy admired the pride and skill exhibited by his father. He described mining as a complete way of life — one that reflected a high level of craftsmanship as well as social identity.)

2. To what class in American society were miners considered to belong?
(Miners were autonomous craft workers who possessed a great deal of independence. Miners usually provided their own tools, worked at their own pace,

and quit early when they chose. Hence, a sense of "brotherhood" emerged between miners.)

Writing Assignments

1. Compare and contrast Brophy's account of mining with other contemporary occupations. According to Brophy, was mining a "profession"?

2. What do Brophy's comments reflect about workers' sense of place within the American industrial economy?

AMERICAN VOICES

Rose Schneiderman: Trade Unionist (p. 509)

Document Discussion

1. What expectations did Schneiderman gain as she studied her working conditions?
(She recognized that she was bringing value to her employer and that some of the hardships she faced were unnecessary. She also wanted men and women in the factory to be treated equally.)

2. How did Schneiderman gain support for her effort?
(She began by organizing a small committee of her friends. Then, with instructions from the union, Schneiderman's committee petitioned other women as they came and went to work in the factories. She sought collective participation, the essence of unionism.)

Writing Assignments

1. Does the attitude of Schneiderman's mother provide any insight into late nineteenth-century gender roles? Explain.

2. What are the advantages and disadvantages of trade unions for women? Consider the perspective of workers, employers, and consumers.

Skill-Building Map Exercises

Map 17.2: The Expansion of the Railroad System, 1870–1890 (p. 490)

1. Why do most of the railroads west of the Mississippi run east to west rather than north to south?
(The direction of the railroads reflects the fact that farmers and ranchers in the West shipped their products via rail to grain processors and packing plants in midwestern cities like St. Louis, Kansas City, Omaha, and Chicago.)

2. How did railroads affect the growth of cities?

(Notice that major cities emerged at the intersection of rail lines. Dallas, Minneapolis–St. Paul, Chicago, Omaha, and Kansas City are examples evident on the map. In turn, cities promoted railroad expansion. This dynamic affected not only large cities but smaller towns as well.)

Map 17.4: The New South, 1900 (p. 496)

1. Which southern states were bypassed by industrial development?

(Arkansas, Florida, Mississippi, and South Carolina.)

2. What does the presence of a robust railroad network indicate about the state of economic development in the South?

(The emergence of a rail network indicates that southern industries were rebounding. The movement of goods by rail is typically a function of wholesale purchase and sale of goods that can only be accomplished by large producers and factories.)

Topic for Research

The Making of the Modern Labor Movement

For much of the nineteenth century, American workers debated a defining question: what should be the goal of the labor movement? By the 1880s, two answers had emerged: labor reform — the demand of the Knights of Labor for fundamental changes in the economic system — and pure and simple unionism — the efforts of the American Federation of Labor to extract the best possible terms for workers from the existing system. Choose either the Knights or the AFL as the subject of your investigation. What were the organization's main goals, and why did it adopt those positions? What were some of the steps it took to achieve its goals, and how successful was it? Compare and contrast both organizations, and explain why the "pure and simple" strategy of the AFL eventually prevailed.

The standard book on the struggle between labor reform and trade unionism is Gerald N. Grob, *Workers and Utopia, 1865–1900* (1961). For the Knights of Labor, it should be supplemented by Leon Fink, *Workingmen's Democracy: The Knights of Labor and American Politics* (1983), which captures the cultural dimensions of labor reform not addressed by earlier historians. The pioneering work on the American labor movement is John R. Commons et al., *History of Labor in the United States* (4 vols., 1918–1935); volumes 2 and 4 cover the period of this chapter. The most recent survey, incorporating much

of the latest scholarship, is Bruce Laurie, *Artisans into Workers: Labor in Nineteenth-Century America* (1989). The clash of ideas, however, is best understood through the words of the two leading exponents, Terence V. Powderly of the Knights and Samuel Gompers of the AFL. Both left autobiographies: Powderly's *The Path I Trod* (1940) and Gompers's *Seventy Years of Life and Labor* (2 vols., 1925). Moreover, the letters and papers of Gompers are being published in an authoritative, multivolume edition by Stuart B. Kaufman. The volumes covering the 1880s have been published, and they contain a rich documentary record of dispute. In Melvyn Dubofsky and Warren Van Time, eds., *Labor Leaders in America* (1986), there are excellent brief biographies of Powderly and Gompers, with up-to-date bibliographical guides for further reading.

You may prefer to examine the views of the Knights and the AFL on another issue: the place of women and blacks in the labor movement. The starting points are two books by Philip S. Foner, *Women and the American Labor Movement from Colonial Times to the Eve of World War I* (1979) and *Organized Labor and the Black Worker* (1974).

Other works that examine various aspects of the American economy and society include Herbert Gutman, *Work, Culture, and Society in Industrializing America* (1976); Elizabeth Ewen, *Immigrant Women in the Land of Dollars* (1990); William Cronon, *Nature's Metropolis* (1992); and Walter LaFeber, *The New Empire* (1998).

Suggested Themes

1. What were the main goals and policies of the American Federation of Labor? Explain the relative success of the AFL in an environment generally hostile to organized labor.

2. What were the chief objectives of the Knights of Labor? Discuss the reasons for the failure of the Knights to organize and represent American labor in the 1870s and 1880s.

3. Compare the views of the Knights and the AFL on the place of women and blacks in the labor movement. Why did the two groups differ on this issue?

4. Compare the leadership qualities of Terence V. Powderly and Samuel Gompers in their roles as chiefs of the Knights of Labor and the AFL, respectively.

How to Use the Ancillaries Available with *America's History*

Refer to the Preface to *America's History* at the front of the book for descriptions of instructor resources, including the Instructor's Resource CD-ROM, Computerized Test Bank, transparencies, and *Using the Bedford Series in History and Culture in the U.S. History Survey*. Student resources, also described in the Preface, include the Online Study Guide and *Documents to Accompany* America's History, a primary-source reader.

For Instructors

Using the Bedford Series in History and Culture in the U.S. History Survey

This brief online guide by Scott Hovey provides practical suggestions for incorporating volumes from the highly regarded Bedford Series in History and Culture into your survey course. Titles that complement the material covered in Chapter 17 include *The McGuffey Readers: Selections from the 1879 Edition*, edited with an introduction by Elliot J. Gorn; *A Traveler from Altruria by William Dean Howells*, edited with an introduction by David W. Levy; and *Looking Backward: 2000-1887 by Edward Bellamy*, edited with an introduction by Daniel H. Borus. For descriptions of these titles and how you might use them in your course, visit **bedfordstmartins .com/usingseries**.

For Students

Online Study Guide at bedfordstmartins.com/henretta

Each of the activities listed below includes short-answer questions. After submitting their answers, students can compare them to the model answers provided.

Map Activity

The map activity presents Map 17.3: The Dressed Meat Industry, 1900 (p. 494), and asks students to analyze its contents.

Visual Activity

The visual activity presents an advertisement for Kellogg's Corn Flakes (p. 495) and asks students to analyze the intended message of the imagery used in the ad.

Reading Historical Documents

The document activity provides a brief introduction to the documents John Brophy: A Miner's Son (p. 504) and Rose Schneiderman: Trade Unionist (p. 509) and asks students to analyze their content, thinking critically about the sources.

Documents to Accompany *America's History*

Each of the documents listed is introduced by a headnote, which places the document in context, and is followed by questions, which help students to analyze the piece.

Sources for Chapter 17 are
Henry George, *Progress and Poverty* (1879)
Andrew Carnegie, *Gospel of Wealth* (1889)
Lilly B. Chase Wyman, *Studies of Factory Life: Among the Women* (1888)
Anonymous (A Black Domestic), *More Slavery at the South* (c. 1912)
Frederick Winslow Taylor, *The Principles of Scientific Management* (1911)
Terrence V. Powderly, *The Army of Unemployed* (1887)
Eugene V. Debs, *How I Became a Socialist* (1902)
Testimony before the U.S. Strike Commission on the Pullman Strike (1894)

CHAPTER 18

The Politics of Late-Nineteenth-Century America

Chapter Instructional Objectives

After you have taught this chapter, your students should be able to answer the following questions:

1. Explain the role of parties in domestic politics before 1900. What choices did the parties afford voters?

2. How and why did political affairs play a central role in American culture in the late nineteenth century? How did women participate in political culture?

3. Analyze and discuss the origins and aims of the Populist movement.

4. Describe the political structure in the South after 1877, and explain how blacks were gradually disenfranchised.

5. How and why did racial segregation intensify in the late nineteenth century?

Chapter Summary

Political stalemate was the rule for most of the last quarter of the nineteenth century. After the end of Reconstruction, national politics became less oriented around vital issues. Neither Republicans nor Democrats could muster the power to dominate national politics. In this environment, laissez-faire government prevailed, a system most Americans willingly accepted. Yet post-Reconstruction politics displayed great vigor at the local level. The number of citizens who voted was high, and local politics was the arena in which the nation's ethnic and religious conflicts were fought out. Also, party machines performed critical civic functions that properly belonged to, but were still beyond the capacity of, governmental bodies.

Many of the wealthy, and those who aspired to become wealthy, adopted the tenets of social Darwinism, which touted prosperity as a sign of personal and social "fitness," defamed poverty as the fate of those unfit for society, and attacked government aid to the needy as destructive to social evolution. Social Darwinists believed government's main duty was to protect property rights. From the 1870s onward the courts increasingly took on this cause while simultaneously curbing state activism on behalf of the poor and needy.

Beneath the placid surface of national politics, however, serious issues lurked. In the heyday of machine politics, rampant political corruption inspired reform movements. Woman suffrage advocates chafed at the male-controlled political process and sought a broadened platform of social reform. Ethnic groups protested rulings concerning religion in the schools, observance of the Sabbath, and the temperance movement. In the South, "redeemer" Democrats appealed to sectional pride and white supremacy in order to establish one-party rule. Their rule did not, however, check class tensions. Racial and class animosity partnered with Populism to challenge conservative Democratic rule but was defeated. To stifle this challenge once and for all, southern Democrats disenfranchised African Americans, completed a social system of strict segregation of the races through Jim Crow laws, and let loose a cycle of violence. Lynching and the intimidation of blacks became commonplace throughout the South.

Populism grew out of farmers' alliance groups and quickly attracted nonfarmers who shared the need for a party ready to act on their interests. In the Midwest, Populism was popular because of declining crop prices; the Populists joined with politicians who favored a bimetallic standard, frightening those who wanted to maintain the status quo. The hard-fought election of 1896 coincided with the return of prosperity, and the Populists, whose ideas had been co-opted by the Democrats, passed into history. The Republican victory ended the party stalemate of the previous two decades and returned reform politics to the national stage.

Chapter Annotated Outline

I. The Politics of the Status Quo, 1877–1893
    A. The National Scene
       1. There were five presidents from 1877 to 1893: Rutherford B. Hayes (R), James A. Garfield (R), Chester A. Arthur (R), Grover Cleveland (D), and Benjamin Harrison (R).
       2. The president's biggest job was to dispense political patronage; after the assassination of President Garfield in 1881, reform of the spoils system became urgent even though the spoils system was not the immediate motive for the murder.
       3. The Pendleton Act of 1883 created a list of jobs to be filled on the basis of examinations administered by the new Civil Service Commission, but patronage still accounted for the bulk of government posts.
       4. The biggest job of the executive branch was delivering the mail; in 1880, 56 percent of federal employees worked for the post office.
       5. One of the most troublesome issues of the 1880s was how to reduce the federal funding surplus created by customs duties and excise taxes.
       6. Congress had more control over national policy than the presidents; even so, on most issues of the day, divisions on policy occurred within the parties, not between them.
       7. The tariff remained a fighting issue in Congress as the Democrats attacked Republican protectionism; each tariff bill was a patchwork of bargains among special interests.
       8. Every presidential election from 1876 to 1892 was decided by a thin margin, and neither party gained permanent command of Congress.
       9. The weakening of principled politics was evident after 1877, as Republicans backpedaled on the race issue and abandoned blacks to their own fate.
    B. The Ideology of Individualism
       1. In the 1880s the economic doctrine of laissez-faire was the belief that the less government did, the better.
       2. Popular writings abounded with rags-to-riches stories, like the novels of Horatio Alger and innumerable success manuals. Also popular were

Carnegie's autobiography *Triumphant Democracy* and sermons praising wealth, including Bishop Lawrence's assurance that "Godliness is in leage with riches" and Russell H. Conwell's "Acres of Diamonds."
       3. Charles Darwin's *Origin of Species* (1859) explained a process of evolution called natural selection and created a revolution in biology.
       4. Herbert Spencer's theory of social Darwinism spun out an elaborate analysis of how human society had evolved through competition and "survival of the fittest" — millionaires being the fittest.
       5. Social Darwinists regarded any governmental interference on behalf of the "unfit" as destructive to "natural" social processes.
    C. The Supremacy of the Courts
       1. Suspicion of government paralyzed political initiative and shifted power away from the executive and legislative branches.
       2. From the 1870s onward, the courts increasingly became the guardians of the rights of private property against the grasping tentacles of government, especially state governments.
       3. State governments had primary responsibility for social welfare and economic regulation, but it was difficult to strike a balance between state responsibility and the rights of individuals.
       4. Used by the Supreme Court, the Fourteenth Amendment was a powerful restraint on the states in the use of their police powers in order to regulate private business.
       5. Judicial supremacy reflected how dominant the ideology of individualism had become and also how low American politicians had fallen in the esteem of their countrymen.

II. Politics and the People
    A. Cultural Politics: Party, Religion, and Ethnicity
       1. Proportionately more voters turned out in presidential elections from 1876 to 1892 than at any other time in American history.
       2. In an age before movies and radio, politics ranked as one of the great American forms of entertainment, yet party loyalty was a deadly serious matter.
       3. Sectional differences, religion, and ethnicity often determined party loyalty; northern Democrats tended to be foreign-born and Catholic, and Republicans tended to be native-born and Protestant.
       4. Hot social issues — education, the liquor question, and observance of the Sabbath — were also party issues and lent deep significance to party affiliation.

B. Organizational Politics

1. By the 1870s, both parties had evolved formal, well-organized structures.

2. The parties were run by unofficial internal organizations — "political machines" — that consisted of insiders willing to do party work in exchange for public jobs or connections.

3. Power brokerage being their main interest, party bosses treated public issues as somewhat irrelevant.

4. There was intense factionalism within the parties; in 1877 the Republican Party divided into the Stalwarts and the Halfbreeds, who were really fighting over the spoils of party politics.

5. Veterans of machine politics proved to be effective legislators and congressmen, and party machines did informally much of what governmental systems left undone. However, political machines never won widespread approval.

6. In 1884, some Republicans left their party and became known as *Mugwumps*, a term referring to pompous or self-important persons.

7. The Mugwumps controlled newspapers and journals that shaped public opinion. They registered their biggest success in the battle for the secret ballot. Adopted in the early 1890s, the secret ballot freed voters from party surveillance as they exercised the right to vote.

8. Mugwumps were reformers but not on behalf of working people or the poor; true to the spirit of the age, they believed that the government that governed least, governed best.

C. Women's Political Culture

1. Due to the nature of party politics, it was considered to be no place for women.

2. The woman suffrage movement met fierce opposition; suffragists abandoned their efforts to get a constitutional amendment and concentrated on state campaigns.

3. Since many of the women's social goals required state intervention, women's organizations became politically active and sought to create their own political sphere.

4. Women's organizations worked to end prostitution, assisted the poor, agitated for prison reform, and tried to improve educational opportunities for women.

5. The Women's Christian Temperance Union (WCTU) was formed in 1874 to combat alcoholism, and later, under the guidance of Frances Willard, the WCTU adopted a "Do Everything" policy.

6. The WCTU was drawn to woman suffrage, arguing that women needed the vote in order to fulfill their social and spiritual responsibilities as women — an argument that did not pose a threat to masculine pride.

7. By linking women's social concerns to women's political participation, the WCTU helped to lay the groundwork for a fresh attack on male electoral politics in the early twentieth century.

III. Race and Politics in the New South

A. Biracial Politics

1. When Reconstruction ended in 1877, blacks had not been driven from politics — but they did not participate on equal terms with whites and were routinely intimidated during political campaigns.

2. After the Civil War, southern Democrats felt they had "redeemed" the South from Republican domination; hence, they adopted the name "Redeemers."

3. The Republican Party in the South soldiered on, aided by a key Democrat vulnerability: the gap between the Redemption claims of universality and its actual domination by the South's economic elite.

4. The Civil War brought out differences between the planter elite and the farmers who were called on to shed blood for a slaveholding system in which they had no interest.

5. After the Civil War, class tensions were exacerbated by the spread of farm tenancy, instead of farm ownership, and the emergence of the low-wage factory.

6. In Virginia, the "Readjusters" expressed agrarian discontent by opposing repayment of Reconstruction debts to speculators.

7. As an insurgence against the Democrats accelerated, the question of black participation in politics and interracial solidarity became critical.

8. Black farmers developed a political structure of their own, the Colored Farmers' Alliance, which made black voters a factor in the political calculations of southern Populists.

B. One-Party Rule Triumphant

1. The conservative Democrats paraded as the "white man's party" and denounced the Populists for promoting "Negro rule," yet they shamelessly competed for the black vote.

2. Mischief at the polls — counting the votes of blacks that were dead or gone — enabled the Democrats to beat back the Populists in the 1892 elections.

3. Disenfranchising the blacks became a potent movement in the South; in 1890, Mississippi adopted a literacy test that effectively drove blacks out of politics.

4. Poor whites turned their fury on the blacks; they did not want to be disenfranchised by their own lack of education and expected lenient enforcement of the literacy test.

5. Tom Watson, once a fervent Georgia Populist, reversed his position, largely to save his political career. Rallying poor whites, he appealed not to their class interests but to their racial prejudices.

6. Segregated seating in trains in the late 1880s set a precedent for the legal separation of the races; Jim Crow laws soon applied to every type of public facility.

7. In *Plessy v. Ferguson* (1896), the Supreme Court upheld the constitutionality of "separate-but-equal" segregation.

8. *Williams v. Mississippi* (1898) validated the disenfranchising devices of southern states, as long as race was not a specified criterion for disfranchisement.

9. Race hatred in the South manifested itself in a wave of lynching and race riots, and public vilification of blacks became commonplace.

C. Resisting White Supremacy

1. Southern blacks resisted white supremacy as best they could; beginning in 1891, blacks boycotted segregated streetcars in at least twenty-five cities; Ida Wells began her antilynching campaign.

2. Some blacks were drawn to the Back to Africa movement, but emigration was not a viable choice.

3. The foremost black leader of his day, Booker T. Washington, spread a doctrine that was seen as being "accommodationist"; it was known as the Atlanta Compromise.

4. Washington's Tuskegee Institute in Alabama advocated industrial education, and Washington thought that black economic progress was the key to winning political and civil rights.

5. Younger educated blacks thought Washington was conceding too much, and blacks became impatient with his silence on segregation and lynching.

6. By 1915, Washington's approach had been replaced with a more militant strategy, relying on the courts and political protest rather than black self-help and accommodation.

IV. The Crisis of American Politics: The 1890s

A. The Populist Revolt

1. Farmers needed organization to overcome their social isolation and to provide economic services — hence, the appeal of the Granger movement and later the farmers' alliances.

2. Two dominant organizations emerged: the Farmers' Alliance of the Northwest and the National (or Southern) Farmers' Alliance.

3. The Texas Alliance struck out in politics independently after its subtreasury plan was rejected by the Democratic Party as being too radical.

4. As state alliances grew stronger and more impatient, they began to field independent slates; the national People's (Populist) Party was formed in 1892.

5. In 1892 the Populist's presidential candidate, James B. Weaver, captured enough votes to make it clear that the agrarian protest could be a challenge to the two-party system.

6. Although the Populist Party welcomed women, its platform was silent on woman suffrage.

7. Populism differed from the two mainstream parties in that it had a positive attitude toward government, and it acknowledged the conflict between capital and labor.

8. Free silver emerged as the overriding demand of the Populist Party and the Omaha Platform; embattled farmers hoped that an increase in the money supply would raise farm prices and give them relief.

9. Social Democrats and agrarian radicals argued that if free silver became the defining party issue, it would undercut the broader Populist program and alienate wage earners.

10. The practical appeal of silver was too great, and the Populists fatally compromised their party's capacity to maintain an independent existence.

B. Money and Politics

1. The U.S. Banking Act of 1863 curtailed the issuance of banknotes, and in 1875 the circulation of greenbacks came to an end. The United States entered an era of chronic deflation.

2. The United States had always operated on a bimetallic standard, but silver became more valuable as metal than as money; in 1873, silver was officially dropped as a medium of exchange.

3. When silver prices plummeted, inflationists began to agitate for a resumption of the bimetallic policy; modest victories were won with the Bland-Allison Act of 1878 and the Sherman Silver Purchase Act of 1890.

4. When the crash of 1893 hit, the silver issue divided politics along party lines, with the Democrats bearing the brunt of the responsibility for handling the economic crisis.

5. Grover Cleveland, a sound-money man, did a poor job of handling the crisis; he had to aban-

don a silver-based currency and had Congress repeal the Sherman Silver Purchase Act.

6. Cleveland's secret negotiations with Wall Street to arrange for gold purchases in order to replenish the treasury enraged Democrats and completed his isolation from his party.

7. In his "Cross of Gold" speech in 1896, the Democratic nomination of William Jennings Bryan established the Democrats as the party of free silver.

8. The Populists accepted Bryan as their candidate and found themselves for all practical purposes absorbed into the Democratic silver campaign.

9. The Republicans' candidate, William McKinley, won the election; McKinley stood solidly for high tariffs, honest money, and prosperity.

10. When McKinley won the election, Republicans became the nation's majority party, and electoral politics regained its place as an arena for national debate.

11. Populism faded away, as did the issue of free silver — the issue upon which the party had staked its fate.

12. In 1897 the world market for agricultural commodities turned favorable and a new spirit of optimism took hold in the "golden age" of American agriculture before World War I.

Lecture Strategies

1. Discuss the American political scene from the presidency of Rutherford B. Hayes to the election of William McKinley. Points to cover include the limited function of the federal government and the presidency; the Mugwumps; party deadlock, especially in Congress; ethnocultural politics; the Populists; and the developing woman suffrage movement.

2. Analyze the "ideology of individualism." Define "individualism" as it was understood at the time. Explain the principles of social Darwinism and the activities of the courts in this regard. Explore the connection between the ideology of individualism and the idea of the American dream.

3. Explain the American fascination with politics in the 1870s and 1880s and note the importance of party loyalty. Explain how the parties divided along ethnic and religious lines as well as people's attitudes toward public morality issues.

4. A lecture on the Populist revolt provides a good opportunity to bring together discordant points in the chapter. For example, one can tie the quest for woman suffrage to the significant role women played

in the Populist movement. Similarly, the hardships of agriculture can be linked to the issue of race, as exemplified by the Colored Farmers' Alliance's coexistence with the Southern Farmers' Alliance. The rural-urban or farmer-wage earner split is a natural point to make. The contrast between the diminishing economic importance of the agricultural sector and the rise of industrialism should be discussed.

5. The importance of the 1896 presidential election makes it a worthwhile lecture topic. Significant points to emphasize include how the election broke a political deadlock and created a Republican ascendancy, the sectional nature of the voting, the role of the currency standard in the campaign, the importance of the economy to voters, and a comparison of the campaigns of William Jennings Bryan and William McKinley.

Class Discussion Starters

1. **Why did the presidents from 1877 to 1897 not make a larger mark on history?**

Possible answers:
   a. Government was conservative in size and scope, initiating and providing very few services.
   b. Government did not have a showy national agenda. Tariffs and patronage, although important, did not capture the public's imagination.
   c. Presidents were not given much latitude by the office; their biggest job was dispensing political patronage.
   d. With the two major political parties so evenly matched, presidents were wary of undertaking any action that might benefit the other party.
   e. There was no war going on to focus attention on the president as the national figurehead.

2. **Why was local politics so interesting to Americans in the late nineteenth century?**

Possible answers:
   a. Politics was a form of mass entertainment.
   b. Certain issues of the day (temperance, education, religious questions) galvanized the electorate. Later, the Populists and the silver issue excited voters.
   c. Sometimes bitter factional disputes — the Mugwump uprising and the Stalwarts versus the Halfbreeds — raised intense interest.

3. **What was the positive side of machine politics?**

Possible answers:
   a. Because of machine politics, professionalism and discipline improved the performance of state and national legislatures.

b. Party machines filled a void — doing what traditional government left undone — and fulfilled people's basic needs, especially in the cities.

c. Party machines provided citizens with civic identity and the ability to influence local matters.

4. What was the negative side of machine politics?

Possible answers:

a. Because of machine politics, small numbers of people, many of whom were unelected or holding no official office, wielded extraordinary political power.

b. Party machines competed with legitimate government agencies for power and influence.

c. Constitutional electoral processes were disrupted by party machine interference.

5. Explain the rise of the woman suffrage movement.

Possible answers:

a. Dedicated feminists such as Susan B. Anthony worked ceaselessly to promote women's rights.

b. Women had begun to make progress in winning the vote: suffrage for women had been granted in four western states.

c. The temperance movement mobilized women to wield social power and taught them important skills in political organizing.

d. The relative absence of other issues meant that the movement didn't have to take a back seat to other contentious issues, such as slavery, or the Civil War. The relative prosperity of the nation meant that there were women with the means, time, and drive to devote to the movement.

6. What differentiated Populists from Republicans and Democrats?

Possible answers:

a. Populism directly appealed to classes and segments of society not served by the other parties.

b. Women played an important role in the Populist movement, while they were essentially excluded from the two major parties.

c. Populists believed that the government had positive responsibilities to the people; they advocated government programs that the two major parties shied away from.

d. Populists lacked the organization and structure of the established parties.

e. Populists lacked the demagogic weapons of the Republicans and Democrats (the "bloody shirt" and "redemption").

7. Why did the question of silver become a national issue?

Possible answers:

a. Farmers supported silver coinage. Large supplies of silver could be used to back currency. With more currency in circulation, inflation would lower farmers' debts.

b. Silver became a political question as silver-state politicians joined the Populists in promoting its use.

c. Silver frightened "sound-money" proponents, who were alarmed by the prospect of crazed agrarians supporting a bimetallic standard that might undermine gold and a strong dollar.

d. Business cycle fluctuations, especially the Panic of 1893, strengthened prosilver sentiment.

e. William Jennings Bryan captivated and agitated the populace with his "Cross of Gold" speech, and silver became the pivotal issue in the 1896 presidential campaign.

8. Why did agrarian radicalism decline after the 1896 election?

Possible answers:

a. Bryan and the silver Democrats lost the election decisively.

b. Agricultural prices moved upward; as commodity prices rose, American farmers entered a "golden age" that lasted through World War I.

c. Large gold finds had the inflationary effects for which the free-silver faction had clamored.

d. Farming's overall importance in the economy was declining as more workers made a living in commerce and manufacturing.

9. Explain the loss of black rights in the South.

Possible answers:

a. With the memory of the Civil War receding, the victorious North lost interest in supporting black rights.

b. The Supreme Court made a number of decisions that undermined civil rights.

c. Congress failed to protect blacks by passing civil rights legislation.

d. Redeemers used the race question to check black-white political cooperation in the 1880s and 1890s.

e. Scientific theories of racial inequality were widely accepted.

10. What was the black response to racist developments in the South?

Possible answers:

a. Resistance, as exemplified by Ida B. Wells and her outspoken and eloquent denunciation of lynching and violence used to intimidate blacks.

b. Accommodation, as exemplified by the teachings of Booker T. Washington.

Chapter Writing Assignments

1. Identify and explain the circumstances that have led to the historical obscurity of the five presidents between 1877 and 1897.

2. If late-nineteenth-century presidents were a bland lot, explain why so many Americans were enthralled with politics.

3. Explain the origins of women's political culture. Consider the relative importance of the West, the Women's Christian Temperance Union, and Populism.

4. What were the origins of Populism, and of what consequence was the Populist revolt? Why didn't Populism emerge earlier?

5. Why did silver and gold become economic and political issues late in the nineteenth century? Why did interest in the silver and gold questions subside after 1896?

6. What factors determined the failure of biracial politics, and why was the quest for racial equality repudiated?

7. Who was Booker T. Washington and why was he such a central figure in race relations in America?

Document Exercises

VOICES FROM ABROAD

Ernst Below: Beer and German American Politics (p. 522)

Document Discussion

1. **What is the political activity under way at the *Turner* festival to which Below objects?**
(Below describes a local social event during which a candidate for mayor orders a round of drinks despite his declared desire to close saloons on Sundays. The event subsequently ended with much drinking and merrymaking. It is difficult to determine whether Below disapproves of the candidate's vote pandering or his position of temperance.)

2. **What does the *Turner* festival suggest about the German-American community in Kansas City?**
(The fact that a crowd from the local German American community gathered at the festival suggests that they continued to identify with at least some customs from their homeland. The presence of a former mayor and mayoral candidate indicates that German American votes were important to winning local political offices.)

Writing Assignments

1. Did associations such as the *Turnverein* contribute to the well-being of immigrant populations in America, or did they hinder their integration as Americans?

2. Examine the role of German immigrants in late nineteenth-century American politics.

AMERICAN VOICES

Helen Potter: The Case for Women's Political Rights (p. 527)

Document Discussion

1. **What was Helen Potter's case for expanding women's political rights?**
(In the short term, Potter thought that politicians would no longer be able to ignore women's issues, the political tone of the nation would improve, and women would get equal pay for equal work. Overall, Potter believed that when women enjoyed full political rights, government would be more responsive to the needs of the entire population. Likewise, women's participation in government would purify civic life.)

2. **Potter thought that woman suffrage would "purify politics, at least for the next two hundred years." Has politics changed as Potter predicted?**
(The nature of political processes and the dynamics that politicians maintain among themselves, the populace, and business interests have persisted. To date, men and women have not organized themselves by gender but continue to identify with issues, or parties, or specific personalities of political leaders.)

Writing Assignments

1. Discuss and analyze the reasons for Potter's belief that suffrage would emancipate women and make them equal to men in the cultural sphere of American life.

2. Evaluate Potter's comment that women should get the vote so that "They would get equal pay for equal work of equal value." How was woman suffrage to translate to economic parity?

AMERICAN VOICES

Tom Watson: The Case for Interracial Unity (p. 528)

Document Discussion

1. **What is Watson's message to poor blacks and poor whites?**

(Watson points out that the material interests of the races are identical. He notes that in terms of economic standing, poor whites and blacks face similar obstacles in trying to better their situation. They each pay high prices for commodities and receive low wages for the products of their labor. Watson attributes racial antagonism to moneyed interests who foster hostility to continue their economic exploitation of the poor.)

2. **What does Watson state about social interaction between whites and blacks?**
   (Watson maintains that the races share a community of economic interests around which they should align. He emphasizes however, that individuals enjoy the prerogative of voluntary association. Watson does not advocate notions of racial supremacy and declares that no law can mandate social standing.)

Writing Assignments

1. Examine the record of the People's Party or another Populist political organization to illustrate the concerns of Populism in the 1890s. How did Populists treat civil rights issues?

2. Identify the core principles of Watson's message, and compare his ideas to the tenets presented in the Declaration of Independence. From such a perspective, was Watson's argument consonant with the nation's founding political ideology or a radical departure?

AMERICAN LIVES

Robert Charles: Black Militant (p. 532)

Document Discussion

1. **What forces shaped Robert Charles? Why do you think he reacted as he did on the night of July 24, 1900?**
   (Charles's life had been characterized by grinding poverty, discrimination, hopelessness, and the fear of lynching. When the police confronted Charles, he snapped.)

2. **According to Ida Wells-Barnett, why would Charles "always be regarded as the hero of New Orleans"? What evidence is there to support this viewpoint?**
   (Charles had fought back against white brutality and thus was a heroic figure. The mere fact that he did not become yet another helpless victim set him apart from black activists who were beaten into submission or lynched. Further evidence of Charles's standing came with the shooting death of Fred Clark, who had betrayed him to the police.)

Writing Assignments

1. How did Charles end up in an extended gunfight with white police officers? What forces might have influenced Charles to resist arrest?

2. What evidence was there that he was a black militant? Did Charles's political ideas make his case an instance of rebellion or one of inept police work and happenstance?

Skill-Building Map Exercises

Map 18.4: The Heyday of Western Populism, 1892 (p. 537)

1. **Why do you think the Populist candidate James B. Weaver did so poorly in the 1892 election in California and Montana and so well in the rest of the West?**
   (Possibly because California's agriculture was so diverse. In Montana, mining and timber were very important, and those interests might not have been won over by Weaver's message.)

Map 18.5: Presidential Elections of 1892 and 1896 (p. 540)

1. **Explain the regional nature of the presidential election of 1896.**
   (Agriculture was dominant or very important in almost all the states that voted for Bryan; manufacturing, trade, and commerce generally dominated the states that supported McKinley.)

2. **What regions of the country possessed the most influence in the electoral college during this election?**
   (Notice that the Northeast and upper Midwest contain the preponderance of electoral college votes. States that today wield influence — such as California, Texas, and Florida — were lightly populated in 1896.)

Topic for Research

The Mugwump Critique of American Politics

In the years following the Civil War, the Mugwumps mounted a powerful critique of American party politics. What kind of people were the liberal reformers? What did they find objectionable in the machine system of politics? What was their attitude toward the immigrants who sustained the machine system? What was their attitude toward universal manhood suffrage? What kind of politics did they advocate, and what was their impact on the political process of the late nineteenth century? Among the many books that explore these questions, the most useful are Geoffrey T. Blodgett, *Gentle Reformers: Massachusetts Democrats in the Cleveland Era* (1966); John G. Sproat, *The "Best Men": Liberal Reformers in the Gilded Age* (1965); Gerald W. McFarland, *Mugwumps, Morals, and Politics, 1884–1920* (1975); and Ari Hoogenboom, *Outlawing the Spoils: The Civil Service Reform Movement, 1865–1883* (1961). A good introduction to the subject, with ample notes on sources, is Chapter 3 in Michael E. McGerr, *The Decline of Popular Politics: The American North, 1865–1928* (1986). The Mugwumps were highly literate people, and they left an ample record of their views. You can find representative essays in 1880s issues of such journals as *The Nation*, *The North American Review*, and *Atlantic Monthly*, copies of which are available in many college libraries. Other accessible sources are the books or collected letters of many Mugwumps, such as Simon Sterne, Moorfield Storey, George William Curtis, and Henry Adams. (Citations to many of these published works can be found in McGerr's notes to Chapter 3 of his *Decline of Popular Politics*.) Adams's satirical novel *Democracy* (1880) conveys, in lively fictional form, the Mugwump critique of machine politics.

Suggested Themes

1. Summarize the Mugwumps' critique of American politics. What did they find objectionable in the machine system of politics and the prevalence of political corruption?

2. Using Chapter 18 and at least two of the sources cited above, compile a statistical profile of five to ten leading Mugwumps, looking at year of birth, gender, social origins, residence, occupation, religion, and attitude toward race and woman suffrage. What did these Mugwumps have in common?

How to Use the Ancillaries Available with *America's History*

Refer to the Preface to *America's History* at the front of the book for descriptions of instructor resources, including the Instructor's Resource CD-ROM, Computerized Test Bank, transparencies, and *Using the Bedford Series in History and Culture in the U.S. History Survey*. Student resources, also described in the Preface, include the Online Study Guide and *Documents to Accompany* America's History, a primary-source reader.

For Instructors

Using the Bedford Series in History and Culture in the U.S. History Survey
This brief online guide by Scott Hovey provides practical suggestions for incorporating volumes from the highly regarded Bedford Series in History and Culture into your survey course. Titles that complement the material covered in Chapter 18 include *Southern Horrors and Other Writings: The Antilynching Campaign of Ida B. Wells, 1892–1900*, edited with an introduction by Jacqueline Jones Royster; *The Souls of Black Folk by W. E. B. DuBois*, edited with an introduction by David W. Blight and Robert Gooding-Williams; *Up from Slavery by Booker T. Washington, with Related Documents*, edited with an introduction by W. Fitzhugh Brundage; and Plessy v. Ferguson: *A Brief History with Documents*, edited with an introduction by Brook Thomas. For descriptions of these titles and how you might use them in your course, visit **bedfordstmartins.com/usingseries**.

For Students

Online Study Guide at bedfordstmartins.com/henretta
Each of the activities listed below includes short-answer questions. After submitting their answers, students can compare them to the model answers provided.

Map Activity
The map activity presents Map 18.3: Disfranchisement in the New South (p. 529) and asks students to analyze the process by which white southerners stripped voting rights from blacks in the late nineteenth century.

Visual Activity
The visual activity presents a photograph of Booker T. Washington (p. 534) and asks students to compare this image with Washington's overall approach to fighting for social, political, and economic rights for blacks.

Reading Historical Documents
The document activity provides a brief introduction to the documents Tom Watson: The Case for Interracial Unity (p. 528) and Helen Potter: The Case for Women's Political Rights (p. 527) and asks students to analyze their content, thinking critically about the sources.

Documents to Accompany *America's History*
Each of the documents listed is introduced by a headnote, which places the document in context, and is followed by questions, which help students to analyze the piece.

Sources for Chapter 18 are
James Bryce, *The American Commonwealth* (1888)
William Graham Sumner, *The Forgotten Man* (1883)

Visual Document: Thomas Nast, "'The Promised Land,' As Seen from the Dome of St. Peter's Rome" (1870)

Republican and Democratic State Platforms on the Bennett English-Language School Law (Wisconsin, 1890) and *The Liquor Question* (Iowa, 1889)

Frances E. Willard, *Woman and Temperance* (1876)

Elizabeth Cady Stanton, *The Solitude of Self* (1892)

The 1890 Mississippi Constitution

Ida B. Wells, *Lynching at the Curve* (1892)

Booker T. Washington, *Atlanta Exposition Address* (1895)

W. E. B. Du Bois, *Of Mr. Booker T. Washington and Others* (1903)

Democrat and Republican National Platforms on the Currency, the Tariff, and Federal Elections (1892)

People's (Populist) Party National Platform (1892)

Henry Demarest Lloyd, *Wealth against Commonwealth* (1894)

William Jennings Bryan, *Cross of Gold Speech* (1896)

CHAPTER 19

The Rise of the City

Chapter Instructional Objectives

After you have taught this chapter, your students should be able to answer the following questions:

1. What enabled American cities to grow so dramatically during the nineteenth century?

2. How did industrialization affect urbanization?

3. How did class structure, ethnicity, and gender affect urban political affairs?

4. Describe the emergence of an urban culture with distinctive living and working patterns, civic and religious institutions, family life, and leisure pursuits.

Chapter Summary

In the nineteenth century, the United States became increasingly urban; in 1900, one in five Americans lived in cities with a population over 100,000. Cities grew rapidly because of economic and technological changes. Industry was concentrated in large population centers that housed the legions of workers needed for labor-intensive manufacturing enterprises that also relied on an extensive railroad network for the movement of raw materials and finished goods. The development of rapid mass transit, the construction of skyscrapers and bridges, and the growing use of electricity and telephones made it practical for cities to grow larger than earlier "walking" cities. Although American cities had good infrastructures, private interests and philanthropists such as Andrew Carnegie undertook most urban development. Thus poor residents often were jammed together in tenements, and too little land was used for parks and other public amenities.

Corrupt political machines ran city governments. The boss of the machine and his aldermen used civic fa-

vors and social services as barter for power. The corruption was sometimes as direct at bribe taking and sometimes as indirect as using insider information to make profitable business deals.

The population of these cities increasingly comprised southern and Eastern European immigrants. These new urban Americans belonged to Catholic churches and Orthodox Jewish synagogues and tended to cluster in their own areas, assimilating only slowly and partially. Protestant sanctuaries were abandoned as their congregations moved into greener, less crowded areas on the fringes of the cities. African American Protestant churches were the center of life in black neighborhoods, which contained their own professional and middle-class residents.

City dwellers lived in a distinctively urban style. They attended professional baseball games; went to vaudeville houses; sought thrills in amusement parks; and enjoyed museums, exhibitions, and revival meetings. They read realistic and naturalistic literature by popular authors such as Stephen Crane, Henry Blake Fuller, William Dean Howells, and Mark Twain. They read sensationalized newspapers and pulp fiction by Horatio Alger. Books were available in a growing number of libraries in the cities. Urban life was particularly pleasant for the wealthy, who lived in magnificent homes and held glittering and conspicuous social gatherings.

A fast-growing middle class composed of managers and professionals tended to live on the outskirts of cities, where they were insulated from the competition of the workplace in the urban centers. The middle class cultivated the private world of the family, in which wives adhered to the cult of domesticity idealized in women's magazines. Nonetheless, a more relaxed attitude toward female sexuality emerged. Men followed their own cult of masculinity, and children, their labor no longer necessary to support the family, found their childhoods extending through adolescence. Their lives contrasted sharply with those of the immigrant masses squeezed into the heart of the noisy, dirty, and crowded cities. There, children's wages and the wages of mothers were needed to support a family as much as the fathers'.

Chapter Annotated Outline

I.   Urbanization
   A.   Industrial Sources of City Growth
      1.   Until the Civil War, cities were centers of commerce, and factories were largely rural.
      2.   With the invention of the steam engine and the use of coal as a fuel, factories relocated to the places most convenient to suppliers and markets.
      3.   The growth of factories contributed to urban growth; large factories employing many workers created small cities within their vicinities.
      4.   Many firms set up their plants near a large city so that they could draw on the city's labor supply and transportation systems.
      5.   Sometimes a metropolis spread and absorbed nearby factory towns; elsewhere, the lines between industrial towns blurred and an extended urban-industrial area emerged.
      6.   Older commercial cities became more industrial because warehouse districts could readily be converted to small-scale manufacturing.
   B.   City Innovation
      1.   The commercial cities of the early nineteenth century were densely settled around harbors or riverfronts.
      2.   A downtown area emerged, and industrial development followed the arteries of transportation to the outskirts of the city where concentrations of industry were formed.
      3.   American cities had lower population densities than did European cities, and it was urgent that they develop efficient transportation systems.
      4.   In 1887, Frank J. Sprague's electric trolley car became the main mode of transportation in the cities; the trolley car had replaced the horsecar, which had in turn replaced the omnibus.
      5.   Congestion in the cities led to the development of elevated and underground transportation; with Manhattan's subway, mass transit became rapid transit.
      6.   With steel girders and passenger elevators available by the 1880s, Chicago soon pioneered skyscraper construction, though New York took the lead after the mid-1890s.
      7.   The first use of electricity was for better city lighting, and Thomas Edison's invention of a serviceable incandescent bulb in 1879 put electric lighting in American homes.
      8.   By 1900, Alexander Graham Bell's newly invented telephone linked urban people in a network of instant communication.
   C.   Private City, Public City
      1.   America was the birthplace of the "private city," shaped primarily by the actions of many individuals, each pursuing his own goals and bent on making money.
      2.   People believed that city functions handled through private enterprise would far exceed what the community could accomplish through public effort.
      3.   Municipal government became more centralized, better administered, and more expansive in the functions it undertook.
      4.   City streets, however, soon became filthy and poorly maintained, smog was a problem, and families lived in crowded tenement housing.
      5.   New York's Tenement House Law of 1901 did little to ease the problems of existing housing, and only high-density, cheaply built housing earned a profit for landlords of the poor.
      6.   Frederick Law Olmsted's projects gave rise to the "City Beautiful" movement; the result was larger park systems, broad boulevards, and zoning laws and planned suburbs.
      7.   Cities usually heeded urban planners too little and too late; the American city placed its faith in the dynamics of the marketplace, not the restraints of a planned future.
II. Upper Class, Middle Class
   A.   The Urban Elite
      1.   In cities, the interpersonal marks of class began to lose their force, and people began to rely on external signs, such as choice of neighborhood, to confer status.
      2.   As commercial development engulfed downtown residential areas, many well-to-do people began an exodus out of the city.
      3.   Some of the richest people preferred to stay in the heart of the city — for example, on New York's Fifth Avenue.
      4.   Great wealth did not automatically confer social standing; in some cities, an established elite, or "old" money, dominated the social heights.
      5.   New York attracted the wealthy not only because it was an important financial center but also because of the opportunities it offered for display and social recognition.
      6.   Ward McAllister's *Social Register* served as a list of all persons deemed eligible for New York society.

7. Americans were adept at making money, but they lacked the aristocratic taste of Europeans for spending it.

B. The Suburban World
1. American industrialism spawned a new salaried middle class; more than a fourth of all employed Americans were white-collar workers in 1910.
2. Some of the middle class lived in row houses or apartments, but most preferred to escape to the suburbs.
3. Unlike its American counterpart, the European middle class was not attracted to the rural ideal and valued urban life for its own sake.
4. The geography of the suburbs was a map of class structure; the farther from the city, the finer the house and the larger the lot.
5. Suburban boundaries were ever-shifting, and each family's move usually represented an advance in living standard.
6. In the suburbs, unlike the cities, home ownership was the norm.
7. The need for community lost some of its urgency for middle-class Americans; work and family had become more important.

C. Middle-Class Families
1. By 1900, a "family" typically consisted of a husband, wife, and three children; the family relationship was usually intense and affectionate — a sharp contrast to the impersonal business world.
2. The duties of domesticity fell on the wife, and it was nearly unheard of for her to seek outside employment.
3. The *American Woman's Home, Ladies' Home Journal*, and *Good Housekeeping* told wives that they were responsible for bringing sensibility, love, and beauty to the household.
4. Custom dictated a wife's submission to her husband, yet some women rebelled against marriage.
5. Middle-class bachelors neither had families to exert patriarchal hold over, nor did they have control over their jobs. A palpable anxiety arose that the American male was becoming weak and effeminate; men began engaging in competitive sports to combat this image.
6. From the 1870s onward, contraceptive devices and birth control information were legally classified as obscene, and abortion became illegal except to save the mother's life.
7. During the 1890s the image of a "new woman" began to emerge, one that was proud of her female form and sexuality and who was emerging from her dependence on her father or husband for financial support.

8. Parents no longer expected their children to work; instead, families were responsible for providing a nurturing environment.
9. Preparation for adulthood became linked to formal education, and as a youth culture began to take shape, adolescence shifted much of the socializing role from parents to peer groups.

III. City Life
A. Newcomers
1. At the turn of the century, upwards of 30 percent of the residents of New York, Chicago, Boston, Minneapolis, and San Francisco were foreign-born.
2. The later arrivals from southern and Eastern Europe had little choice about where they lived; they needed inexpensive housing near their jobs.
3. Capitalizing on fellow feeling within ethnic groups, immigrants built a rich and functional institutional life in urban America.
4. A great African American migration from the rural South to northern cities began at the turn of the century, but urban blacks could not escape discrimination; job opportunities were few, and they retreated into ghettos to live.
5. Urban blacks built their own communities with middle-class businesses and black churches, and the preacher was the most important local citizen.

B. Ward Politics
1. Politics integrated newcomers into urban society; each migrant to a city became a ward resident and immediately acquired a spokesman at city hall in his local alderman.
2. Urban political machines depended on a loyal grassroots constituency, so each ward was divided into election districts of a few blocks.
3. The machine served as a social service agency for city dwellers, providing jobs, lending help, and interceding against the city bureaucracy.
4. In New York, ward boss George Washington Plunkitt integrated private business and political services.
5. For city businesses, the machine served a similar purpose, but it exacted a price in return for its favors: tenement dwellers gave a vote, businesses wrote a check.
6. For the young and ambitious — whether white, black, or foreign-born — machine politics was the most democratic of American institutions; it served an integrating function that cut across ethnic lines.

C. Religion in the City
1. For many city dwellers the church was a central institution of urban life, although all the great

faiths of the time found it difficult to reconcile religious belief with urban secular demands.

2. The monocultural environment upon which strict religious observance depended could not be re-created in the city. Orthodox Judaism survived by reducing its claim on the lives of its faithful.

3. The Catholic Church managed to satisfy the immigrant faithful and made itself a central institution for the expression of ethnic identity in urban America.

4. To counter a decline in the number of its members, city-center Protestant churches turned to evangelizing as well as becoming instruments of social uplift.

5. For single people new to the city, there were Young Men's and Women's Christian Associations; no other association so effectively combined activities with evangelizing appeal through nondenominational worship and a religious atmosphere.

6. Beginning in the mid-1870s, revival meetings swept through the cities, pioneered by figures such as Dwight L. Moody and Billy Sunday.

D. City Amusements

1. City people needed amusement as a reward for working and to prove to themselves that life was better in the New World.

2. Amusement parks and theaters were built to entertain families, and working-class youth forged a culture of sexual interaction and pleasure seeking.

3. Prostitution became less closeted and more intermingled with other forms of public entertainment.

4. A robust gay subculture could be found in certain parts of the city, with a full array of saloons and clubs supported by gay patrons.

5. Baseball grew into more than just an afternoon of fun; by rooting for the home team, fans found a way of identifying with the cities in which they lived.

6. Newspapers were sensitive to the public they served and catered to city people's hunger for information and sensational news.

E. The Higher Culture

1. The Corcoran Gallery of Art opened in 1869, followed by the Metropolitan Museum of Art in 1871, the Boston Museum of Fine Arts in 1876, and Chicago's Art Institute in 1879.

2. Symphony orchestras appeared first in New York in the 1870s and in Boston and Chicago during the next decade.

3. Public libraries, many established by Andrew Carnegie, grew into major urban institutions.

4. Generous with their wealth, new millionaires patronized the arts partly to establish themselves in society, partly out of a sense of civic duty and partly out of a sense of national pride.

5. Mark Twain and Charles Dudley Warner published *A Gilded Age* (1873) to satirize America as a land of money grubbers and speculators.

6. The idea of culture took on an elitist cast and simultaneously became feminized; men represented the "force principle" and women the "beauty principle."

7. The "genteel tradition" dominated universities and publishers from the 1860s onward.

8. By the early 1900s, the city had entered the American imagination and had become a main theme of American art and literature — the city had also become an overriding concern of reformers.

Lecture Strategies

1. While being careful to define terms and give illustrations, explain how "city people" became "distinctively and recognizably urban." Describe the way urban residents lived, the diversions they enjoyed, and the stresses they faced.

2. Discuss the growth of nineteenth-century American cities. Explain the factors that enabled them to expand so dramatically. Compare American cities with those in Europe in terms of population density, the availability of everyday conveniences, and cultural amenities.

3. Give a lecture about the social impact of immigration on the American city. Among the points to be covered are religious change in the cities, the role of churches in urban areas, the development of ethnic enclaves, the migration of more settled groups into suburbs, the impact of immigration on urban blacks, and the way in which urban living affected the American family.

4. Explore the interrelationship of poverty, ethnicity, and class structure and the rise of political machines in American cities.

5. Lecture on wealth and poverty in American cities. Contrast the lives of the rich and the poor from birth to death. Compare the educational attainment, housing, social activities, cultural interests, and religious practices of the two classes.

6. Discuss the impact of city life on the family. Note the changing roles of men, women, and children in turn-of-the-century urban America. Compare the family in the modern United States to the family a century earlier.

Class Discussion Starters

1. **Why did American cities grow so rapidly during this period?**

Possible answers:
   a. New industries built factories in metropolitan areas because of convenient railroad service; workers went where jobs were plentiful.
   b. New technologies and improved engineering. For example, the construction of skyscrapers and bridges allowed cities to overcome natural barriers to growth.
   c. A significant African American migration from the South began at the turn of the century.
   d. European immigration to the port cities continued, particularly from southern and Eastern Europe.

2. **How did the introduction of mass transit and electricity affect urban life?**

Possible answers:
   a. Mass transit — trolleys, subways, and urban railways — made it convenient for people to live far from their workplaces, thus promoting the growth of suburbs.
   b. Electricity made urban life easier and more pleasant; illumination, for example, made streets safer and allowed citizens to work late and enjoy their private interests at night.
   c. Electricity made the skyscraper possible. Until the invention of electric elevators, buildings could be no more than four or five stories tall.
   d. Electricity made the telegraph and telephone possible, which, in turn, boosted communication.

3. **What was the African American experience in urban areas?**

Possible answers:
   a. Urban blacks experienced racism, including residential segregation.
   b. Skilled job opportunities evaporated for urban blacks, and they were forced to compete with white immigrants for jobs.
   c. Amid adversity, urban blacks built their own tightly knit communities and churches.

4. **What role did ward politicians play in the lives of immigrants?**

Possible answers:
   a. Ward politics was an avenue of advancement for immigrants.
   b. Immigrants received assistance at crucial times, and their votes kept ward politicians in office.
   c. Ward politicians helped to integrate immigrants into American life.
   d. Ward politicians, by bowing to ethnic customs and a sense of ethnic pride, endorsed ethnic divisions.

5. **How did wealthy Americans display their affluence?**

Possible answers:
   a. Through the conspicuous display of lavish houses, clothes, and entertaining other rich people.
   b. By joining elite clubs or fraternal organizations.
   c. By living in the "right" neighborhood.
   d. Through the funding of public works such as parks, libraries, museums, and concert halls.

6. **What impact did industrialization have on the family?**

Possible answers:
   a. The family ceased being an interdependent economic unit.
   b. Families became smaller, and relations within the family grew more intense.
   c. Husbands became breadwinners, frequently absent from the home for extended periods. Wives became household managers, and children went to school longer.
   d. The divorce rate increased. Unmarried men were no longer stigmatized.
   e. Fewer women married than in preceding generations.
   f. When child labor laws were enacted, a greater portion of poor women were forced to find jobs.

7. **What were some developments that indicated the spread of "higher culture"?**

Possible answers:
   a. The establishment of major museums.
   b. The proliferation of public libraries.
   c. The appearance of symphony orchestras.
   d. The "city beautiful" movement that wanted to keep citizens' senses from being dulled by dirt and ugliness.

Chapter Writing Assignments

1. Discuss how key technological advances — mass transit, the skyscraper, bridges, electricity, and the telephone — transformed the way people lived in American cities. Include why cities continued to grow, where and why people located their homes, and how the workplace and social diversions changed.

2. Examine the impact on urban American life of southern and Eastern European immigrants and African American migrants. Why did immigrant groups move to and remain in American cities? How

did their presence affect the economic and social organization of cities?

3. Compare the occupations, residential patterns, and family life of upper-class and middle-class Americans around 1900. In particular, describe the measures taken by members of the upper class to mark their distinctiveness. How fluid was social class in this era?

Document Exercises

AMERICAN VOICES

M. Carey Thomas: "We Did Not Know . . . Whether Women's Health Could Stand the Strain of College Education" (p. 555)

Document Discussion

1. **Why did Thomas fear that women could not endure the rigors of a college education?**
   (Thomas's fears reflected the medical theories prevalent at the turn of the century. She had little personal experience of women who pursued an education; she knew that her family and acquaintances frowned on the thought; and she was aware of biblical passages urging the inferiority of women. Thus the thought that women could and should succeed at college was truly revolutionary.)

2. **Do you think that Thomas and other women like her were aware that a college education would have an impact on the economic independence of women?**
   (Before going to college, it appears that women did not realize the impact that an education would have. They seem to have wanted to get an education for the sake of learning, and only after the fact did they realize that it might lead to economic independence.)

Writing Assignments

1. What historical examples of the public roles of women might Thomas have turned to for support? Or, besides the often quoted letters of St. Paul, what might Thomas have found in the Bible to support her quest for knowledge and a place of her own in society?

2. Discuss the possible reasons for the belief that women's health "could not stand the strain of college education." Do you think that there was an actual concern for women's health, or was it a ploy to keep women uneducated and therefore subordinate to men?

AMERICAN VOICES

Anonymous: Bintel Brief (p. 561)

Document Discussion

1. **What common dilemmas did the writers to the Bintel Brief confront?**
   (These immigrant writers all faced the challenge of preserving their religious and cultural traditions within a larger American society that embodied a degree of intellectual diversity to which they were not accustomed.)

2. **What does the letter about the girl with a dimple in her chin reveal about the letter's writer?**
   (That he was very superstitious and willing to give up the girl over what he considered a "flaw." The reply to his letter lets him know how ridiculous it is to be superstitious. Some of the letters address broader issues of cultural assimilation, but others, like this one, merely reflect the personal issues of the author.)

Writing Assignments

1. What types of solutions does the editor of the *Jewish Daily Forward* offer to the correspondents?

2. Compare and contrast the types of concerns one might find addressed in a modern-day paper with those concerns addressed in the *Jewish Daily Forward*.

AMERICAN LIVES

Big Tim Sullivan: Tammany Politician (p. 564)

Document Discussion

1. **Why did Sullivan enter politics? Why was he such an effective political leader?**
   (By achieving success in the newspaper business, which he had entered at age seven, Sullivan apparently captured the attention of the Democrats, who nominated him for political office. He won and then went on to greater accomplishments. He was an effective politico — his constituents identified with him, and he carefully and methodically courted the different ethnic groups that kept him in office.)

2. **Were Sullivan's political practices an example of what he called "honest graft," or was he simply a corrupt politician?**
   (As Sullivan practiced "honest graft," he used his position and knowledge to derive economic benefits from businesses in which he had a personal stake. Ac-

cording to Sullivan's own testimony, he would never partake of tainted money — from prostitution, for example. While he drew these distinctions, modern political ethics do not draw them, and today Sullivan would be viewed as corrupt.)

Writing Assignments

1. What benefits did Tammany politicians such as Sullivan give their constituents? What were the costs of "honest graft"? Considering both sides of the coin and the future development of city politics, explain why you think the urban machines were beneficial or detrimental to American society and democracy.

2. Discuss Tammany Hall and its political operations as a prototype for other party machines in the industrial United States or to the operation of the national parties of the day.

VOICES FROM ABROAD

José Martí: Coney Island, 1881 (p. 567)

Document Discussion

1. **What aspects of American behavior amuse Martí?**
   (Martí comments at length that Americans desire personal gain and entertainment. The Yankees, he observes, exhibit little interest in the attainment of theoretical ideals but rather seek various manner of stimulation. Martí's estimate of Americans is that they are a brassy and expressive people.)

2. **How did Martí characterize American society?**
   (Martí was impressed with Americans' desire for gain and the consequent leisure that prosperity entailed and contrasted this with Europeans' more subdued behavior. He marveled at the frenetic activity and overt pursuit of pleasure in which the crowds engaged. Martí was equally impressed with the industrial engines that allowed such hedonism to occur: the trains, trolleys, and facilities that moved the crowds between New York and Coney Island.)

Writing Assignments

1. Martí, although admiring Americans at play, also said that America is a nation "void of spirit." Why did he make this claim? Does the rest of the chapter support him?

2. Compare and contrast Martí's description of Americans enjoying their leisure time in 1881 with the description a visitor might give of Americans enjoying leisure time today. How has the American outlook on life and leisure changed? How has it remained the same?

Skill-Building Map Exercises

Map 19.1: America's Cities, 1900 (p. 545)

1. **What were the six largest cities in the United States in 1900?**
   (New York, Chicago, Philadelphia, Boston, Baltimore, and St. Louis.)

2. **Why do you think urban growth was most pronounced in New England and the Middle Atlantic and Great Lakes states?**
   (Major industries moved to those areas because of ease of transportation, access to resources, and the presence of a large labor force. Immigrants from Europe were most likely to settle in those regions.)

Map 19.4: The Lower East Side, New York City, in 1900 (p. 559)

1. **Why do you think the geographical expression "Lower East Side" gained a special distinction in American history?**
   (Jews living in the area created quite an ambience as they went on to achieve great success in the United States. Plays, stories, and movies made the Lower East Side a special place known to many Americans far removed from New York City.)

2. **Why do you think European Jews flocked to the Lower East Side?**
   (Racial and ethnic groups tended to follow in the wake of pioneer settlers from their own groups. Thus Eastern European Jews followed early Jewish immigrants to New York's Lower East Side, where they established their own synagogues, heard their own languages, and could buy their own specialized foods.)

Topic for Research

The City Boss

How did machine politics come to play the key role in governing the industrial cities of the late nineteenth century? There is a rich contemporary literature describing the boss system by critics looking in from the outside — for example, James Bryce, *The American Commonwealth* (1888); Josiah Strong, *Our Country* (1891); and (on Boston) Robert A. Woods, *The City Wilderness* (1898). Historical studies of the subject include Zane Miller, *Boss Cox's Cincinnati* (1968); Humbert S. Nelli, "John Powers and the Italians: Politics in a Chicago Ward, 1896–1921,"

Journal of American History (June 1970); David C. Hammack, *Power and Society: Greater New York at the Turn of the Century* (1982); and Bruce M. Stave, ed., *Urban Bosses, Machines, and Progressive Reformers* (1972). But how did the system look from the inside? How did the bosses see their roles? What values did they hold? How did they explain the loyalty they engendered in the immigrant wards? How did they justify the "graft" that rewarded them for their labors? One Tammany boss — George Washington Plunkitt — gave a series of interviews in which he candidly addressed these questions. See William L. Riordon, ed., *Plunkitt of Tammany Hall* (1948). You might want to compare Plunkitt's views with those of contemporary critics such as Bryce, Strong, or Woods, or try to place Plunkitt's views in a more analytical context by reading one or more historical accounts of city machine politics. Plunkitt might be compared with Big Tim Sullivan, whose biography is recounted in Daniel Czitrom, "Underworlds and Underdogs: Big Tim Sullivan and Metropolitan Politics in New York, 1889–1913," *Journal of American History* (September 1991), 536–558.

Suggested Themes

1. Investigate the views of a city boss such as George Washington Plunkitt. How did he see his role? What values did he hold, and how did he justify the graft characteristic of machine politics?

2. Compare the discussion of a particular city in one of the contemporary accounts of late nineteenth-century America (Bryce, Strong, or Woods) with the treatment of the same topic in one of the more recent studies (Miller, Nelli, Hammack, or Stave). How perceptive were the contemporary observers? What, if anything, did they miss?

How to Use the Ancillaries Available with *America's History*

Refer to the Preface to *America's History* at the front of the book for descriptions of instructor resources, including the Instructor's Resource CD-ROM, Computerized Test Bank, transparencies, and *Using the Bedford Series in History and Culture in the U.S. History Survey*. Student resources, also described in the Preface, include the Online Study Guide and *Documents to Accompany* America's History, a primary-source reader.

For Instructors

Using the Bedford Series in History and Culture in the U.S. History Survey
This brief online guide by Scott Hovey provides practical suggestions for incorporating volumes from the highly regarded Bedford Series in History and Culture into your survey course. Titles that complement the material covered in Chapter 19 include *How the Other Half Lives: Studies among the Tenements of New York by Jacob A. Riis*, edited with an introduction by David Leviatin, and *Plunkitt of Tammany Hall* by William L. Riordan, edited with an introduction by Terrence J. McDonald. For descriptions of these titles and how you might use them in your course, visit **bedfordstmartins.com/usingseries**.

For Students

Online Study Guide at bedfordstmartins.com/henretta
Each of the activities listed below includes short-answer questions. After submitting their answers, students can compare them to the model answers provided.

Map Activity
The map activity presents Map 19.1: America's Cities, 1900 (p. 545), and asks students to analyze the growth of cities at the turn of the century.

Visual Activity
The visual activity presents a photograph of Mulberry Street in New York City (p. 542) and asks students to analyze how the scene represents the new American city.

Reading Historical Documents
The document activity provides a brief introduction to the documents M. Carey Thomas: "We Did Not Know . . . Whether Women's Health Could Stand the Strain of College Education" (p. 555) and Bintel Brief (p. 561), and asks students to analyze their content, thinking critically about the sources.

Documents to Accompany *America's History*
Each of the documents listed is introduced by a headnote, which places the document in context, and is followed by questions, which help students to analyze the piece.

Sources for Chapter 19 are
Julian Ralph, *Colorado and Its Capital* (1893)
Louis H. Sullivan, *The Skyscraper* (1896)
Thorstein Veblen, *Conspicuous Consumption* (1899)
Henry Adams, *The Columbian Exposition of 1893*
Catherine E. Beecher, *The Christian Family* (1869)
Theodore Dreiser, *Sister Carrie* (1900)
The Immigrant Experience: Letters Home (1901–1903)
Giuseppe Giacosa, *A Visitor in Chicago* (1892)
William L. Riordan, *Plunkitt of Tammany Hall* (1905)
Josiah Strong, *The Dangers of Cities* (1886)

CHAPTER 20

The Progressive Era

Chapter Instructional Objectives

After you have taught this chapter, your students should be able to answer the following questions:

1. How did progressivism and organized interest groups reflect the new political choices of Americans?

2. Why did progressives believe in the ability of individuals to affect positive change? How has this idea manifested itself in political reform efforts?

3. What reforms did American women, urbanites, and African Americans seek?

4. Evaluate and explain how and why President Roosevelt expanded the federal government's power within the economy.

5. How did President Wilson seek to accommodate his progressive principles to the realities of political power?

Chapter Summary

The unhindered capitalism of the late nineteenth century had created great wealth for some Americans, but poverty persisted for many others. Members of the growing middle class, having recovered from the recession of the mid-1890s, wanted to improve the quality of life both for themselves and for the less fortunate. Their determination laid the foundation for a movement called progressivism, and its ideas of reform dominated the nation's public discourse for the next two decades.

With few precedents to guide them, progressives cobbled together a variety of reforms that had the simple goal of making life better for the American people. They were bolstered in their efforts by the appearance of a so-

cial science and a philosophy that rejected formalism in favor of pragmatic solutions to social problems. Crusading journalists exposed the corruption and excesses of those who held political and financial power. The task of correcting the abuses revealed by these muckrakers fell to reforming politicians, who, in an ironic development, tried to establish sound business and managerial practices at the state and municipal levels.

Women reformers began to play an active role in areas closely related to women's traditional sphere — working in settlement houses and trying to improve the working conditions of women in the labor force. Feminists declared equality for women and joined longtime suffragists in seeking the vote, but disagreements over principles divided the women's movement.

Urban political machines began to realize that the welfare of their constituents depended on state action in order to eliminate dangerous working and living conditions. Joining with organized labor, urban liberals began to rely on the Democratic Party to support their reforming activities. The Democrats cultivated the immigrant vote and, as cities continued to grow, became the majority political party in American cities.

The plight of African Americans continued to worsen as academics developed new theories of white racial superiority, which white society in the North and the South accepted with varying degrees of zeal. Black activists recognized the need to organize against racial inequality but were divided on the question of biracial involvement. Although most white progressives shared the racial prejudices of the dominant culture, brutality against blacks — notably the Springfield Riot — led some white and African American leaders to jointly organize the National Association for the Advancement of Colored People (NAACP) and the National Urban League. Together, these leaders hoped to gather the numbers and influence needed to campaign effectively against racial discrimination and injustice.

While reformers tackled cases of local importance, they required federal government involvement to counter the influence of giant industrial and financial powers. The progressive presidents Theodore Roosevelt and Woodrow Wilson proved eager to curb the abuses brought about by great concentrations of wealth. Neither president was antibusiness, however, so their trust-busting activities aimed to regulate corporate excesses, not reduce the power of big business. By the end of the Progressive Era, government and big business had come to accept a cooperative relationship aimed at fostering competition and protecting the public interest.

Muckraking journalists caught the nation's attention by pointing out to consumers many deficiencies in the food packaging and processing industries. Progressive legislators approved several federal laws, and, more importantly, they established the Food and Drug Administration (FDA) in order to set and enforce safety standards. The federal government was expanding to fill an activist role that it would continue to pursue through the twentieth century.

Chapter Annotated Outline

I. The Course of Reform
    A. The Progressive Mind
       1. The term *progressivism* embraces a widespread, many-sided effort after 1900 to build a better society; there was no single progressive constituency, agenda, or unifying organization.
       2. Progressives placed great faith in scientific management and academic expertise; they also felt that it was important to resist ways of thinking that discouraged purposeful action.
       3. "Institutional economists" used statistics and history to reveal how the economy functioned and why the strong would devour the weak in the absence of trade unions and regulation.
       4. Progressives opposed the reigning legal concept that treated laws as if they arose from eternal principles neither rooted in nor to be tested by social reality.
       5. Justice Oliver Wendell Holmes's reasoning, known as legal realism, rested on his conviction that "the life of the law has not been its logic; it has been its experience."
       6. The philosophical underpinnings for legal realism came from William James's philosophy of pragmatism, which judged ideas by their consequences.
       7. The most important source of progressive idealism was religion. The major doctrine known as the Social Gospel came about as the

churches' concerns for the plight of the poor expanded the concept of piety to include work for social improvement.
       8. The progressive mode of thought, which valued acquisition of facts, nurtured a new kind of reform journalism; at the turn of the century, editors discovered that readers were most interested in the exposure of mischief in America.
       9. The term *muckraker* was given to journalists who exposed the underside of American life; however, in making the public aware of social ills, muckrakers called the people to action.
    B. Women Progressives
       1. Middle-class women, who had long carried the burden of humanitarian work in American cities, were among the first to respond to the idea of progressivism.
       2. Josephine Shaw Lowell founded the New York Consumers' League in 1890 to improve the wages and working conditions for female clerks in the city stores by "white listing" progressive businesses.
       3. The league spread to other cities and became the National Consumers' League, a powerful lobby for protective legislation for women and children.
       4. *Muller v. Oregon* (1908), which limited women's workday to ten hours, cleared the way for a wave of protective laws across the country; in their decision, the justices gave more weight to the damage done to women's lives than to narrow issues of constitutionality.
       5. Settlement houses, such as Hull House, helped to alleviate social problems in the slums and also helped to satisfy the middle-class residents' need for meaningful lives.
       6. Women from the National Women's Trade Union League identified their cause with the broader struggle for women's rights, such as the right to vote.
       7. Alice Paul's National Women's Party and the National American Woman Suffrage Association (NAWSA) organized a broad-based campaign to push for a constitutional amendment for woman suffrage.
       8. Feminists were militantly prosuffrage because they considered themselves fully equal to men, not a weaker sex entitled to men's protection.
       9. Feminism and broader progressivism came together in the work of Margaret Sanger, who opened the first birth control clinic in the United States.
      10. Disputes led to the fracturing of the women's movement, dividing the older generation of

progressives from their feminist successors who prized gender equality higher than any social benefit.

C. Reforming Politics

1. Progressive politicians, especially Robert LaFollette, felt that the key to reforming party machines was to reclaim the power to choose candidates. The progressives took that power away from the bosses and gave it to voters in a direct primary.

2. The ballot initiative enabled citizens to seek direct redress for issues important to them, and the recall empowered them to remove office-holders in whom they had lost confidence.

3. Like the direct primary, the initiative and the recall had as much to do with power relations as with democratic idealism, since many progressives excelled at garnering popular support.

4. Many cities demanded more efficient government. By making aldermanic elections city-wide, municipal reformers attacked the ward politics that underlay the corrupting patronage system.

5. Combining an elected commission with an appointed city manager became the model for municipal reformers; the commission-manager system aimed at running the city in the same way as a private business corporation.

6. After the Triangle Shirtwaist Factory fire, it was clear that urban social problems had become too big to be handled informally by party machines; some machine politicians led the way in making laws and regulations in order to improve labor conditions.

7. Urban liberals advocated intervention by the state to better the lives of the laboring masses of American cities.

8. Combining campaign magic and popular programs, progressive mayors won over the urban masses; city machines adopted urban liberalism without much ideological struggle.

9. When social experts warned that the numbers of southern and Eastern Europeans immigrating into the United States would bring about "mongrelization" and moral decay, moral reformers expanded their agenda to stop the influx; the Immigration Restriction League spearheaded a movement to end America's open-door policy.

10. Urban liberals denounced prohibition and anti-immigrant proposals as attacks on the personal liberty and decency of urban immigrants.

11. During the progressive years, the unions' self-reliant "voluntarism" weakened substantially as the labor movement came under attack by the courts.

12. Judges granted injunctions to prohibit unions from striking, and, in the *Danbury Hatters* case, the Supreme Court's decision rendered trade unions vulnerable to antitrust suits.

13. After the American Federation of Labor's "Bill of Grievances" was rebuffed by Congress, unions became more politically active.

14. Organized labor joined the battle for progressive legislation and became its strongest advocate, especially for workers' compensation for industrial accidents.

15. Between 1910 and 1917, all industrial states enacted insurance laws covering on-the-job injuries, yet health insurance and unemployment compensation scarcely made it into the American political agenda.

16. Old-age pensions met resistance because the United States already had a pension system for Civil War veterans and their survivors whose enforcement was extremely lax. Easy access to these veterans' benefits prompted fears that a new generation of workers could become dependent upon state payments.

D. Racism and Reform

1. The southern direct primary was ostensibly an attack on back-room party rule, but it also served to deprive blacks of their political rights.

2. In the North, racism was on the rise as thousands of blacks migrated from the South to the North.

3. The Niagara Movement, led by William Monroe Trotter and W. E. B. Du Bois, defined the African American struggle for rights: they proclaimed black pride, insisted on full civic and political equality, and resolutely rejected submissiveness.

4. A few white reformers joined the African American cause; one of their meetings led to the formation of the National Association for the Advancement of Colored People in 1909.

5. The NAACP's national leadership was dominated by white leadership. But the editor of the *Crisis*, W. E. B. Du Bois, was an African American, and he used that platform to demand equal rights for blacks.

6. Like the NAACP, the National Urban League was interracial, and it became the leading organization in social welfare.

7. In the South, social welfare was the province of black women; they utilized the National Association of Colored Women's Clubs, which was established in 1896.

II. Progressivism and National Politics
  A. The Making of a Progressive President
    1. Like many budding progressives, Theodore Roosevelt was motivated by a high-minded Christian upbringing, but he did not scorn power and its uses.
    2. During his term as governor of New York, Roosevelt asserted his confidence in the government's capacity to improve the life of the people.
    3. In 1901, Roosevelt, who was vice president at the time, became president after the assassination of William McKinley.
    4. As president, Roosevelt backed the Newlands Reclamation Act, expanded the national forests, upgraded land management, and prosecuted violators of federal land laws.
    5. In an unprecedented step, Roosevelt intervened personally in a strike by the United Mine Workers in 1902 and appointed an arbitration commission to end it.
    6. Roosevelt was prepared to use all his presidential authority against the "tyranny" of "irresponsible" business.
  B. Regulating the Marketplace
    1. Roosevelt was troubled by the threat that big business posed to competitive markets.
    2. The mergers of individual businesses into trusts decreased competition; bigger business meant power to control markets.
    3. With the passage of the Sherman Antitrust Act of 1890, the federal government had enabled itself to enforce firmly established common laws in cases involving interstate commerce, but the power had not been exercised.
    4. In 1903, Roosevelt established the Bureau of Corporations in order to investigate business practices and to support the Justice Department's capacity to mount antitrust suits.
    5. After winning the presidential election, Roosevelt became the nation's trust-buster, taking on corporations such as Standard Oil, American Tobacco, and Du Pont.
    6. In the *Trans-Missouri* decision of 1897, the Supreme Court held that actions restraining or monopolizing trade automatically violated the Sherman Antitrust Act.
    7. Roosevelt was not antibusiness, and he did not want the courts to punish "good" trusts, so he exercised his presidential prerogative to decide whether or not to prosecute a trust.
    8. By distinguishing between good and bad trusts, Roosevelt reconciled the Sherman Act with the economic reality of corporate concentration.
    9. Roosevelt was convinced that the railroads rates and bookkeeping needed firmer oversight, so he pushed through the Elkins Act (1903) and the Hepburn Railway Act (1906), achieving a landmark expansion of the government's regulatory powers over business.
    10. Roosevelt authorized a federal investigation into the stockyards; the Pure Food and Drug and the Meat Inspection Acts were passed, and the Food and Drug Administration was created.
    11. During Roosevelt's campaign he called his program the Square Deal, meaning that when companies abused their corporate power, the government would intercede to assure Americans a fair arrangement.
  C. The Fracturing of Republican Progressivism
    1. William Howard Taft had served Roosevelt loyally as governor-general of the Philippines and as secretary of war. He was an avowed Square Dealer, but he was not a progressive politician.
    2. Taft won the election against William Jennings Bryan in 1908 with a mandate to pick up where Roosevelt left off; however, this was not to be.
    3. Progressives felt that Roosevelt had been too easy on business, and with him no longer in the White House, they intended to make up for lost time.
    4. Although Taft had campaigned for tariff reform, he ended up approving the protectionist Payne-Aldrich Tariff Act of 1909.
    5. After the Pinchot-Ballinger affair, in which he fired Pinchot for whistle-blowing on a conspiracy to hand public land to a private syndicate, the progressives saw Taft as a friend of the "interests" bent on plundering the nation's resources.
    6. Galvanized by Taft's defection, the reformers in the Republican Party became a dissident faction, calling themselves the "Progressives" or "Insurgents."
    7. The Progressives formed the National Progressive Republican League and began a drive to take over the Republican Party; they knew they needed Roosevelt to topple Taft.
    8. Roosevelt knew that a party split would benefit the Democrats, but he was driven to set aside party loyalty when he clashed with Taft over the question of trusts.
    9. Unlike Roosevelt, Taft was unwilling to pick and choose trusts for prosecution; he instead relied on the letter of the Sherman Act.
    10. In the *Standard Oil* decision of 1911, the Supreme Court once again asserted the rule of reason, which meant that the courts, not the

president, would distinguish between good and bad trusts.

11. Taft's attorney general brought suit against U.S. Steel, basing the antimonopoly charges in part on an acquisition approved by Roosevelt, who could not, without dishonor, ignore what amounted to a personal attack.

12. Roosevelt made the case for what he called the New Nationalism, its central tenet being that human welfare had priority over property rights. The government would become "the steward of the public welfare."

13. Roosevelt believed that the courts stood in the way of reform and proposed sharp curbs on their powers.

14. Roosevelt was too reformist for party regulars who handed Taft the Republican presidential nomination for the 1912 election, so Roosevelt led his followers into a new Progressive Party, nicknamed the "Bull Moose" Party.

D. Woodrow Wilson and the New Freedom

1. As Republicans battled among themselves, Democrats made dramatic gains in 1910, taking over the House of Representatives and capturing a number of traditionally Republican governorships.

2. While governor of New Jersey, Woodrow Wilson compiled a sterling reform record; he then went on to win the Democratic presidential nomination in 1912.

3. Wilson warned that the New Nationalism represented a future of collectivism, whereas his own New Freedom policy would preserve political and economic liberty.

4. Wilson and Roosevelt differed over *how* government should restrain private power.

5. Wilson won the election of 1812, but his program of the New Freedom did not receive a clear mandate from the people.

6. However, the election did prove decisive in the history of economic reform; Wilson attacked the problems of tariff and banking reform.

7. The Underwood Tariff Act of 1913 pared rates down from 40 percent to 25 percent; the trust-dominated industries were targeted to foster competition and reduce prices for consumers.

8. The Federal Reserve Act of 1913 gave the nation a banking system that was resistant to financial panic, delegating financial functions to twelve district reserve banks. This strengthened the banking system and placed a measure of restraint on Wall Street.

9. To deal with the problem of corporate power, the Clayton Antitrust Act of 1914 amended the Sherman Act; the Clayton Act's definition of il-

legal practices was left flexible to distinguish whether or not an action stifled competition or created a monopoly.

10. The Federal Trade Commission was established in 1914, and it received broad powers to investigate companies and issue "cease and desist" orders against unfair trade practices.

11. The labor vote had grown increasingly important to the Democratic Party, and before his second campaign, Wilson championed a host of bills beneficial to American workers.

12. Wilson had encountered the same dilemma that confronted all successful progressives: how to balance the claims of moral principle with the unyielding realities of political life. Progressives prided themselves on being realists as well as moralists.

Lecture Strategies

1. What factors contributed to the emergence of progressivism? Describe how concentrated power was used to corrupt or oppress segments of American society. Specific readings from the muckrakers about political corruption or corporate excesses can help in this task.

2. The influence of academics on progressive policy began in this period. The ways in which social science and philosophy meshed with the progressive politicians' need for objective social analysis should be explored, with concrete examples given. The importance of this development for the subsequent work of public intellectuals can be pointed out. A comparison with the contemporary role of academic intellectuals and think tanks in developing policy may help to illustrate this issue.

3. Discuss the role of women progressives in this period. Perhaps biography is the most effective way of exploring the achievement of female reformers; fortunately, extensive material is available. The stories of Jane Addams at Hull House, Florence Kelley of the National Consumers' League, and the family planning activities of Margaret Sanger illustrate the areas to which progressive women gravitated. Students should also be aware of the important ways in which first-wave feminists differed from other activist women. This understanding might assist students in sorting out future rifts within the women's movement.

4. Students will be interested in the process by which the urban political machine shifted its emphasis from the ward to the state. The failure of traditional machines to protect workers and regulate conditions in the workplace forced urban Democratic politi-

cians to seek state intervention on behalf of their constituents. This common cause allowed progressive politicians to be assisted by the machines. Students should also understand how organized labor, after deliberately avoiding political involvement, found it necessary to engage in partisan politics. The process by which organized labor became a major constituency in the Democratic Party can be seen in the development of urban liberalism and events such as the Triangle Shirtwaist fire.

5. Although several lectures could be given on the careers of Theodore Roosevelt and Woodrow Wilson, a comparison of their personalities and the implications of their personal styles for their policies will interest students. Roosevelt was an outgoing, charismatic, enthusiastic individual who personalized his policies. Wilson was, in sharp contrast, reserved, scholarly, and well suited to direct a bureaucracy. Students should consider the effects of their personalities on their policies; for example, Roosevelt jawboned corporate leaders, whereas Wilson established the Federal Trade Commission in order to deal with corporate abuse. Other issues may also be used to illustrate the contrast, such as Roosevelt on consumers and Wilson on banking.

6. Any discussion of progressivism must deal with the intrinsic limitations of the movement. Its middle-class base led it to accept the system, both economic and political, in which it operated. In contrast to socialists, progressives had no desire to overturn or drastically reshape the economic system but wanted only to make it equitable. In exploring this issue, a concrete comparison between progressivism and socialism can be instructive. The question of whether reform in America can or should go beyond progressivism should provoke a lively discussion among students. Some attention might also be paid to progressivism's top-down emphasis. Students should be encouraged to think of other limitations.

Class Discussion Starters

1. **What were the hallmarks of the Progressive Era?**

Possible answers:
a. Reform became a major, self-sustaining phenomenon.
b. The old order was challenged and changed both politically and economically.
c. Reformers believed that problems could be addressed through scientific investigation and that people had the ability to master their environment.
d. Educated women found a congenial intellectual environment in which to play an active public role.
e. Religion played an underlying role in much reform activity.
f. There was a drive for information gathering and a high degree of confidence in academic expertise.

2. **What impact did the muckrakers have on American society?**

Possible answers:
a. Inexpensive general-circulation magazines containing exposés became popular reading material.
b. Investigative journalism established itself as a legitimate enterprise.
c. Muckraking publications attracted new converts to progressive reform.
d. Exposure of municipal corruption gave rise to reform on the local level.
e. Exposés, such as Upton Sinclair's *The Jungle*, spurred federal regulation of dangerous industrial practices.

3. **What role did religion play in the Progressive Era?**

Possible answers:
a. Most reformers had been raised in Christian families and had imbibed Christian ethical principles.
b. Leaders of the Social Gospel movement helped to formulate progressive principles.
c. Some urban churches opened centers that served as settlement houses.

4. **How did women capitalize on, or participate in, the progressive movement?**

Possible answers:
a. Women's organizations became powerful lobbies for the rights of women and children.
b. The nature of the work of those organizations made women's public activities more acceptable in a patriarchal world.
c. The prominence of certain women progressives allowed them to serve as role models for the younger generation.
d. The movement for woman suffrage was reinvigorated by progressive activists.
e. The feminist movement for complete gender equality was founded.
f. Women made concrete improvements in labor safety, family planning, and other significant fields.

5. **What critical events in African American history occurred during the Progressive Era?**

Possible answers:
a. The adoption of the white primary in southern states completed the process of disfranchisement.
b. Blacks migrated in increasing numbers from the rural South to northern cities.

c. The all-black Niagara Movement of African American intellectuals was organized in 1906 to seek racial equality.

d. White progressives joined black activists to form the National Association for the Advancement of Colored People in 1909.

e. The National Urban League was organized in 1911 by black and white social workers in order to assist black migrants who relocated to the cities.

f. Southern black women worked for progressive reform through civic organizations, filling the vacuum left by the disfranchisement of black men.

6. In what ways did Theodore Roosevelt's progressivism express itself?

Possible answers:

a. He sought to protect wilderness areas from inappropriate development so that they would be available for use by the public.

b. He threatened a government takeover of coal mines if their owners refused union recognition.

c. He personally intervened to control the abuses of what he called bad trusts.

d. He supported the passage of the Hepburn Railway Act, which empowered the Interstate Commerce Commission to curb discriminatory railroad rates.

e. He helped to enact consumer-protection legislation such as the Pure Food and Drug and the Meat Inspection Acts.

7. What were the elements of Woodrow Wilson's New Freedom?

Possible answers:

a. A determination to avoid the social legislation favored by Roosevelt.

b. The establishment of the Federal Trade Commission in order to regulate corporate behavior.

c. A lowering of tariffs to reduce consumer prices.

d. The establishment of the Federal Reserve System in order to reduce the likelihood of financial panics.

e. The passage of a number of bills that benefited labor, such as workers' compensation, child labor restrictions, and the eight-hour workday.

8. How did progressivism lead to an increase in the intervention of state power in economic, political, and social affairs?

Possible answers:

a. Corporate influence had become too powerful to be restricted without state authority.

b. Voluntary associations such as labor unions were not effective in protecting their interests.

c. Political corruption was too widespread and entrenched to be controlled by citizens' groups.

d. The state was able to call on expert scientific testimony in order to reveal the existing system's failure to protect the public interest.

Chapter Writing Assignments

1. What were the intellectual elements of the progressive outlook? Summarize the interaction of progressive ideas with the academic disciplines of economics, philosophy, psychology, and law.

2. Compare and contrast the ideas and activities of woman progressives with those of earlier female reformers, such as those in the abolitionist and woman suffrage movements. Did progressive women really "progress," or were they essentially working on the same types of issues (work, education, family) as their predecessors?

3. Describe the successes and failures of the labor movement during the Progressive Era. In what ways was this a turning point for the labor movement?

4. Describe the struggles of African Americans to secure their rights during the Progressive Era. What aspects of progressive reform undermined blacks' rights?

5. Compare and contrast the administrations of Theodore Roosevelt and Woodrow Wilson. What principles did they share? How did they differ in setting goals and carrying them out?

6. Trace the role of the Supreme Court in striking down and upholding progressive legislation in cases such as *Lochner v. New York* (1905), *Muller v. Oregon* (1908), and *United States v. Standard Oil* (1911). Were these rulings excessively activist, or were they an appropriate exercise of the Court's jurisdiction?

Document Exercises

AMERICAN VOICES

Charles Edward Russell: Muckraking (p. 576)

Document Discussion

1. **What objections did Russell have to the men who had amassed vast fortunes in the Gilded Age?**
   (He felt that they had engaged in illegal activities and had deprived other people of economic advancement. Russell also suggested that he opposed society's obsession with the collection of riches. He mentions a general suspicion that concentrations of

wealth in the hands of a few meant that others were being denied opportunity.)

2. **Why was the work of the muckrakers important?**
(The excesses of unregulated capitalism gave powerful people an unfair advantage over smaller businessmen and allowed them to defraud and injure the general public with impunity. The muckrakers exposed their activities, and that exposure occasionally led to reform.)

Writing Assignments

1. What reforms were enacted as a result of the work of the muckrakers?

2. The introduction to the article states that Mr. Russell never did "get back to writing music." What type of attraction might muckraking have held for journalists of his time?

AMERICAN LIVES

Frances Kellor: Woman Progressive (p. 580)

Document Discussion

1. **What drove Frances Kellor?**
(Kellor's upbringing was a major influence in her life. She had personal experience with poverty and the pitiful options open for women like her mother who needed work. In Coldwater, Michigan, she was exposed to reformers and their ideas during her formative years. The political atmosphere of progressivism certainly affected her.)

2. **Examine the various barriers to women that Kellor faced in her academic and political career. How and to what extent did she overcome them?**
(Kellor was not born into the middle class, but she found patrons and friends who assisted her to better herself. She did this without the support of a father or husband. Kellor was a pioneer in postgraduate study for women. She was interested in athletics when other girls were not encouraged to be athletes and fought for women's crew at Cornell. She chose to work in criminology, which was not considered a "ladylike" profession. Her first-rate work in the field, however, made her eminent. She overcame barriers through her achievements but not the barrier of racism put up by her teachers and reinforced by her studies. She was not allowed to vote, but her sound research and courage earned her government posts.)

Writing Assignments

1. Was Kellor a typical or an atypical progressive?

2. Examine the attitudes of Kellor's female contemporaries. What did women think about the types of choices Kellor and fellow progressives pursued?

AMERICAN VOICES

Dr. Alice Hamilton: Tracking Down Lead Poisoning (p. 588)

Document Discussion

1. **Why was Hamilton studying industrial diseases?**
(Very little was known about how working conditions affected the health of laborers in American cities. By the 1890s, the Industrial Revolution had transformed the national economy so that millions of Americans worked daily within factories or at industrial trades that exposed them to numerous dangers. The objective of Hamilton's project was to learn about the materials and practices used by workers in an urban environment.)

2. **What was the government's response to the problem of industrial hazards?**
(Government action to safeguard working conditions was expanding at the end of the nineteenth century but was still in its infancy. Hamilton mentions several official bodies, including the Occupational Disease Commission and the Factory Inspector's Office. A framework for political response existed, although the expertise and resources of such organizations was minimal.)

Writing Assignments

1. Associate the ideals and ambitions that Hamilton expresses with the progressive movement in American politics. How successfully were progressive ideas changing American attitudes regarding health and work?

2. Hamilton opens with comment that "it was all new, this exploring of the poor quarters of a big city," and that life for the poor was an "unknown" part of American life. From these observations, what can you conclude about the structure of American society? Assess matters such as rural and urban lifestyles, social mobility, wealth, and education.

VOICES FROM ABROAD

James Bryce: America in 1905: "Business Is King" (p. 594)

Document Discussion

1. **How do Bryce's fears regarding the risks of prosperity and material development echo many simi-**

lar claims today? Was Bryce correct? Why or why not?

(Bryce's lament that "rural districts are being studded with villages, the villages are growing into cities, the cities are stretching out long arms of suburbs, which follow the lines of road and railway in every direction," should sound strikingly familiar to students. This claim is frequently heard in the media today and often finds voice with local officials through zoning ordinances, environmental regulation, and so on.)

2. **Bryce warns that American society is losing its sense of "individualism" through the "power of wealth." Why does he think this is a danger? Is he convincing?**

(Bryce fears that wealth will ultimately be gathered into the hands of the few, which will expose the consumer to predatory practices. But he ignores the many benefits that a widening prosperity allows for an individual. He fails to acknowledge that the fortunes he sees being built are attained by people who were not previously wealthy. Thus to a degree Bryce contradicts himself: he asserts that many are attaining fortunes but also that many are at risk of being exploited by the few.)

Writing Assignments

1. Compare Bryce's concerns about material progress with the statements of the transcendentalists of the 1820s and 1830s. The writing of Thoreau would provide an interesting starting point. How are they similar, and how are they different? Why?

2. Bryce claimed that commerce and finance in America were overcoming all other interests. Was he right? How can you account for the persistence of religion, sports, leisure activities, or the family?

Skill-Building Map Exercises

Map 20.1: Woman Suffrage, 1890–1919 (p. 582)

1. **Why was woman suffrage accepted in the West first?**
(Hardship, demographics, and women's contributions combined to make the western states more likely to consider woman suffrage.)

2. **Why was the most stubborn resistance to woman suffrage in the South?**
(The South was the region of the country that was most conservative and unwilling to change social

roles and behaviors. The South's tradition of a well-defined social hierarchy and the religious convictions of many residents restrained suffrage.)

Topic for Research

The Muckrakers

No group was more instrumental in stimulating reform activity than the muckraking journalists. They investigated political corruption, child labor, adulterated food, business fraud, racial conflict, prostitution, and many other evils. Ellen F. Fitzpatrick, ed., *Muckraking* (1994), presents three landmark articles from Ray Stamard Baker, Lincoln Steffens, and Ida Tarbell — three of the great American journalists of the twentieth century. Important full-length muckraking books include Lincoln Steffens, *The Shame of the Cities* (1904), and Ida M. Tarbell, *The History of the Standard Oil Company* (1904). Most famous of the muckraking novels is Upton Sinclair, *The Jungle* (1906). Others are Jacob Riis, *How the Other Half Lives* (1890); Frank Norris, *The Octopus* (1901) and *The Pit* (1903); David Graham Phillips, *The Great God Success* (1901), *The Plum Tree* (1905), and *Susan Lenox* (1917); and Robert Herrick, *The Memoirs of an American Citizen* (1905). Finally, the ideas and experiences of the muckrakers might be explored through their autobiographies, the best of which is *The Autobiography of Lincoln Steffens* (1931).

Suggested Themes

1. Lincoln Steffens was one of the most famous muckrakers. Using his *Autobiography* (1931), summarize Steffens's activities in the pre–World War I period, and explain his drift from optimism to cynicism.

2. Compare and contrast the backgrounds and ideas of four prominent muckrakers. Is there an overriding concern or theme that offers a clue as to why they all became muckrakers?

How to Use the Ancillaries Available with *America's History*

Refer to the Preface to *America's History* at the front of the book for descriptions of instructor resources, including the Instructor's Resource CD-ROM, Computerized Test Bank, transparencies, and *Using the Bedford Series in History and Culture in the U.S. History Survey*. Student resources, also described in the Preface, include the Online Study Guide and *Documents to Accompany* America's History, a primary-source reader.

For Instructors

Using the Bedford Series in History and Culture in the U.S. History Survey

This brief online guide by Scott Hovey provides practical suggestions for incorporating volumes from the highly regarded Bedford Series in History and Culture into your survey course. Titles that complement the material covered in Chapter 20 include *Looking Backward: 2000–1887 by Edward Bellamy*, edited with an introduction by Daniel H. Borus; *A Traveler from Altruria by William Dean Howells*, edited with an introduction by David W. Levy; *Who Were the Progressives*, by Glenda Elizabeth Gilmore; *The 1912 Election and the Power of Progressivism: A Brief History with Documents*, by Brett Flehinger; *The Rebuilding of Old Commonwealths and Other Documents of Social Reform in the Progressive Era South*, edited with an introduction by William A. Link; *Muckraking: Three Landmark Articles*, edited with an introduction by Ellen F. Fitzpatrick; *Twenty Years at Hull-House by Jane Adams*, edited with an introduction by Victoria Bissell Brown; *Muller v. Oregon: A Brief History with Documents*, by Nancy Woloch; and *Other People's Money and How the Bankers Use It by Louis D. Brandeis*, edited with an introduction by Melvin I. Urofsky. For descriptions of these titles and how you might use them in your course, visit **bedfordstmartins.com/usingseries**.

For Students

Online Study Guide at bedfordstmartins.com/henretta

Each of the activities listed below includes short-answer questions. After submitting their answers, students can compare them to the model answers provided.

Map Activity

The map activity presents Map 20.1: Woman Suffrage, 1890–1919 (p. 582), and asks students to analyze the geo-graphic variations in states' granting women the right to vote.

Visual Activity

The visual activity presents the cartoon "Jack and the Wall Street Giants" (p. 593) and asks students to analyze the depiction of Theodore Roosevelt and the leaders of industry.

Reading Historical Documents

The document activity provides a brief introduction to the documents Charles Edward Russell: Muckraking (p. 576) and Dr. Alice Hamilton: Tracking Down Lead Poisoning (p. 588) and asks students to analyze their content, thinking critically about the sources.

Documents to Accompany *America's History*

Each of the documents listed is introduced by a headnote, which places the document in context, and is followed by questions, which help students to analyze the piece.

Sources for Chapter 20 are
Oliver Wendell Holmes Jr., *Dissenting Opinion,* Lochner v. New York (1905)
Walter Rauschenbusch, *The Church and the Social Movement* (1907)
Lincoln Steffens, *The Shame of the Cities* (1904)
Benjamin Barr Lindsey, *The Beast* (1910)
Jane Addams, *Twenty Years at Hull-House* (1910)
Margaret Sanger, *The Case for Birth Control* (1917)
Progressivism and Compulsory Sterilization (1907)
Robert M. La Follette, *Autobiography* (1913)
Theodore Roosevelt, *The Struggle for Social Justice* (1912)
Woodrow Wilson, *The New Freedom* (1912)
Louis D. Brandeis, *In Defense of Competition* (1912)
Walter Lipmann, *Drift and Mastery* (1914)

CHAPTER 21

An Emerging World Power
1877–1914

Chapter Instructional Objectives

After you have taught this chapter, your students should be able to answer the following questions:

1. How did economic interests affect American involvement in overseas expansion?

2. What were the causes and consequences of the Spanish-American War?

3. Explain and assess President Wilson's attempts to reconcile America's foreign policy with the nation's political ideals.

4. Describe the American foreign policy that developed between 1877 and 1914.

Chapter Summary

In 1877 the United States was, by any economic or demographic measure, already a great power. But America was inward looking. The absence of significant overseas concerns led to lax conduct of its foreign policy and neglect of its naval power. However, America's rapid economic development began to force the country to look outward, particularly in search of markets for surplus goods.

By the early 1890s, a new strategic outlook had taken hold, shaped in large part by the writings of Alfred T. Mahan, who called for a battleship navy, an interoceanic canal, and overseas bases. This dramatic shift was underpinned by economic, military, and intellectual justifications. Arguments drawn from social Darwinism and America's earlier tradition of Manifest Destiny supported this new expansionism.

The United States went to war with Spain in 1898, acquired distant possessions in the peace settlement, and set about becoming a colonial power. American troops put down a rebellion in the Philippines and participated in the multinational suppression of the Boxer Rebellion in China in 1900. The United States sought to limit foreign control of China and keep China's markets accessible in the Open Door notes of 1899 and 1900. Relying on Theodore Roosevelt's unilateral addition to the Monroe Doctrine, the United States policed the Caribbean basin. In 1914 and 1916, American troops were sent into revolutionary Mexico.

World power status came with penalties, however, and America paid the price: men were killed or wounded in the war with Spain and the Philippine insurrection, government spending increased, and the newly acquired colonial territories far removed from the Western Hemisphere were vulnerable to unfriendly powers. Suddenly, rivalries that had gone unnoticed became significant to the American government, as did the British move toward rapprochement. The United States had become a world power just as war was about to erupt in Europe.

Chapter Annotated Outline

I. The Roots of Expansion
   A. Diplomacy in the Gilded Age
      1. In 1880 the United States had a population of 50 million, and the nation's industrial production ranked second only to Britain's.
      2. The Civil War had put the United States at odds with Britain and France; the United States opposed France's attempt to establish a puppet regime in Mexico; with Britain, the issues involved damages to Union shipping by the Alabama and other Confederate sea raiders operating from English ports.
      3. In the years after the Civil War, the United States lapsed into diplomatic inactivity as the

building of the nation's industrial economy turned Americans' attention inward.

4. Americans shared a sense of security and isolation from the rest of the world, even though new international telegraphic cables provided overseas communication after the 1860s.

5. The U.S. Navy fleet gradually deteriorated; the administration of Chester A. Arthur (1881–1885) began a modest upgrading program, but the navy remained small.

6. Domestic politics made it difficult to develop a coherent foreign policy, and appointment to the foreign service was mostly through the spoils system.

7. The State Department tended to be inactive and exerted little control over either policy or its missions abroad; the American presence often consisted of independent religious missionaries.

8. Diplomatic activity quickened when James G. Blaine became secretary of state in 1881; he tried his hand at settling disputes in South America, and he called the first Pan-American conference.

9. After the McKinley Tariff of 1890 cancelled Hawaii's favored access to the American market, sugar planters backed by the Harrison administration planned an American takeover, but Grover Cleveland halted the annexation that would, he said, have violated America's "honor and morality" and nonimperial tradition.

10. In 1867 the United States purchased Alaska from imperial Russia, and to the south it secured rights in 1878 to a coaling station in Pago Pago Harbor in the Samoan Islands.

11. American diplomacy during the Gilded Age has been characterized as a series of incidents rather than the pursuit of a clear foreign policy.

B. The Economy of Expansionism

1. America's gross domestic product quadrupled between 1870 and 1900, and as the industrial economy expanded, so did factory exports.

2. American firms such as the Singer Sewing Machine Company and Standard Oil began to establish their factories overseas.

3. Foreign trade was important for reasons of international finance: to balance its foreign debt account, the United States needed to export more goods than it imported.

4. Many thought that the nation's capacity to produce had outpaced its capacity to consume, so the United States needed buyers in foreign markets to purchase its surplus products.

5. Europe and Canada represented the bulk of American export trade in the late nineteenth century, and Asia and Latin America represented a modest part.

6. The importance of the non-Western markets was not so much their current value as their future promise, especially the China trade, which many felt would one day be the key to American prosperity.

7. The pace of European imperialism accelerated in the mid-1880s: Africa was carved up after the Berlin Conference, and European powers challenged American interests in Latin America.

8. The Panic of 1893 set in motion industrial strikes and agrarian protests that many Americans took to be symptoms of revolution.

9. Securing the markets of Latin America and Asia became an urgent necessity and inspired the expansionist diplomacy of the 1890s.

C. The Making of a "Large" Foreign Policy

1. In his book *The Influence of Seapower upon History* (1890), Captain Alfred T. Mahan, a leading naval strategist, argued that the key to imperial power was control of the seas.

2. Traversing the oceans required a robust merchant marine, a powerful navy to protect American commerce, and strategic overseas bases.

3. Mahan called for a canal across Central America to connect the Atlantic and Pacific Oceans, with control over strategic points in defense of American trading interests.

4. Politicians accepted Mahan's underlying logic, and pushed for a "large policy"; from 1889 onward, a surprising consistency began to emerge in the conduct of American foreign policy.

5. In 1890, under Benjamin Harrison's administration, Congress appropriated funds for three battleships as the first installment on a two-ocean navy.

6. Grover Cleveland's administration cancelled Harrison's scheme for annexing Hawaii but picked up the naval program; the nation's commercial vitality depended on its naval power.

7. For years, a border dispute simmered between Venezuela and British Guiana, and the United States demanded that the British resolve it.

8. Invoking the Monroe Doctrine, Secretary of State Richard Olney warned Britain that the United States would brook no challenge to its vital interests in the Caribbean.

9. Realizing that the Cleveland administration meant business, the British agreed to arbitration of the border dispute.

10. Secretary of State Olney asserted that other countries would now have to accommodate America's need for access to "more markets and larger markets."

D. The Ideology of Expansionism

1. One source of expansionist dogma was the social Darwinism theory: if the United States wanted to survive, it had to expand.

2. Linked to social Darwinism was a spreading belief in the inherent superiority of the Anglo-Saxon race.

3. John Fiske's "Manifest Destiny" lecture espoused the belief that every land on the earth's surface should become English in its language, religion, political habits, and bloodline.

4. Frederick Jackson Turner suggested a link between the closing of the western frontier and overseas expansion, and as Turner predicted, American confidence in Manifest Destiny turned outward.

II. An American Empire

A. The Cuban Crisis

1. In February 1895, Cuban patriots rebelled and began a guerrilla war for their freedom from Spain; the Spanish commander, Valeriano Weyler, adopted a policy of "reconcentration."

2. The Junta, a key group of exiles, tried to make a case for the *Cuba Libre* in New York; William Randolph Hearst put Cuba's plight on the front page of the *New York Journal.*

3. Americans felt concern and sympathy for the Cubans, and their anger against Spain came to be known as "jingoism."

4. Congress began calling for Cuban independence, but Grover Cleveland was more concerned that the Cuban civil war was disrupting trade and harming American property interests.

5. William McKinley, like Cleveland, felt that the United States was the dominant Caribbean power with vital interests to be protected, but McKinley was tougher on the Spaniards.

6. McKinley was sensitive to business fears that any rash action might disrupt an economy just recovering from the depression.

7. On September 18, 1897, the United States informed the Spanish government that it was time to end the war, or the United States would take steps to end it.

8. Spain backed away from reconcentration and offered Cuba a degree of self-rule, but the Cuban rebels demanded full independence.

9. The *New York Journal* published the private letter of Dupuy de Lôme, the Spanish minister to the United States, which called President McKinley weak and implied that the Spanish government did not take American demands seriously.

10. A week later the U.S. battle cruiser *Maine* blew up and sank in Havana Harbor, killing 260 seamen; now, McKinley had to contend with popular clamor for a war against Spain.

11. Spain rejected McKinley's demands for an immediate armistice, abandonment of the practice of reconcentration, and peace negotiations.

12. The War Hawks in Congress chafed under McKinley's cautious progress, but the president did not lose control.

13. The resolutions authorizing intervention in Cuba contained an amendment disclaiming any intention by the United States of taking possession of Cuba.

14. It was not *because* of expansionist ambitions that McKinley forced Spain into a corner, but once war came, McKinley saw it as an opportunity for expansion.

B. The Spoils of War

1. When Spain declared war on April 24, 1898, Theodore Roosevelt was commissioned lieutenant colonel in the volunteer cavalry regiment known as the Rough Riders.

2. Confusion reigned in the swelling volunteer army: uniforms did not arrive, the food was bad, the sanitation was worse, rifles were in short supply, and no provisions had been made for getting troops to Cuba.

3. The small regular army provided a nucleus for the civilians who had to be turned into soldiers inside of a few weeks.

4. The navy was in better shape, as Spain had nothing to match American battleships and armored cruisers.

5. On May 1, American ships cornered the Spanish fleet in Manila Bay and destroyed it; Manila, the Philippine capital, fell on August 13, 1898.

6. After Commodore George Dewey's naval victory, Americans were not going to let the Philippine Islands go; the Philippines made a strategic base in the western Pacific and projected American power into Asia and its markets.

7. Hawaiian annexation went through Congress by joint resolution in July 1898; now, Hawaii was a crucial halfway station on the way to the Philippines.

8. The navy also pressed for a coaling base in Guam in the central Pacific and a base in Puerto Rico in the Caribbean.

9. The main battle in the campaign in Cuba occurred near Santiago on the heights commanded by San Juan Hill; convinced that Santiago could not be saved, Spanish forces surrendered.

10. In an armistice, Spain agreed to liberate Cuba and cede Puerto Rico and Guam to the United States, and American forces occupied Manila pending a peace treaty.

C. The Imperial Experiment

1. As to the question of what to do with the Philippines, not even avid American expansionists advocated colonial rule over subject peoples.

2. McKinley and his advisors felt that they could neither return the islands to harsh Spanish rule nor did they believe that the Filipinos were fit to rule themselves.

3. In the Treaty of Paris, the Spanish ceded the Philippines to the United States for a payment of $20 million.

4. Opponents of the treaty invoked American republican principles, declaring that the federal government could not conquer an alien people and hold them in subjugation.

5. In November 1890, a social elite of old-line Mugwump reformers from Boston formed the first of the Anti-Imperialist Leagues that began to spring up around the country.

6. The anti-imperialists never developed a popular movement: they shared little other interests, and they lacked "the common touch."

7. Before the Senate ratified the Treaty of Paris, fighting broke out between American and Filipino patrols; confronted with American annexation, Cubans turned their guns on American forces.

8. Fighting tenacious Philippine guerrillas, the U.S. Army resorted to the reconcentration tactic the Spaniards had used in Cuba.

9. The fighting ended in 1902, and, as governor-general, William Howard Taft intended to make the Philippines a model of American road building and sanitary engineering.

10. Americans had not anticipated the brutal methods needed to subdue the Filipino guerrillas; the Jones Act (1916) formally committed the United States to granting Philippine independence but set no date.

11. In a few years the United States had acquired the makings of an overseas empire and had moved into a position of what is commonly called a world power.

III. Onto the World Stage

A. A Power among Powers

1. Roosevelt justified American dominance in the Caribbean by saying that it was incumbent upon the civilized powers to insist on the proper policing of the world and the maintenance of the balance of power.

2. Britain's position in Europe was steadily worsening, challenged by a Germany bent on imperial supremacy and weakened by soured relations with France and Russia. Now, Great Britain had a new and clear need of rapprochement with the United States.

3. In the Hay-Pauncefote Agreement of 1901, the British gave up their rights to participate in any Central American canal project.

4. There was no formal alliance, but Anglo-American friendship had been placed on such a firm basis that it was assumed that the Americans and the British would never have a parricidal war.

5. In regard to American power, especially naval power, Roosevelt said, "Speak softly and carry a big stick."

6. Roosevelt was furious when the Columbian legislature voted down his proposal to lease land for a canal; he contemplated outright seizure of Panama but instead lent covert assistance that ensured a bloodless Panamanian revolution against Columbia.

7. On November 7, 1901, the United States recognized Panama and two weeks later received a perpetually renewable lease on a canal zone.

8. The U.S. Army Corps of Engineers finished the Panama Canal in 1914, giving the United States a commanding commercial and strategic position in the Western Hemisphere.

9. A condition for Cuban independence had been a proviso called the Platt Amendment, which gave the United States the right to intervene if Cuba's independence or internal order was threatened.

10. The Roosevelt Corollary to the Monroe Doctrine translated into an unrestricted American right to regulate Caribbean affairs.

11. On occasions when Caribbean domestic order broke down, the U.S. Marines occupied Cuba in 1906, Nicaragua in 1909, and Haiti and the Dominican Republic in later years.

B. The Open Door in Asia

1. In 1890, U.S. secretary of state John Hay sent the powers occupying China an "open door" note claiming the right of equal trade access for all nations that wanted to do business there.

2. In 1900, the United States joined a multinational campaign to break the Boxers' siege of the diplomatic missions in Peking.

3. As long as the legal fiction of an independent China survived, so would American claims to equal access to the China market.

4. Britain, Germany, France, and Russia were strongly entrenched in East Asia and not inclined to defer to American interests.

5. Anxious to restore some semblance of power, Roosevelt mediated a settlement of the Russo-Japanese War in 1905; Japan emerged as the predominant power in East Asia.

6. A surge of anti-Asian sentiment in California complicated Roosevelt's efforts to achieve Asian accommodation for American interests in the Pacific.

7. The Root-Takahira Agreement confirmed the status quo in the Pacific as well as the principles of free oceanic commerce and equal trade opportunity in China.

8. William Howard Taft hoped that with "dollar diplomacy" American capital would counterbalance Japanese power and pave the way for increased commercial activities.

9. When the Chinese Revolution of 1911 toppled the Manchu dynasty, Taft supported the victorious Chinese nationalists, and the United States entered a long-term rivalry with Japan.

C. Wilson and Mexico

1. Woodrow Wilson opposed dollar diplomacy, which he believed bullied weaker countries financially and gave undue advantage to American business.

2. Wilson insisted that the United States should conduct its foreign policy in conformity with its democratic principles.

3. Porfirio Diaz, Mexico's dictator, was overthrown by Francisco Madero, who spoke for liberty and constitutionalism much as did Wilson.

4. But before Madero could carry out his reforms, he was deposed and murdered in 1913 by Victoriano Huerta.

5. Although other powers were quick to recognize Huerta's provisional government, Wilson abhorred him, and the United States did not recognize his government.

6. Wilson intended to force Huerta out and to put the Mexican revolution back on the constitutional path started by Madero.

7. Venustiano Carranza, leading a Constitutionalist movement in northern Mexico, did not want American intervention; he only wanted recognition so that he could purchase U.S. weapons.

8. In 1914, American weapons began to flow to Carranza's troops; but as it became clear that Huerta was not going to fall, Wilson ordered the American occupation of the port of Veracruz.

9. Huerta's regime began to crumble, yet Carranza nonetheless condemned the United States, and his forces came close to engaging the Americans. Carranza's rival Pancho Villa did engage Americans, so Wilson sent troops under General John J. Pershing into Mexico, which further antagonized Mexico to the point that war was only narrowly averted.

D. The Gathering Storm in Europe

1. In Europe, there was rivalry between Germany, France, and Britain; in the Balkans, Austria-Hungary and Russia were maneuvering for dominance.

2. These conflicts created two groups of allies: Germany, Austria-Hungary, and Italy made up the Triple Alliance, and France and Russia made up the Dual Alliance.

3. Britain reached an entente with France and Russia by 1907, laying the foundation for a Triple Entente; a war between two great European power blocs became more likely.

4. On becoming president, Roosevelt took a lively interest in European affairs, and as the head of a Great Power, he was eager to make a contribution to the cause of peace there.

5. At an international conference in 1906 at Algeciras, Spain, the U.S. role was defined: the United States would be the apostle of peace, distinguished by a lack of selfish interest in European affairs.

6. The Hague Peace Conference of 1899 offered a new hope for the peaceful settlement of international disputes in the Permanent Court of Arbitration.

7. Both Roosevelt and Taft negotiated arbitration treaties with other countries, only to have them crippled by a Senate afraid of any erosion of the nation's sovereignty.

8. William Jennings Bryan's "cooling off" treaties with other countries were admirable but had no bearing on the explosive power politics of Europe.

Lecture Strategies

1. Contrast the diplomacy that was practiced before the 1890s with the diplomacy that emerged toward the end of the century. Explain why neither the United States nor foreign nations originally viewed diplomatic matters with great concern, and articulate how circumstances changed.

2. A lecture on Alfred Thayer Mahan and American sea power would be worthwhile. Some points to include

are the American naval policy before Mahan, the sources of Mahan's ideas on sea power, the reasons for Mahan's rise to prominence here and abroad, Mahan's influence compared with that of other contemporary naval advocates, and Mahan's relationship with those who favored American expansion.

3. Discuss the noneconomic sources of American expansionism. Note factors such as the activities and influence of missionaries, the impact of international rivalries on American expansionist thought, the appearance of Pan-Americanism in the 1880s, the central place of expansionism earlier in American history, and the importance of social Darwinism and Anglo-Saxonism in the changing foreign policy climate late in the nineteenth century.

4. Evaluate William McKinley. Some points to cover: Did he shape events, or did events determine his course? What influenced McKinley's ideas about expansionism? Was he an effective leader during the crisis and war with Spain? Did McKinley consider the long-term consequences of expansionism?

5. A lecture on the Spanish-American War can involve many subtopics: the military situations of the United States and Spain, the conduct of the invasion of Cuba, the campaign in Puerto Rico and how the United States was drawn into the Philippines, and the decisive factors in the American victory.

6. Discuss the Philippine insurrection. Explain how the United States became involved in the archipelago, note the reasons the United States chose to remain in the islands, and detail how the fighting between Filipinos and Americans started. Trace the course of the insurrection and discuss the tactics employed by the American military and the way the United States achieved victory. Finally, examine the human costs of pacification.

7. Many Americans had deep misgivings about the acquisition of an overseas empire. Consult anti-imperialist literature and outline the case of the anti-imperialists.

8. Discuss the Panama Canal. Describe the French attempt to build the canal and their motives for doing so. Explain America's historic interest in the region, elaborate on Theodore Roosevelt's determination to construct and control an isthmian canal, and analyze the Panamanian revolution and America's role in it. Have students compare the pluses and minuses of the American presence in Panama and the Canal Zone.

9. Discuss the Anglo-American rapprochement of the early twentieth century. Points to include in the lecture: Britain's deteriorating position in Europe, British investment in the United States, the impact of

the growth of American power on Britain, Anglo-American diplomacy from the Venezuelan crisis to the Alaska boundary settlement, and the attitudes of the American ruling elite toward Britain.

10. Compare American open-door diplomacy toward China under William McKinley with Japanese-American relations during the administrations of Theodore Roosevelt and William Howard Taft. Explore the notion of dollar diplomacy, and show how it influenced differing policies.

11. Examine Woodrow Wilson's Latin American policy between 1913 and 1916. Reconcile the president's initial renunciation of territorial ambitions with the frequent interventions that occurred in the Caribbean region. Note Wilson's interest in Mexico, how the two nations almost drifted into war, and the means by which hostilities were avoided. Ask what lessons can be learned from Wilson's record.

Class Discussion Starters

1. **What evidence exists for America's lack of interest in foreign affairs before the 1890s?**

Possible answers:
   a. Before 1890, prominent citizens, even the young Theodore Roosevelt, expressed negative sentiments about overseas involvements.
   b. American military forces were scattered throughout the West and committed to fighting Indians.
   c. The decline of the American navy after the Civil War.
   d. The generally low quality of diplomatic appointments both by the United States and by foreign countries to the United States.

2. **What were the economic sources of expansionism?**

Possible answers:
   a. Insufficient domestic markets existed to absorb the burgeoning output of American industry.
   b. Export outlets were desirable in periods of economic downturn; the more output that was sent abroad in bad times, the fewer workers that would need to be dismissed.
   c. Although exports to selected non-Western areas might be relatively small, the potential — in China, for example — was enormous.
   d. Exports needed to be boosted to balance the repatriation of the earnings of foreign investors in America.

3. **What were some of Alfred Thayer Mahan's ideas?**

Possible answers:
   a. Historically, great nations or empires had been major naval powers.

b. Sea powers had to have strategic overseas bases to sustain their naval forces and commerce.

c. A strong navy with secure overseas bases and the ability to move rapidly from one ocean to another could protect the nation's merchant marine, safeguarding foreign trade.

d. With an expanded, modern fleet, the United States could de-emphasize shore defenses.

e. An interoceanic canal linking the Atlantic and the Pacific was indispensable to America's playing a larger role in international affairs.

4. **What was the significance of the Venezuela crisis?**

Possible answers:

a. The United States invoked the Monroe Doctrine, warning against European interference in the Western Hemisphere.

b. The Venezuelan episode was a logical step in American foreign policy's outward thrust.

c. The crisis confirmed American domination of the Western Hemisphere.

d. American self-assertion reminded Britain that the United States was a valuable ally.

5. **What were the elements of the ideology of American expansionism?**

Possible answers:

a. Social Darwinist thought promoted the idea that great nations must expand; America, being a great nation, inevitably had to create an empire.

b. The United States was mainly an Anglo-Saxon nation, and Anglo-Saxons had proved themselves to be of superior racial stock. If the United States expanded abroad, it would have the higher motive of helping lesser races develop.

c. Americans realized that the domestic frontier had closed. In the words of the historian Frederick Jackson Turner, a "wider field," the international arena, was the new frontier.

6. **Why did America declare war on Spain?**

Possible answers:

a. Spain had been unable to crush the Cuban insurrection even though Spanish troops resorted to cruel and barbarous treatment of the Cuban populace.

b. A media blitz involving the publishing empires of Joseph Pulitzer and William Randolph Hearst featured stories sympathetic to the Cubans and made the American people support intervention.

c. The fighting was hurting American investments in Cuba.

d. The United States wished to end Caribbean instability, a goal that could be partially accomplished by resolving the Cuban imbroglio.

e. Neither Spain nor the United States could agree on a satisfactory negotiated end to the Cuban insurrection.

f. The blowing up of the battleship *Maine* and the publication of the Spanish envoy Dupuy de Lôme's indiscreet criticisms of President McKinley made already tense relations worse.

7. **How and why did America acquire the Philippines?**

Possible answers:

a. Commodore George Dewey's victory at the Battle of Manila Bay handed America a plum possession in the western Pacific.

b. Having defeated Spain, the United States could not return the islands to that nation.

c. The partitioning of the Philippines among the imperial powers — seen as a real danger in Washington — could jeopardize America's Pacific commerce.

d. Control of the Philippines gave the United States more influence on international policy in nearby China and easier access to Chinese markets.

e. It was thought that the Filipinos had to be "civilized"; the natives needed to be schooled in the science of government. The islands could be granted independence later.

8. **Why was there an Anglo-American rapprochement, and what signs were there of the two English-speaking nations drawing closer together?**

Possible answers:

a. Britain's diplomatic isolation dictated a more conciliatory policy toward America.

b. The American policymaking elite developed more tolerant attitudes toward Britain.

c. The British conceded any right to the Panama Canal, consenting to American control there as well as American dominance in the Caribbean.

d. The British sacrificed the interests and dreams of their Canadian subjects and agreed to an Alaskan boundary settlement favorable to the United States.

e. The British and Americans shared a common language and a common belief in Anglo-Saxon superiority.

9. **Where and why did the United States intervene in the Caribbean between 1898 and 1916?**

Possible answers:

a. In Venezuela in 1898 to end a border dispute with Great Britain.

b. In Cuba and Puerto Rico in 1898 to end Spanish control, and twice more in Cuba (1906 and 1917) because of political instability there.

c. In Panama in 1903 to end Colombian control and build an isthmian canal.

d. In the Dominican Republic in 1905 and 1916 to promote economic and political stability. Similar intervention provoked a rebellion in Nicaragua in 1912, resulting in occupation by American troops.

e. In Mexico in 1914 because of an incident involving American sailors in Tampico and again in 1916–1917 because of violation of the American border by Mexican forces.

f. In Haiti in 1915 because of political instability.

10. Why did the American expansion across the Pacific lose some of its luster early in the twentieth century?

Possible answers:

a. The Open Door notes of 1899 and 1900 were not honored by other nations.

b. The China market never materialized.

c. Japan emerged as a significant East Asian force that was potentially threatening to America's Philippine colony.

d. "Dollar diplomacy" in China failed during Taft's presidency.

e. News of brutality inflicted by American troops on Filipinos nullified claims of a civilizing mission.

Chapter Writing Assignments

1. Examine the economic and ideological roots of American expansionism. Was Frederick Jackson Turner correct in linking the closing of the frontier in 1890 to subsequent expansion overseas?

2. Describe the sequence of events that led to the Spanish-American War and the negotiations that concluded it. To what extent were U.S. policymakers carrying out a deliberate policy, and to what extent were they merely reacting to events?

3. Summarize the most important interventions of the United States in the Caribbean and Mexico during the presidencies of Theodore Roosevelt, Taft, and Wilson. How did each president justify his actions? Do you find echoes of these justifications in recent interventions, such as the invasions of Iraq and Kosovo in the 1990s?

Document Exercises

NEW TECHNOLOGY

The Battleship (p. 610)

Document Discussion

1. **What were the strengths and weaknesses of the battleship?**

(The most important capability of the battleship was its high-volume, large-caliber firepower. The battleship was the largest ship in the fleet, could maintain good speed, and was capable of absorbing punishment from an enemy and still staying afloat. Overall, the battleship was a lethal fighting platform. Drawbacks to the battleship included its substantial cost to build and operate, the large number of trained crew members required to maintain the ship, and the prodigious supply of fuel necessary to power it.)

2. **What was the military purpose of a battleship?**

(The purpose of the battleship was to close with and destroy enemy capital ships and to disrupt or destroy lesser warships and merchant vessels. The multiple direct-fire weapon systems of the battleship meant that it was effective across a broad engagement range against many types of opponents. An important characteristic beyond its direct military application was politicians' propensity to deploy a battleship in order to serve as a diplomatic tool signaling national resolve.)

Writing Assignments

1. Using the case of the battleship as evidence, examine the nature of technological change. Explain whether battleships were the product of evolutionary or revolutionary development.

2. This selection mentions Captain Alfred T. Mahan's advice to build capital ships. Mahan was indeed influential and contributed significantly to naval doctrine in the last decades of the nineteenth century. After surveying Mahan's writing, explain the role he assigned to navies in the service of a nation state.

AMERICAN LIVES

William Randolph Hearst: Jingo (p. 614)

Document Discussion

1. **How did Hearst increase the circulation of his newspapers?**

(According to Hearst, it was a matter of "SENSATION, SENSATION, SENSATION." He focused on items that would cause his readers to become emotionally aroused and involved in the stories.)

2. **Why did Hearst stir up the public about the rebellion in Cuba?**

(Hearst was not particularly interested in foreign affairs for their own sake but cared about circulation. He saw the Cuba situation as one that would allow him to focus on sensational [and often fictional] episodes and thus lead to an increase in circulation.)

Writing Assignments

1. Did newspapers like the *New York Journal* and the *San Francisco Examiner* fashion public opinion to suit the priorities of their editors and owners, or did they simply reflect the interests of their readers?

2. What does the popularity of newspapers suggest about the rate of literacy, and hence progress of primary education, in America?

AMERICAN VOICES

George W. Prioleau: Black Soldiers in a White Man's War (p. 619)

Document Discussion

1. **Is Prioleau suggesting that white racism was universal in the United States?**
   (He gives a mixed answer. He wonders if America is any better than Spain, and he indicts the nation for mistreating black children. Yet he notes that spectators in the North were supportive and that the crowds cheered black soldiers until the Ninth Cavalry reached Nashville, Tennessee.)

2. **What irony does Prioleau note for veterans of the black regiments who fought in Cuba?**
   (They fought to free Cuba of Spanish control only to return to the United States to fight their own battle against racism and prejudice.)

Writing Assignments

1. Discuss the discrimination experienced by black soldiers in the Spanish-American War. Were conditions in the army any different from those in society at large? Should they have been?

2. Drawing on the textbook and the sources cited in the bibliography, discuss the black role in the Spanish-American War.

AMERICAN VOICES

Daniel J. Evans and Seiward J. Norton: Fighting the Filipinos (p. 621)

Document Discussion

1. **Why did the American soldiers behave so harshly toward their enemy?**
   (The conduct of these particular troops was reprehensible and a violation of American army practice and training. The war in the Philippines was the nation's first major overseas conflict and the first time

that American troops engaged in a guerrilla war operating in a foreign country. In many respects, the civilians who ordered the troops to the islands, the leaders who attempted to craft a military strategy, and the soldiers who were on duty were equally unprepared for the vicious fighting that ensued.)

2. **Was the behavior of American soldiers as described in this text representative of U.S. troops' behavior toward native residents of the Philippines?**
   (The overwhelming number of American military units and soldiers did not mistreat prisoners or noncombatants. Such events did occur within the context of the war in the Philippines, but they were the exception and must be considered in the context of low-intensity warfare. American forces easily defeated their Spanish opponent only to confront a native movement that sought to eliminate all forms of Western governance. These fighters waged a guerrilla campaign against American troops, which resulted in a bloody and prolonged affair.)

Writing Assignments

1. Examine the morality of warfare. How can war be waged morally? Can only nation states fight legitimately? What is the standing of "rebel" forces?

2. Assess American foreign policy at the beginning of the twentieth century. Did the Spanish-American War fulfill America's objectives overseas and at home?

VOICES FROM ABROAD

Jean Hess, Émile Zola, and Ruben Dario: American Goliath (p. 624)

1. **What specific criticisms of U.S. expansionism do these writers express?**
   (Hess argues that United States became involved in the Philippines for economic gain rather than to secure liberty for the Filipinos. Zola claims that the United States has caught "war fever" and characterizes the Spanish-American War as a sign that the U.S. is more likely to engage in military conflict in the future, jeopardizing peace around the globe. Dario highlights both the strengths and frailties of the American nation as a poetic reminder that it is not infallible.

Writing Assignments

1. Do you think that these three writers were representative of world opinion regarding American expansionism? Why or why not? How might a politician, a peasant, or a soldier agree or disagree?

2. Compare the pieces by Hess and Zola to the Dario poem. Which do you find more effective and why?

Skill-Building Map Exercises

Map 21.1: The Spanish-American War of 1898 (p. 617)

1. **Why do you think the United States sent an invasion force to Cuba but not to the Philippines?**
   (Cuba was closer to America's bases, and Spain had forces on the ground there; the defeat of the Spanish troops on the island was more feasible and thus of more interest to American military planners and the public. In the Philippines, Commodore Dewey's victory in the Battle of Manila Bay seemingly precluded the need for infantry.)

2. **Why was there an American naval fleet in the South China Sea in 1898?**
   (Dewey's fleet was in the region to protect growing American interests in the Pacific. European competition for colonial markets was intense, China remained vulnerable, and the Japanese were becoming more powerful. America's economic, political, and military elite were beginning to pay much closer attention to the region.)

Map 21.4: Policemen of the Caribbean, 1895–1941 (p. 626)

1. **How might one interpret the interventions noted on the map?**
   (Clearly, the United States was seeking stability in, if not domination of, the Caribbean and Mexico.)

2. **Under which president did most interventions occur?**
   (Woodrow Wilson.)

Topic for Research

The Anti-Imperialists (1898–1900)

During the 1890s, the attention grabbers were those advocating American expansionism. But America also had a long tradition of anti-imperialism — of opposition to the rule of other peoples by the United States — and this tradition was very much revived by the Spanish-American War and the sudden acquisition of an overseas empire. Although they had little political success, the anti-imperialists mounted a powerful critique of expansionism and, in particular, of the taking and subsequent

bloody suppression of the Philippines. What were the ideas and arguments these anti-imperialists leveled against their nation's imperial adventure? The starting point for such an inquiry is Robert L. Beisner, *Twelve against Empire: The Anti-Imperialists, 1898–1900* (1968), in particular the chapters on the philosopher William James, the industrialist Andrew Carnegie, the journalist E. L. Godkin (editor of *The Nation*), and the Yankee businessman and historian Charles Francis Adams. A guide to the writings of these anti-imperialists is to be found in Beisner's "Note on Sources." Beisner links anti-imperialism to the Mugwump tradition. There were, however, many anti-imperialists outside that tradition. For labor, one might study the anti-imperialist Samuel Gompers; for a woman's perspective, Jane Addams; and, to see how humor was brought to bear on the pretensions of the expansionists, Mark Twain.

As victims of racism, African Americans had particularly ambiguous feelings about the events of 1898–1900, and these might be explored in the writings of Booker T. Washington or in the contemporary black press. A useful source is Philip S. Foner and Richard C. Winchester, eds., *The Anti-Imperialist Reader: A Documentary History of Anti-Imperialism in the United States* (1984).

Suggested Themes

1. Summarize the anti-imperialist case made by one of the former Mugwumps against the acquisition of empire. How does the argument differ from that made by one of the non-Mugwumps: Samuel Gompers, Jane Addams, or Booker T. Washington?

2. According to the textbook, those who opposed the Spanish-American War belonged to a long tradition of American anti-imperialism. Examine what the anti-imperialists of 1900 owed to earlier writers and politicians, and explain what was new in their arguments.

How to Use the Ancillaries Available with *America's History*

Refer to the Preface to *America's History* at the front of the book for descriptions of instructor resources, including the Instructor's Resource CD-ROM, Computerized Test Bank, transparencies, and *Using the Bedford Series in History and Culture in the U.S. History Survey*. Student resources, also described in the Preface, include the Online Study Guide and *Documents to Accompany America's History*, a primary-source reader.

For Students

Online Study Guide at bedfordstmartins.com/henretta Each of the activities listed below includes short-answer questions. After submitting their answers, students can compare them to the model answers provided.

Map Activity

The map activity presents Map 21.1: The Spanish-American War of 1898 (p. 617) and asks students to analyze different aspects of this conflict.

Visual Activity

The visual activity presents an illustration from *Life* magazine that satirizes American imperialism (p. 623) and asks students to place this image in the debate over the nation's expanding imperial interests.

Reading Historical Documents

The document activity provides a brief introduction to the documents George W. Prioleau: Black Soldiers in a White Man's War (p. 619) and Daniel J. Evans and Seiward J. Norton: Fighting the Filipinos (p. 621) and asks students to analyze their content, thinking critically about the sources.

Documents to Accompany *America's History*

Each of the documents listed is introduced by a headnote, which places the document in context, and is followed by questions, which help students to analyze the piece.

Sources for Chapter 21 are
Alfred Thayer Mahan, *The Influence of Sea Power upon History* (1890)

Frederick Jackson Turner, *The Significance of the Frontier in American History* (1893)
Albert J. Beveridge, *The March of the Flag* (1898)
William James, *The Philippines Tangle* (1899)
Visual Document: R. C. Bowman, *Cartoon on the Philippines and Cuba* (1901)
John Hay, *Open Door Notes* (1899, 1900)
Mark Twain, *To the Person Sitting in the Darkness* (1901)
Theodore Roosevelt, *The Roosevelt Corollary to the Monroe Doctrine* (1904, 1905)

Thinking about History: The Fate of the Great Plains (p. 632)

Discussion Questions

1. What did American settlers expect to find in the Great Plains? Why did they go there?

2. Examine the role of the federal government in the settlement of the West.

3. Construct an alternative history of the settlement of the American interior that preserves Native American culture.

PART FIVE

The Modern State and Society

1914–1945

Part Instructional Objectives

After you have taught this part, your students should be able to answer the following questions:

1. How and why did the United States fight in World War I? How did the settlement of the war affect the next two decades?

2. What were the dramatic changes and upheavals experienced by the American economy?

3. How and why did the federal government increase its power and expand its authority in response to domestic economic, political, and social challenges?

4. How and why did a mass national culture in America emerge?

5. How and why did America transform from an isolationist state to leader of the Allied coalition in World War II?

6. How and why did the Allied Powers execute and win World War II?

Thematic Timeline

	GOVERNMENT	DIPLOMACY	ECONOMY	SOCIETY	CULTURE
	The Rise of the State	From Isolation to World Leadership	Prosperity, Depression, and War	Nativism, Migration, and Social Change	The Emergence of a Mass National Culture
1914	▸ Wartime agencies expand power of federal government	▸ United States enter World War I (1917) Wilson's Fourteen Points (1918)	▸ Shift from debtor to creditor nation Agricultural glut	▸ Southern blacks begin migration to northern cities	▸ Silent screen; Hollywood becomes movie capital of the world
1920	▸ Republican ascendancy Prohibition (1920–1933) Business-government partnership Nineteenth Amendment gives women the vote	▸ Treaty of Versailles rejected by U.S. Senate (1920) Washington Conference sets naval limits (1922)	▸ Economic recession (1920–1921) Booming prosperity (1922–1929) Rise of welfare capitalism	▸ Rise of nativism National Origins Act (1924) Mexican American immigration increases	▸ Consumer culture—advertising, radio, magazines, movies—flourishes Consumer culture promotes image of emancipated womanhood, the Flapper
1930	▸ Franklin D. Roosevelt becomes president (1933) The New Deal: unprecedented government intervention in economy, social welfare, arts	▸ Roosevelt's Good Neighbor Policy toward Latin America (1933) Abraham Lincoln Brigade fights in Spanish civil war U.S. neutrality proclaimed (1939)	▸ Great Depression (1929–1941) Rise of labor movement Married women increasingly participate in workforce	▸ Farming familes migrate from dust bowl states to California and the West Indian New Deal	▸ Documentary impulse Federal patronage of the arts
1940	▸ Government mobilizes industry for war production and rationing	▸ United States enters World War II (1941) Allies defeat Axis powers; bombing of Hiroshima (1945)	▸ War mobilization ends depression	▸ Rural whites and blacks migrate to war jobs in cities Civil Rights movement revitalized	▸ Film industry enlisted to aid war effort

By 1914, industrialization, economic expansion abroad, massive immigration, and the growth of a vibrant urban culture had set the foundations for distinctly modern American society. In all facets of politics, the economy, and daily life, American society was becoming more organized, more bureaucratic, and more complex. By 1945, after having fought in two world wars and weathering a dozen years of economic depression, the edifice of the new society was largely complete.

Government   First, an essential building block of modern American society was a strong national state. This state came late and haltingly to America compared with that of the industrialized countries of Western Europe. American participation in World War I called forth an unprecedented mobilization of the domestic economy, but policymakers quickly dismantled the centralized wartime bureaucracies in 1919. During the 1920s the Harding and Coolidge administrations embraced a philosophy of business-government partnership, believing that unrestricted corporate capitalism would provide for the welfare of the American people. Ultimately, the Great Depression, with its countless business failures and unprecedented levels of unemployment, overthrew that long-cherished idea. Franklin D. Roosevelt's New Deal dramatically expanded federal responsibility for the economy and the welfare of ordinary citizens. An even greater expansion of the national state resulted from the massive mobilization necessitated by America's entry into World War II. Unlike the experience after World War I, the new state apparatus remained in place when the war ended.

Diplomacy   Second, America was slowly and somewhat reluctantly drawn into a position of world leadership, which it continues to hold today. World War I provided the major impetus: before 1914, the world had been dominated by Europe, but from that point on the United States increasingly dominated the world. In 1918, American troops provided the margin of victory for the Allies, and President Wilson helped to shape the treaties that ended the war. The United States, however, refused to join the League of Nations. America's dominant economic position guaranteed an active role in world affairs in the 1920s and 1930s nonetheless. The globalization of America accelerated in 1941, when the nation threw all its energies into a second world war that had its roots in the imperfect settlement of the first one. Of all the powers that participated in this most devastating of global conflagrations, only America emerged physically unscathed from World War II. The country was also the only one to possess a dangerous new weapon — the atomic bomb. Within wartime decisions and strategies lay the roots of the cold war that followed.

Economy   Third, modern America developed a strong domestic economy. In fact, between 1914 and 1945 the nation's industrial economy was the most productive in the world. Even the Great Depression, which hit the United States harder than any other industrialized nation, did not permanently affect America's global economic standing. Indeed, American businesses successfully competed in world markets, and American financial institutions played the leading role in international economic affairs. Large-scale corporate organizations replaced smaller family-run businesses. The automobile industry symbolized the ascendancy of mass-production techniques. Many workers shared in the general prosperity but also bore the brunt of economic downturns. These uncertainties fueled the dramatic growth of the labor movement in the 1930s.

Society   Fourth, American society was transformed by the great wave of European immigration and the movement from farms to cities. The growth of metropolitan areas gave the nation an increasingly urban tone, and geographical mobility broke down regional differences. Many old-stock white Americans viewed these processes with alarm; in 1924, nativists succeeded in all but eliminating immigration except from within the Western Hemisphere, where migration across the border from Mexico continued to shape the West and Southwest. In other ways, internal migration changed the face of America as African Americans moved north and west to take factory jobs, and dust bowl farmers in the 1930s moved to the Far West to find better livelihoods. World War II accelerated these migration patterns even more.

Culture   Fifth, modern America saw the emergence of a mass national culture. By the 1920s, Americans were increasingly drawn into a web of interlocking cultural experiences. Advertising and the new entertainment media — movies, radio, and magazines — disseminated the new values of consumerism; the movies exported this vision of the American experience worldwide. Not even the Great Depression could divert Americans from their desire for leisure, self-fulfillment, and consumer goods. The emphasis on consumption and a quest for a rising standard of living would define the American experience for the rest of the twentieth century.

CHAPTER 22

War and the American State
1914–1920

Chapter Instructional Objectives

After you have taught this chapter, your students should be able to answer the following questions:

1. How and why did World War I begin?

2. Evaluate and discuss President Wilson's decision to enter the war in 1917.

3. Why was World War I considered a "total war"?

4. How did the war affect economic affairs and social relationships in America?

5. How and why did President Wilson attempt to shape the Treaty of Versailles?

6. Assess and discuss the failure of the Settlement of 1919–1920 to achieve a lasting peace in America and in Europe.

Chapter Summary

Before the outbreak of the Great War in 1914, the world had been dominated by the nation-states of Europe. In the postwar world the United States increasingly dominated the political, economic, and cultural affairs of many countries.

In keeping with the American tradition of noninvolvement in foreign affairs, President Wilson issued a neutrality proclamation at the outbreak of World War I. As the war progressed, however, enormous strains were placed on the United States, the most serious being violations of American neutrality rights. The German sinking of the British liner *Lusitania*, with the loss of more than a hundred American lives, epitomized those strains. Neutrality was not abandoned, however, until early 1917, when imperial Germany resumed unrestricted submarine warfare. With public opinion aroused by the con-

tents of the Zimmermann telegram, political opposition to entering the war evaporated, and the United States declared war on Germany.

The public expected a limited naval conflict, but the enormously destructive war led to the mobilization, training, and movement of several million young Americans to European battlefields, where their numbers proved decisive in the defeat of Germany. On the home front, the Wilson administration vastly expanded the government's powers in order to coordinate economic production and to popularize the war through propaganda. Ambivalence about expanding state power, coupled with pressures of wartime mobilization, severely damaged the impetus for progressive reforms that had characterized the prewar era. Yet even in the context of international crisis, some reformers expected the war to serve the cause of improving American society.

The wartime environment facilitated the passage of Prohibition and woman suffrage amendments to the Constitution. Reformers concerned for the welfare of children, health, and public morality found an ally in the military, which wanted to promote discipline. But as a spirit of conformity pervaded the home front, many Americans found themselves suspected of fomenting treason and revolution. Public officials curbed civil liberties and tolerated little criticism of patriotic values and established institutions.

President Wilson, although not oblivious to problems on the home front, concentrated on pursuing a nonpunitive peace settlement with Germany and approval of an international organization called the League of Nations. When the Republican Senate refused to ratify the Treaty of Versailles, Wilson refused to compromise. Many wartime issues, including reparations and the division of colonies among European states, were left unresolved and established conditions for another war in Europe.

In America, workers of all races harbored hopes for a better life after the war. The war years had brought better pay, shorter hours, and improved working conditions. Many African Americans were determined to stand up for their rights, which contributed to a spirit of militancy. Workers' strikes, black activism, and long-standing anxiety among whites about unassimilated immigrants led to increased social tensions and heightened fears of radicalism that culminated in race riots, the Red Scare, and renewed government suppression of union strikes.

Chapter Annotated Outline

I.   The Great War, 1914–1918
   A. War in Europe
      1. When war erupted, most Americans saw no reason to involve themselves in the struggle among Europe's imperialist powers; the United States had a good relationship with both sides.
      2. Many Americans believed in "U.S. exceptionalism," the feeling that democratic values and institutions made their country immune from the corruption and chaos of other nations.
      3. Almost from the moment the Triple Entente was formed in 1907 to counter the Triple Alliance, European leaders began to prepare for an inevitable conflict.
      4. Austria's seizure of Bosnia and Herzegovina in 1908 enraged Russia and Serbia; Serbian terrorists recruited Bosnians to agitate against Austrian rule.
      5. On June 28, 1914, Gavrilo Princip, a Bosnian, assassinated Franz Ferdinand, the heir to the Austro-Hungarian throne, and his wife in the town of Sarajevo.
      6. After the assassination, the complex European alliance system drew all the major powers into war within a few days.
      7. The two rival blocs faced off: Great Britain, France, Japan, Russia, and Italy formed the Allied Powers, while Germany, Austria-Hungary, Turkey, and Bulgaria formed the Central Powers.
      8. The worldwide scope of the conflict came to be known as "the Great War," or later, World War I.
      9. World War I was the first war in which extensive harm was done to civilians; new military technology, much of it from the United States, made armies more deadly than before.
      10. Trench warfare produced unprecedented numbers of casualties; between February and December of 1916, the French suffered 550,000 casualties and the Germans 450,000.
   B. The Perils of Neutrality
      1. After the war began in Europe, President Woodrow Wilson made it clear that America would remain neutral; he believed that he could arbitrate and influence a European settlement.
      2. The United States had divided loyalties concerning the war; many Americans felt deep cultural ties to the Allies, while others, especially Irish and German immigrants, had strong pro-German sentiments.
      3. Progressive leaders opposed American participation in the European conflict, new pacifist groups mobilized popular opposition, the political left condemned the war as imperialistic, and some industrialists, like Henry Ford, bankrolled antiwar activities.
      4. African American leaders saw the war as a conflict of the white race only.
      5. The British imposed a naval blockade that in effect prevented neutral nations, including the United States, from trading with Germany and its Allies.
      6. The resulting trade imbalance translated into closer U.S. economic ties with the Allies, despite America's official posture of neutrality.
      7. The German navy launched a devastating new weapon, the U-boat, and issued a warning to civilians that all ships flying the flags of Britain or its Allies were liable to be destroyed.
      8. On May 7, 1915, the British luxury liner *Lusitania* was torpedoed by a German U-boat off the coast of Ireland; 128 Americans were among the 1,198 people killed.
      9. In September 1915, Germany announced that its submarines would no longer attack passenger ships without warning.
      10. Wilson worried that the United States might be drawn into the conflict, so he endorsed a $1 billion buildup of the army and the navy.
      11. Congress passed the National Defense Act, which created the Council of National Defense, an agency charged with planning industrial mobilization in the event of war.
      12. Public opposition to entering the war made the election of 1916 a contest between two anti-war candidates; Wilson won the election but eventually lost his hopes of staying out of the war.
      13. The resumption of unrestricted submarine warfare, in conjunction with the Zimmermann telegram, inflamed anti-German sentiment in America.
      14. Throughout March 1917, German U-boats attacked and sank American ships without

warning; on April 2, Wilson asked Congress for a declaration of war; the United States formally declared war on Germany on April 6, 1917.

C. "Over There"

1. Many Americans assumed that their participation in the war would be limited to military and economic aid and were surprised to find that American troops would be sent to Europe.
2. To field an adequate fighting force, the American government conscripted almost 4 million men and women with the passage of the Selective Service Act in May 1917.
3. The Selective Service system combined central direction from Washington with local administration and civilian control; thus it preserved individual freedom and local autonomy.
4. General John J. Pershing was head of the American Expeditionary Force (AEF), but the new recruits had to be trained before being transported across the submarine-infested Atlantic.
5. The government countered the U-boats by sending armed convoys across the Atlantic; the plan worked: no American soldiers were killed on the way to Europe.
6. Pershing was reluctant to put his men under foreign commanders; thus, until May 1918, the French and the British still bore the brunt of the fighting.
7. Under the Treaty of Brest-Litovsk, the new Bolshevik regime under Vladimir Ilych Lenin surrendered about one-third of Russia's territories in return for peace with the Central Powers.
8. At the request of Allied leaders, Pershing committed about 60,000 Americans to help the French repel the Germans in the battles of Château-Thierry and Belleau Wood.
9. American and Allied forces brought the German offensive to a halt in mid-July; the counteroffensive began with a campaign to push the Germans back from the Marne River.
10. The Meuse-Argonne campaign pushed the enemy back across the Selle River near Verdun and broke the German defenses, at the cost of over 26,000 American lives.
11. German and Allied representatives signed an armistice on November 11, 1918, ending World War I.
12. America's decisive contribution shifted international power: European dominance declined, and the United States emerged as a world leader.

D. The American Fighting Force

1. The United States lost 48,000 American servicemen in the fighting, and another 27,000 died from other causes; the Allies and Central Powers lost 8 million soldiers.
2. The ethnic diversity of the American military worried some observers, but most optimistically predicted that service in the armed forces would promote the Americanization of immigrants.
3. The Stanford-Binet intelligence test used by the armed forces reinforced stereotypes about the supposed intellectual inferiority of blacks and immigrants; in fact, the lower scores stemmed from the cultural and environmental biases of the tests.
4. The Americanization of the army was imperfect at best; African Americans were in segregated units under the control of white officers and were assigned to the most menial tasks. The French were more egalitarian, socializing with black troops and awarding hundreds of them the Croix de Guerre.
5. A group of former AEF soldiers formed the first American Legion in 1919 in order to preserve the "memories and incidents" of their association in the Great War.

II. War on the Home Front

A. Mobilizing Industry and the Economy

1. As the Allies paid in gold for American grain and military supplies, the United States reversed its historical position as a debtor and became a leading creditor.
2. The government paid for the war by using the Federal Reserve System to expand the money supply, by enacting the War Revenue Bills of 1917 and 1918, and by collecting excess-profits taxes from corporations.
3. The central agency for coordinating wartime production, the War Industries Board (WIB), epitomized an unparalleled expansion of the federal government's powers.
4. Despite higher taxes, corporate profits soared, aided by the suspension of antitrust laws and the institution of price guarantees for war work.
5. To ease a fuel shortage in the winter of 1917–18, the Fuel Administration ordered the temporary closing of factories, and the Railroad War Board took temporary control of the railroads when traffic slowed troop movement.
6. The Food Administration encouraged farmers to expand production and encouraged housewives to conserve food; at no time was it necessary for the government to contemplate domestic food rationing.

7. With the signing of the armistice in 1918, the WIB was disbanded; most Americans could tolerate government planning power during an emergency but not permanently.

8. The U. S. participation in the war lasted just eighteen months, but it left an enduring legacy: the modern bureaucratic state.

B. Mobilizing American Workers

1. The National War Labor Board (NWLB) and acute labor shortages helped to improve labor's position with eight-hour days, time-and-a-half pay for overtime, and equal pay for women.

2. After the war, the NWLB quickly disbanded; wartime inflation ate up most of the wage hikes, and a postwar antiunion movement caused a decline in union membership.

3. During the war emergency, northern factories actively recruited African Americans, spawning the "Great Migration" from the South.

4. Wartime labor shortages prompted many Mexican Americans to leave farm labor for industrial jobs in rapidly growing southwestern cities.

5. About 1 million women joined the labor force for the first time, and many of the 8 million already working switched from low-paying fields to higher-paying industrial work.

C. Wartime Reform: Woman Suffrage and Prohibition

1. Members of the National American Woman Suffrage Association (NAWSA) felt that women's patriotic service could advance the cause of woman suffrage.

2. Members of the National Woman's Party (NWP) were arrested and jailed for picketing the White House; they became martyrs and drew attention to the issue of woman suffrage.

3. In January 1918, Woodrow Wilson withdrew his opposition to a federal woman suffrage amendment; on August 26, 1920, the goal of woman suffrage was finally achieved with the Nineteenth Amendment.

4. Throughout the mobilization period, reformers pushed for social reforms: addressing children's welfare, launching a campaign against sexually transmitted diseases, and lobbying for a ban on drinking.

5. Prohibition met with resistance in the cities because alcoholic beverages played an important role in the social life of certain ethnic cultures.

6. Many states already had Prohibition laws, and the Eighteenth Amendment to the Constitution demonstrated the government's widening influence on personal behavior.

7. Federal agencies were quickly disbanded after the war was over, reflecting the unease most Americans felt about a strong bureaucratic state.

8. The wartime collaboration between government and business gave corporate leaders more influence in shaping the economy and government policy.

D. Promoting National Unity

1. Formed in 1917, the Committee on Public Information (CPI) promoted public support for the war and acted as a nationalizing force by promoting the development of a national ideology.

2. During the war, the CPI touched the lives of practically every American, and in its zeal, it often ventured into hatemongering against the Germans.

3. Many Americans found themselves targets of suspicion as self-appointed agents of the American Protective League spied on neighbors and coworkers.

4. The CPI encouraged ethnic groups to give up their Old World customs in the spirit of "One Hundred Percent Americanism," an insistence on conformity and an intolerance of dissent.

5. Law enforcement officials tolerated little criticism of established values and institutions; legal tools for curbing dissent included the Espionage Act of 1917 and the Sedition Act of 1918.

6. The acts, which defined treason and sedition loosely, led to the conviction of more than a thousand people, and the courts rarely resisted wartime legal excesses.

7. In *Schenck v. United States*, the Supreme Court upheld limits on freedom of speech that would not have been acceptable in peacetime.

III. An Unsettled Peace, 1919–1920

A. The Treaty of Versailles

1. In January 1917, President Wilson proposed a "peace without victory," and the keystone of his postwar plans was a permanent League of Nations.

2. The Allies accepted Wilson's Fourteen Points as the basis for the peace negotiations for the Treaty of Versailles that began in January 1919.

3. Wilson called for open diplomacy, freedom of navigation upon the seas, arms reduction, the removal of trade barriers, and an international commitment to national self-determination.

4. According to Article X of the peace treaty, the League of Nations would curb aggressor countries through collective military action and mediate disputes to prevent future wars.

5. The Fourteen Points were imbued with the spirit of progressivism, but the lofty goals and ideals for world reformation proved too far reaching for the Old World powers, which had less high-minded goals of their own.

6. Representatives from twenty-seven countries attended the peace conference in Versailles, but representatives from Germany and Russia were not invited.

7. France, Italy, and Great Britain wanted to treat themselves to the spoils of war by demanding heavy reparations; they had made secret agreements to divide up the German colonies.

8. National self-determination bore fruit in the creation of the independent states of Austria, Hungary, Poland, Yugoslavia, and Czechoslovakia.

9. The creation of the new nations of Finland, Estonia, Lithuania, and Latvia upheld the principle of self-determination, while also isolating Soviet Russia from the rest of Europe.

10. Wilson won only limited concessions regarding the colonial empires, and topics such as freedom of the seas and free trade never came up because of Allied resistance.

11. A peace treaty was signed in Versailles on June 28, 1919, but when Wilson presented the treaty to the U.S. Senate, it did not receive the necessary two-thirds vote for ratification.

12. Progressive senators felt that the treaty was too conservative, "irreconcilables" disapproved of U.S. participation in European affairs, and Republicans wanted to amend Article X.

13. In September of 1919, Wilson went on a speaking tour to defend the treaty, but the tour was cut short because he suffered a severe stroke.

14. Wilson remained inflexible in his refusal to compromise, but the treaty was not ratified when it came up for a vote in the Senate in 1919 and again in 1920.

15. Wartime issues were only partially resolved; some unresolved problems played a major role in the coming of World War II, and some, like the competing ethnic nationalism in the Balkans, remain unsolved today.

B. Racial Strife, Labor Unrest, and the Red Scare

1. Many African Americans emerged from the war determined to stand up for their rights and contributed to a spirit of resistance to oppression that characterized the early 1920s.

2. Blacks who had migrated to the North and blacks who had served in the war had high expectations that exacerbated white racism; lynching nearly doubled in the South, and race riots broke out in the North.

3. A variety of tensions were present in northern cities where violence erupted: black voters determined the winners of close elections, and blacks competed with whites for jobs and housing.

4. Workers of all races had hopes for a better life, but after the war employers resumed attacks on union activity, and rapidly rising inflation threatened to wipe out wage increases.

5. As a result of workers' determination and employers' resistance, one in every five workers went on strike in 1919; strikes were held by steelworkers, shipyard workers in Seattle, and policemen in Boston.

6. Governor Calvin Coolidge of Massachusetts fired the entire Boston police force, and that strike failed; Coolidge was rewarded with the Republican vice presidential nomination in 1920.

7. Americans harbored a pervasive fear of radicalism and a long-standing anxiety about unassimilated immigrants, an anxiety that had been made worse by the war.

8. The Russian Revolution of 1917 so alarmed the Allies that Wilson sent several thousand troops to Russia in hopes of weakening the Bolshevik regime.

9. American fears of communism were deepened as the labor unrest coincided with the founding of the Bolsheviks' Third International (or Comintern) to export Communist doctrine and revolution to the rest of the world.

10. Ironically, as public concern about domestic Bolshevism increased, the U.S. Communist Party and the Communist Labor Party were rapidly losing members and political power.

11. Tensions mounted with a series of bombings in the early spring of 1919; in November, Attorney General A. Mitchell Palmer staged the first of what were known as "Palmer raids."

12. Lacking the protection of U.S. citizenship, thousands of aliens faced deportation without formal trial or indictment.

13. Palmer predicted that a conspiracy attempt to overthrow the government would occur in May 1920; when the incident never occurred, the hysteria of the Red Scare began to abate.

14. At the height of the Red Scare, Nicola Sacco and Bartolomeo Vanzetti — alien draft evaders — were arrested for robbery and murder, were denied a new trial even though evidence surfaced that suggested their innocence, and were executed in 1927.

15. With few casualties and no physical destruction at home, America emerged from the war

stronger than ever — a major international power with exceptional industrial productivity.

Lecture Strategies

1. The American decision to go to war is a natural lecture topic. Several points can be developed, including the Eurocentric nature of the United States; the cultural influence of Great Britain and, to a lesser degree, France; the negative image of Imperial Germany; the impact of Allied propaganda in this country; the economic relationship of the United States with the Allies; American conceptions of international law and neutrality rights; and the impact of President Wilson's vision of a cooperative postwar world.

2. The American military's role in World War I may interest students. American unpreparedness — owing to tradition, Mexican border problems, and the assumption that troops would not have to be sent abroad — could be part of the lecture. A second part could examine the buildup of the army through conscription, the screening of recruits, segregation, and training. The third part of the lecture could focus on the American Expeditionary Force in action and could include a time frame, numbers, battles, casualties, and the role American forces played in securing the victory.

3. Another lecture subject is the war's impact on U.S. industry: a quarter of the gross national product went for war production. With an eye toward the 1920s, the government's cozy relationship with business through takeovers and regulation should be explored. Similarly, the government's brief honeymoon with labor should be described.

4. Focusing on civil liberties during and after the war is useful. Topics to explore include the pressure used to generate support for the war and the treatment of "slackers," government as an engine of oppression through the Committee on Public Information and the Sedition Act, and the activities of the Wilson administration during the Red Scare. The Sacco-Vanzetti case can be used to finish the lecture.

5. The defeat of the Treaty of Versailles constitutes an important subject. Although it is tempting to dwell on the adversarial relationship between President Wilson and Senator Henry Cabot Lodge, it would be better to articulate other reasons for the Senate's refusal to approve the League of Nations. A major stumbling block was fear that an international organization would limit American sovereignty. Many people believed that the war had been won and that America's job had been completed. Wilson's haughtiness and arrogance toward the Senate also hurt his chances of securing approval of membership in the league. The treatment of Germany at the peace conference also stirred Senate opposition to the league.

6. The war's consequences for the nation should be examined. The United States became a creditor nation and replaced Great Britain as the leader in global finance. The negative impact of the war — the Allies squabbling among themselves and perpetuating power politics — should be probed. The yearning for "normalcy" that followed eight years of progressivism and war must be explained. The war's costs in money and lives should be emphasized.

7. Lecture on racial unrest on the home front. Topics to touch on include the effect of black migration to the North, prevailing racism, the black experience in the armed forces, the black experience in the military abroad, and the race riots of 1919. Expanded subjects could address the movement of Mexican Americans into industrial jobs and the creation of segregated neighborhoods in urban areas. Ask students to question the origins and resilience of racial stereotypes.

8. The progress of women, who also sought to take advantage of wartime opportunities, might interest students. Many women joined the labor force in large numbers for the first time, and others switched to higher-paying work in the industrial sector, although men and women often viewed this transformation as only a temporary, wartime measure. Ask students to question the origins and resilience of gender stereotypes.

Class Discussion Starters

1. **Why did the United States enter World War I?**

    Possible answers:
    a. Germany's unrestricted submarine warfare and the threat it posed to neutrality rights.
    b. American economic interests.
    c. Cultural ties with Great Britain and France.
    d. The Zimmermann telegram.
    e. The sinking of the *Lusitania*.

2. **How did the United States help the Allies win World War I?**

    Possible answers:
    a. American entry into the war gave the Allies an enormous psychological boost.
    b. The U.S. Navy helped to suppress the U-boat menace in the North Atlantic so that an expeditionary force could be dispatched safely to Europe.
    c. The rapid buildup of American troop strength in the summer of 1918 helped to halt the final Ger-

man offensive and then permitted the Allies to begin a ground offensive that brought the war to an end.

3. What was the economic legacy of World War I?

Possible answers:
a. Internationally, the United States became a creditor nation.
b. Reduced international trade led to the War Revenue Bills of 1916 and 1917, which established the first income taxes in American history.
c. With the war's cost at $33 billion, the national debt increased to previously unseen heights.

4. How did the federal government's powers expand during World War I?

Possible answers:
a. The government exercised control over the citizenry through the draft.
b. The government intervened in the economy on a massive scale through agencies such as the War Industries Board and the National War Labor Board.
c. The government curbed civil liberties.

5. What were some of the social effects of the war?

Possible answers:
a. Over 400,000 southern blacks moved to northern cities to fill the increasing demand for labor.
b. There were more job opportunities for Mexican Americans in industry.
c. The war helped the suffrage movement because women made significant contributions to the victory.
d. The war helped to speed the passage of Prohibition as supporters pointed to the benefits of a sober labor force.

6. Why were there large-scale violations of civil liberties during World War I?

Possible answers:
a. The government's attempt to promote a "national ideology" fanned public fears through the activities of the Committee on Public Information.
b. The wartime atmosphere contributed to the organization of quasi-vigilante groups such as the American Protective League, which enforced support for the war.
c. Measures such as the Espionage Act of 1917 and the Sedition Act of 1918 were passed.
d. An ocean away from the real fighting, civilians directed their aggression at targets that they could see: local dissenters.

7. What were some of the changes in Europe after World War I?

Possible answers:
a. The breakup of the Austro-Hungarian, German, Ottoman, and Russian empires and the appearance of new independent states.
b. The isolation of the Soviet Union due to its Communist revolution.
c. The absorption of German colonies by Britain and France under the protectorate rubric.

8. What caused racial clashes in the United States from 1917 to 1919?

Possible answers:
a. The migration northward of thousands of blacks to previously white areas.
b. Competition for jobs and housing.
c. The black military experience, including fighting for the nation and being treated more equally abroad.

9. What were the origins of the Red Scare?

Possible answers:
a. The Bolshevik Revolution in Russia had brought to power a regime that called for worldwide revolution.
b. The racial and labor strife associated with the war and suspicions that "Reds" were behind those occurrences.
c. A series of mail bombings and attempted bombings in 1919.
d. Overzealousness on the part of officials, as exemplified by the "Palmer raids" of Wilson's attorney general.

10. Why was the Eighteenth Amendment adopted?

Possible answers:
a. Prohibition had historical roots; many states were already enforcing it.
b. There was strong support for the measure in rural areas and in certain Protestant churches.
c. Prohibition was regarded as a progressive measure: for example, it would aid the fight against urban poverty.
d. There was an anti-German tone to the drive, as several major brewers had German names.
e. Prohibition would help to conserve food such as wheat and barley to feed Europe's population and win the war.

Chapter Writing Assignments

1. Some historians believe that Woodrow Wilson did a remarkable job keeping the United States neutral for almost three years. Others contend that America's intervention was necessary but tardy under Wilson. After examining the difficulties faced by the presi-

dent between 1914 and 1917, explain why you agree or disagree with this view of Wilson's leadership.

2. What were the causes of American intervention in World War I? Was any factor of primary importance in explaining why the United States went to war in April 1917?

3. If the positive side of American entry into World War I was the military defeat of the Axis powers, discuss and analyze the negative consequences of America going to war. Include a consideration of international political and economic conditions before and after the war.

4. Examine how effectively the nation mobilized its industrial base and manpower to fight World War I. Contrast the effort after 1914 with the federal government's deployment of forces for the Spanish-American War. Why was there such a difference?

5. Discuss the war's impact on American women and the suffrage movement. Why did the suffrage movement win a Constitutional amendment?

6. Discuss the erosion of civil liberties during World War I. Explain the paradox of the United States fighting to make the world safe for democracy while it infringed on individual rights at home.

7. Discuss the Senate's rejection of the Treaty of Versailles. Ultimately, where did responsibility lie — with Wilson or the Senate or the Europeans — for the rebuff of the treaty and American participation in the League of Nations?

8. What were the sources of the civil strife that erupted in postwar America? How were those troubles resolved?

Document Exercises

AMERICAN VOICES

Harry Curtin: Trench Warfare (p. 641)

Document Discussion

1. **What does Curtin's story suggest about daily life in the trenches?**
(Curtin's description reveals that inside the trenches soldiers encountered a world in many ways divorced from the normalcy of civil life. Combat, violence, and death could occur at any moment. Soldiers had to endure extreme physical hardships. They were exposed to the elements and could never escape the mud, vermin, and filth that living underground entailed.)

2. **How did men like Curtin cope with the harsh conditions they faced daily?**

(When soldiers initially enlisted for World War I, they did so with a great deal of enthusiasm. Even though Americans had three years to observe the carnage being wrought on European battlefields, most American recruits were eager to demonstrate the strength of their idealism. However, fighting for principles soon became secondary once a soldier entered the brutal world of the trenches. There, soldiers like Curtin drew on their training, hard-won experience, and their commitment to their unit to survive. They overlooked the present to focus on the future. Troops took enormous pride in their performance of duty and dedicated themselves to returning home.)

Writing Assignments

1. Why did the armies of World War I find themselves fighting trench warfare in 1918? What had military leaders expected when the war began in 1914?

2. What were the effects, both psychological and physical, on soldiers who were subjected to the trench warfare of World War I?

VOICES FROM ABROAD

A German Propaganda Appeal to Black Soldiers (p. 648)

Document Discussion

1. **What arguments did the Germans use to convince black American soldiers to defect?**
(The Germans reminded black soldiers of the racial discrimination they faced in the United States and then urged them to reject such treatment by fleeing to the German lines, where they would be given increased opportunities. The Germans emphasized the contradiction between the stated American goals of democracy and the reality of discrimination. They also told the soldiers that if their leaders would betray them at home, then the lies being told about the state of affairs in Germany could not be believed either.)

2. **Why didn't the black soldiers defect?**
(Despite the German appeal, the message that life would be better for minorities in Germany failed to convince the soldiers for several reasons. First, the soldiers tended to feel a strong bond of responsibility toward one another that, the larger issues of war aside, was difficult to break. They understood that defection as a very personal sort of betrayal. Second, these soldiers, despite their poor treatment by many whites, no doubt considered themselves to be Americans and felt that the American ideals of democracy, although not yet fully implemented, were worth their continued perseverance.)

Writing Assignments

1. How might the Germans have changed their propaganda so that American soldiers would have found it more convincing?

2. What kind of message would you craft to send to the German lines in an effort to inspire German soldiers to defect to the Allied side?

AMERICAN VOICES

Southern Migrants (p. 652)

Document Discussion

1. **The female author seems quite satisfied with her new circumstances. Why?**
(Beyond her new job and living arrangements, this author emphasizes a positive communal climate. She is living with her brother and his wife and appears pleased that her daughter is working for the same company as she. Furthermore, despite the long hours, the author takes comfort in finding what she believes to be God's path for her. Matters of religion seem important: a revival is mentioned, and the author mentions God several times. She also seems interested in what has happened in her hometown and sends greetings to family and friends from whom she is separated.)

2. **What kinds of information seem to be important to the male writer?**
(Matters of employment figure prominently in this letter. The author mentions his occupation and how much he earns. He seems pleased that he does not have to bow down to whites and that he is treated more equally at his place of employment.)

Writing Assignments

1. How important to migrants was correspondence? Why did migrants maintain networks of communication with others in similar situations?

2. To what degree did letters like this one inspire other migrants to move to northern cities? What kinds of expectations did informal correspondence like this establish?

AMERICAN LIVES

George Creel: Holding Fast the Inner Lines (p. 656)

Document Discussion

1. **Why did Creel agree to work for the Wilson administration?**

(Although Creel had been impressed with Wilson's idealism a full decade before the outbreak of World War I, and had backed Wilson's candidacy in 1912 and reelection in 1916, Creel did not want a position in Washington. Only when America was on the verge of entering the war did he agree to oversee the Committee on Public Information (CPI). Creel's motivation for doing so was to promote the American cause in the war. Creel had been actively working on behalf of progressive issues since he was a young man. He was eager to shape public opinion and zealously undertook numerous muckracking activities. Wilson's professed optimism impressed Creel.)

2. **Under Creel's leadership, what did the CPI achieve?**
(The success of the CPI during the war stimulated the advertising and film industries, each of which became major contributors to the growth of an American consumer society during the 1920s. The printed publicity orchestrated by Creel played a crucial role in reaching and binding together a diverse nation. Overseas, the foreign section of the CPI exported positive ideas about American life to neutral nations, American allies, and civilian populations of the Central Powers.)

Writing Assignments

1. George Creel seemed to reflect contradictory impulses. He was a muckraking, progressive journalist who earned his professional reputation uncovering the ills of American society. Yet he went on to serve the Wilson administration by promoting America to both domestic and foreign media outlets. How do you account for Creel's behavior?

2. Examine the relationship between journalists and the government, particularly in a time of war. What were the responsibilities and objectives of each?

Skill-Building Map Exercises

Map 22.2: U.S. Participation on the Western Front, 1918 (p. 644)

1. **Was war waged on German territory?**
(Only in far southwestern Germany, in the disputed region called Alsace. Southern Belgium and northern France were the main scenes of the fighting.)

2. **What does this map reveal about the nature of combat during World War I?**
(Note that the front lines of 1918 were in most places only about fifty to seventy miles from the trench lines of 1915, which were established during the opening campaigns of the war. For over three years the oppos-

ing armies had fought from the squalor of their trenches with few territorial gains to show for the tremendous loss of life.)

Map 22.4: Prohibition on the Eve of the Eighteenth Amendment, 1919 (p. 654)

1. **Do you think there was a link between the choice for local option and the religion and population makeup of the local-option states?**
    (Local-option states were in the Northeast, the Middle Atlantic, and the Great Lakes region. These were areas with major industries manned by Catholic and immigrant labor.)

2. **What caused most of the states to choose Prohibition in 1916 and 1917?**
    (The war was on, and Progressive Era America viewed Prohibition as a patriotic, moral, and worthwhile measure.)

Topic for Research

Free Speech in Wartime

How far does the First Amendment go in protecting the right of free speech? Does the state have a legitimate interest in imposing stringent regulation on public expression during wartime? Carefully analyze the reasoning of the Supreme Court in the 1919 cases of *Schenck v. United States* (249 U.S. 47) and *Abrams v. United States* (250 U.S. 616). What are the facts in each case? How is the doctrine of "clear and present danger" presented? Why did Justices Oliver Wendell Holmes and Louis Brandeis vote with the unanimous majority in *Schenck* but dissent in the *Abrams* case? Is there an absolute right to free speech? If not, then what are acceptable limits in a democratic society?

For background, Zechariah Chaffee Jr.'s classic *Free Speech in the United States* (1941) can be supplemented by Richard Polenberg, *Fighting Faiths: The Abrams Case, the Supreme Court, and Free Speech* (1987). For further historical context, consult Harold C. Peterson and Gilbert Fite, *Opponents of War, 1917–1918* (1968); Donald Johnson, *The Challenge to American Freedoms: World War I and the Rise of the American Civil Liberties Union* (1963); William Preston Jr., *Aliens and Dissenters: Federal Suppression of Radicals, 1903–1933* (1963); and Harry Schreiber, *The Wilson Administration and Civil Liberties, 1917–1921* (1960).

Suggested Themes

1. What misdeeds had the defendants Schenck, Debs, and Abrams committed? From today's perspective, were their actions heinous?

2. "The most stringent protection of free speech should not protect a man in falsely shouting fire in a theatre and causing a panic," Oliver Wendell Holmes wrote in the case *Schenck v. United States*. How relevant is Holmes's analogy? Was Schenck's "crime" comparable to panicking a theater audience?

3. What are the limits of free speech in wartime? Has the question been settled yet?

How to Use the Ancillaries Available with *America's History*

Refer to the Preface to *America's History* at the front of the book for descriptions of instructor resources, including the Instructor's Resource CD-ROM, Computerized Test Bank, transparencies, and *Using the Bedford Series in History and Culture in the U.S. History Survey*. Student resources, also described in the Preface, include the Online Study Guide and *Documents to Accompany* America's History, a primary-source reader.

For Instructors

Using the Bedford Series in History and Culture in the U.S. History Survey
This brief online guide by Scott Hovey provides practical suggestions for incorporating volumes from the highly regarded Bedford Series in History and Culture into your survey course. Titles that complement the material covered in Chapter 23 include *Black Protest and the Great Migration: A Brief History with Documents*, edited with an introduction Eric Arnesen. For a description of this title and how you might use it in your course, visit **bedfordstmartins.com/usingseries**.

For Students

Online Study Guide at bedfordstmartins.com/henretta
Each of the activities listed below includes short-answer questions. After submitting their answers, students can compare them to the model answers provided.

Map Activity
The map activity presents Map 22.3: The Great Migration and Beyond (p. 650) and asks students to analyze the movement of blacks to northern cities during World War I.

Visual Activity
The visual activity presents a war poster for Liberty bonds (p. 649) and asks students to analyze how it specifically encourages immigrants to support the war effort

Reading Historical Documents
The document activity provides a brief introduction to the documents Harry Curtin: Trench Warfare (p. 641)

and Southern Migrants (p. 652) and asks students to analyze their content, thinking critically about the sources.

Documents to Accompany *America's History*
Each of the documents listed is introduced by a headnote, which places the document in context, and is followed by questions, which help students to analyze the piece.

Sources for Chapter 22 are
The Zimmermann Telegram (1917)
Woodrow Wilson, *War Message* (1917)
Robert M. LaFollette, *Antiwar Speech* (1917)
Hervey Allen, *German Dugouts* (1918)
Bernard M. Baruch, *The War Industries Board* (1917–1918)

Visual Document: *Posters from the Anti-Venereal Disease Campaign* (1917–1918)
Marcus L. Hansen, *The Home Front: The Young Women's Christian Association* (1920)
Visual Document: Wartime Propaganda Poster
George Creel, *The Home Front: The Four Minute Men* (1920)
Help Us to Help, from The Crisis (1917)
Woodrow Wilson, *Fourteen Points* (1918)
Treaty of Versailles, *Select Articles* (1919)
Henry Cabot Lodge, *Speech before the Senate* (1919)
Woodrow Wilson, *Speech in Indianapolis, Indiana* (1919)
Report on the Chicago Race Riot (1919)
W. E. B. DuBois, *Returning Soldiers* (1919)

CHAPTER 23

Modern Times

The 1920s

Chapter Instructional Objectives

After you have taught this chapter, your students should be able to answer the following questions:

1. How and why did business and government become allies in the 1920s? How did this partnership affect the American economy?

2. Evaluate and discuss American foreign policy in the 1920s.

3. Discuss the emergence of a mass national culture after World War I.

4. How and why did cultural conflict break out in response to the new secular values of the decade?

5. How and why did intellectuals, writers, and artists react to the postwar era?

Chapter Summary

The American economy generally flourished in the 1920s, driven by innovations in mass production and mass consumption. However, agriculture and several "sick industries" did not share in the general prosperity, and the problems in those sectors foreshadowed the difficulties facing the whole economy in the 1930s.

The Republican Party dominated national politics in the 1920s. Most Americans were comfortable with the Republicans' promotion of business interests and advocacy of limited government. A series of scandals in the mid-1920s was not enough to drive the Republicans from power. The Democrats, as was often the case in the twentieth century, were divided between northern, urban, liberal interests and a southern, rural-conservative wing. The Progressive Party made an attempt to capture the

White House in 1924 but was soundly defeated. Women were active in 1920s politics but were unable to achieve any long-term reforms. The problems of minority groups were largely ignored.

The modern corporation was a prominent feature of American life in the 1920s. Most industries were dominated by a few large producers. Business leaders enjoyed enormous popularity and respect compared with most of the politicians of the period. Corporations improved their images in the minds of the public by developing "welfare capitalism."

The United States was not completely isolationist in the 1920s. It had emerged from World War I as a powerful modern state and could not withdraw from international involvement. Instead, the nation became selectively involved in foreign affairs, usually choosing to do so when American economic interests were at stake.

A new emphasis on leisure, along with innovations in mass communication, gave rise to a mass culture in America. Magazine and radio advertising, automobiles, chain stores, motion pictures, and spectator sports helped to transform American values and consumption patterns. However, not all segments of the population participated in this mass culture.

Not all Americans accepted the secular values that characterized the mass-consumption society of the 1920s. One response to the rapid change in values was nativism. Congress passed strict new immigration-restriction quotas that favored northern and Western Europeans and discriminated against Asians and southern and Eastern Europeans. The Ku Klux Klan became popular not just in the South but also in the Midwest and other sections of the country. Protestant fundamentalists gained a large following by challenging scientific thought and modern notions of morality.

Literature and the arts reflected the disillusionment felt by many intellectuals about the direction in which American life and institutions were moving in the 1920s. Many American writers criticized the futility and waste of World War I, whereas others attacked the blandness of middle-class American life. A short-lived but dramatic flowering of black artistic talent occurred in Harlem in the 1920s.

Prohibition was the law of the land in the 1920s, but it was not always enforced. Americans reduced their total consumption of alcohol, but thousands of ordinary citizens became lawbreakers when they drank or served liquor. By the end of the decade, even Prohibition's most ardent defenders conceded that the law was not working and was encouraging the rise of organized crime.

The 1928 presidential election demonstrated that many Americans were not ready to support a Catholic for the presidency. The Republicans won easily, but the election also demonstrated the Democratic Party's growing strength among urban voters.

Chapter Annotated Outline

I. Business-Government Partnership of the 1920s
    A. Politics in the Republican "New Era"
       1. In the 1920 election, Republicans Warren G. Harding and Calvin Coolidge promised a return to "normalcy," which meant a strong probusiness stance and conservative cultural values.
       2. Central to what Republicans termed the "New Era" was business-government cooperation.
       3. A new tax cut benefited wealthy individuals and corporations, and for the most part, the Federal Trade Commission ignored the antitrust laws.
       4. The Department of Commerce, headed by Herbert Hoover, assisted private trade associations by cooperating in such areas as product standardization and wage and price controls.
       5. When President Harding died of a heart attack in August 1923, evidence of widespread fraud and corruption in his administration had just come to light.
       6. Secretary of the Interior Albert Fall became the first cabinet officer in American history to serve a prison sentence; he took bribes in connection with oil reserves in Wyoming and California.
       7. Vice President Calvin Coolidge took Harding's place as president and soon announced his candidacy for the presidency in 1924.
       8. Democrats disagreed over Prohibition, immigration restriction, and the mounting power of the racist and anti-immigrant Ku Klux Klan.
       9. Democrats nominated John W. Davis for president and Charles W. Bryan for vice president, and in a third-party challenge, Senator Robert M. La Follette ran on the Progressive ticket.
       10. Although there was a decline in voter turnout — due to a long-term drop in voting by men and not to the absence of votes by newly enfranchised women — Coolidge won decisively.
       11. Many women tried to break into party politics, but Democrats and Republicans granted them only token positions on party committees; women were more influential as lobbyists.
       12. The Women's Joint Congressional Committee lobbied actively for reform legislation, and its major accomplishment was the short-lived Sheppard-Towner Federal Maternity and Infancy Act. Congress cut the act's funding when politicians realized that women did not vote in a bloc.
       13. Americans were unenthusiastic about increased taxation and more governmental bureaucracy after enduring years of progressive reforms and an expanded federal presence in World War I.
    B. The Economy
       1. In the immediate postwar years, the nation suffered rampant inflation accompanied by intense business activity; federal efforts to halt inflation produced the recession of 1920 to 1921.
       2. In 1922, stimulated by an abundance of consumer products, the economy began a recovery that continued through 1929.
       3. The federal government was soon recording a budget surplus, and this economic expansion provided the backdrop for the partnership between business and government.
       4. New techniques of management and mass production led to growth in manufacturing output; demand for goods and services kept unemployment low.
       5. The spending power of many Americans increased, yet income distribution reflected significant disparity: 5 percent of American families received one-third of all income.
       6. Agriculture and the coal and textiles industries expanded in response to wartime demand, which dropped sharply at war's end; their troubles foreshadowed the Great Depression.
    C. The Heyday of Big Business
       1. Throughout the 1920s, business leaders enjoyed enormous popularity and respect; the most revered businessman of the decade was Henry Ford.

2. Oligopolies became the norm in manufacturing, and financial institutions also expanded and consolidated.

3. The 1920s saw large-scale corporate organizations with bureaucratic structures of authority replace family-run enterprises.

4. Members of the working class enjoyed higher wages and a better standard of living, but scientific management techniques reduced workers' control over their labor.

5. "Welfare capitalism," the American Plan (or nonunion shop), and Supreme Court decisions that limited workers' ability to strike all helped to erode the strength of unions.

D. Economic Expansion Abroad

1. During the 1920s the United States was the most productive country in the world and competed in foreign markets that eagerly desired American consumer products.

2. American companies, such as General Electric, Ford, and Standard Oil, aggressively sought investment opportunities abroad.

3. Other American companies invested internationally during the 1920s to take advantage of lower production costs or to produce raw materials and supplies, concentrating mainly on Latin America.

4. The United States became the world's largest creditor nation, causing a dramatic shift of power in the world's capital markets.

5. European countries had difficulty repaying their war debts to the United States due to tariffs such as the Fordney-McCumber Tariff of 1922 and the Hawley-Smoot Tariff of 1930.

6. The Dawes Plan of 1924 offered Germany substantial loans from American banks and a reduction in the amount of reparations owed to the Allies.

E. Foreign Policy in the 1920s

1. U.S. officials continued the quest for peaceful ways to dominate the Western Hemisphere but retreated slightly from military intervention in Latin America.

2. International cooperation on the American side came through forums such as the 1921 Washington Naval Arms Conference.

3. By placing limits on naval expansion, policymakers hoped to encourage stability in areas such as the Far East and to protect the fragile postwar economy from an expensive arms race.

4. Through the Kellogg-Briand Peace Act, the United States joined other nations in condemning militarism; critics complained that the act lacked mechanisms for enforcement.

5. U.S. policymakers vacillated between wanting to play a larger role in world events and fearing that treaties and responsibilities would limit their ability to act unilaterally.

II. A New National Culture

A. A Consumer Culture

1. Although millions of Americans shared similar daily experiences, participation in commercial mass culture was not universal, nor did it mean mainstream conversion to materialistic values.

2. Many Americans stretched their incomes by buying consumer goods on the newly devised installment plan.

3. Electric appliances made housewives' chores easier, yet their leisure time did not dramatically increase, since more middle-class housewives did their own housework and laundry.

4. The advertising industry spent billions of dollars annually to entice consumers into buying their goods; advertisers made consumption a socially acceptable ideal for most of the middle class.

B. The Automobile Culture

1. Mass production of automobiles stimulated the prosperity of the 1920s, and by the end of the decade, Americans owned about 80 percent of the world's automobiles.

2. Auto production stimulated the steel, petroleum, chemical, rubber, and glass industries and caused an increase in highway construction.

3. Car ownership spurred the growth of suburbs, contributed to real estate speculation, and led to the building of the first shopping center.

4. The American Automobile Association, founded in 1902, reported in 1929 that almost a third of the population took vacations by automobile.

C. Mass Media and New Patterns of Leisure

1. Silent movies such as *The Great Train Robbery* began to run in nickelodeons around the turn of the century; mostly working-class Americans attended the shows.

2. By the end of World War I, the United States was producing 90 percent of the world's movies; when studios began making feature films and showing them in large ornate theaters, middle-class Americans began to attend.

3. Clara Bow, the "It Girl," and other "flappers" burst onto the American scene as Hollywood's symbol of emancipated womanhood, although in actuality they reflected only a tiny minority of women.

4. The advent of "talkies" made movies even more powerful influences; *The Jazz Singer*

(1927) was the first feature-length film to offer sound.

5. Jazz often expressed black dissent in the face of mainstream white values, yet it was such a popular part of the new mass culture that the 1920s are often referred to as the "Jazz Age."

6. Jazz music had its roots in African American music forms, such as ragtime and blues, and most of the early jazz musicians were African Americans who brought southern music to northern cities. Some of the best-known black jazz performers were "Jelly Roll" Morton, Louis Armstrong, Bessie Smith, and Duke Ellington.

7. In the 1920s tabloid newspapers and magazines like *The Saturday Evening Post*, *Reader's Digest*, and *Good Housekeeping* helped to establish national standards of taste and behavior.

8. Professional radio broadcasting began in 1920, and by 1929, about 40 percent of households owned a radio and tuned in to sports events and radio shows such as *Amos 'n' Andy*.

9. Leisure became increasingly tied to consumption and mass media, as Americans had more time and energy to spend on recreation.

10. Baseball continued to be a national pastime with the rise of stars such as Babe Ruth; black athletes such as Satchel Paige played in Negro leagues.

11. Charles Lindbergh captivated the nation when he flew *The Spirit of St. Louis* on the first successful nonstop flight between New York and Paris in 1927.

12. *Time*'s first "Man of the Year," Lindbergh combined his mastery of new technology with the pioneer virtues of individualism, self-reliance, and hard work.

III. Dissenting Values and Cultural Conflict
A. The Rise of Nativism
1. Some of the innovations of the new era worried more tradition-minded people, and tensions surfaced in conflicts over immigration, religion, Prohibition, and race relations.
2. As farmers struggled with severe economic problems, rural communities lost residents to the cities at an alarming rate.
3. The mass media generally reflected the cosmopolitan values of cities, and many Americans worried that the cities, and the immigrants living there, would soon dominate the nation and its culture.
4. Nativist animosity fueled a new drive against immigration, and in 1921, Congress passed a bill based on a quota system that limited the number of immigrants entering the United States.
5. In 1924 the National Origins Act reduced immigration even further, and after 1927 the law set a cap of 150,000 immigrants per year; Japanese immigrants were excluded entirely.
6. Nativists and organized labor lobbied Congress to close a loophole in the immigration law that allowed Mexican immigrants to enter America.
7. The Ku Klux Klan of the 1920s harassed Catholics and Jews as well as blacks, and this modern Klan appealed to both rural and urban people. After 1925 the Klan declined rapidly.

B. Legislating Values: The *Scopes* Trial and Prohibition
1. "Modernists" reconciled their religious faith with Darwin's theory of evolution, but "fundamentalists" interpreted the Bible literally.
2. Religious controversy entered the political arena when some states enacted legislation to block the teaching of evolution in schools.
3. The *John T. Scopes* trial of 1925 epitomized the clash between the two competing value systems: modernist and fundamentalist.
4. Prohibition summoned the power of the state to enforce social values; drinking declined after passage of the Eighteenth Amendment, but noncompliance was widespread in cities.
5. The "drys" supported the Eighteenth Amendment, but the "wets" argued that Prohibition undermined respect for the law and impinged upon individuals' liberties; the amendment was repealed on December 5, 1933.

C. Intellectual Crosscurrents
1. Some writers and intellectuals of the 1920s were so repelled by what they saw as the complacent, moralistic, and anti-intellectual tone of American life that they settled in Europe.
2. The war inspired John Dos Passos's *The Three Soldiers* and *1919* and Ernest Hemingway's *In Our Time*, *The Sun Also Rises*, and *A Farewell to Arms*. T. S. Eliot's *The Waste Land* summed up a general postwar disillusionment with modern culture as a whole.
3. The modernist movement, which was marked by skepticism and technical experimentation in literature, invigorated American writing abroad and at home.
4. In his *American Mercury*, H. L. Mencken championed writers such as Sherwood Anderson, Sinclair Lewis, and Theodore Dreiser, who satirized the provincialism of American society.

5. In the 1920s, poetry enjoyed a renaissance in the works of Robert Frost, Wallace Stevens, Marianne Moore, and William Carlos Williams.

6. The creative energy of writers such as Edith Wharton, F. Scott Fitzgerald, and William Faulkner led to masterpieces like *The Age of Innocence*, *The Great Gatsby*, and *The Sound and the Fury*, respectively.

7. The influence of Freudian psychology was evident in the experimental plays *The Hairy Ape* and *Desire under the Elms* by Eugene O'Neill.

8. The "Harlem Renaissance" was a movement among young writers and artists who broke with older genteel traditions of black literature in order to reclaim a cultural identity with African roots.

9. Authors such as Claude McKay and Zora Neale Hurston represented the "New Negro" in fiction; Countee Cullen and Langston Hughes turned to poetry and Augusta Savage to sculpture.

10. The Universal Negro Improvement Association was the black working class's first mass movement; under Marcus Garvey it published *Negro World* and supported black enterprise. The movement collapsed when Garvey was deported for fund-raising irregularities involving the Black Star Line company.

D. Cultural Clash in the Election of 1928

1. The 1924 Democratic National Convention revealed an intensely polarized party, split between the urban machines and its rural wing.

2. In 1928 the urban wing nominated Alfred E. Smith; a descendant of Irish immigrants, a product of Tammany Hall, and a Catholic, Smith alienated many Democratic voters — as did his stance on Prohibition.

3. For Smith's supporters, he embodied a new America; to them, his nomination signified that perhaps the country would embrace a more pluralistic conception of American identity.

4. Republican Herbert Hoover embodied the new managerial and technological elite that was restructuring the nation's economic order; he was seen as more progressive than Smith.

5. Although they lost the election, Democratic voter turnout increased substantially in urban areas; the Democrats were on their way to fashioning a new identity as the party of the urban masses.

6. Having claimed credit for the prosperity of the 1920s, Republicans could not escape the blame for the depression; it was twenty-four years before a Republican won the presidency again.

7. Despite cultural conflicts and workplace issues, as Hoover began his presidency in 1929, Americans were generally optimistic and expected prosperity and progress to continue.

Lecture Strategies

1. When many Americans think of the 1920s, they imagine the Jazz Age, flappers, and speakeasies. A lecture on this period could contrast the clichés of the Roaring Twenties with the realities of life for the majority of Americans. Some time should be spent examining some of the unique and fascinating aspects of the 1920s — Prohibition, organized crimes, jazz music, and changing sexual values — but one should also emphasize how "average" Americans lived and how many people, including immigrants, minorities, and rural Americans, faced challenges in the 1920s.

2. The definitions of mass production and mass consumption are important to understanding the economy of the 1920s. The automobile industry, which was so important to the era's prosperity, provides an excellent case study of the various innovations of the period, including the assembly line, research and development, scientific management, mass advertising, and credit purchases.

3. The politics of the 1920s, especially government-business cooperation, lends itself to comparisons with the 1950s. Compare some of the programs and policies of the three decades to see how much they had in common. One could also determine which aspects of the 1920s were unique to the period. Special attention should be given to the political philosophy of Herbert Hoover, who envisioned a new industrial order predicated on expert government commissions and cooperation among trade associations. Hoover dominated government-business relations in the 1920s.

4. Many instructors of American history survey courses find it convenient to treat the foreign policies of the 1920s in the same lecture as the foreign policies of the 1930s and the origins of World War II. Older interpretations of the period emphasized America's reluctance to become involved in world affairs when, in fact, the United States was very active in its efforts to secure profits for American businesses operating overseas. The quest for foreign oil concessions makes a good case study for trends in American foreign relations in the 1920s and anticipates some of the problems of American foreign relations in the second half of the twentieth century.

5. The cultural and intellectual trends of the 1920s lend themselves to fascinating lecture material. After describing some of the themes of the period's famous

novels, such as *The Sun also Rises*, examine the literary achievements and social impact of the Harlem Renaissance, with special attention given to the writings of Claude McKay, Langston Hughes, Zora Neale Hurston, and Jean Toomer. Two sources for additional material on this subject are David Levering Lewis's *When Harlem Was in Vogue* (1979) and Page Smith's *Redeeming the Time* (1987).

6. One of the darker sides of the 1920s was the rise of nativism and the Ku Klux Klan. This issue can be brought into greater focus for students by citing examples of local Klan activity or other kinds of political persecution in the university's community in the 1920s.

7. An approach that may interest students is to point out that some historians see the 1920s as a watershed decade in the creation of "modernity" in America. In the last chapter, students learned that, with the conclusion of World War I and President Wilson's ambition to create a League of Nations, the United States became committed to international involvement and worldwide influence, which it still upholds today. Likewise, American culture changed in ways that continue to shape our lives. Mass marketing and advertising, the extension of private credit, widespread use of mechanized transport, travel, and involvement in the stock market are all examples of these changes. Ask students to define the term *modern*, and examine why the innovations of the 1920s are still with us today.

Class Discussion Starters

1. **Why did the American people embrace the Republicans' "politics of normalcy" in the 1920s?**

Possible answers:
   a. The Democrats were blamed for the strikes, the Red Scare, the racial violence, and the economic disruptions that occurred in the years after World War I.
   b. Harding and Coolidge appeared to be respectable candidates whose promises of limited reforms and a healing of the nation's wounds were safe and reassuring.
   c. American politics seems to follow a cyclical pattern, oscillating between periods of government activism and reform. The pendulum was due to swing in the conservative direction.

2. **How did the automobile epitomize the new values of mass consumption and the changing patterns of leisure in America?**

Possible answers:
   a. The automobile afforded people unprecedented freedom and mobility for shopping, travel, and entertainment.

   b. The automobile became a status symbol. Advertisers convinced Americans that they needed a car.
   c. Americans began to accept credit purchases as part of their normal consumption behavior.
   d. More Americans took extended vacations, and they traveled farther away from home than ever before.
   e. Young people used cars as a way to escape parental supervision. Cars changed dating patterns throughout America.

3. **What examples are given in the textbook to demonstrate that the United States was not truly an isolationist country in the 1920s?**

Possible answers:
   a. The United States continued to dominate the economic affairs of the Western Hemisphere.
   b. The United States sponsored the Washington Naval Arms Conference, which imposed limits on the size of the Great Powers' navies and made arrangements for keeping the peace in East Asia.
   c. The United States sponsored the Kellogg-Briand Pact, which renounced war as an instrument of national policy.
   d. The United States sponsored the Dawes Plan, which assisted German economic recovery and promoted European financial stability.

4. **What explains the rise and fall of the new Ku Klux Klan in the 1920s?**

Possible answers:
   a. Americans who were reacting against the pace of modernization saw in the Klan a means to control the most "objectionable" aspects of social change.
   b. The Klan benefited from the rise of nativism and the desire to promote "100 percent Americanism" that had begun during World War I.
   c. The Klan promoted a sense of community and belonging, which seemed to be eroding in small towns across America.
   d. The Klan declined in power and popularity because of scandals involving its leadership and because immigration restriction eliminated one of its most potent issues.

Chapter Writing Assignments

1. Explain why American businessmen became some of the most respected public figures of the 1920s. Be sure to describe the performance of the economy and the government's policy toward big business. Also, discuss the achievements of public relations and welfare capitalism.

2. Explain why the development of a mass national culture accelerated during the 1920s. Be sure to describe

innovations in advertising and the rise of the consumer society. What was the role of technological advances, especially in transportation, the media, and entertainment?

3. How did individuals and groups who were dissatisfied with aspects of American society express their discontent during the 1920s? What had changed about American culture to allow a variety of dissent to be aired, such as that expressed by nativist activists, the Ku Klux Klan, and religious fundamentalists. Include the very different critiques offered by "lost generation" writers and black intellectuals and activists.

4. Review the reasons for Prohibition, discuss why it failed, and explain what its most important effects were before and after its repeal. Be sure to describe the impact of Prohibition on the social habits of ordinary Americans, the government's attempts to enforce it, and its relationship to the rise of organized crime.

Document Exercises

AMERICAN VOICES

Women Write the Children's Bureau (p. 669)

Document Discussion

1. **What reaction greeted the first letter writer's attempt to provide sex education for her eighteen-year-old stepson?**
(Family members criticized her for doing so. Speaking to children about sex was not socially acceptable in her family or in most families during this period. Adolescent sexual behavior, then as now, raised in many peoples' minds the specter of unwanted pregnancy and social shame. Some thought that discussing the topic equated to condoning sexual conduct.)

2. **What did the second letter writer want from the Children's Bureau, and what does she say about attempts to cap doctor's fees?**
(She hoped to get advice on how to get medical and dental care that she could not afford to pay for. She believes that the state has put limits on the fees but that the doctors charge more than is allowed; she is looking for information on the subject.)

Writing Assignments

1. Does the second letter writer believe she should get medical care even though she cannot pay for it? Why would she feel that she deserves something she can't afford?

2. What kinds of medical services were available to the poor in the 1920s? How do those services compare with what is available today to the same segment of the population?

VOICES FROM ABROAD

The Ford Miracle: "Slaves" to the Assembly Line (p. 671)

Document Discussion

1. **Adams mentions that only ten men out of a hundred require technical skill in the factory. Who are these men? What does he characterize as the future of manufacturing?**
(Adams identifies mechanics and toolmakers, the ones who install and service the machines of the production line, as the only men in the workshop requiring skill. He makes the claim that other industries will follow a similar progression. At the time, mass-production techniques were a novel means of systematizing industrial organization. Other forms of technological skill that have become components of more recent service and "information" economies did not yet exist.)

2. **To what does Adams object about American factory work?**
(Adams criticizes the redundant, simple, unending nature of labor on a mass production line. He bemoans the loss of workers' skills, which are no longer required to function on an assembly line. In effect, Adams sees men acting as machines or at least being slaves to machines as they merely repeat tasks day after day without prospect of relief. Over time, Adams believes this routine will crush individual initiative and identity.)

Writing Assignments

1. Has labor in America become as bland and monotonous as Adams depicted? Why or why not?

2. Adams declares that a fundamental conflict exists between America's ethos of industrial labor and its ideal of individualism. Defend or refute Adams's position.

AMERICAN LIVES

Clara Bow: The "It" Girl (p. 678)

Document Discussion

1. **How did Elinor Glyn define "it," the characteristic that the public identified with Clara Bow in the 1920s?**

(Glyn defined "it" as a "strange magnetism which attracts both sexes," a physical attraction without a trace of conceit or self-consciousness. "It" meant trendy, up-to-date, and cutting edge — characteristics that cultural icons of any era are credited as having.)

2. **How did Hollywood typically portray the flapper in the 1920s?**
(The ideal Hollywood flapper exhibited youth, beauty, sophistication, and a willingness to take chances, especially in her love life. The flapper was a cultural icon because she exhibited each of the ideals of the period in proper proportion.)

Writing Assignments

1. What aspects of Bow's style and personality accounted for her huge success in the 1920s? Why was her career so short lived?

2. The Roaring Twenties has a distinct image in the popular mind even today, eighty years later. What role did movies — those made in the 1920s as well as those made later about the 1920s — play in shaping that image?

NEW TECHNOLOGY

Aviation (p. 682)

Document Discussion

1. **In what ways did aviation affect Americans' lives in the 1920s?**
(Most people felt inspired after witnessing airplane flight for the first time. Aviation held great portent for military use, but after World War I, Americans turned their attention to other pursuits, and the airplane quickly became an icon for freedom, power, and modern progress in American culture. Although it took most of the decade and beyond to make the aviation industry profitable, Americans were captivated by the antics of stunt pilots who performed at air shows and races. Aviation stories were a staple of the print and film industries. It would take until the 1930s before aviation became sufficiently reliable and cost effective to allow passenger travel.)

2. **How did the federal government assist the growth of aviation?**
(An important milestone was the 1925 Contract Mail Act, whereby the federal government awarded contracts for airmail delivery on a competitive basis. These contracts were essential to modern airlines because they offered a guaranteed income during a period when there was neither sufficient technology nor demand for commercial passenger traffic.)

Writing Assignments

1. Explain how and why aviation was able to complete in just over a decade the "cycle of pioneering, merger, regulation, and stabilization," whereas it took railroads nearly a half century to accomplish the same.

2. What role did aviation play in World War I?

AMERICAN VOICES

Kazuo Kawai: A Foreigner in America (p. 686)

Document Discussion

1. **What distressed Kawai when he thought of his trip to Japan?**
(Kawai felt that he was an American. His language, customs, and ideals were American, yet he was not treated like a true American. When he thought of his trip to Japan, he realized that he was not truly Japanese either; he had no country to which he felt he completely belonged.)

2. **Why was there tension between Kawai's aspirations and American society?**
(Kawai was frustrated on two levels. First, many American customs and laws reflected a racial bias. Hence, Kawai could not play tennis where he wanted, nor could he own a house or have his hair cut in any establishment he chose. This angered and perplexed him. Second, Kawai wished for what amounted to full citizenship on the basis of his agreement with American ideals and language.)

Writing Assignments

1. What does Kawai's lament suggest about the relationship between race and national citizenship?

2. Do you see any possible solutions to Kawai's dilemma?

Skill-Building Map Exercises

Map 23.1: The Shift from Rural to Urban Population, 1920–1930 (p. 681)

1. **What regions seemed to gain the most population in the 1920s?**
(The areas of highest population growth were areas that were opening up to new agriculture: southern Florida, southern Texas, the southern Great Plains, the Southwest, and southern California.)

2. What were the chief destinations for migrating southern blacks in the 1920s?

(Blacks went to northern cities to work in industrial jobs previously filled by European immigrants. Washington, D.C., Baltimore, Philadelphia, New York, St. Louis, Chicago, and Detroit were among the most popular destinations.)

Map 23.3: The Election of 1928 (p. 692)

1. What accounted for Hoover's overwhelming victory?

(Most Americans were confident that a Republican in the White House would mean continued prosperity. Hoover had a very positive image as a capable administrator. Also, many Americans were disturbed by Smith's religion and urban values.)

2. Given his Catholic faith and opposition to Prohibition, how do you account for Smith winning six of the states of the Deep South?

(The Deep South was virtually a one-party region in the 1920s. For many people, it was still a crime to vote for the party of Lincoln and Reconstruction.)

Topic for Research

Advertising Modernity

Nothing conveys the tone of modernity in the 1920s better than advertising, but ads (like movies) are not a simple mirror of society. Nonetheless, they are an excellent source for chronicling the emergence of a mass-consumption economy. Pick a specific consumer good such as the automobile, radio, an electrical appliance, cigarettes, or a hygiene product such as deodorant or mouthwash. Look for advertisements from the 1920s in a magazine like *The Saturday Evening Post, Ladies' Home Journal, Literary Digest, Fortune,* or *True Story.* How was the product marketed? Were any unusual stylistic or artistic devices used to sell the product? Who was the ad's audience? How representative of American society were the models or situations shown in the ads? What do the advertisements say about societal attitudes about race, class, and gender?

To place your own observations into a broader context, consult histories of advertising such as Roland Marchand, *Advertising the American Dream: Making Way for Modernity, 1920–1940* (1985); Daniel Pope, *The Making of Modern Advertising* (1983); and T. J. Jackson Lears, "From Salvation to Self-Realization: Advertising and the Therapeutic Roots of the Consumer Culture, 1880–1930" in Richard Wightman Fox and T. J. Jackson Lears, *The*

Culture of Consumption (1983). Trade journals such as *Printers' Ink* and *Advertising Age* supply the industry's perspective.

How to Use the Ancillaries Available with *America's History*

Refer to the Preface to *America's History* at the front of the book for descriptions of instructor resources, including the Instructor's Resource CD-ROM, Computerized Test Bank, transparencies, and *Using the Bedford Series in History and Culture in the U.S. History Survey.* Student resources, also described in the Preface, include the Online Study Guide and *Documents to Accompany America's History,* a primary-source reader.

For Instructors

Using the Bedford Series in History and Culture in the U.S. History Survey

This brief online guide by Scott Hovey provides practical suggestions for incorporating volumes from the highly regarded Bedford Series in History and Culture into your survey course. Titles that complement the material covered in Chapter 23 include *The Scopes Trial: A Brief History with Documents,* by Jeffrey P. Moran. For a description of this title and how you might use it in your course, visit **bedfordstmartins.com/usingseries.**

For Students

Online Study Guide at bedfordstmartins.com/henretta

Each of the activities listed below includes short-answer questions. After submitting their answers, students can compare them to the model answers provided.

Map Activity

The map activity presents Map 23.1: The Shift from Rural to Urban Population, 1920–1930 (p. 681), and asks students to analyze how geographic mobility shaped American society.

Visual Activity

The visual activity presents a photograph of Ku Klux Klan women marching in Washington, D.C. (p. 687), and asks students to analyze the resurgence of the Klan during the 1920s.

Reading Historical Documents

The document activity provides a brief introduction to the documents Women Write the Children's Bureau (p. 669) and Kazuo Kawai: A Foreigner in America (p. 686) and asks students to analyze their content, thinking critically about the sources.

Documents to Accompany *America's History*
Each of the documents listed is introduced by a head-note, which places the document in context, and is followed by questions, which help students to analyze the piece.

Sources for Chapter 23 are
Herbert Hoover, *American Individualism* (1922)
Andrew W. Mellon, *Fundamental Principles of Taxation* (1924)
Bruce Barton, *The Man Nobody Knows* (1925)
Visual Document: *Advertisement for Listerine* (1923)

Visual Document: *Advertisement for the Wanderer* (1926)
Robert S. Lynd and Helen Merrel Lynd, *Middletown* (1929)
Jane Addams, *A Decade of Prohibition* (1930)
Madison Grant, *Nativism in the Twenties* (1930)
Meyer v. Nebraska (1923)
The Ku Klux Klan, *The Good Citizen* (1924)
William Jennings Bryan, *The Scopes Trial* (1925)
Visual Document: *Cabinet Meeting — If Al Were President* (1928)
Marcus Garvey, *Editorial in* Negro World (1924)
Louis D. Rubin, *A Statement of Southern Principles* (1930)

CHAPTER 24

The Great Depression

Chapter Instructional Objectives

After you have taught this chapter, your students should be able to answer the following questions:

1. What were the origins and consequences of the Great Depression?

2. How did American families react to the deprivations of the Great Depression?

3. Describe popular American culture of the early 1930s.

4. Evaluate President Hoover's response to the Great Depression.

5. How and why did the national election of 1932 mark a turning point in American politics?

Chapter Summary

The Great Depression was the worst peacetime disaster in American history and dominated the political, social, and cultural developments of the 1930s. The crash of 1929 destroyed the faith of those who viewed the stock market as the crowning symbol of American prosperity, precipitating a crisis of confidence that prolonged the depression.

Economic historians have not reached a consensus on the causes of the depression. The stock market crash of October 1929 cannot alone account for the length and severity of the slump. Structural weaknesses in the economy, including "sick industries" and a depressed agricultural sector, were major contributors. Also, the increasingly unequal distribution of wealth meant that not enough people could afford to spend the money necessary to revive the economy. Finally, economic national-

ism in the form of the high Hawley-Smoot Tariff of 1930 made a bad situation worse by lowering the level of world trade.

The depression led to hardship for many Americans. Thousands had no jobs; thousands more experienced downward mobility. Commercial banks had invested heavily in stocks and, as banks failed, many middle-class Americans lost their life savings.

The damage to individual lives cannot be measured solely in dollars; the detrimental impact of not being able to provide for one's family was great. After exhausting their savings and credit, many families faced the humiliation of going on relief. Hardships left an "invisible scar," and for the majority of Americans, the crux of the Great Depression was the fear of losing control over their lives.

During the depression, the marriage rate dropped, and the popularity of birth control increased, resulting in a declining birth rate. Women workers did not fare well, but gender divisions of labor insulated some working women from unemployment. White workers pushed minorities out of menial jobs. The depression also had a negative and sometimes permanent impact on the lives of young people, whose career aspirations were often delayed or unfulfilled.

Popular culture played an important role in getting the United States through the trauma of the Great Depression. The mass culture that had taken root during the 1920s, especially the movies and radio, flourished spectacularly in the 1930s. Americans spent their time and money differently during the depression. Things once considered luxuries — cigarettes, movies, and radios — became necessities to help counteract the bleak times.

The depression hit some groups harder than others. Thousands of farmers were forced to flee the Great Plains in the face of the dust bowl and ruinous competition with mechanized agriculture. There was growing black allegiance to the Democratic Party in the 1930s as the New Deal channeled significant amounts of relief money toward blacks outside the South. With fear of competition from foreign workers at a peak, many Mexican Americans left California and returned to Mexico. Others joined labor unions and became more involved in American politics, important steps in the creation of a distinctive Mexican American ethnic identity.

Herbert Hoover had the misfortune of being president in the worst years of the depression. He eventually took a number of aggressive and creative steps to combat the crisis, including deficit spending on public works and government home loans. Ultimately, however, he accepted conventional wisdom and encouraged Congress to pass higher taxes, which made the depression worse. He also refused to consider direct federal relief for the unemployed. As the depression persisted, more and more people blamed Hoover. His reputation as a cold, heartless leader was confirmed for many when he ordered the eviction from Washington of the "Bonus Army," a group of unemployed veterans of World War I lobbying for immediate bonus payments. In 1932, Franklin D. Roosevelt defeated Hoover in a landslide.

Chapter Annotated Outline

I. The Coming of the Great Depression
    A. Causes of the Depression
        1. Since the beginning of the Industrial Revolution, the United States had experienced recessions or panics at least every twenty years, but none as severe as the Great Depression of the 1930s.
        2. After 1927, consumer spending declined, and housing construction slowed. In 1928, manufacturers cut back on production and began to lay off workers.
        3. The stock market had become the symbol of the nation's prosperity, yet only about 10 percent of the nation's households owned stock.
        4. In 1928 and 1929, stock prices rose an average of 40 percent; market activity, such as margin buying, was essentially unregulated.
        5. On "Black Thursday," October 24, and "Black Tuesday," October 29, 1929, overextended investors began to sell their portfolios; waves of panic selling ensued.
        6. Commercial banks and speculators had invested in stocks; the impact of the Great Crash was felt across the nation as banks failed and many middle-class Americans lost their life savings.
        7. The crash destroyed the faith of those who viewed the stock market as the crowning symbol of American prosperity, precipitating a cri-

sis of confidence that prolonged the depression.
        8. Long-standing weaknesses in the economy accounted for the length and severity of the Great Depression; agriculture and certain basic industries had suffered setbacks in the 1920s.
        9. Once the depression began, America's unequal income distribution left the majority of people unable to spend the amount of money needed to revive the economy.
    B. The Deepening Economic Crisis
        1. The more the economy contracted, the more people expected the depression to last; the longer they expected it to last, the more afraid they became to spend or invest their money.
        2. In 1930, many farmers went bankrupt, causing rural banks to fail; the rural banks defaulted on their obligations to urban banks, which also began to collapse.
        3. In 1931, the Federal Reserve System significantly increased the discount rate, squeezing the money supply, forcing prices down, and depriving businesses of funds for investment.
        4. Americans kept their dollars stashed away rather than deposited, further tightening the money supply.
    C. The Worldwide Depression
        1. Domestic factors far outweighed international causes of America's protracted decline, yet the economic problems of the rest of the world affected the United States and vice versa.
        2. By the late 1920s, European economies were staggering under the weight of huge debts and trade imbalances with the United States; by 1931, most European economies had collapsed.
        3. In response to the Hawley-Smoot Tariff of 1930, foreign governments imposed their own trade restrictions, further intensifying the worldwide depression.
        4. From 1929 to 1933, the U.S. gross national product fell by almost half, private investment plummeted 88 percent, and unemployment rose to a staggering 24.9 percent; those who had jobs faced wage cuts or layoffs.
II. Hard Times
    A. The Invisible Scar
        1. Race, ethnicity, age, class, and gender all influenced how Americans experienced the depression.
        2. People who believed the ethic of upward mobility through hard work suddenly found themselves floundering in a society that no longer had a job for them.

3. After exhausting their savings and credit, many families faced the humiliation of going on relief, and, even then, the amount they received was a pittance.

4. Hardships left an "invisible scar," and for the majority of Americans, the fear of losing control over their lives was the crux of the Great Depression.

B. Families Face the Depression

1. On the whole, far more families stayed together during the depression than broke apart.

2. Men considered themselves failures if they were no longer breadwinners, while women's sense of importance increased as they struggled to keep their families afloat.

3. Americans as a whole maintained a fairly high level of consumption during the depression; deflation lowered the cost of living, and buying on credit stretched reduced incomes.

4. Americans spent their money differently during the depression; things once considered luxuries — cigarettes, movies, and radios — became necessities to help counteract the bleak times.

5. One measure of the depression's impact on family life was the change in demographic trends: the marriage rate fell, the divorce rate fell, and the birth rate dropped drastically.

6. In *United States v. One Package of Japanese Pessaries* (1936), a federal court struck down all federal restrictions on the dissemination of contraceptive information.

7. Abortion remained illegal, but the number of women undergoing the procedure increased.

8. Margaret Sanger pioneered the establishment of professionally staffed birth control clinics and in 1937 won the American Medical Association's endorsement of contraception.

9. In the 1930s the total number of married women employed outside the home rose 50 percent; working women faced resentment and discrimination in the workplace.

10. Many fields where women workers already had been concentrated suffered less from economic contraction than did the heavy industries, which employed men almost exclusively.

11. Observers paid little attention to the impact of the depression on the black family, as white men and women willingly sought out jobs usually held by blacks or other minorities.

12. Some of America's young people became so demoralized by the depression that they became hobos or "sisters of the road."

13. College was a privilege for a distinct minority, and many college students became involved in

political movements; the Student Strike against War drew student support across the country.

14. Youths enjoyed more education in the 1930s, yet men who entered their twenties during the depression era had less successful careers than those who came before or after them.

C. Popular Culture Views the Depression

1. Americans turned to popular culture in order to alleviate the trauma of the depression.

2. In response to public outcry against immorality in the movies, the industry established a means of self-censorship — the Production Code Administration.

3. Many movies contained messages that reflected a sense of the social crisis engulfing the nation and reaffirmed traditional values like democracy, individualism, and egalitarianism; others contained criticisms that the system wasn't working.

4. Popular gangster movies suggested that incompetent or corrupt politicians, police, and businessmen were as much to blame for organized crime as the gangsters.

5. Depression-era films by Frank Capra pitted the virtuous small-town hero against corrupt urban shysters whose machinations subverted the nation's ideals.

6. Radio offered more than escape; the business failures of radio characters mirrored the lives of many Americans and reaffirmed the traditional values of diligence, saving, and generosity.

7. In a resurgence of traditionalism, attendance at religious services rose, and the home was once again the center for pleasurable pastimes such as playing Monopoly, reading aloud, and talking.

III. Harder Times

A. African Americans in the Depression

1. African Americans, who had always known discrimination and limited opportunities, viewed the depression differently from most whites.

2. Despite the black migration to the cities of the North, most African Americans still lived in the South and earned less than a quarter of the annual average wages of a factory worker.

3. Throughout the 1920s, southern agriculture suffered from falling prices and overproduction, so the depression made an already desperate situation worse.

4. The Southern Tenant Farmers' Union, which some black farmers joined, could do little to reform an agricultural system based on deep economic and racial inequalities.

5. The hasty trials and the harsh sentences in a 1931 Scottsboro, Alabama, rape case prompted the International Labor Defense to take over the defense of the accused, who were black men.

6. The Communist Party targeted the struggle against racism as a priority in the early 1930s, but it made little headway in recruiting African Americans.

7. The Scottsboro case, along with an increase in lynching in the early 1930s, gave blacks a strong incentive to head for the North and the Midwest.

8. In 1935, Harlem was the setting of the only major race riot of the decade, when anger exploded over the lack of jobs, a slowdown in relief services, and economic exploitation of blacks.

9. There was growing black allegiance to the Democratic Party in the 1930s, which in return offered African Americans some hope for their future.

10. The New Deal channeled significant amounts of relief money toward blacks outside the South, and the NAACP continued to challenge the status quo of race relations.

B. Dust Bowl Migrations

1. The years 1930 to 1941 witnessed the worst drought in America's history, but low rainfall alone did not cause the dust bowl.

2. To maximize profit, farmers stripped the land of its natural vegetation, destroying the ecological balance of the plains; when the rains dried up, there was nothing to hold the soil.

3. John Steinbeck's *Grapes of Wrath* immortalized the Okies, ruined by the ecological disaster and unable to compete with large-scale corporate farms, who headed west in response to promises of good jobs in California.

4. A few Okies were professionals, business proprietors, or white-collar workers, and the drive west was fairly easy along Route 66.

5. California agriculture was large-scale, intensive, and diversified, and its massive irrigation system laid the groundwork for serious future environmental problems.

6. Key California crops had staggered harvest times and required a great deal of transient labor; a steady supply of cheap migrant labor made this type of farming feasible.

7. At first, migrants met hostility from old-time Californians, but they stayed and filled important roles in California's expanding economy.

C. Mexican American Communities

1. With fear of competition from foreign workers at a peak, many Mexican Americans left California and returned to Mexico.

2. Forced "repatriation" slowed after 1932, but deportation of Mexican Americans was still a constant threat and a reminder of their fragile status in the United States.

3. Discrimination and exploitation were omnipresent in the Mexican community; César Chávez, a Mexican American, became one of the twentieth century's most influential labor organizers.

4. Many Mexican Americans worked as miners or held industrial jobs where they established a vibrant tradition of labor activism.

5. Mexican American women played a leading role in the formation of the United Cannery, Agricultural, Packing, and Allied Workers of America union.

6. Joining labor unions and becoming more involved in American politics were important steps in the creation of a distinctive Mexican American ethnic identity.

D. Asian Americans Face the Depression

1. Men and women of Asian descent constituted a minority that concentrated primarily in the western states.

2. Despite being educated, Asians found relatively few professional jobs open to them, as white firms refused to hire them.

3. Asian Americans had carved out a modest success by the time of the depression, but a California law prohibited Japanese immigrants from owning land.

4. Chinese Americans clustered in ethnic enterprises in the city's Chinatown; although Chinatown's businesses suffered during the depression, they bounced back more quickly.

5. In hard times the Chinese turned inward to the community, getting assistance from traditional Chinese social organizations and kin networks.

6. Filipinos were not affected by the ban on Asian immigration passed in 1924 because the Philippines were a U.S. territory.

7. In 1936, Filipinos and Mexican workers came together in a Field Workers Union chartered by the American Federation of Labor.

8. The Tydings-McDuffie Act declared the Philippines an independent nation, classified all Filipinos in the United States as aliens, and restricted immigration; as aliens, Filipinos were not eligible for citizenship or most assistance programs.

IV. Herbert Hoover and the Great Depression

A. Hoover Responds

1. Hoover's response to the depression was slow because he failed to view the situation realistically.

2. Hoping to avoid coercive measures on the part of the federal government, Herbert Hoover asked businesses to maintain wages and production levels voluntarily during the depression.

3. Hoover cut federal taxes, asked governments to increase public construction projects, signed the Agricultural Marketing Act, and declared a moratorium on payment of the Allied debts.

4. A 33-percent tax increase, designed to balance the budget, choked investment and contributed significantly to the continuation of the depression.

5. Hoover pushed Congress to create a system of government home-loan banks and supported the Glass-Steagall Banking Act, which temporarily propped up the ailing banking system.

6. The Reconstruction Finance Corporation (RFC) was the first federal institution created to intervene directly in the economy during peacetime.

7. Although the RFC's trickle-down effect was minimal, it represented a watershed in American political history and the growth of the federal government.

8. Hoover believed that privately organized charities were sufficient to meet the nation's social welfare needs and refused to consider plans for direct federal relief for those out of work.

B. Rising Discontent

1. Many citizens began to harbor hard feelings against Hoover; his willingness to bail out banks and businesses, though not individuals, added to his reputation of cold-heartedness.

2. New terms entered the American vocabulary: "Hoovervilles" were shanty towns; "Hoover flags" were empty pockets turned inside out; and "Hoover blankets" were newspapers.

3. Even as some Americans were going hungry, farmers formed the Farm Holiday Association and destroyed food rather than accepting prices that would not cover their costs.

4. Bitter labor strikes occurred in the depths of the depression, despite the threat that strikers would lose their jobs.

5. In 1931 and 1932, violence broke out in cities as the unemployed battled local authorities over inadequate relief; some of the actions were organized by the Communist Party.

6. Hoover's reputation was further damaged in 1932 as newsreels showed the U.S. Army moving against its own veterans, the "Bonus Army," in Washington.

C. The 1932 Election: A New Order

1. As the 1932 election approached, the nation overall was not in a revolutionary mood;

Americans initially blamed themselves rather than the system for their hardships.

2. The Republicans nominated Hoover once again for president, and the Democrats nominated Governor Franklin Delano Roosevelt of New York.

3. In 1921, Roosevelt had suffered an attack of polio that left both his legs paralyzed, yet he emerged from the illness a stronger, more resilient man.

4. Roosevelt won the election, yet in his campaign, he hinted only vaguely at new approaches to alleviate the depression. People voted as much against Hoover as for Roosevelt.

5. The 1932 election marked the emergence of a Democratic coalition that would help to shape national politics for the next four decades.

6. In the worst winter of the depression, unemployment stood at 20 to 25 percent, and the nation's banking system was close to collapse.

7. The depression had totally overwhelmed public welfare institutions, and private charity and public relief reached only a fraction of the needy; hunger haunted both cities and rural areas.

Lecture Strategies

1. Although the Great Crash of 1929 is often overrated as the chief cause of the Great Depression, it is nevertheless an important and colorful episode that deserves attention. Some time should be spent explaining the nature of stock market speculation in the late 1920s, how it caused the crash, and its effects on investors and ordinary Americans.

2. The various explanations for the length and severity of the Great Depression should be discussed. These include the structural weaknesses in the 1920s economy, including the already depressed farm sector and several "sick industries"; the unequal distribution of wealth, which contributed to underconsumption; international economic problems made worse by a trade war with Europe that the United States helped to start; and federal monetary and fiscal policies during the Hoover administration that reduced consumer purchasing power, which, if increased, could have been the key to restoring prosperity.

3. Explain how the Great Depression affected the American economy, using statistics on unemployment and other economic indexes. Explain the problems of gathering accurate measurements on unemployment, and show why it is believed that conditions were worse than the statistics indicate.

4. Analyze the impact of the Great Depression on ordinary American men and women. Note the special problems of various ethnic groups, the elderly, and the young. You should also discuss the psychological damage the depression caused for millions of Americans. Useful sources for individual accounts of the effects of the depression include Ann Banks's *First-Person America* (1980) and Studs Terkel's *Hard Times* (1970).

5. Describe some of the cultural changes in America during the 1930s. Particular attention should be paid to the movies and radio. You should discuss the social functions of mass entertainment, including diverting people's attention from the burdens of the depression.

6. Our understanding of Herbert Hoover's presidency has undergone more revision than has that of most past presidencies. Hoover is now generally regarded as a transition figure between the passive presidencies of the 1920s and the more dynamic Roosevelt administration. His philosophies and policies should be discussed in detail. Explain Hoover's aversion to direct federal relief, and describe how his position has been criticized.

7. Examine the issues and personalities of the 1932 presidential election. Explain what voters expected from Franklin D. Roosevelt and why they turned against Hoover so overwhelmingly. Note the details of the election results and the creation of the Democratic coalition. Finally, discuss the problems of the period after the election.

Class Discussion Starters

1. What were the causes of the Great Depression?

Possible answers:
a. The Great Crash of October 1929 wiped out the savings of thousands of Americans and destroyed consumers' optimism. Many investors had bought stock on margin while the prices were inflated and lost money when they were forced to sell at prices below what they had paid.
b. Structural weaknesses in the economy, especially in agriculture and "sick industries" such as coal, textiles, shipping, and railroads, made the economy vulnerable to a crisis in the financial markets.
c. The unequal distribution of wealth made it impossible to sustain the expansive economic growth of the late 1920s. In the 1920s the share of national income going to upper- and middle-income families had increased, so that in 1929 the lowest 40 percent of the population received only 12.5 percent of the national income. Once the depression began, not enough people could afford to spend the money necessary in order to revive the economy, a phenomenon known as underconsumption.
d. The reduced flow of American capital to world markets after the Great Crash and the trade war initiated by the Hawley-Smoot Tariff of 1930 led to a decline in world trade that made the depression worse.

2. What was the "invisible scar" of the Great Depression?

Possible answers:
a. Many Americans suffered silently in the 1930s, living on less income and accepting lower-paying, more menial jobs. The loss of identity that resulted from unemployment, moving to poorer neighborhoods, or accepting charity was also psychologically damaging for both breadwinners and their spouses.
b. The depression left a legacy of fear for many Americans that they might someday lose control of their lives again.
c. The depression limited the success of young men who entered their twenties during the depression. Robbed of time and opportunity to build careers, they were described as "runners, delayed at the gun."

3. What functions did movies perform for Americans in the 1930s?

Possible answers:
a. The movies were the most popular form of entertainment in America; more than 60 percent of the population saw at least one movie a week.
b. With their exciting plots, glamorous stars, and exotic locations, they were a means for escaping from daily life in the depression.
c. The movies also reflected and reinforced values and customs.

4. What were the stages of the 1930s dust bowl disaster?

Possible answers:
a. A severe drought on the Great Plains, after years of ill-advised farming techniques, created severe wind erosion and a series of dust storms. In May 1934 the storms reached the Upper Midwest and even the East, where they blackened the skies.
b. The dust bowl was one of the reasons for the great migration of "Okies" from the region. (The other was the eviction of farmworkers from the land due to the growth of large-scale agriculture.)
c. "Okie" descendants came to make up a large proportion of California's population, especially in the San Joaquin Valley.

5. **What were the most dramatic episodes of protest during the Hoover years, and what do they tell us about the depression?**

Possible answers:
   a. A strike of coal miners in Harlan County, Kentucky, featured police violence and resulted in the crushing of the union.
   b. A demonstration at Ford's River Rouge plant in 1932 resulted in three deaths and fifty serious injuries.
   c. In 1932, a group of midwestern farmers formed the Farm Holiday Association and dumped food on the roads rather than to see it reach the market at prices below production costs.
   d. A group of unemployed World War I veterans calling themselves the Bonus Army marched on Washington and remained encamped in the city after Congress failed to pass a relief bill for them. They were violently evicted by federal troops.
   e. Frustration and despair reached many corners of American society during the depression. For the most part the voices of protest were silenced by the authorities.
   f. The Communist Party organized and participated in some of the protests but remained a small organization with only 12,000 members.

6. **How did Herbert Hoover try to combat the depression?**

Possible answers:
   a. Hoover did not embrace a laissez-faire approach; he called on business leaders to hold the line on wages.
   b. He cut taxes and increased public works spending (policies in line with what would later be called Keynesian remedies for a depression).
   c. He imposed a moratorium on foreign-debt payments in order to stimulate world trade.
   d. He later raised taxes to lower interest rates and balance the budget, and that hurt the economy.
   e. He encouraged the creation of the Reconstruction Finance Corporation, which lent money to banks and large companies in the hope that their increased production would "trickle down" to the rest of the economy.
   f. Most significantly, Hoover refused to sanction direct federal relief for the needy, claiming that this would create a permanent class of dependent citizens, something he believed would be worse than the continued deprivations of the depression.

Chapter Writing Assignments

1. Explain why the Great Crash of October 1929 is considered the beginning of the Great Depression. Be sure to describe the reasons for the crash and indicate who was affected. How significant was the Great Crash compared to other domestic and international factors in causing the depression in the United States?

2. Identify and discuss the characteristics of mass culture in the 1930s. What distinguished this decade from previous ones? Why were movies so popular? Was it their themes or the types of film or some other reason?

3. Examine the impact of the Great Depression on one of the groups of Americans discussed in the text — unemployed male breadwinners, housewives and working women, young people, African Americans, dust bowl migrants, or Mexican Americans.

4. During the Great Depression, many men blamed themselves for their economic plight and refused to seek public assistance. Is there a similarity with this notion of individual responsibility and Hoover's response to the opening years of the depression? Was Hoover's response inadequate? Why was he personally vilified for his decisions?

Document Exercises

VOICES FROM ABROAD

Mary Agnes Hamilton: Breadlines and Beggars (p. 700)

Document Discussion

1. **What did Hamilton note in the cities she visited that indicated the depth of the economic depression in the United States?**
   (Hamilton was moved by the long queues of unemployed men that she encountered during her travels. These men dressed shabbily and seemed mostly apathetic about their circumstances. Overall, she painted a scene of abject poverty and grim resignation in America.)

2. **In one respect, Hamilton criticized the unemployed. Why?**
   (Hamilton noted that despite the destitution of the unemployed, cigarettes were still being sold in abundance. Apparently, Hamilton thought that the money spent on such an indulgence could be better used for the purchase of necessities. She thought that Americans were wasteful and, despite the depression, had not rid themselves of that characteristic.)

Writing Assignments

1. Hamilton mentions an "obscure alarm" among the unemployed poor, suggesting that they might take radical

action if their suffering was not alleviated. Yet no violent revolution occurred. What did Hamilton misunderstand about the Great Depression in America?

2. Were Hamilton's assertions regarding the economic suffering of Europe and the United States accurate? Why or why not?

AMERICAN VOICES

Larry Van Dusen: A Working-Class Family Encounters the Great Depression (p. 703)

Document Discussion

1. **What memories about the Great Depression were most vivid for Van Dusen?**
(Van Dusen's account related the emotional and economic consequences of his father's employment. When his father could earn a wage, the family enjoyed a brief interlude of satisfaction and security, but those times when a job could not be found led to despair and bitterness. Adding to the trepidation Van Dusen felt was the fact that his father was often absent from home, searching for work in other cities.)

2. **In this account, Van Dusen did not mention that his mother sought employment. Why?**
(Van Dusen could have failed to mention his mother for any number of personal reasons. But it is likely that his mother did not seek outside employment because none was available. Van Dusen may have assumed that his interviewer understood this. Having children at home would have severely limited his mother's ability to work in any case.)

Writing Assignments

1. What does Van Dusen's account suggest was the most significant challenge facing political leaders of the 1930s?

2. Van Dusen mentions that his father drank, and the family would often wonder if he would make it home with his paycheck. Why would the breadwinner of the household waste money on drinking during such tough economic times?

AMERICAN LIVES

Bert Corona and the Mexican American Generation (p. 712)

Document Discussion

1. **What factors contributed to the development of Corona's labor activism?**

(His father had fought with the revolutionaries in Mexico, Bert had encountered prejudice and discrimination in school, and he had seen the impact of poverty on both Mexican Americans and Anglo-Americans during the depression. He later credited those influences with making him an activist.)

2. **What issues united the "Mexican American Generation"?**
(Its members were political activists of Mexican descent who came of age in the 1930s and 1940s. They were conscious of being both American and Mexican. Many were progressive political activists involved in trying to improve the lives of their fellow Mexican Americans.)

Writing Assignments

1. Investigate the lives of *los repatriados*, Mexicans in the United States who returned to Mexico during the depression of the 1930s.

2. How important was Hispanic participation in labor organizations like the Congress of Industrialized Organizations (CIO)?

AMERICAN VOICES

Public Assistance Fails a Southern Farm Family (p. 716)

Document Discussion

1. **Why is the mother frustrated with the government?**
(Her husband is working, but his wage is too small to provide for the family's needs. Yet she can gain no further relief money because of her husband's employment. With limited skills and education of her own, she can see few options to improve her family's condition. It is likely that her and her husband's ability to provide for themselves and their six children was only marginal under the best of economic conditions. During the 1930s, their situation was extremely bleak.)

2. **Why did relief jobs, such as the one employing the husband, pay so little for a father with six children?**
(A variety of relief programs were operative during the depression, but many did not take into consideration the particular circumstances of a family. Rather, wages were fixed for the type of employment. One of the most intractable problems of the period was a low-wage rate for nearly all types of work in both the public and private sectors.)

Writing Assignments

1. What is the solution to this woman's problem(s)? Who is responsible for her plight? How could it be

avoided? How would President Hoover have responded to her?

2. The woman claims both that she doesn't know anyone who can help her and that there are thousands who could help if they only knew of her plight. Which is the more accurate assessment?

Skill-Building Map Exercises

Map 24.3:
The Dust Bowl, 1930–1941 (p. 710)

1. **Where was the dust bowl?**
   (It was in the southern Great Plains, centered in the Oklahoma Panhandle, and including the surrounding areas of Texas, New Mexico, Colorado, and Kansas. These states contained large areas of farmland that had been overworked by farmers.)

2. **Why is Route 66 included on this map?**
   (This was the route taken to California by many victims of the dust bowl and farm foreclosures. Note that many of the migrants came from eastern Oklahoma, which was not part of the dust bowl.)

Map 24.4: The Election of 1932 (p. 718)

1. **Compare the 1932 election results to those of 1928. What caused the dramatic turnaround in voter allegiance?**
   (Most voters blamed Hoover and the Republicans for the Great Depression and were so eager to embrace another leader that Hoover was able to carry only the most staunchly Republican states, all of which were in the Northeast.)

2. **Was the election of 1932 the biggest landslide in American presidential history?**
   (No. Roosevelt won an even greater victory in 1936, with a margin in the electoral college of 523 to 8. The record for the highest percentage of the popular vote belongs to Lyndon Johnson, who won 61.1 percent in 1964.)

Topic for Research

Remembering the Great Depression

One historian who studied the oral histories collected in the 1930s expressed surprise at how rarely people mentioned the Great Depression by name. "The depression was not the singular event it appears in retrospect," she concluded. "It was one more hardship." On the other hand, the depression loomed larger in oral histories collected well after the event. As the years went by between hard times and the present, people's recollections of the depression's impact grew.

Test that hypothesis by comparing oral histories collected during the 1930s and those done later. Does the Great Depression take on an independent and different meaning as time goes by? How aware were people in the 1930s that they were living through "the Great Depression"? What does this tell us about the role that historical memory plays in shaping our relation to the past? For an excellent introduction to Works Progress Administration (WPA) oral histories collected in the 1930s, see Ann Banks, ed., *First-Person America* (1980). Also of interest are the Federal Writers' Project, *These Are Our Lives* (1939) and Tom Terrill and Jerrold Hirsch, eds., *Such As Us: Southern Voices of the Thirties* (1978). The interviews Studs Terkel collected for *Hard Times: An Oral History of the Great Depression* (1970) provide an interesting counterpoint.

Other works that illuminate various aspects of the depression era include: Paul Conkin, *The New Deal* (1975); Jeane Westin, *Making Do: How Women Survived the '30s* (1976); David Lowenthal, *The Past Is a Foreign Country* (1985); Irving Bernstein, *The Lean Years: A History of the American Worker, 1920–1933* (1988); William E. Leuchtenberg, *Franklin D. Roosevelt and the New Deal, 1932–1940* (1989); Harvard Sitkoff, *A New Deal for Blacks* (1990); Joan Hoff-Wilson, *Herbert Hoover, Forgotten Progressive* (1992); Lizabeth Cohen, *Making a New Deal: Industrial Workers in Chicago, 1919–1939* (1992); and William E. Leuchtenberg and Daniel J. Boorstin, *Perils of Prosperity, 1914–1932* (1993).

How to Use the Ancillaries
Available with *America's History*

Refer to the Preface to *America's History* at the front of the book for descriptions of instructor resources, including the Instructor's Resource CD-ROM, Computerized Test Bank, transparencies, and *Using the Bedford Series in History and Culture in the U.S. History Survey*. Student resources, also described in the Preface, include the Online Study Guide and *Documents to Accompany* America's History, a primary-source reader.

For Instructors

Using the Bedford Series in History and Culture in the U.S. History Survey
This brief online guide by Scott Hovey provides practical suggestions for incorporating volumes from the highly regarded Bedford Series in History and Culture into your survey course. Titles that complement the material cov-

ered in Chapter 24 include *Confronting Southern Poverty in the Great Depression: The Report on Economic Conditions of the South with Related Documents*, edited with an introduction by David L. Carlton and Peter A. Coclanis. For a description of this title and how you might use it in your course, visit **bedfordstmartins.com/usingseries**.

For Students

Online Study Guide at bedfordstmartins.com/henretta
Each of the activities listed below includes short-answer questions. After submitting their answers, students can compare them to the model answers provided.

Map Activity
The map activity presents Map 24.3: The Dust Bowl, 1930–1941 (p. 710), and asks students to analyze this devastating environmental disaster.

Visual Activity
The visual activity presents a photograph of drought refugees (p. 710) and asks students to analyze how they are depicted and how they typify the hardship brought on by the Great Depression.

Reading Historical Documents
The document activity provides a brief introduction to the documents Public Assistance Fails a Southern Farm Family (p. 716) and Larry Van Dusen: A Working-Class Family Encounters the Great Depression (p. 703) and asks students to analyze their content, thinking critically about the sources.

Documents to Accompany *America's History*
Each of the documents listed is introduced by a headnote, which places the document in context, and is followed by questions, which help students to analyze the piece.

Sources for Chapter 24 are
John Dewey, *The House Divided against Itself* (1930)
John J. Raskob, *Everybody Ought to be Rich* (1929)
Stuart Chase, *Balancing the Books* (1929)
B. C. Forbes and Julius Klein, *Proposals for Recovery* (1930–1931)
Visual Document: John T. McCutcheon, *A Wise Economist Asks a Question* (1932)
Mirra Komarovsky, *The Unemployed Man and His Family* (1940)
Meridel Le Sueur, *Women on the Breadlines* (1932)
Hilda Crosby Standish, *Birth Control in Connecticut during the Depression* (1935–1939)
A Report on the Harlem Riot of 1935
Richard Wright, *Communism in the 1930s*
A Letter to Eleanor Roosevelt (1934)
John Steinbeck, *The Grapes of Wrath* (1939)
Herbert Hoover's Plan (1931)
Milo Reno, *Why the Farmers' Holiday?* (1932)

CHAPTER 25

The New Deal
1933–1939

Chapter Instructional Objectives

After you have taught this chapter, your students should be able to answer the following questions:

1. How and why did the federal government influence American economic and political issues during the 1930s?

2. How did President Roosevelt respond to economic depression, and why did he respond in this manner?

3. How did the New Deal affect American society both during the 1930s and thereafter?

Chapter Summary

Roosevelt's New Deal came to stand for a complex set of responses to the nation's economic collapse. The New Deal was meant to relieve suffering yet conserve the nation's political and economic institutions. Through unprecedented intervention by the national government, Roosevelt's programs put people to work, instilling hope and restoring the nation's confidence. Roosevelt made his administration's programs respond to shifting political and economic conditions rather than adhering to a set ideology or plan. He established a close rapport with the American people; his use of radio-broadcasted "fireside chats" fostered a sense of intimacy. Roosevelt's approach expanded the power of the executive branch to initiate policy, thereby helping to create the modern presidency.

Roosevelt's promise to act quickly was embodied in the legislation of the "hundred days." Programs were quickly established to aid agriculture and industry, and direct relief was provided to millions of suffering families. Federal job projects aided millions more. Although those actions did not end the depression, they offered both hope and sustenance to many. Legislation regulating banks and the stock market sought to eliminate some of the financial excesses of the 1920s that had contributed to the depression.

Popular leaders accused the New Deal of moving too slowly in redistributing wealth and caring for the elderly. This pressure from the left caused FDR to inaugurate the "Second New Deal" — a program that offered support for organized labor and Social Security legislation that included unemployment insurance and aid to those who couldn't work. Persistent and pervasive unemployment led to the establishment of the Works Progress Administration (WPA), an agency that would provide millions of federally funded jobs through the remainder of the decade.

The New Deal accelerated the expansion of the federal bureaucracy, and power was increasingly centered in the nation's capital, not in the states. During the 1930s the federal government operated as a broker state, mediating between contending groups seeking power and benefits.

After FDR's reelection in 1936, the New Deal began to falter. An abortive attempt to alter the structure of the Supreme Court undercut FDR's popularity, and his premature reductions in federal spending led to the "Roosevelt recession" of 1937 to 1938. Roosevelt's attempt to "purge" the Democratic Party of some of his most conservative opponents only widened the liberal-conservative rift as the 1938 election approached. Fresh out of ideas and with the nation still in a depression, FDR's basic conservatism became more apparent. Tinkering with the system had not led to economic recovery; something more drastic would be required.

Even though the New Deal did not end the depression, it ushered in an unprecedented expansion of the federal government that redefined its role. By seeking to spread benefits more equitably among neglected portions of the population, the New Deal attracted African Americans, professional women, and organized labor to the Democratic Party. For the first time, organized labor had federal support, and prominent blacks and women were brought into government service. The New Deal laid the foundation for a modified welfare state and created a political coalition that would dominate national politics for most of the next three decades.

The Great Depression saw a flowering of American culture. The WPA employed many writers and artists to produce works that celebrated the lives of ordinary people throughout the nation. A hallmark of the era was the "documentary impulse," a presentation in photography, graphic arts, music, and film of a social reality designed to elicit public empathy.

As Europe moved toward war and Japan expanded its incursions in the Far East, Roosevelt focused less on domestic reform and more on international relations.

Chapter Annotated Outline

I.   The New Deal Takes Over, 1933–1935
    A. The Roosevelt Style of Leadership
        1. Roosevelt's proposed New Deal eventually came to stand for his administration's complex set of responses to the nation's economic collapse.
        2. The New Deal was meant to relieve suffering yet conserve the nation's political and economic institutions through unprecedented activity on the part of the national government.
        3. The Great Depression destroyed Herbert Hoover's reputation and helped to establish Roosevelt's.
        4. Roosevelt's ideology was not vastly different from Hoover's, but he was willing to experiment with new programs to address the current crisis. His programs put people to work and instilled hope in the future.
        5. Roosevelt crafted his administration's programs in response to shifting political and economic conditions rather than according to a set ideology or plan.
        6. Roosevelt established a close rapport with the American people; his use of radio-broadcasted "fireside chats" fostered a sense of intimacy.
        7. Roosevelt's personal charisma allowed him to dramatically expand the role of the executive branch in initiating policy, thereby helping to create the modern presidency.
        8. During the interregnum, Roosevelt relied so heavily on the advice of certain Columbia University professors that the press dubbed them the "Brain Trust."
        9. Roosevelt turned to advisors and administrators scattered throughout the New Deal bureaucracy when searching for fresh new ideas; it was said to have been "a glorious time for obscure people."
    B. The Hundred Days
        1. After the Emergency Banking Act was passed, the president reassured citizens that the banks were safe; when the banks reopened, there were more deposits than withdrawals.
        2. A legislative session, known as the "hundred days," saw fifteen pieces of major legislation enacted and remains one of the most productive legislative sessions ever.
        3. Congress created the Homeowners Loan Corporation to refinance home mortgages and the Glass-Steagall Act to curb speculation and create the Federal Deposit Insurance Corporation.
        4. The Civilian Conservation Corps was created, and the Tennessee Valley Authority (TVA) received approval for its plan of government-sponsored regional development and public energy.
        5. In a move that lifted public spirits, beer was legalized. Full repeal of Prohibition came in December of 1933.
        6. The Agricultural Adjustment Act's benefits were distributed unevenly; it harmed marginal farmers while it consolidated the economic and political clout of larger landholders.
        7. The National Industrial Recovery Act launched the National Recovery Administration (NRA), which established a system of self-government to handle the problems of overproduction, cutthroat competition, and price instability.
        8. The NRA's codes established minimum wages and maximum hours, outlawed child labor, and gave workers union rights.
        9. Trade associations, controlled by large companies, tended to dominate the NRA's code-drafting process, thus solidifying the power of large businesses at the expense of smaller ones.
        10. The Federal Emergency Relief Administration (FERA), set up in May 1933, offered federal money to states for relief programs.
        11. Due to a tentative leader, the effectiveness of the Public Works Administration was limited, but the director of the Civil Works Administration (CWA) put 2.6 million men and women to work within thirty days.
        12. Abandoning the international gold standard allowed the Federal Reserve System to manipulate the value of the dollar in response to fluctuating economic conditions.

13. In 1934 the Securities and Exchange Commission was established in order to regulate the stock market and prevent abuses.

14. The Banking Act of 1935 placed the control of money-market policies at the federal level rather than with regional banks and encouraged centralization of the nation's banking system.

C. The New Deal under Attack

1. Business leaders and conservative Democrats formed the Liberty League in 1934 to lobby against the New Deal and its "reckless spending" and "socialist" reforms.

2. In *Schechter v. United States*, the Supreme Court ruled that the National Industrial Recovery Act represented an unconstitutional delegation of legislative power to the executive branch.

3. Citizens like Francis Townsend thought that the New Deal had not gone far enough; Townsend proposed the Old Age Revolving Pension Plan.

4. In 1935, Father Charles Coughlin organized the National Union for Social Justice to attack the Roosevelt's New Deal and demand a national banking system.

5. Because he was Canadian-born and a priest, Coughlin was not likely to run for president — the most direct threat to Roosevelt came from Senator Huey Long.

6. In 1934, Senator Long broke with the New Deal and established his own national movement, the Share Our Wealth Society.

7. Coughlin and Long offered feeble solutions to the depression and quick-fix plans that addressed only part of problem. Both men showed little respect for the principles of representative government.

II. The Second New Deal, 1935–1938

A. Legislative Accomplishments

1. As the Depression continued and attacks on the New Deal mounted, Roosevelt — with his eye on the 1936 election — began to construct a new coalition and broaden the scope of his response to the depression.

2. The Second New Deal emphasized reform and promoted legislation to increase the role of the federal government in providing for the welfare of citizens.

3. The Wagner Act of 1935 upheld the right of industrial workers to join a union and established the nonpartisan National Labor Relations Board to further protect workers' rights.

4. With the 1935 Social Security Act, the United States joined countries such as Great Britain and Germany in providing old-age pensions and unemployment compensation to citizens.

5. Categorical assistance programs for those who clearly could not support themselves expanded over the years until they became an integral part of the American welfare system.

6. The Works Progress Administration became the main federal relief agency and put relief workers directly onto the federal payroll.

7. The Revenue Act of 1935 increased estate and corporate taxes and instituted higher personal income tax rates in the top brackets.

B. The 1936 Election

1. The broad range of New Deal programs brought new voters into the Democratic coalition as the 1936 election approached.

2. Roosevelt beat out the Republicans' Alfred M. Landon in a landslide; there was no third-party threat since the Union Party garnered less than 2 percent of the votes.

C. Stalemate

1. Because he felt the future of New Deal reforms might be in doubt, Roosevelt asked for fundamental changes in the structure of the Supreme Court only two weeks after his inauguration.

2. Roosevelt proposed the addition of one new justice for each sitting justice over the age of seventy; opponents protested that he was trying to "pack" the Court with justices who favored the New Deal.

3. The issue became a moot point when the Supreme Court upheld several key pieces of New Deal legislation and a series of resignations created vacancies on the Court.

4. Roosevelt managed to reshape the Supreme Court to suit his liberal philosophy through seven new appointments, but his handling of the Court issue was a costly political blunder.

5. Though a conservative coalition tried to impede social legislation, two reform acts did pass: the National Housing Act of 1937 and the Fair Labor Standards Act of 1938.

6. The economic crisis gave the president influence in proposing and passing legislation, and the executive branch's influence was also expanded by the administration of the New Deal programs; Congress resisted this accrual of power.

7. A bill passed in 1939 allowed Roosevelt to create the Executive Office of the President and name six administrative assistants to the White House staff. The White House also took control of the budget process.

8. A steady improvement of the economy prompted Roosevelt to slash the federal budget in 1937, Congress to cut the WPA's funding in half, and the Federal Reserve to tighten credit.

9. Unemployment soared to 19 percent; having taken credit for the recovery between 1933 and 1937, Roosevelt also had to take the blame for the "Roosevelt recession."

10. Roosevelt spent his way out of the downturn; he and his economic advisors were groping toward John Maynard Keynes's theory of using deficit spending in order to stimulate the economy.

11. Roosevelt's attempt to "purge" the Democratic Party of some of his most conservative opponents only widened the liberal-conservative rift as the 1938 election approached.

III. The New Deal's Impact on Society
   A. New Deal Constituencies and the Broker State
      1. The New Deal accelerated the expansion of the federal bureaucracy, and power was increasingly centered in the nation's capital, not in the states.
      2. During the 1930s the federal government operated as a broker state, mediating between contending pressure groups seeking power and benefits.
      3. Organized labor won the battle for recognition, higher wages, seniority systems, and grievance procedures.
      4. The Congress of Industrial Organizations (CIO) served as the cutting edge of the union movement by promoting "industrial unionism" — organizing all the workers in one industry, both skilled and unskilled, into one union.
      5. While few workers in the CIO's unions actually joined the Communist Party, it had a great influence in labor organizing in the 1930s.
      6. The CIO recognized that in order to succeed, unions had to become more inclusive, and they worked deliberately to attract new groups to the labor movement.
      7. The CIO scored its first two major victories with the United Automobile Workers at General Motors and the Steel Workers Organizing Committee at the U.S. Steel Corporation.
      8. Hoping to use its influence to elect candidates that were sympathetic to labor and social justice, the CIO quickly allied itself with the Democratic Party.
      9. The labor movement still had not developed into a dominant force in American life, and many workers remained indifferent or even hostile to unionization.

10. Under the experimental climate of the New Deal, Roosevelt appointed the first female cabinet member, the first female director of the mint, and a female judge to the court of appeals.

11. Eleanor Roosevelt had worked to increase women's power in political parties, labor unions, and education; as first lady, she pushed the president and the New Deal to do more.

12. New Deal programs were marred by grave flaws; some NRA codes set a lower minimum wage for women than men, and the Civilian Conservation Corps (CCC) did not hire women at all.

13. Although some New Deal programs reflected prevailing racist attitudes, blacks received significant benefits from programs that were for the poor, regardless of race.

14. The Resettlement Act fought for the rights of black farmers, and many blacks reasoned that the aid from Washington outweighed the discrimination present in many federal programs.

15. Mary McLeod Bethune headed the "black cabinet," an informal network that worked for fairer treatment of blacks by New Deal agencies.

16. Blacks had voted Republican since the Civil War, but in 1936, blacks outside the South gave Roosevelt 71 percent of their votes. Blacks have remained overwhelmingly Democratic ever since.

17. Under the New Deal, Mexican Americans benefited from relief programs; Democrats made it clear that they considered Mexican Americans to be an important part of the New Deal coalition.

18. The Indian Reorganization Act of 1934 and other changes in federal policies under the "Indian New Deal" were well intentioned but did little to improve the lives of Native Americans.

   B. The New Deal and the Land
      1. The expansion of federal responsibilities in the 1930s created a climate conducive to conservation efforts, as did public concern heightened by the devastation in the dust bowl.
      2. The Tennessee Valley Authority integrated flood control, reforestation, and agricultural and industrial development; a hydroelectric grid provided cheap power for the valley's residents.
      3. Agents from the Soil Conservation Service in the Department of Agriculture taught farmers the proper technique for tilling hillsides.
      4. Government agronomists tried to prevent soil erosion through better agricultural practices and windbreaks like the Shelterbelts.

5. Cabins, shelters, picnic areas, and lodges in American state parks, built in a "government rustic" style, are witness to the New Deal ethos of recreation coexisting with conservation.

6. The New Deal was ahead of its time in attention to conservation, but many of the tactics used in its projects are now considered to be intrusive.

C. The New Deal and the Arts

1. A WPA project known as "Federal One" put unemployed artists, actors, and writers to work; "art for the millions" became a popular New Deal slogan.

2. The Federal Art Project commissioned murals for public buildings and post offices across the country.

3. Under the Federal Music Project, government-sponsored orchestras toured the country and presented free concerts that emphasized American themes.

4. The Federal Writer's Project, at its height, employed about 5,000 writers, some of whom later achieved great fame.

5. The only time that America had a federally supported national theater was during the Federal Theatre Project; talented directors, actors, and playwrights offered their services.

6. The documentary, probably the decade's most distinctive genre, influenced practically every aspect of American culture: literature, photography, art, music, film, dance, theater, and radio.

7. The *March of Time* newsreels, which were shown to audiences before feature films, presented the news of the world for the pretelevision age.

8. The Resettlement Administration's historical section documented and photographed American life for the government; their photos depicted life in the United States during the depression years.

D. The Legacies of the New Deal

1. For the first time, Americans experienced the federal government as a part of their everyday lives through Social Security payments, farm loans, relief work, and mortgage guarantees.

2. The government made a commitment to intervene when the private sector could not guarantee economic stability, and federal regulation brought order and regularity to economic life.

3. The federal government accepted primary responsibility for the individual and collective welfare of the people with the development of the welfare state.

4. One shortcoming of the welfare system stemmed from the ideal of "family wage," which assumed that men were workers and women were homemakers.

5. The New Deal Democratic coalition contained potentially fatal contradictions mainly involving the issue of race, and the resulting fissures would eventually weaken the coalition.

6. As Europe moved toward war and Japan seized more territory in the Far East, Roosevelt put domestic reform on the back burner and focused on international relations.

Lecture Strategies

1. A good way to begin this section is with an analysis of FDR's first inaugural address. The psychological impact of the address should be considered. For example, the famous phrase "the only thing we have to fear is fear itself," highlights the psychological malaise that Roosevelt saw at the center of the nation's economic crisis. The public's positive response to the address and to his "fireside chat" on the banking crisis indicated that people were ready to respond to his leadership.

2. The impact of the "hundred days" legislation should be made clear. Areas where it broke from tradition should be indicated. The Federal Emergency Relief Administration provided states with funds for direct relief — the dole. Students should understand the controversy over the dole, an argument that continues today. The ambiguous impact of the Agricultural Adjustment Act (AAA) needs to be noted — landlords received support, but many sharecroppers and tenants were driven off the land. The Civilian Conservation Corps was popular because it got troublesome youths off the streets and into the countryside. Note that much of the hundred days legislation was designed to last only until the expected economic recovery. The psychological and economic impact of those rapidly passed laws helped to create an atmosphere of hope among many Americans.

3. Students are often fascinated by challenges to FDR from the left. The rise of the Townsend movement shows how an interest group can quickly form and wield power. In dealing with the more complex challenges by Coughlin and Long, the use of recordings and documentary films is helpful. At this point, there should be a discussion of the difference between a popular leader and a demagogue. Did these movements provide a serious challenge to FDR's presidency, or were they merely annoyances? In what ways was the Second New Deal designed to counteract the influence of Townsend, Coughlin, and Long? What other factors might have pushed FDR to the left?

4. Work relief programs need to be analyzed. Why were they so unpopular (except for the CCC) with Americans who did not participate in them? Recap the argument between those who believed that private industry, and not government, should provide jobs and those who saw the government as the employer of last resort. Many current examples of the same debate can be cited. The extensive public works projects of the WPA should be described so that students can see the benefit they provided for the nation. The even more controversial writers' and artists' projects should be evaluated. Discuss the continuing debate over federal funding for the arts in order to help students understand this issue.

5. The impact of the Wagner (National Labor Relations) Act of 1935 should be considered. What was the significance of the federal government's first overture to support workers' right to organize? To illustrate this issue, discuss the Flint, Michigan, sit-down strike against General Motors. This dramatic confrontation can be explored effectively through documentary films. The emergence of the Congress of Industrial Organizations and its successes in organizing industrial workers in the waning years of the decade were important developments in securing labor's support for the Democratic Party.

6. The emergence of the "documentary impulse" is one of the easiest depression developments to present to students. The availability of prints of the New Deal propaganda films *The Plow that Broke the Plains* and *The River* make it possible for students to see how the New Deal publicized its programs. Many volumes of photographs taken under the auspices of the Resettlement Administration (RA) and the Farm Security Administration (FSA) are available, as are slides from the government's archives. It is interesting to note how the subjects of the photographs changed in response to complaints about what were seen as a "negative" emphasis in the earlier photos. Students should discuss the use of what was (and still is) seen as the "biased" portrayal of social reality in documentary material.

7. Given the general public's disapproval of communism, the role of left-wing political and intellectual movements in the 1930s should be explored. The activities of American Communists in organizing unemployment councils might be noted. More controversial is the "popular front" period during which the noncommunist left and Communists coalesced around the issue of antifascism.

8. How does one evaluate the New Deal? Liberals and radicals have been critical of its failure to restructure the American economic system in a more egalitarian way. Conservatives have criticized it for the intrusion of the federal government into the everyday lives of the American people. To what extent did it lay the foundations for a welfare state? Much of the expansion of the federal government often attributed to the New Deal actually took place during World War II. Was FDR too timid or too conservative to pursue a more radical solution to the depression? Was the depression bound to run its course no matter what the government tried? Hoover never understood why Roosevelt remained so popular, even though he was unable to end the depression. Can students offer Hoover an answer? What did the New Deal accomplish that leads most historians to view the 1930s as a watershed period in American history?

Class Discussion Starters

1. **What were some of the major problems faced by Roosevelt as he took office?**

   Possible answers:
   a. The rate of unemployment stood at about 25 percent.
   b. American industry was stagnant.
   c. People were literally starving to death.
   d. Thousands of banks had failed, and others were facing bankruptcy.
   e. Many Americans had lost faith in the economic system.

2. **In what ways did the "hundred days" legislation deal with critical areas of the depressed economy?**

   Possible answers:
   a. FERA provided funds that states could offer as direct relief so that people could eat and pay their rent.
   b. The AAA tried to stabilize and support farm prices by reducing overproduction.
   c. The CCC provided work relief for young men.
   d. The Emergency Banking Act helped to stabilize the banking system, and people redeposited their money.
   e. The PWA provided funds for public works projects that would put the unemployed to work.
   f. The NRA was established in an effort to get manufacturing under way.

3. **What kinds of national programs did prominent political activists seek to organize in order to alleviate some of the hardships of the 1930s?**

   Possible answers:
   a. Dr. Francis Townsend organized retired people in an effort to get the government to provide old-age pensions.
   b. Father Charles Coughlin sought the nationalization of the banking system.

c. Coughlin also wanted an expansion of the money supply.

d. Huey Long sought a redistribution of wealth that was to be accomplished by a confiscatory tax on all incomes over $1 million.

e. Long also wanted the establishment of a federally guaranteed minimum family income.

4. **What important elements of the Second New Deal broke new ground in providing for the needs of the American people?**

Possible answers:

a. The National Labor Relations Act gave government support for the first time to workers attempting to organize unions.

b. The Social Security Act provided for an old-age pension system and unemployment insurance.

c. The Social Security Act also provided for aid to the blind, the deaf, the disabled, and dependent children.

d. The Works Progress Administration provided millions of Americans with federally funded jobs through the remainder of the depression.

5. **What factors signified the decline of the New Deal after Roosevelt's reelection in 1936?**

Possible answers:

a. The New Deal programs had failed to put an end to the depression.

b. FDR's failed attempt to "pack" the Supreme Court increased the confidence of his congressional opposition.

c. Conservatives in Congress became more aggressive in opposing social and economic reforms.

d. FDR's reduction of federal spending helped to create the "Roosevelt recession" of 1937 to 1938.

e. Roosevelt's basic conservatism prevented him from suggesting more radical approaches to end the depression; the New Deal ran out of steam.

6. **What was the impact of the New Deal on African Americans?**

Possible answers:

a. The Resettlement Administration helped many black sharecroppers and tenant farmers to resettle after the AAA caused them to be evicted.

b. Prominent African Americans were brought into government service and formed an informal "black cabinet."

c. Blacks benefited from relief programs that targeted the poor without regard to race or ethnic background.

d. Unemployed blacks were hired on WPA projects at a rate higher than their percentage in the population.

e. African Americans shifted their political allegiance from the Republican Party (the party of Lincoln) to the Democratic Party (the party of Eleanor Roosevelt).

7. **In what ways did conservation become a major motif of New Deal programs?**

Possible answers:

a. The environmental devastation of the dust bowl was countered by the planting of millions of trees to serve as windbreaks on the Great Plains.

b. Scientific farming methods were adopted in an attempt to halt soil erosion.

c. New Deal construction projects improved the national parks system and made the parks more accessible to citizens.

d. The TVA established a series of flood control dams in the watershed of the Tennessee River, helping to control erosion.

e. The AAA established procedures that helped farmers to restore the productivity of the soil.

8. **Evaluate the impact of the New Deal on American society and polity.**

Possible answers:

a. The New Deal provided immediate relief for many of those suffering under the economic conditions that prevailed in 1933.

b. The New Deal laid the foundation for a modified welfare state with the adoption of Social Security, unemployment insurance, and aid to the dependent.

c. The New Deal demonstrated that successful governmental action depended to a large extent on the quality of leadership exercised by the president.

d. The New Deal expanded the political role of the federal government in the everyday lives of the American people.

Chapter Writing Assignments

1. Discuss the ways in which the legislation of the "hundred days" dealt with the problems facing the Roosevelt administration on taking office. Were the "hundred days" effective in the short term?

2. Compare the First and Second New Deals. Which has had the more pronounced effect on American society?

3. Evaluate work relief as a response to depressed economic conditions — was it a success or failure and why? Consider the specific work relief programs of the New Deal (CWA, CCC, PWA). Pay attention to which constituencies they served, how they were funded, and what they accomplished.

4. How did the New Deal court the following constituencies: (1) women, (2) African Americans, (3) organized labor, (4) farmers, and (5) Mexican Americans? Was the New Deal used as a vote-getter for the Democratic Party, or were these constituencies just particularly hard-hit by the depression?

Document Exercises

AMERICAN VOICES

Joe Marcus: A New Deal Activist (p. 723)

Document Discussion

1. **How did Marcus react to the New Deal?**
   (Marcus was clearly enthusiastic about the opportunities afforded by the New Deal. He saw the federal government as a place of opportunity and action. Marcus welcomed the chance to make positive and immediate changes in people's lives.)

2. **Why does Marcus's account of the New Deal seem so different from many others of the 1930s?**
   (Perhaps because Marcus doesn't appear to have personally suffered many deprivations, his view of the decade is somewhat unique. Note that he was graduated from college in 1935, which suggests he entered shortly after the depression began. His having had the resources to complete college at such a time hints at an economic background that probably shielded him and his family from the downturn.)

Writing Assignments

1. Marcus seems to contradict himself when he states that "we weren't thinking of remaking society," and yet asserts, "what was happening was a complete change in social attitudes at the central government level." How can you account for these two contradictory claims?

2. Marcus suggests the ways in which the Roosevelt administration expanded opportunities for Jews like himself. Why would Roosevelt and the New Deal have reached out to American Jews? Why would they have responded favorably?

AMERICAN LIVES

Mary McLeod Bethune: Black Braintruster (p. 736)

Document Discussion

1. **How did Bethune seek to improve the condition of African Americans?**

(Bethune pursued a number of projects to promote her agenda regarding race, education, and women. She opened a college in 1904 and participated in numerous national black women's organizations during the 1920s. She struck a friendship with Eleanor Roosevelt that permitted her access to national policymakers. Bethune's strategy was to gain policymaking positions for African Americans and thereby improve the treatment blacks received at the hands of government.)

2. **Why was New Deal legislation not explicitly committed to the civil rights of minorities?**
   (New Deal legislation was formulated in order to stimulate economic growth and improve personal incomes of workers. While legislation was not discriminatory, during a time of economic distress, Roosevelt could not politically afford to appear to be purposefully advancing the cause of minority rights, especially in the workplace.)

Writing Assignments

1. What does Bethune's experience suggest underlay many white Americans' racism in the first half of the twentieth century?

2. Compare Bethune's philosophy to the career and teachings of Booker T. Washington? Were Bethune and Washington successful?

AMERICAN VOICES

Susana Archuleta: A Chicana Youth Gets New Deal Work (p. 739)

Document Discussion

1. **How did Archuleta's family earn an income during the depression?**
   (Archuleta's mother took in washing, and the children helped by picking up the clothing and assisting with the ironing and folding. These types of low-skill jobs were all that were available to people without training or education.)

2. **Archuleta states that upon Roosevelt's election the depression "began to take a turn." To what is she referring?**
   (Archuleta admires the various work projects available to her and her siblings. She appears grateful for the opportunity to earn wages and gain experience at a very difficult time. Note that the programs Archuleta encountered took into account family size when determining employment priority.)

Writing Assignments

1. How does Archuleta feel about "giveaway programs like welfare"? Why?

2. How does the adolescence that Archuleta describes contrast with the experiences of today's youth? Are there more similarities or differences?

VOICES FROM ABROAD

Odette Keun: A Foreigner Looks at the Tennessee Valley Authority (p. 742)

Document Discussion

1. **Why did Keun admire the TVA?**
    (Keun praised the TVA for marshaling the assets of an entire region in order to improve the economic welfare of the people living there. Keun viewed the TVA as helping to preserve liberalism by providing for the economic needs of a region and decreasing its susceptibility to dictatorship.)

2. **Keun viewed the TVA as a sensible, middle-of-the-road approach, yet many Americans opposed it. Why?**
    (For Keun, the TVA was a successful application of governmental power to ensure the livelihood of an entire population. Keun feared the emergence of dictatorship and thought that when governments provided for the material needs of people, dictators could not emerge. Many Americans, on the other hand, were wary of a government project on such a large scale.)

Writing Assignments

1. Keun asserts that dictatorships come from the "total incapacity" of parliamentary government and the "failure of the economic machine to function properly." Germany failed on these two points in the 1920s and 1930s, but America did not. Why?

2. Keun defined liberalism as being in "opposition to extremes" and embracing the "practice of graduated change." Was this "middle of the road in time and space" the experience of America?

NEW TECHNOLOGY

Rural Electrification (p. 744)

Document Discussion

1. **Why did electricity come so late to rural America?**
    (Private power companies were not willing to spend the money to run electric lines deep into rural America.)

2. **Which farm tasks were eased by the coming of electricity?**

(Household tasks such as washing, ironing, and cleaning were eased. In some ways the most important task performed by electricity was pumping water from a well into the house, making running water and indoor bathrooms possible. The arrival of electricity marked a profound change in the lives of rural Americans.)

Writing Assignments

1. The Rural Electrification Administration was one example of a government initiative that improved the economic standing of farmers. How did other government agencies and New Deal legislation contribute to the welfare of the agricultural sector of the American economy?

2. Was rural electrification more important to men, women, or children living in the countryside? Why? Did gender roles or age roles change with the new technology? Why or why not?

Skill-Building Map Exercises

Map 25.4: The Tennessee Valley Authority, 1933–1952 (p. 741)

1. **The TVA was mainly an environmental project, but its benefits extended far beyond the natural environment. What environmental needs did the Tennessee Valley have? How did meeting these needs benefit people living in the area?**
    (The Tennessee River Valley watershed contains a number of rivers — the Cumberland, the Duck, the Tennessee, the Holston, and the Clinch — that would often flood due to heavy rainfall. Numerous dams were built to prevent the flooding; the map shows a total of 23 new dams. This construction created thousands of jobs for local people, many of whom were desperate for gainful employment. The hydroelectric power was harnessed in order to provide cheap electricity to many rural areas, improving the quality of life for residents.)

2. **What does this map demonstrate about the ability of the federal government, versus individual states, to address large-scale environmental and infrastructure problems?**
    (Environmental problems are not limited to one state; they often affect an entire region that may span several states. For example, note the scope of the Tennessee River Valley watershed. According to the map, the TVA built dams, power plants, and chemical plants and/or provided electricity to Tennessee, Kentucky, Georgia, Alabama, and Mississippi. Without

federal oversight, it might have been difficult for states to coordinate a successful response to this complex problem.)

Topic for Research

The New Deal and Your Community

Historians say that the New Deal affected virtually every locality in the country. What did it mean to yours? Find examples of the impact of New Deal projects on your local area. Likely candidates include buildings, highways, or public works projects funded by the WPA; post office murals painted by the Federal Arts Project; a nearby state park or recreation area, including playgrounds and golf courses; forestry or Shelterbelt projects, perhaps in connection with a CCC camp; or a traveling art project or theatrical performance funded by the WPA. As you play historical detective, consider these questions: What did it mean to the community to have the federal government enter its life? Did the federal presence mean different things to different segments of the community?

Several overviews suggest the kinds of places to start your research. Phoebe Cutler, *The Public Landscape of the New Deal* (1985), cites examples throughout the country. Marlene Park and Gerald Markowitz, *Democratic Vistas: Post Offices and Public Art in the New Deal* (1984), surveys New Deal murals and art. Carl Fleischhaeuer and Beverly Brannan, *Documenting America, 1935–1943* (1988), samples New Deal photography. For your community, visit the local historical society or library, check town records and old newspaper clippings from the 1930s, and seek out senior citizens. If your town does not have enough material, investigate the New Deal's impact on a large urban area such as New York or San Francisco.

Suggested Themes

1. Using newspaper files from the 1930s and other available sources (guidebooks, for example), identify the projects in your area that were completed under the auspices of the work relief programs of the New Deal. Evaluate the significance of those projects for your community.

2. Seek out and interview people in your community who participated in work relief programs. How did their participation in those programs help them to cope with the depression? How would they feel if the federal government were to provide the same kinds of programs for today's unemployed individuals?

How to Use the Ancillaries Available with *America's History*

Refer to the Preface to *America's History* at the front of the book for descriptions of instructor resources, including the Instructor's Resource CD-ROM, Computerized Test Bank, transparencies, and *Using the Bedford Series in History and Culture in the U.S. History Survey*. Student resources, also described in the Preface, include the Online Study Guide and *Documents to Accompany* America's History, a primary-source reader.

For Instructors

Using the Bedford Series in History and Culture in the U.S. History Survey
This brief online guide by Scott Hovey provides practical suggestions for incorporating volumes from the highly regarded Bedford Series in History and Culture into your survey course. Titles that complement the material covered in Chapter 25 include *The Era of Franklin D. Roosevelt: A Brief History with Documents*, by Richard Polenberg, and *Confronting Southern Poverty in the Great Depression: The Report on Economic Conditions of the South with Related Documents*, edited with an introduction by David L. Carlton and Peter A. Coclanis. For descriptions of these titles and how you might use them in your course, visit **bedfordstmartins.com/usingseries**.

For Students

Online Study Guide at bedfordstmartins.com/henretta
Each of the activities listed below includes short-answer questions. After submitting their answers, students can compare them to the model answers provided.

Map Activity
The map activity presents Map 25.4: The Tennessee Valley Authority, 1933–1952 (p. 741), and asks students to analyze the impact of the New Deal program.

Visual Activity
The visual activity presents a poster for the Steel Workers Organizing Committee (p. 733) and asks students to analyze the images used to portray organized labor.

Reading Historical Documents
The document activity provides a brief introduction to the documents Joe Marcus: A New Deal Activist (p. 723) and Susana Archuleta: A Chicana Youth Gets New Deal Work (p. 739) and asks students to analyze their content, thinking critically about the sources.

Documents to Accompany *America's History*
Each of the documents listed is introduced by a head-note, which places the document in context, and is followed by questions, which help students to analyze the piece.

Sources for Chapter 25 are
Franklin D. Roosevelt, *First Inaugural Address* (1933)
Rexford G. Tugwell, *Design for Government* (1933)
Franklin D. Roosevelt, *Criticism of the* Schechter v. United States *Decision* (1935)

Huey P. Long, *The Long Plan* (1933)
Harlan F. Stone, *Dissenting Opinion,* U.S. v. Butler (1936)
Republican and Democratic National Platforms (1936)
Norman Thomas, *What Was the New Deal?* (1936)
The Federal Antilynching Bills (1938)
Eleanor Roosevelt, *The State's Responsibility for Fair Working Conditions* (1933)
Mary Heaton Vorse, *The Sit-Down Strike at General Motors* (1937)
Lorena Hickok's Report on Arizona to Harry L. Hopkins (1934)

CHAPTER 26

The World at War
1939–1945

Chapter Instructional Objectives

After you have taught this chapter, your students should be able to answer the following questions:

1. What were the key elements of American foreign policy prior to World War II?

2. How and why did America edge closer to war between 1939 and 1941?

3. How did mobilization and war affect American society?

4. How did the Allies fight and win World War II?

5. How did American war aims affect plans for postwar settlement?

Chapter Summary

Disillusioned after World War I, the American people retreated into isolationism in the 1930s. During the first years of World War II, the United States tried to remain neutral but found itself drawn closer to Great Britain by a president who favored internationalism over isolationism.

The nation's neutrality was undermined by the wars begun by Germany, Italy, and Japan, all determined to expand their borders and their power. After winning an unprecedented third term as president in 1940, Roosevelt concentrated on persuading the American people to increase aid to Britain. Congress passed the Lend-Lease Act and the United States began supplying arms to Great Britain and the Soviet Union. This marked the unofficial entrance of the United States into the European war.

Japanese bombers attacked Pearl Harbor in December 1941, and Congress voted to declare war on Japan.

Three days later, Germany and Italy declared war on the United States, and the United States in turn declared war on them.

A dramatic expansion of power occurred at the presidential level when Congress passed the War Powers Act of 1941. During the war, the federal budget expanded tenfold, and the national debt grew by 600 percent. The number of civilians employed by the government quadrupled. Mobilization on such a gigantic scale gave a huge boost to the economy, but the new capitalist system relied heavily on the federal government's participation.

By the end of World War II, the armed forces of the United States numbered 15 million. The military segregated African Americans and assigned them the most menial jobs; Mexican Americans and Native Americans were never officially segregated. About 350,000 women served in agencies such as the Women's Army Corps (WACS) and Women Appointed for Volunteer Emergency Service (WAVES), although they were barred from combat. The War Manpower Commission sought to remedy the war-induced labor shortage by urging women to join the workforce.

The lure of high-paying defense jobs encouraged people to move; 15 million Americans migrated during the war years. In many towns with defense industries, housing was scarce and public transportation inadequate; conflicts arose between old-timers and newcomers. Latchkey kids became the norm, and juvenile delinquency seemed to be reaching epidemic proportions.

In July 1943, Mussolini's fascist regime fell, and Italy's new government joined the Allies. D-Day, the Allied invasion of France, came on June 6, 1944. Under General Eisenhower's command, more than 1.5 million American, British, and Canadian troops crossed the English Channel. In August 1944, Allied troops helped to liberate Paris; by September, they had driven the Germans out of most of France and Belgium. Germany surrendered in May 1945. As Allied troops advanced into Germany, they came upon the extermination camps where 6 million Jews, along with 6 million other "undesirables," had been put to death.

After Pearl Harbor, Japan continued its conquests in the Far East. In May 1942, in the Battle of the Coral Sea, American naval forces halted the Japanese offensive against Australia. Over the next eighteen months, General Douglas MacArthur and Admiral Chester W. Nimitz led the offensive in the Pacific.

When Roosevelt, Churchill, and Stalin met at Yalta in February 1945, victory in Europe and the Pacific was in sight, but no agreement had been reached on the peace to come. One source of conflict was Stalin's desire for a band of Soviet-controlled satellite states to protect the Soviet Union's western border. Roosevelt and Churchill agreed in principle on the idea of a Soviet sphere of influence in Eastern Europe but deliberately left its dimensions vague. When Harry Truman took over the presidency, he ordered the dropping of atomic bombs on the Japanese cities of Hiroshima and Nagasaki, assuring the Japanese surrender in August 1945. World War II had ended, but a new era of political and military confrontation with the Soviet Union — the cold war — was dawning.

Chapter Annotated Outline

I.   The Road to War
   A. The Rise of Fascism
     1. The nation's neutrality was challenged by the aggressive actions of Germany, Italy, and Japan, all determined to expand their borders and their influence.
     2. In 1931 Japan occupied Manchuria; then in 1937 it launched a full-scale invasion of China. The League of Nations condemned the aggression, and Japan withdrew from the League.
     3. In 1935 Italy invaded Ethiopia, and by 1936, the Italian subjugation of Ethiopia was complete.
     4. Adolf Hitler and his National Socialist (Nazi) Party, who took control of Germany in 1933, believed that "inferior races" and other "undesirables" had to make way for the "master race."
     5. Hitler began to overturn the territorial settlements of the Versailles treaty and to annex large areas of Eastern Europe.
     6. Hitler's first concentration camp was established in 1933, and once the war started, he began the extermination of the Jews.
     7. Wanting to avoid a war with Germany, Britain and France were proponents of what became known as "appeasement."

     8. Germany withdrew from the League of Nations in 1933, and Hitler's 1935 announcement of plans to rearm Germany — in violation of the Versailles treaty — met with no resistance.
     9. Germany reoccupied the Rhineland in 1936, and later that year Hitler and Italy's Benito Mussolini joined forces in the Rome-Berlin Axis.
   10. Germany and Japan signed the Anti-Comintern Pact, a precursor to the military alliance between Japan and the Axis that was formalized in 1940.
   11. In 1938 Hitler annexed Austria, and within six months of the Munich Conference that same year, German forces had overrun Czechoslovakia.
   12. In August 1939, Hitler and the Soviet Union signed the Nonaggression Pact; just two days after Germany attacked Poland on September 1, Britain and France declared war on Germany.
   B. Depression-Era Isolationism
     1. During the early years of the New Deal, America limited its involvement in international affairs.
     2. One of Roosevelt's few diplomatic initiatives was the formal recognition of the Soviet Union in 1933.
     3. Although Congress repealed the Platt Amendment, the Good Neighbor Policy had its limits, evidenced by the fact that the U.S. Navy kept a base at Cuba's Guantanamo Bay and continued to meddle in Cuban politics.
     4. Partly due to disillusionment with American participation in World War I, isolationism built in Congress and the nation throughout the 1920s.
     5. The Neutrality Act of 1935 imposed an embargo on arms trading with countries at war and declared that American citizens traveled on the ships of belligerent nations at their own risk.
     6. In 1936 the Neutrality Act was expanded to ban loans to belligerents, and in 1937, it adopted a "cash-and-carry" provision.
     7. Despite their Loyalist sympathies, the neutral stance of the United States, Great Britain, and France virtually assured a fascist victory in the 1936 Spanish civil war.
   C. Retreat from Isolationism
     1. President Roosevelt, with the support of most Americans, sought to keep the United States neutral.
     2. By mid-1940, Germany had overrun Western Europe, leaving Great Britain as the only power in Europe fighting Hitler.

3. In America, the Committee to Defend America by Aiding the Allies led the interventionists, while the isolationists formed the America First Committee, which had the support of the conservative press, to keep America out of the war.

4. The National Defense Advisory Commission and the Council of National Defense were created in 1940 to put America's economy and government on a defense footing.

5. Also in 1940, the United States traded destroyers to Britain for the right to build military bases on British possessions and instituted a peacetime draft registration and conscription.

6. After winning an unprecedented third term as president in 1940, Roosevelt concentrated on persuading the American people to increase aid to Britain.

7. Roosevelt connected the Lend-Lease Act and his "Four Freedoms": freedom of speech and expression, freedom of worship, freedom from want, and freedom from fear.

8. The "lend-lease" was extended to the Soviet Union, which became part of the Allied coalition after it was invaded by Germany; this marked the unofficial entrance of the United States into the European war.

9. The United States and Britain's Atlantic Charter called for economic collaboration between the two countries and for guarantees of political stability after the end of the war.

10. When the Americans started supplying the Allies, Germany attacked American and Allied ships; still, Roosevelt hesitated to ask Congress for a declaration of war.

D. The Attack on Pearl Harbor

1. During the sack of Nanking in 1937, the Japanese sunk the American gunboat *Panay*; the United States accepted Japan's apology and more than $2 million in damages.

2. Japan craved the conquest of more territory and signed the Tri-Partite Act with Germany and Italy in 1940.

3. After Japan occupied part of French Indochina, Roosevelt retaliated with trade restrictions and embargos on aviation fuel and scrap metal.

4. When Japanese troops occupied the rest of Indochina, Roosevelt froze Japanese assets in the United States and instituted an embargo on trade with Japan, including oil shipments.

5. The United States knew that Japan was planning an attack but did not know when or where; on December 7, 1941, Japanese bombers attacked Pearl Harbor.

6. On December 8, Congress voted to declare war on Japan; three days later, Germany and Italy declared war on the United States, and the United States in turn declared war on them.

II. Organizing for Victory

A. Financing the War

1. Presidential power expanded dramatically when Congress passed the War Powers Act of December 18, 1941. The act gave Roosevelt unprecedented authority over all aspects of the war.

2. During the war, the federal budget expanded tenfold, and the national debt grew by 600 percent.

3. The Revenue Act of 1942 taxed not only the wealthy and corporations, but also, for the first time, average citizens.

4. The number of civilians employed by the government increased almost fourfold; leadership of federal agencies was turned over to volunteer business executives, so-called "dollar-a-year men."

5. The Office of Price Administration (OPA) supervised the domestic economy, allocating resources and trying to keep inflation down.

6. The War Production Board (WPB) awarded defense contracts, evaluated military and civilian requests for scarce resources, and oversaw the conversion of industry to military production.

7. The WPB preferred to deal with major corporations; these very large businesses would later form the very core of the military-industrial complex of the postwar years.

8. Mobilization on such a gigantic scale gave a huge boost to the economy, nearly doubling the gross national product (GNP), but the new capitalist system relied heavily on the federal government's participation.

B. Mobilizing the American Fighting Force

1. The government's mobilization of a fighting force expanded state presence in Americans' lives; by the end of World War II, the armed forces of the United States numbered 15 million.

2. The military segregated African Americans and assigned them the most menial jobs; Mexican Americans and Native Americans were never officially segregated.

3. Women found both opportunities and discrimination in the armed forces; not until 1977 did a congressional act accord the Women's Airforce Service Pilots (WASPS) veteran's benefits.

4. About 350,000 women served in agencies such as the Women's Army Corps and Women Ap-

pointed for Volunteer Emergency Service, although they were barred from combat.

C. Workers and the War Effort

1. The War Manpower Commission sought to remedy the war-induced labor shortage by urging women into the workforce.

2. Government planners and employers regarded women as just "filling in" while the men were away; despite their new opportunities, they still faced discrimination in the jobs they were assigned and the pay they received.

3. Women's participation in the labor force dropped temporarily when the war ended, but it rebounded steadily for the rest of the 1940s.

4. The National War Labor Board established wages, hours, and working conditions and had the authority to seize plants that did not comply.

5. Although incomes jumped 70 percent for workers during the war, they felt cheated as they watched corporate profits soar in relation to wages.

6. John L. Lewis led the United Mine Workers on a strike; Congress passed the antiunion Smith-Connally Labor Act over Roosevelt's veto, and strikes were entirely prohibited in defense industries.

D. Civil Rights during Wartime

1. African American leaders pointed out parallels between anti-Semitism in Germany and racial discrimination in America; they pledged themselves to a "Double V" campaign.

2. In response to the threat of a black "March on Washington," Roosevelt issued Executive Order 8802 and established the Fair Employment Practices Commission (FEPC).

3. The FEPC did not affect segregation in the armed forces, and the committee only resolved about a third of the complaints it received.

4. The League of United Latin American Citizens built on their communities' patriotic contributions to the defense industry and the armed services to challenge discrimination and exclusion.

5. African American groups flourished; the NAACP grew ninefold by 1945, and the Congress of Racial Equality became known nationwide for its demonstrations and sit-ins.

E. Politics in Wartime

1. Roosevelt began to drop New Deal programs once mobilization began to bring full employment.

2. Later into the war, Roosevelt called for a second bill of rights, yet his commitment to it remained largely rhetorical since it received no congressional support.

3. The Servicemen's Readjustment Act (1944), known as the GI Bill, provided education, job training, medical care, pensions, and mortgage loans for those who had served during the war.

4. Roosevelt's call for social legislation was part of a plan to woo Democratic voters; the 1942 elections saw Republicans gain seats in both houses and increase their share of governorships.

5. Seeking a fourth term because of the war, Roosevelt teamed with Harry S. Truman to run against Governor Thomas E. Dewey of New York.

6. Roosevelt received only 53.5 percent of the popular vote; the party's margin of victory came from the cities, and a significant segment of this urban support came from organized labor.

III. Life on the Home Front

A. "For the Duration"

1. The Office of War Information (OWI) strove to disseminate information and promote patriotism; the OWI urged advertising agencies to link their clients' products to the "four freedoms."

2. Many movies had patriotic themes or demonstrated the heroism or patriotism of ordinary citizens; others warned of the dangers of fascism at home and abroad.

3. Federal defense spending had solved the depression: unemployment had disappeared, and per capita income had risen from $691 in 1939 to $1,515 in 1945.

4. The Office of Price Administration subjected to rationing or regulation almost everything Americans ate, wore, or used during the war.

5. The war affected where people lived; families followed service members to training bases or points of debarkation, and the lure of high-paying defense jobs encouraged others to move.

6. As a center of defense production, California was affected by the wartime migration more than any other state, experiencing a 53 percent growth in population.

7. In many towns with defense industries, housing was scarce and public transportation inadequate; conflicts arose between old-timers and newcomers.

8. Latchkey kids became the norm, and juvenile delinquency seemed to be reaching epidemic proportions.

9. As more than a million African Americans migrated to defense centers in California, Illinois, Michigan, Ohio, and Pennsylvania, racial conflicts arose over jobs and housing.

10. Many young people wore "zoot suits" as a symbol of alienation and self-assertion, but to adults and Anglos, the zoot suit symbolized wartime juvenile delinquency.

11. German Americans and Italian Americans usually did not experience intense prejudice, and leftists and Communists faced little repression after the Soviet Union became an ally.

B. Japanese Internment

1. In 1942, Roosevelt approved a War Department plan to intern Japanese Americans in relocation camps for the rest of the war.

2. Despite the lack of any evidence of Nissei or Issei disloyalty or sedition, few public figures opposed the plan.

3. The War Relocation Authority rounded up Japanese Americans and sent them to internment camps in California, Arizona, Utah, Colorado, Wyoming, Idaho, and Arkansas.

4. The Japanese Americans who made up one-third of the population of Hawaii were not interned; the Hawaiian economy could not function without them.

5. Furloughs for seasonal workers, attendance at a college, and enlistment in the armed services were some routes out of the internment camps.

6. In *Hirabayashi v. United States* and *Korematsu v. United States*, the Supreme Court upheld the constitutionality of internment as a legitimate exercise of power during wartime.

IV. Fighting and Winning the War

A. Wartime Aims and Strategies

1. The Russians argued for opening a second front in Europe — preferably in France — because it would draw German troops away from Russian soil.

2. In November 1943, Roosevelt and Winston Churchill agreed to open a second front in return for Joseph Stalin's promise to fight against Japan when the war in Europe ended.

3. The delay in creating the second front meant that the Soviet Union bore the brunt of the land battle against Germany; Stalin's mistrust of the United States and Great Britain carried over into the cold war.

B. The War in Europe

1. During the first six months of the war, the Allies suffered severe defeats on land and sea both in Europe and Asia.

2. The turning point in the war came when the Soviets halted the German advance in the Battle of Stalingrad; by 1944, Stalin's forces had driven the Germans out of the Soviet Union.

3. In North Africa, Allied troops, under the leadership of General Dwight D. Eisenhower and General George S. Patton, defeated Germany's Afrika Korps led by General Erwin Rommel.

4. The Allied command moved to attack the Axis through Sicily and the Italian peninsula; in July 1943, Mussolini's fascist regime fell, and Italy's new government joined the Allies.

5. The invasion of France came on D-Day, June 6, 1944; under General Eisenhower's command, more than 1.5 million American, British, and Canadian troops crossed the English Channel.

6. In August 1944, Allied troops helped to liberate Paris; by September, they had driven the Germans out of most of France and Belgium.

7. In December 1944, after ten days of fighting, the Allies pushed the Germans back across the Rhine River in the Battle of the Bulge, the final German offensive.

8. As American, British, and Soviet troops advanced toward Berlin, Hitler committed suicide in his bunker on April 30; Germany surrendered on May 8, 1945, now known as V-E Day.

9. As Allied troops advanced into Germany, they came upon the extermination camps where 6 million Jews, along with 6 million other people, were put to death.

10. The Roosevelt administration had information about the camps as early as 1942, but so few Jews escaped the Holocaust because the United States and the rest of the world would not take in the Jews.

11. The War Refugee Board, established in 1944, eventually helped to save about 200,000 Jews who were placed in refugee camps in countries such as Morocco and Switzerland.

C. War in the Pacific

1. After Pearl Harbor, Japan continued its conquests in the Far East and began to threaten Australia and India.

2. In May 1942, in the Battle of the Coral Sea, American naval forces halted the Japanese offensive against Australia, and in June, Americans inflicted crucial damage on the Japanese fleet at Midway.

3. Over the next eighteen months, General Douglas MacArthur and Admiral Chester W. Nimitz led the offensive in the Pacific, advancing from one island to the next.

4. The reconquest of the Philippines began with a victory in the Battle of Leyte Gulf; by early 1945, triumph over Japan was in sight, with American victories at Iwo Jima and Okinawa.

5. The use of kamikaze missions, combined with the Japanese refusal to surrender, suggested to military strategists that Japan would continue to fight despite overwhelming losses.

D. Planning the Postwar World

1. When Roosevelt, Churchill, and Stalin met at Yalta in February 1945, victory in Europe and the Pacific was in sight, but no agreement had been reached on the peace to come.

2. One source of conflict was Stalin's desire for a band of Soviet-controlled satellite states to protect the Soviet Union's western border.

3. Roosevelt and Churchill agreed in principle on the idea of a Soviet sphere of influence in Eastern Europe but deliberately left its dimensions vague.

4. Germany was to be divided into four zones to be controlled by the United States, Great Britain, France, and the Soviet Union; Berlin would be partitioned among the four.

5. The Security Council of the United Nations would include the five major Allied powers, plus six other nations participating on a rotating basis.

6. The international organization of the United Nations was to convene in San Francisco on April 25, 1945; Roosevelt suffered a cerebral hemorrhage and died on April 12, 1945.

E. The Onset of the Atomic Age and the War's End

1. When Harry Truman took over the presidency, he learned of the top-secret Manhattan Project, charged with developing the atomic bomb.

2. Truman ordered the dropping of atomic bombs on the Japanese cities of Hiroshima, on August 6, and Nagasaki, on August 9.

3. Japan offered to surrender on August 10 and signed a formal treaty of surrender on September 2, 1945.

Lecture Strategies

1. The evolution of American foreign policy in the years 1939 to 1941 provides an interesting case study of American politics: President Roosevelt used every tool at his disposal — all within his constitutional powers — to move the country in a direction decidedly different from what the people and Congress seemed to want. The United States evolved from neutral to nonbelligerent to belligerent in only two years, after a decade or more of isolationism.

2. Over the past half century, historians have discussed and debated the intriguing question: did Roosevelt take the "back door" to war, that is, get into the war in Europe through the Pacific "door"? On one side, pro-ponents of the "warmonger" thesis suggest that Roosevelt wanted to join Great Britain in fighting Germany early on but could not provoke Hitler into declaring war. The president's defenders counter that FDR was too wise to risk the loss of American possessions in the Pacific in the opening moments of a war and that he could not depend on Hitler to join his Axis partner, Japan, in a war against the United States. Present both sides of this issue and then ask students to choose one side or the other in a class discussion, a small-group activity, or a writing assignment.

3. World War II provided opportunities for women and African Americans that might not have been available in peacetime. The Great Depression had forced women out of the workplace and shut the door of opportunity to all people of color. Mobilization for war reversed that trend. Developing this topic not only allows you to explore issues of gender and race during the war but also can provide a springboard into discussions of the widespread support for the war among the American people.

4. Life on the home front in World War II offers a good contrast to discussions of the military conduct of the war. American society at home changed to support wartime demands. You might present World War II recruiting posters, ration books, war bonds, and other artifacts. Time spent showing World War II films, or snippets of several films, will explain better than lectures alone how Hollywood contributed to the war effort at home.

5. You may wish to explore the contradictions between the fight for freedom abroad and the internment of Japanese Americans within the United States. Students may find a discussion of the suppression of civil liberties during wartime particularly relevant. Emphasize the personal experiences of Japanese Americans through autobiography. Memoirs and oral histories (for example, Monica Sone's recollections in American Voices, p. 767) are readily available as primary sources.

6. The outcome of World War II — an Allied victory — is a firm part of most students' knowledge of the war. They might assume that the Allied victory was inevitable, but, of course, it was not. You can discuss how the American armed forces rapidly changed their training and doctrine to defeat the Axis powers. Describe the close working relationship among Allied leaders, especially between Roosevelt and Churchill. Contrast this with the lack of communication on the Axis side. Tell students about the superior industrial capacity of the United States and the fact that American factories never suffered the destruction from bombing that weakened the other belliger-

ents. The commitment of the American people to a total war — rationing of goods, popular culture focusing on the war, and so forth — is another part of this story.

7. A nation's successes and failures are often bound up with the personalities and characteristics of its leaders. Perhaps nowhere is this shown better than in a comparison and contrast of Franklin Roosevelt in the United States and Adolf Hitler in Germany. These were two of the great players of World War II, who dominated their own countries' and the Western world's fate. Although they came from quite different backgrounds, both began to rise to power in the 1920s and then took command of their countries in 1933; both wrestled with troubles caused by economic turmoil but chose different paths to solve the problems of the depression; both commanded great military machines; and both died in April 1945, within days of each other.

8. The story of the Manhattan Project offers a great mixture of high drama — science and technology at the cutting edge, intrigue and secrecy, and decision making in a high-stakes setting. This lecture can be structured in various ways. You can run through the story from Albert Einstein's famous letter to FDR to the bomb runs over Hiroshima and Nagasaki. Or you can focus on personalities such as President Roosevelt, J. Robert Oppenheimer, and General Leslie Groves. Or you can compare the race between the United States and Germany to get the bomb first. This topic also has the advantage of providing a bridge between World War II and the cold war — the atomic bomb ended one era and opened another.

Class Discussion Starters

1. **In a climate of isolationism, President Roosevelt provided a strong voice for internationalism. How did the president show his preference for American involvement abroad before Pearl Harbor?**

Possible answers:
   a. American recognition of the Soviet Union in 1933 was a sign that under FDR the country would have a wider world vision than it had during the Republican presidencies of the 1920s.
   b. The Good Neighbor Policy ensured that the United States would pursue an activist approach in the Western Hemisphere but was willing to moderate the gun-boat diplomacy practiced earlier.
   c. In 1937, in the face of Japanese expansionism in Asia, FDR proposed that the United States join with other nations to "quarantine" aggressor states. The public forced him to back down, but the speech gave evidence of his attitude.

   d. From the start of the war in Asia in 1937 and in Europe in 1939, Roosevelt showed determination to assist friendly countries — especially Great Britain — in their wars against aggressors that threatened American interests.
   e. Roosevelt used his personal popularity to set up justification for war by making his sympathies known, denouncing Japan as "the present reign of terror and international lawlessness" and saying that he could not ask Americans to remain neutral in their thoughts about Hitler's aggression. His four freedoms speech defined America's ideological difference from its future enemies.

2. **What steps did the United States take between March and December 1941 to mark out a path toward war?**

Possible answers:
   a. Approval of the Lend-Lease Act in March.
   b. Extension of lend-lease to the Soviet Union in June, after the Germans invaded.
   c. FDR froze Japanese assets in the United States and initiated a trade embargo against Japanese goods in July.
   d. Roosevelt and Churchill announced the Atlantic Charter in August.
   e. The U.S. Navy began fighting an undeclared war against Nazi naval forces in September.

3. **What sorts of roles did American women play during World War II to support the nation's war effort?**

Possible answers:
   a. Although their numbers were relatively low, some women volunteered for military duty during the war. Under law, women could not be involved in combat. Still, some were near the front lines as nurses, and others played active roles as WACS, WAVES, SPARS (of the Coast Guard Women's Reserve), and WASPS.
   b. Women played a critical role in war industries, and their work proved indispensable in providing arms, munitions, aircraft, and other commodities that were vital in the war.
   c. Seeing their husbands off to war, many women became, in effect, single parents. They stayed home to raise children and continued to occupy relatively domestic roles, but they were imbued with a sense of contributing to the larger cause.

4. **What roles did minority group members play in the conduct of World War II? How did the war change the lives of American minorities?**

Possible answers:
   a. Although the war did little to bring lasting change for Mexican Americans, economic expansion in

western states, especially California, provided job opportunities in the defense industry.

b. African Americans played an important role in defense industries during the war. Many blacks migrated from the South and from rural areas into industrial cities in the North and West to work in war industries. The results were mixed: economic opportunities were often countered by racial violence. Although the armed forces were segregated, some African Americans volunteered for military service and served with distinction. The war years also inspired a new mood of militancy among black Americans; membership in the NAACP increased dramatically, and new organizations such as CORE joined in efforts to promote civil rights.

c. Although their native countries were engaged in war against the United States, German and Italian Americans did not come under extensive suspicion during the war. Japanese Americans, on the other hand, were subjected to abuse, discrimination, and internment because they were perceived as threats to public safety and national security. More than 100,000 Japanese and Americans of Japanese ancestry were relocated from their homes along the Pacific coast to internment camps in the interior. In the late 1980s the U.S. Congress approved the payment of indemnities to the survivors of internment but could not erase the memory of this shameful episode.

5. Why do historians consider 1942 to be a pivotal year for the outcome of the war?

Possible answers:

a. In the Pacific war, the Allies — led by the United States — reclaimed the initiative from Japan. Victory in the Coral Sea guaranteed that Australia would remain free of Japanese control. The Battle of Midway, sometimes called "the turning point in the Pacific war," cost Japan naval control of the Pacific (with the loss of four aircraft carriers). In late summer, American marines began the arduous task of moving the Japanese out of the Pacific island groups between Hawaii and the mainland of Asia.

b. At the Battle of Stalingrad in the fall of 1942, Russian forces turned back Hitler's advance into the Soviet Union. After Stalingrad, German armies were in retreat back toward their homeland, with Russian forces in pursuit from the east.

c. In late 1942, American forces cooperated with British troops in advances across North Africa that exposed the "soft underbelly" of Europe. The American army gained valuable lessons that they applied successfully during their invasion of Italy in 1943 and France in 1944.

Chapter Writing Assignments

1. According to most historians, the origins of World War II can be found in the consequences of World War I. Explain.

2. In the 1930s, American foreign policy tended toward an isolationist position. Which groups in the United States promoted this policy? Which groups opposed isolationism? In the context of the 1930s, was isolationism a realistic or a shortsighted policy to follow?

3. According to the oral historian Studs Terkel, World War II was a "good war." Do you agree with this assessment? Explain.

4. After the attack on Pearl Harbor, the United States acted quickly to become involved in the war. How was the United States able to make such a smooth transition from peace to war?

5. Overall, what sort of impact — positive or negative — did World War II have on women and minority groups in the United States?

6. How did the American people manifest their support for the nation's involvement in World War II? Was there any serious opposition to the war in the United States?

Document Exercises

AMERICAN LIVES

Henry J. Kaiser: World War II's "Miracle Man" (p. 756)

Document Discussion

1. **Henry J. Kaiser was called the "Miracle Man" for his speedy delivery of Liberty ships during World War II. What were some of the other activities that occupied Kaiser's public life and career?**
(Kaiser aided in opening the American West through several major engineering projects, including Hoover Dam on the Colorado River, the San Francisco–Oakland Bay Bridge, and the Grand Coulee Dam on the Columbia River. He applied the subassembly system to shipbuilding, allowing for faster and more efficient production. He adopted several innovative benefits for his workers, notably day care and health care, the latter being his most lasting contribution in the form of today's Kaiser Permanente health-care system.)

2. **Henry Kaiser's popularity is similar to the hero status of Andrew Carnegie. Compare these two figures.**

(Both Carnegie and Kaiser were born to European parents. Both men pioneered innovation — but not inventions — in their chosen industries. Carnegie adopted the Bessemer process for producing steel and created one of the giant corporations in the Gilded Age when America's economy came of age. Kaiser used a variety of ideas borrowed from others to become the "Miracle Man" of shipbuilding. In their later years, both men broke from their chosen fields to work in other areas. Carnegie became prominent in philanthropy, funding public libraries, teacher training schools, and other programs that benefited the American population. In a blending of philanthropy and pragmatism, Kaiser became associated with innovations in labor relations, especially health care. Carnegie seemed to embody business when business was idolized. Kaiser embodied a public-spirited energy at the end of an economic depression that had estranged many Americans from big business.)

Writing Assignments

1. Write an obituary for Henry J. Kaiser that could run in the first edition of a newspaper on the day of his death. What information will you provide your readers that might convey the wide range of roles he played in his public life?

2. Do the accomplishments of men and women who rise to lead their industry as Kaiser did constitute uniquely American stories? If so, how? If not, why?

VOICES FROM ABROAD

German POWs: American Race Relations (p. 761)

Document Discussion

1. **What kinds of jobs were the German prisoners of war (POWs) assigned? In performing these tasks, what types of Americans did they encounter?**
(The German POWs performed menial labor. As recounted here, they picked cotton, canned peas, and scavenged garbage. This type of work placed the POWs in a position to observe the lower orders of American society. They mingled with a variety of people who were struggling to succeed against very real obstacles in America.)

2. **What did the POWs think about American race relations?**
(Although these soldiers do not render a substantive judgment, their observations indicate that much racial bias persisted in American society. Most of the nonwhite people the POWs encountered were oppressed or disadvantaged.)

Writing Assignments

1. A major component of National Socialist (Nazi) Party ideology was racial prejudice. Do you see any ironies regarding race in the comments made by these German soldiers?

2. Why do you think the people of German origin were the most dissatisfied with and unfriendly to the soldiers?

AMERICAN VOICES

Monica Sone: Japanese Relocation (p. 767)

Document Discussion

1. **According to Sone, how were the Japanese treated in the internment camps?**
(Sone does not recount any direct physical abuse, but the internment itself was difficult and tragic. Accommodations were poor at best, and internees, many of whom were American citizens, were kept under observation and restricted to a life within the compound.)

2. **As distressing as the physical incarceration was to Sone and her family, what seems to distress her even more?**
(Sone feels that in many respects she has lost her identity. She does not understand why she has been interned, particularly since she is an American citizen. Sone points out that the ideas of democracy only operate when people have the faith and confidence to enact them in their daily lives.)

Writing Assignments

1. You are a reporter for the *Los Angeles Times*, and your assignment editor has asked you to write an op-ed piece (an editorial-opinion essay) to justify the American policy of relocating and interning Japanese Americans who had been living along the West Coast. What points will you make to defend this policy?

2. Now write an op-ed piece in which you oppose relocation and internment.

AMERICAN VOICES

Anton Bilek: The War in the Pacific (p. 774)

Document Discussion

1. **What were conditions like for American soldiers and marines taken as POWs by the Japanese?**

(Food was allotted at only half rations or less, even for long marches from one camp to another; medical treatment was denied or limited, even for debilitating diseases such as malaria, dysentery, and beriberi. The conditions were horrific, and the death count among Americans and Filipinos ran into the thousands.)

2. **How did American POWs manage to combat their mistreatment and survive the conditions of the camps and the rigors of the "death marches"?**
(The most critical instruments for surviving as POWs in inhumane conditions were a strong will to live — a commitment not to break under the physical strain and emotional pressure — and a dogged determination to rejoin family members and friends someday. POWs developed close bonds that tied them together in a common crisis. They encouraged one another; shared what little they had with other POWs who needed help, often to the point of personal sacrifice; and told tales of home life that gave inspiration and encouragement — sometimes even comic relief. By working together, many of the POWs managed to combat even the worst conditions.)

Writing Assignments

1. Why did the Japanese fight so viciously to control the Philippines during World War II?

2. Compare and contrast the treatment of American POWs at the hands of the Japanese in the Philippines with the conditions experienced by Japanese and Japanese Americans relocated in the United States. Include in your answer the responsibilities and privileges of soldiers and noncombatants during wartime. Can either event be justified legally or morally?

Skill-Building Map Exercises

Map 26.3: World War II in Europe, 1941–1943 and Map 26.4: World War II in Europe, 1944–1945 (pp. 760–61)

1. **These two maps show the European Theater of Operations (ETO), including Europe, the Middle East, and North Africa, at different stages of World War II. Using Map 26.3 (1941–1943), ask students to suggest reasons why Great Britain was able to stay free of German control and why Britain was so important to the United States.**
(Great Britain is separated from the mainland of Europe by the English Channel. Even after Germany overran most of Western Europe, Great Britain was

protected by the channel, the Royal Navy, and the Royal Air Force [RAF]. In the Battle of Britain in the summer of 1940, the RAF fought back against the German bombardment of Great Britain. Hitler never could get his armies across the geographic obstacle of the English Channel. The map also shows that beyond Great Britain, only the Atlantic Ocean separated Germany from the United States.

2. **Using Map 26.4 (1944–1945), what do the blue and green arrows that mark Allied advances and air operations tell you about Allied strategy in the European war?**
(The arrows all point toward one location: Germany. The Allied strategy for the ETO was to bring as much pressure to bear on Germany from as many directions as possible. By 1944 the Allies were advancing from the south through southern France, Italy, and the Balkans; from the west through France after the opening of the second front on D-Day; and from the east out of the Soviet Union and through Poland.)

Map 26.5: World War II in the Pacific, 1941–1942 and Map 26.6: World War II in the Pacific, 1943–1945 (pp. 772–73)

1. **Looking at Map 26.5 (1941–1942), what is striking about the extent of Japanese control in the Pacific during that time?**
(Remarkably, the Japanese had brought under their influence the vast majority of land masses within the Pacific realm. Only in the far south, in parts of New Guinea and Australia, and in the Far East, at Midway and Hawaii, are any sizeable territories unconquered. The challenge then facing the Japanese militarily was how to defend them. The farthest reach of the Japanese empire was over four thousand miles from the homeland. Resupplying and communicating at that distance posed an immense obstacle that the Japanese never fully resolved. Poor coordination between Japanese naval and ground forces aided the Allied cause.)

2. **These two maps show the Pacific theater in World War II, charting the farthest advance of the Japanese into the Pacific. Using Map 26.6 (1943–1945), what do the blue arrows that mark the Allied response tell you about Allied strategy in the Pacific?**
(This map of the Pacific region shows that the Allies began their push toward Japan from the South. Early in the war the Allies needed to safeguard their lines of supply and avoid Japanese patrols. Also, the Allies wanted to ensure Australia was secure. Once Allied strength had matured, an offensive across the central Pacific was initiated. Another idea that you can point

out is that the American strategy after the victory at Midway in June 1942, which damaged the Japanese navy's ability to project power, was to use the American army and marines in an island-hopping fashion. With the U.S. Navy providing protective firepower, the ground troops would land on an island, clean out the Japanese defenders, and then units repeat the process on another island, bypassing and isolating those that contained the heaviest Japanese garrisons. To illustrate this strategy, ask students to follow the arrows from the Marshals to Guam in the Marianas and then to Iwo Jima to the northwest and Okinawa to the west.)

Topic for Research

Hollywood Goes to War

After Pearl Harbor, the Office of War Information asked Hollywood to concentrate on six subjects as part of the war effort: the enemy, the Allies, the armed forces, war production, the home front, and the issues. Choose a film made during the war, either a popular film or a documentary, and analyze it as a document about American participation and attitudes about the war. How useful is it as a historical source? Is its historical accuracy, or lack thereof, less important than its role in boosting patriotism and morale? Films about the armed services include *Wake Island* (1942), *Guadalcanal Diary* (1943), *So Proudly We Hail* (1943), *Lifeboat* (1944), *Thirty Seconds over Tokyo* (1945), and *Keep Your Powder Dry* (1945). Frank Capra's *Why We Fight* series and John Huston's *Battle of San Pietro* (1944) are powerful documentaries. The best home front film is probably *Since You Went Away* (1943). A cult classic such as *Casablanca* (1942) looks different when watched through the lens of wartime America.

John E. O'Connor, ed., *Image as Artifact: The Historical Analysis of Film and Television* (1990), is an excellent introduction to using films as historical sources. For Hollywood in the 1940s, see Clayton R. Koppes and Gregory D. Black, *Hollywood Goes to War: How Politics, Profits, and Propaganda Shaped World War II Movies* (1987). See also Douglas Gomery and Robert Allen, *Film History: Theory and Practice* (1985), and David Bordwell, Janet Staiger, and Kristin Thompson, *The Classical Hollywood Cinema: Film Style and Mode of Production to 1960* (1985).

Suggested Themes

1. Oral Histories of World War II: Although the war generation is aging fast, many World War II-era Americans or war zone citizens who immigrated to the United States after the war as refugees or war

brides are available to visit with students. You could assign students — either individually or in small groups — to "visit a vet" or talk with their grandparents or older neighbors about their recollections of the war. They could report back to the class in writing or in an oral presentation. This assignment could be used in several ways: as a required activity (as an alternative, get students to read published oral histories), as an extra-credit activity for bonus points, or as an option/alternative to a traditional research paper.

2. In your opinion, how important are the media in shaping public opinion in a time of crisis? What role did Hollywood play in supporting American involvement in World War II?

3. Show selected segments from a World War II-era film such as *Wake Island*. Ask students to identify stereotypes that are used in the film to characterize American fighting men as well as the Japanese enemy. Ask them why stereotyping an enemy can make a war easier to define and an enemy easier to kill.

4. Compare Hollywood's portrayal with the way the war was really fought. For information regarding the fighting on the military front, see Samuel E. Morrison, *The Two-Ocean War* (1963); Charlton Ogburn, *The Marauders* (1982 reprint); Carlo D'Este, *Decision in Normandy* (1983); Charles B. MacDonald, *A Time for Trumpets* (1984); Keith E. Bonn, *When the Odds Were Even* (1994); Richard B. Frank, *Guadalcanal* (1990); Stephen E. Ambrose, Citizen Soldiers (1997); David M. Glantz and Jonathan House, *The Battle of Kursk* (1999); Peter R. Mansoor, *The GI Offensive in Europe* (1999); and Williamson Murray and Allan R. Millett, *A War to Be Won* (2000).

How to Use the Ancillaries Available with *America's History*

Refer to the Preface to *America's History* at the front of the book for descriptions of instructor resources, including the Instructor's Resource CD-ROM, Computerized Test Bank, transparencies, and *Using the Bedford Series in History and Culture in the U.S. History Survey*. Student resources, also described in the Preface, include the Online Study Guide and *Documents to Accompany* America's History, a primary-source reader.

For Instructors

Using the Bedford Series in History and Culture in the U.S. History Survey
This brief online guide by Scott Hovey provides practical suggestions for incorporating volumes from the highly

regarded Bedford Series in History and Culture into your survey course. Titles that complement the material covered in Chapter 26 include *The Era of Franklin D. Roosevelt: A Brief History with Documents*, by Richard Polenberg; *America Views the Holocaust, 1933–1945: A Brief Documentary History*, by Robert H. Abzug; *Pearl Harbor and the Coming of the Pacific War: A Brief History with Documents and Essays*, by Akira Iriye; and *What Did the Internment of Japanese Americans Mean?* by Alice Yang Murray. For descriptions of these titles and how you might use them in your course, visit **bedfordstmartins .com/usingseries.**

For Students

Online Study Guide at bedfordstmartins.com/henretta
Each of the activities listed below includes short-answer questions. After submitting their answers, students can compare them to the model answers provided.

Map Activity
The map activity presents Map 26.3: World War II in Europe, 1941–1943, and Map 26.4: World War II in Europe, 1944–1945 (pp. 760–61), and asks students to analyze the conflict in this theater.

Visual Activity
The visual activity presents a photograph of interned Japanese (p. 766) and asks students to analyze how this image contradicts the American war for democracy abroad.

Reading Historical Documents
The document activity provides a brief introduction to the documents Anton Bilek: The War in the Pacific (p. 774) and Monica Sone: Japanese Relocation (p. 767) and asks students to analyze their content, thinking critically about the sources.

Documents to Accompany *America's History*
Each of the documents listed is introduced by a headnote, which places the document in context, and is followed by questions, which help students to analyze the piece.

Sources for Chapter 26 are
Visual Document: C. D. Batchelor, "The Reluctance to Go to War" (1936)

Franklin D. Roosevelt, *Fireside Chat on the Great Arsenal of Democracy* (1940)
Franklin D. Roosevelt, *Four Freedoms Speech* (1941)
The Atlantic Charter (1941)
Norma Yerger Queen, *Women Working at the Home Front* (1944)
Visual Document: "Mother, When Will You Stay Home Again?" (1944)
Stanley Reed, *The Supreme Court on White Primaries in the South* (1944)
Visual Document: Wartime Posters, "The Japanese and Venereal Disease"
Remembering the War Years on the Home Front (1984)
Executive Order 9066 to Prescribe Military Areas (1942)
Japanese American Exclusion: Korematsu v. United States (1944)
Ernie Pyle, *Street Fighting* (1944)
William McConahey and Dorothy Wahlstrom, *Remembering the Holocaust* (1945)
Cozy Stanley Brown, *Code Talker — Pacific Theater* (1941–1944)
Albert Einstein's Letter to Roosevelt (1939)
Henry L. Stimson, *The Decision to Use the Atomic Bomb* (1945)

Thinking about History: Women, Gender, and the Welfare System (p. 778)

Discussion Questions

1. What distinction did New Dealers make between Social Security and welfare? How has this distinction become blurred today?

2. How and why was the welfare system originally designed to keep women from having to enter the workforce? Compare this original intent with the thrust of current welfare reform.

3. What are some of the contemporary criticisms of the current welfare program? How might its problems be rooted in its history?

PART SIX

America and the World
1945 to the Present

Part Instructional Objectives

After you have taught this part, your students should be able to answer the following questions:

1. Describe the events that led to the cold war. Why did it last so long?

2. What were the objectives of the United States in the cold war? How did the United States try to secure those objectives? Discuss all of the U.S.-Soviet confrontations from the end of World War II through the end of Reagan's presidency.

3. What domestic economic and social issues divided national political leaders during the cold war years? What basic principles did most national leaders share?

4. Why did the civil rights movement come into existence when it did? What did it accomplish? What remains to be done?

5. Explain the emergence of the women's movement in the 1960s. What did it accomplish? Why did it fail to secure the Equal Rights Amendment?

6. Explain the origins and conduct of American involvement in Vietnam. Assess the relationship between events in Vietnam and domestic affairs.

7. How has the role and expectation of the presidency and the federal government changed since 1980?

8. How has the end of the cold war and the emergence of the United States as the world's lone superpower affected American foreign policy? What are the domestic implications for American international leadership?

Thematic Timeline

	DIPLOMACY	GOVERNMENT	ECONOMY	SOCIETY	CULTURE
	The Cold War — and After	Redefining the Role of the State	Ups and Downs of U.S. Economic Dominance	Social Movements and Demographic Diversity	Consumer Culture and the Information Revolution
1945	▸ Truman Doctrine (1947) Marshall Plan (1948) NATO founded (1949)	▸ Truman's Fair Deal liberalism Taft-Hartley Act (1947)	▸ Bretton Woods system established: World Bank, IMF, GATT	▸ Migration to cities accelerates Armed forces desegregated (1948)	▸ End of wartime rationing Rise of television
1950	▸ Permanent mobilization: NSC-68 (1950) Korean War (1950–1953)	▸ Eisenhower's modern Republicanism Warren Court activism	▸ Rise of military-industrial complex Service sector expands	▸ *Brown v. Board of Education* (1954) Montgomery bus boycott (1955)	▸ Growth of suburbia Baby boom
1960	▸ Cuban missile crisis (1962) Nuclear test ban treaty (1963) Vietnam War escalates (1965)	▸ High tide of liberalism: Great Society, War on Poverty Nixon ushers in conservative era	▸ Kennedy-Johnson tax cut, military expenditures fuel economic growth	▸ Student activism Civil Rights Act (1964); Voting Rights Act (1965) Revival of feminism	▸ Shopping malls spread Baby boomers swell college enrollment Youth counterculture
1970	▸ Nixon visits China (1972) SALT initiates détente (1972) Paris Peace accords (1973)	▸ Watergate scandal; Nixon resigns (1974) Deregulation begins under Ford and Carter	▸ Arab oil embargo (1973–1974); inflation surges Deindustrialization brings unemployment to "Rust Belt" Income stagnation	▸ *Roe v. Wade* (1973) Televangelists mobilize evangelical Protestants New Right urges conservative agenda	▸ Rise of consumer and environmental protection movements Gasoline shortages Apple introduces first personal computer (1977)
1980	▸ Reagan begins arms buildup INF treaty (1988) Berlin Wall falls (1989)	▸ Reagan Revolution Supreme Court conservatism	▸ Reagonomics Budget and trade deficits soar Savings and loan bailout	▸ New Latino and Asian immigration AIDS epidemic	▸ MTV debuts Compact discs and cell phones invented
1990–2002	▸ War in the Persian Gulf (1990) Soviet Union disintegrates; end of the cold war U.S. peacekeeping forces in Bosnia Radical Muslim terrorists destroy New York's World Trade Center and attack the Pentagon	▸ Democratic party adopts "moderate" policies Republican Congress shifts federal government tasks to states George W. Bush narrowly elected president	▸ Corporate downsizing Boom of the mid-1990s gives way to weakening economy	▸ "Culture Wars" over affirmative action, feminism, and gay rights Affirmative action challenged Welfare reform	▸ Health care crisis Information superhighway Biotech Revolution

In 1945 the United States entered an era of unprecedented international power. Unlike the period after World War I, American leaders did not avoid international commitments; instead, they aggressively pursued U.S. interests abroad, vowing to contain communism around the globe. The consequences of that struggle profoundly influenced the nation's domestic economy, political affairs, and social and cultural trends for the next half century.

Diplomacy   First, the United States took a leading role in global diplomatic and military affairs. When the Soviet Union challenged America's vision of postwar Europe, the Truman administration responded by crafting the policies and alliances that came to define the cold war. That struggle lasted for more than forty years, spawned two "hot" wars in Korea and Vietnam, and fueled a terrifying nuclear arms race. The cold war mentality prevailed until the collapse of the Soviet Union in 1991. In the absence of bipolar superpower confrontations, international conflicts persisted, arising from regional, religious, and ethnic differences, and brought new challenges to the nation. In 1990, it fought the Gulf War against Iraq and ten years later sent peacekeeping troops to war-torn Bosnia. And, as a devastating attack on New York's World Trade Center in September 2001 so powerfully indicated, the problem of international terrorism looms menacingly.

Government   Second, America's global commitments had dramatic consequences for American government, as liberals and conservatives generally agreed on keeping the country in a state of permanent mobilization and maintaining a large military establishment. The end of the cold war brought modest cutbacks but with new diplomatic challenges; military expenditures remained a high priority and competed with spending for domestic needs. In the area of economic policy, both Republicans and Democrats were willing to intervene in the economy when private initiatives could not maintain steady growth, but liberals also pushed for a larger role for the federal government in the areas of social welfare and environmental protection. In the 1960s, Lyndon B. Johnson's "Great Society" erected an extensive federal and state apparatus to provide for social welfare. In subsequent years, particularly under the presidency of Ronald Reagan in the 1980s and the Republican control of Congress in the mid-1990s, conservatives cut back on many of the major programs and tried to delegate federal powers to the states.

Economy   Third, thanks to the growth of a military-industrial complex and the expansion of consumer culture,

the quarter century after 1945 represented the heyday of American capitalism. Economic dominance abroad translated into unparalleled affluence at home. In the early 1970s, however, competition from other countries began to challenge America's economic supremacy, and for the next two decades, many American workers experienced high levels of unemployment, declining real wages, stagnant incomes, and a standard of living that could not match that of their parents. Following this period of global economic restructuring, the U.S. economy rebounded in the mid-1990s, reclaiming a position of undisputed dominance. By 2002, however, this sense of extraordinary American prosperity was undercut by a weakening economy and a volatile stock market as well as concerns that disparities in wealth and opportunity were growing.

Society   Fourth, the victory over fascism in World War II led to renewed calls for America to make good on its promise of liberty and equality for all. In great waves of protests in the 1950s and 1960s, African Americans — and then women, Latinos, and other groups — challenged the political status quo. The resulting hard-won reforms brought concrete gains for many Americans, but since the late 1970s, conservatives have challenged many of these initiatives. As the century drew to a close, the promise of true equality remained unfulfilled.

Culture   Fifth, American economic power in the postwar era accelerated the development of a consumer society based on suburbanization and technology. As millions of Americans migrated to new suburban developments after World War II, growing baby boom families provided an expanded market for household products of all types. Among the most significant were new technological devices — television, video recorders, and personal computers — that helped break down the isolation of suburban and rural living. In the 1990s the popularization of the Internet initiated an "information revolution" that expanded and challenged the power of corporate-sponsored consumer culture.

Today, more than a half century after the end of World War II, Americans are living in an increasingly interwoven network of national and international forces. Outside events shape ordinary lives in ways that were inconceivable a century ago. As the cold war era fades into history, the United States remains the sole military superpower, but it shares economic leadership in the new interdependent global system.

CHAPTER 27

Cold War America
1945–1960

Chapter Instructional Objectives

After you have taught this chapter, your students should be able to answer the following questions:

1. What were the origins of the cold war? Explain its broad ideological, economic, political, and military components.

2. Analyze and discuss America's plans of containment and economic aid and the consequent events that characterized foreign affairs between 1945 and 1952.

3. What were the causes, conduct, and consequences of the Korean War?

4. How did the cold war affect domestic economic and political affairs in the 1950s?

5. How and why did civil rights emerge as a national domestic issue after 1954?

Chapter Summary

The wartime cooperation between the United States and the Soviet Union ended largely because they disagreed over the future of Eastern Europe and the development of nuclear weapons. At the end of World War II, the Allies *did* agree to disarm Germany, dismantle its military production facilities, and permit the occupying powers to extract reparations. However, plans for future reunification of Germany stalled, leading to its division into East and West Germany.

As tensions mounted, the United States came to see Soviet expansionism as a threat to its own interests and began shaping a new policy of containment. The Truman Doctrine required large-scale military and economic assistance to prevent communism from taking hold in

Greece and Turkey, which in turn lessened the Communist threat in the entire Middle East. This appropriation reversed the postwar trend toward sharp cuts in foreign spending and marked a new level of commitment to the cold war. The Marshall Plan brought relief to devastated European countries, ushering in an economic recovery that made them less susceptible to communism and opening these countries up to new international trade opportunities.

For the next forty years, the ideological conflict between capitalism and communism determined the foreign policy of the United States and the Soviet Union and, later, China. The United States pursued a policy designed to contain Communist expansion in Europe, the Middle East, and Asia.

American policy in Asia was focused on the region's global economic importance as well as the desire to contain communism there. After dismantling Japan's military forces and weaponry, American occupation forces began transforming the country into a bulwark of Asian capitalism. At the end of World War II, both the Soviets and the United States had troops in Korea, which was divided into competing spheres of influence. In June 1950, North Korea invaded South Korea. Truman ordered U.S. troops to repel the invaders, leading to three years of vicious fighting. An armistice, brokered by President Eisenhower, was signed in July 1953. Korea was divided near the original border at the thirty-eighth parallel.

After the Korean War, Eisenhower turned his attention to Europe and the Soviet Union. Soviet repression convinced American policymakers that armed conflict would be the only way to roll back Soviet power in Europe. Under the "New Look" defense policy, the United States began to develop a massive nuclear arsenal, instead of more expensive conventional forces, to deter the Soviet Union.

President Truman attempted to expand the social welfare policies of the New Deal in a program he called the Fair Deal, which aimed to extend a higher standard of living to a greater number of citizens. But conservative Democrats joined with Republicans in order to block the most progressive legislation. Nevertheless, Truman did make some gains in Social Security, the minimum wage, and public housing. Truman turned to executive action to further civil rights, appointing a National Civil Rights Commission in 1946, ordering the Justice Department to support antisegregation cases, and desegregating the armed forces in 1948.

Domestically, the Republican Party accused the Democrats of being "soft on communism." The frustrations of the cold war led to a national persecution of suspected Communists, known as McCarthyism.

In the presidential election of 1952, Eisenhower represented modern Republicanism, the moderate continuation of the welfare-state policies of the Democrats. In foreign policy, Secretary of State John Foster Dulles pursued a vigorous anti-Soviet line even though the death of Stalin had brought about a relative softening of the Soviet stance toward the West. In pursuit of containment, the Central Intelligence Agency (CIA) assisted in the overthrow of legitimate governments that seemed to fall short of staunch anticommunism. The arms race continued with the development of new weapons systems capable of "mutual assured destruction" in case of a nuclear attack.

Chapter Annotated Outline

I. The Cold War Abroad
    A. Descent into Cold War, 1945–1946
       1. Roosevelt had been able to work with Soviet leader Joseph Stalin, and in part as a memorial to Roosevelt, the Senate approved America's participation in the United Nations in 1945.
       2. After Yalta, the Soviets made no move to hold the promised elections and rebuffed western attempts to reorganize Soviet-installed governments in its European "sphere of influence."
       3. At the 1945 Potsdam Conference, President Harry Truman was in a position of strength because the United States had the atom bomb and the Soviets did not, so he took a hard line against Soviet expansion.
       4. At Potsdam, the Allies agreed to disarm Germany, dismantle its military production facilities, and permit the occupying powers to extract reparations.
       5. Plans for future reunification of Germany stalled, and the foundation was laid for what would later become the division of Germany into the capitalist Federal Republic of Germany and the Communist German Democratic Republic.
       6. The failure of the Baruch Plan to maintain a U.S. monopoly on nuclear arms while preventing their development by other nations signaled the beginning of a frenzied nuclear arms race between the two superpowers — the United States and the Soviet Union.
    B. The Truman Doctrine and Containment
       1. As tensions mounted, the United States increasingly perceived Soviet expansionism as a threat to its own interests, and a new policy of containment began to take shape.
       2. The Truman Doctrine called for large-scale military and economic assistance in order to prevent communism from taking hold in Greece and Turkey, which in turn lessened the threat to the entire Middle East.
       3. The appropriation reversed the postwar trend toward sharp cuts in foreign spending and marked a new level of commitment to the cold war.
       4. The Marshall Plan sent relief to devastated European countries and helped to make them less susceptible to communism; the plan required that foreign-aid dollars be spent on U.S. goods and services.
       5. Truman's plan for economic aid to European economies met with opposition in Congress until a Communist coup occurred in Czechoslovakia in February 1948.
       6. Over the next four years, the United States contributed nearly $13 billion to a highly successful recovery; Western European economies revived, opening new opportunities for international trade.
       7. Truman countered a Soviet blockade of West Berlin with airlifts of food and fuel; the blockade, lifted in May 1949, made West Berlin a symbol of resistance to communism.
       8. In April 1949, under the North Atlantic Treaty Organization (NATO) pact, twelve nations agreed that an armed attack against one of them would be considered an attack against all of them.
       9. NATO agreed to the creation of the Federal Republic of Germany (West Germany) in May 1949; in October, the Soviets created the German Democratic Republic (East Germany).
       10. The Soviets organized the Council for Mutual Economic Assistance in 1949 and the military Warsaw Pact in 1955.
       11. In September 1949, American military intelligence had proof that the Soviets had detonated an atomic bomb; this revelation called for a

major reassessment of American foreign policy.

12. The National Security Council (NSC) gave a report, known as NSC-68, that recommended the development of a hydrogen bomb and called for increased taxes in order to finance defense building.

13. The beginning of the Korean War helped to transform the NSC-68 recommendations into reality.

C. Containment in Asia and the Korean War

1. American policy in Asia was based as much on Asia's importance to the world economy as on the desire to contain communism.

2. After dismantling Japan's military forces and weaponry, American occupation forces began the job of transforming the country into a bulwark of Asian capitalism.

3. In China, a civil war had been raging since the 1930s between Communist forces, led by Mao Zedong and Zhou Enlai, and conservative Nationalist forces, under Jiang Jieshi.

4. For a time the Truman administration attempted to help the Nationalists until they proved intransigently corrupt; in October 1949 the People's Republic of China was formally established under Mao, and Jiang's forces fled to Taiwan.

5. The "China lobby" led the United States to refuse to recognize "Red China"; instead, the United States recognized the exiled Nationalist government and blocked China's admission to the United Nations (UN).

6. At the end of World War II, both the Soviets and the United States had troops in Korea; as a result, Korea was divided at the thirty-eighth parallel into competing spheres of influence.

7. The Soviets supported a Communist government, led by Kim Il Sung, in North Korea; and the United States backed a Korean nationalist, Syngman Rhee, in South Korea.

8. On June 25, 1950, North Koreans invaded across the thirty-eighth parallel; Truman asked the United Nations Security Council to authorize a "police action" against the invaders.

9. The Security Council voted to send a "peacekeeping" force to Korea, and Truman ordered U.S. troops to go there; General Douglas MacArthur headed the UN forces.

10. Given domestic opinions and a stalemate in Korea, Truman and his advisors decided to work toward a negotiated peace; they did not want large numbers of U.S. troops tied down in Asia.

11. MacArthur, who believed that the future of the United States lay in Asia and not in Europe, tried to execute his own foreign policy involving Korea and Taiwan and was drawn into a Republican challenge of Truman's conduct of the war. MacArthur was relieved of his command in Korea and Japan; the decision to relieve him was not a popular one at home.

12. Two years after truce talks began, an armistice was signed in July 1953; Korea was divided near the original border at the thirty-eighth parallel, with a demilitarized zone between the countries.

13. Truman committed troops to Korea without congressional approval, setting a precedent for other undeclared wars.

D. Eisenhower and the "New Look" of Foreign Policy

1. Eisenhower's "New Look" in foreign policy continued America's commitment to containment but sought less expensive ways of implementing U.S. dominance in the cold war struggle against international communism.

2. One of Eisenhower's first acts as president was to use his negotiating skills in order to bring an end to the Korean War.

3. Eisenhower then turned his attention to Europe and the Soviet Union; Stalin died in 1953, and after a struggle, Nikita S. Khrushchev emerged as his successor in 1956.

4. Soviet repression of the 1956 Hungarian revolt showed that American policymakers had few options for rolling back Soviet power in Europe, short of going to war with the Soviet Union.

5. Under the "New Look" defense policy, the United States economized by developing a massive nuclear arsenal as an alternative to more expensive conventional forces.

6. The U.S. Strategic Air Command had a Distant Early Warning line of radar stations installed in Alaska and Canada.

7. By 1958, both the United States and the Soviets had intercontinental ballistic missiles (ICBMs), and they were both carrying out atmospheric testing of the hydrogen bomb.

8. The arms race curtailed the social welfare programs of both nations by funneling resources into weapons.

9. The Southeast Asia Treaty Organization (SEATO) was created to complement the NATO alliance in Europe.

10. U.S. policymakers tended to support stable governments, as long as they were not Communist; some American allies were governed by dictatorships or repressive right-wing regimes.

11. The Central Intelligence Agency moved beyond intelligence gathering into active, albeit covert, involvement in the internal affairs of foreign countries.

12. In 1953 the CIA helped to overthrow Iran's nationalist premier after he seized control of British oil properties, and in 1954 the CIA helped to support a coup against a duly elected government in Guatemala.

13. The American policy of containment soon extended to new nations emerging in the Third World.

14. The United States often failed to recognize that indigenous or nationalist movements in emerging nations had their own goals and were not necessarily under the control of Communists.

15. On May 14, 1948, Zionist leaders proclaimed the state of Israel; Truman quickly recognized the new state, alienating the Arabs but winning crucial support from Jewish voters.

16. In early 1957, after the Suez Canal crisis, the Eisenhower Doctrine stated that American forces would assist any nation in the Middle East requiring aid against communism.

17. Eisenhower invoked the doctrine when he sent troops to aid King Hussein of Jordan and when he sent troops to back a pro-United States government in Lebanon.

18. U.S. attention given to developments in the Middle East in the 1950s reflected a growing desire for access to steady supplies of oil, a desire that increasingly affected foreign policy.

II. The Cold War at Home

  A. Postwar Domestic Challenges

    1. Government spending dropped after the war, but consumer spending increased, and unemployment did not soar back up with the shift back to civilian production.

    2. When Truman disbanded the Office of Price Administration and lifted price controls in 1946, prices soared, producing an annual inflation rate of 18.2 percent.

    3. The Employment Act of 1946 introduced federal fiscal planning on a permanent basis to achieve full employment, but the legislation was ineffective because it did not mandate planning measures or set clear economic priorities.

    4. Inflation prompted workers to demand higher wages; workers mounted crippling strikes in the automobile, steel, and coal industries.

    5. Truman ended a strike by the United Mine Workers and one by railroad workers by placing the mines and railroads under federal control; Democrats in organized labor were outraged.

    6. In 1947 the Republican-controlled Congress passed the Taft-Hartley Act, a rollback of several prounion provisions of the 1935 National Labor Relations Act.

    7. Truman's veto of the Taft-Hartley Act countered some workers' hostility to his earlier anti-strike activity and kept labor in the Democratic fold.

    8. In the election of 1948, the Republicans again nominated Thomas E. Dewey for president and nominated Earl Warren for vice president.

    9. Democratic left and right wings split off: the Progressive Party nominated Henry A. Wallace for president; the States' Rights Party (Dixiecrats) nominated Strom Thurmond.

    10. To the nation's surprise, Truman won the election handily, and the Democrats regained control of both houses of Congress.

  B. Fair Deal Liberalism

    1. The Fair Deal was an extension of the New Deal's liberalism, but it gave attention to civil rights, reflecting the growing importance of African Americans to the Democratic coalition.

    2. Congress adopted only parts of Truman's twenty-one point plan: a higher minimum wage, an extension of and increase in Social Security, and the National Housing Act of 1949.

    3. The activities of certain interest groups — Southern conservatives, the American Medical Association, and business lobbyists — helped to block support for the Fair Deal's plan for enlarged federal responsibility for economic and social welfare.

  C. The Great Fear

    1. As American relations with the Soviet Union deteriorated, a fear of communism at home started a widespread campaign of domestic repression, often called "McCarthyism."

    2. In 1938, a group of conservatives had launched the House Un-American Activities Committee (HUAC) to investigate Communist influence in labor unions and New Deal agencies.

    3. In 1947, HUAC intensified the "Great Fear" by holding widely publicized hearings on alleged Communist activity in the film industry.

    4. In March 1947, Truman initiated an investigation into the loyalty of federal employees; other institutions undertook their own anti-subversive campaigns.

    5. Communist members of the labor movement were expelled, as were Communist members of

civil rights organizations such as the NAACP and the National Urban League.

6. In early 1950, Alger Hiss, a State Department official, was convicted of perjury for lying about his Communist affiliations; his trial and conviction lent credibility to the paranoia about a Communist conspiracy and contributed to the rise of Senator Joseph McCarthy.

7. McCarthy's accusations of subversion in the government were meant to embarrass the Democrats; critics who disagreed with him were charged with being "soft" on communism.

8. McCarthy failed to identify a single Communist in government, but cases like Hiss's and the 1951 espionage trial of Julius and Ethel Rosenberg lent weight to McCarthy's allegations.

9. McCarthy's support declined with the end of the Korean War, the death of Stalin, and when his hearings as he investigated subversion in the U.S. Army were televised revealing his smear tactics to the public.

D. "Modern Republicanism"

1. In 1952, Dwight D. Eisenhower secured the Republican nomination and asked Senator Richard M. Nixon to be his running mate.

2. The Eisenhower administration set the tone for "modern Republicanism," an updated party philosophy that emphasized a slowdown, rather than a dismantling, of federal responsibilities.

3. The Democrats nominated Governor Adlai E. Stevenson of Illinois for president and Senator John A. Sparkman for vice president.

4. Eisenhower was popular with his "I Like Ike" slogan, his $K_1 C_2$ (Korea, Communism, Corruption) formula, and his campaign pledge to go to Korea to end the stalemate.

5. As president, Eisenhower hoped to decrease the need for federal intervention in social and economic issues yet simultaneously avoid conservative demands for a complete rollback of the New Deal.

6. The National Aeronautics and Space Administration (NASA) was founded in 1958, the year after the Soviets launched *Sputnik*, the first satellite.

7. To advance U.S. technological expertise, Eisenhower persuaded Congress to appropriate funds for college scholarships and for research and development.

8. The creation of the Department of Health, Education, and Welfare in 1953 consolidated government control of social welfare programs.

9. The Highway Act of 1956 was an enormous public works program that surpassed anything undertaken during the New Deal.

III. The Emergence of Civil Rights as a National Issue

A. Civil Rights under Truman

1. Truman offered support for civil rights not only because he wanted to solidify the Democrats' hold on African American voters but also because he was concerned about America's image abroad.

2. Truman appointed the National Civil Rights Commission in 1946, and he signed an executive order to desegregate the army in 1948.

3. Southern conservatives blocked Truman's proposals for a federal antilynching law, federal protection of voting rights, and a federal agency to guarantee equal employment opportunity.

B. Challenging Segregation

1. Legal segregation of the races still governed southern society in the early 1950s; whites and blacks did not share the same room in restaurants or even the same water fountains.

2. In *Brown v. Board of Education of Topeka* (1954), the Supreme Court overturned the long-standing "separate but equal" doctrine of *Plessy v. Ferguson* (1896).

3. Over the next several years, the Supreme Court used the *Brown* case to overturn segregation in public recreation areas, transportation, and housing.

4. In the Southern Manifesto of 1956, southern members of Congress denounced the *Brown* decision as an abuse of judicial power and encouraged their constituents to defy the ruling.

5. In response to the Little Rock school-integration incident, Eisenhower became the first president since Reconstruction to use federal troops to enforce the civil rights of blacks.

6. Rosa Parks's refusal to give up her bus seat to a white person prompted the Montgomery bus boycott; the Supreme Court declared bus segregation unconstitutional in 1956.

7. Reverend Martin Luther King Jr. was catapulted into national prominence after the bus boycott; in 1957, he and other black clergy founded the Southern Christian Leadership Conference (SCLC) in Atlanta.

8. While the SCLC and the NAACP achieved only limited victories in the 1950s, they laid the organizational groundwork for the dynamic civil rights movement of the 1960s.

C. The Civil Rights Movement and the Cold War

1. The cold war affected civil rights because of the way in which the hunt for internal subver-

sives stifled dissent in American culture in the late 1940s and 1950s.

2. This suppression shaped the direction of the civil rights movement by minimizing the attention given to class and economic issues and focusing instead on the legal discrimination and violence toward African Americans in the south.

3. Black activists invoked the cold war as justification for pursuing racial reform; U.S. presidents increasingly had to view black civil rights at home in the context of international politics.

IV. The Impact of the Cold War

A. Nuclear Proliferation

1. After the 1950s, federal investigators documented a host of illnesses, deaths, and birth defects among families of veterans who had worked on weapons tests and among "downwinders."

2. According to a 1993 Department of Energy report, many subjects used in the Atomic Energy Commission's experiments in the 1940s and 1950s did not know that they were being irradiated.

3. Bomb shelters and civil defense drills were daily reminders of the threat of nuclear war; Eisenhower himself had second thoughts about the Mutual Assured Destruction policy.

4. Eisenhower tried to negotiate an arms limitation agreement with the Soviet Union, but in 1960, progress was cut short when an American spy plane was shot down over Soviet territory.

B. The Military-Industrial Complex

1. The Department of Defense evolved into a massive bureaucracy that profoundly influenced the postwar economy; with the government paying part of the bill, corporations developed products with unprecedented speed.

2. In his final address in 1961, Eisenhower warned against the growing power of what he termed the "military-industrial complex," which by then employed 3.5 million Americans.

Lecture Strategies

1. Students today may have a difficult time understanding the intensity of American-Soviet conflict during the postwar years. A full examination of America as a world power and the international events that challenged American political and economic ideals after World War II is vital to students' appreciation for the

subsequent wars in Korea, Vietnam, and elsewhere. The cold war prompted America's first sustained involvement in foreign matters and necessitated unprecedented economic and political measures domestically.

2. In his first inaugural address, President Roosevelt paid attention primarily to the crisis of the Great Depression; on foreign policy, he limited himself to a statement that the United States would act as a good neighbor in the future. While this topic gets limited attention in the text, you might want to explore it in a short "mini-lecture." Even in a time of isolationism, the United States stayed active in dealing with Latin America, and the Good Neighbor Policy paid important dividends after Pearl Harbor, when the United States got nearly unanimous support (the exception being Argentina) in the war against the Axis.

3. The Vietnam War has eclipsed the Korean War in the memory of many Americans, but students should understand that it was in Korea that the U.S. military was first charged with containing communism by force. Students should know that the secretary of state had declared Korea to be outside the national security concerns of the United States but that Truman needed to strengthen his anti-Communist credentials; Communist North Korea's invasion of the South gave him that opportunity. The fact that American troops have remained in Korea since the end of the war should indicate to students that the decision by the United States to provide an anti-Communist police force for the postwar world remains costly.

4. Most of the social welfare programs of the New Deal were adopted as emergency measures in order to cope with the depression, not as an attempt by the Roosevelt administration to enact a coherent reform agenda. Students should see that Truman's Fair Deal proposals, by contrast, called for a series of social reforms that reflected a coherent progressive ideology. The fact that the depression had ended suggested to the president that the newly affluent society could afford to become a welfare state, providing a national health care program, a full-employment policy, expanded educational opportunities, and improved civil rights. Students should be encouraged to follow the congressional debate over these issues. They will see that the debate did not strictly follow party lines but reflected the deep division in American political life between conservatives and liberals in both parties.

5. Few things are harder to explain to today's students than the anti-Communist hysteria of the 1950s. Sev-

eral cases studies, including the *Rosenberg* case, the HUAC hearings on the entertainment industry, and the Army-McCarthy hearings, are helpful in depicting the intensity of this hysteria. Each of these episodes can be introduced to students through documentary films, which are excellent and widely available. Students watching films of Joseph McCarthy may have a hard time believing that he had any influence in American life. They might consider whether McCarthy would have been as effective in our full-blown television age. Students should also understand that, although Americans in general did not go around looking for Communists, most of them accepted that left-wing subversion was a genuine threat to the American system.

6. The impromptu anti-communist foreign policy of the Truman years became coherent and more aggressive under Eisenhower's secretary of state, John Foster Dulles. Students should understand how the elements of Dulles's policy fit together and made the world seem more dangerous. It is important for students to see that, although Stalin had died and the moderate Khrushchev had called for "peaceful coexistence," Dulles's single-minded anticommunism permitted no relaxation of vigilance. Indeed, in defense of American interests, the United States established alliances with a series of unsavory dictators. Students should see that U.S. foreign policy had become so mired in anticommunism that other issues (human rights and democracy, for example) were ignored. The Eisenhower administration also relied on nuclear deterrence, further escalating the arms race. The use of the CIA to overthrow governments outside the Soviet orbit that were not considered sufficiently anticommunist should be seen as a logical extension — even if poorly conceived and executed — of Dulles's policy.

7. Several factors contributed to the growth of American interest in Third World nations. (Some examples of the decolonization process should be provided for students so that they can see the various forms the process took — Israel, India, and Indonesia, for example.) Students need to see that some of the new nations could provide raw materials and markets, whereas others had strategic geographical locations for the cold war struggle. The refusal of the Dulles State Department to accept neutrality as a legitimate option for Third World nations drove some of them into the Soviet orbit, making them vulnerable to CIA covert action. With even longer-range implications, the United States maintained Israel as a cold war ally in the tumultuous Middle East even though that posed a potential threat to American supplies of oil from anti-Israel Arab states.

Class Discussion Starters

1. **What factors gave rise to the cold war between the United States and the Soviet Union?**

Possible answers:
   a. The Soviet decision to impose Communist governments on the nations of Eastern Europe led the United States to organize NATO to protect the West from a Soviet attack.
   b. The hostility and aggression of Stalin toward the West ensured that confrontation would continue.
   c. Long-standing conflict between the capitalist and Communist ideologies of the superpowers reemerged after the temporary cooperation of World War II.
   d. U.S. demands for open trade throughout Europe after the war made the Soviet Union fear for its economic survival as a Communist state and led it to close Eastern Europe to Western commerce.
   e. The perception among American policymakers that the Soviet Union had expansionist ambitions led the United States to adopt a policy of military and economic containment of communism.

2. **Why were the more radical social reforms of Truman's Fair Deal not enacted?**

Possible answers:
   a. With the country no longer in a depression, people felt that traditional laissez-faire individualism should be allowed to drive economic and social policies.
   b. The Republicans joined conservative southern Democrats to halt what they saw as dangerously liberal social welfare policies.
   c. Lobbyists such as the American Medical Association were able to persuade Congress that some of the proposed reforms were "socialist" in intent.
   d. The outbreak of the Korean War shifted Washington's interest away from domestic policy and toward fighting the cold war.

3. **What was the domestic impact of the anti-Communist crusade of the late 1940s and 1950s?**

Possible answers:
   a. Many famous people in the entertainment industry were blacklisted and unable to find work under their own names.
   b. Progressive political reforms were seen as reflections of Communist influence.
   c. Unsavory politicians were able to rise to power by threatening to expose subversives in the U.S. government.
   d. Spectacular trials, such as those of the Rosenbergs and Hiss, were used to reaffirm the threat of Communist espionage in the United States.

e. A pervasive climate of apprehension led to activities such as defense drills, construction of air raid shelters, and harmful radiation experiments performed on unknowing individuals.

4. What role did nuclear weapons technology play in the developing cold war?

Possible answers:
a. The existence of atomic bombs raised the stakes of postwar foreign policy.
b. The Soviets developed their own atomic bomb to support their expansionist ideology and to secure their hold on Eastern Europe.
c. The successful test of atomic weapons by the Soviet Union drove the United States to seek bigger and more effective nuclear weapons, leading to a costly arms race between the two superpowers.
d. The evidence in the United States that the Soviets had stolen the "secret" of the atomic bomb through espionage fueled the domestic anti-Communist crusade and was used to create an atmosphere of hostility toward and fear of the Soviet Union.

5. In what ways did the cold war affect American policy at home and abroad during this period?

Possible answers:
a. Much of the progressive legislation proposed by the Fair Deal was defeated by those who saw it as a threat to traditional American laissez-faire capitalism.
b. The anti-Communist crusade made dissent from traditional political and social policies appear to be un-American.
c. The decision to contain communism led the United States to make military commitments in Europe and Asia that led to open warfare in Asia.
d. The decision to establish a national security state led the government to invest heavily in defense industries, diverting economic assets from needed domestic social spending.
e. The division of the world into two opposed and armed camps prevented a neutral policy toward the Third World from emerging.

Chapter Writing Assignments

1. Why did civil rights emerge as a national domestic issue in the years after World War II?

2. What impact did NSC-68 and the Korean War have on the development of postwar American defense policy?

3. The sign on Harry Truman's desk said "The Buck Stops Here." The decisiveness implied in that statement characterized many of Truman's actions as president. Discuss and evaluate the impact of his self-proclaimed decisiveness on American foreign and domestic policy. Did he measure up to his own standard?

4. In what ways did the social policies of Truman's Fair Deal build on Roosevelt's New Deal, and in what ways did they try to go beyond it? What were the major sources of opposition to the expansion of governmental social welfare programs?

5. What elements of the federal government were responsible for exposing supposed subversive activities in the United States during the 1940s and 1950s? What was the result of their investigations?

6. Discuss the many overt and covert activities undertaken abroad during the Eisenhower administration's pursuit of communism containment.

Document Exercises

AMERICAN LIVES

George F. Kennan: Architect of Containment (p. 788)

Document Discussion

1. **How did Kennan characterize the Soviet Union's view of the United States?**
   (Kennan argued that the Soviet Union was hostile toward America. In his estimation, the Soviets were insecure in their international position, yet as autocrats they would not consider compromising with the West. In fact, they were determined to export communism through violent means.)

2. **How did Kennan's ideas about containment affect U.S. foreign policy?**
   (Kennan's theory of containment held that the only way the United States could halt Soviet expansionism was to oppose the Soviets directly. Kennan believed that if it were "contained," the Soviet Union would perish from its own contradictions and internal decay. But Kennan's formulation of containment theory was vague in several respects. He did not define what kinds of force the United States should deploy against the Soviets.)

Writing Assignments

1. How and why did Kennan's call for containment manifest itself in the decisions and commitments of American political leaders in the 1950s and 1960s?

2. Other than containment, what strategic choices did American policymakers possess to confront the Soviet Union during the cold war? What were the strengths and weaknesses of each alternative?

VOICES FROM ABROAD

Jean Monnet: Truman's Generous Proposal (p. 790)

Document Discussion

1. **How did Monnet feel about Truman and American aid to Europe?**
(Monnet expressed gratitude and admiration for America's sustained economic support and political involvement in Europe during the years following the war.)

2. **What does Monnet assume to be America's responsibility in postwar Europe?**
(Monnet asserts that the economic plight of the states of Western Europe in 1947 gave to the United States direct responsibility for rebuilding European economies and defending governments against Communist aggression. For the most part, Monnet views American aid in the form of economic relief as being most urgent but includes arms for Turkey and Greece as important elements as well.)

Writing Assignments

1. Use Monnet's statement to contrast America's relationship to Europe after World War II with how America responded to the end of war in Europe in the 1920s.

2. Why did Monnet feel that Europe was at the risk of being overtaken by communism? Why didn't he express more confidence that Europeans could reestablish constitutional government by themselves?

AMERICAN VOICES

Mark Goodson: Red Hunting on the Quiz Shows; or, What's My Party Line? (p. 802)

Document Discussion

1. **Who bore the ultimate responsibility for blacklisting performers in the entertainment industry?**
(It is difficult to assign blame to any individual or corporate position. The anti-Communist attitude of the early 1950s pervaded the industry's hierarchy. Sponsors, ad agencies, network executives, and producers engaged in questioning people's loyalty.)

2. **How did Goodson come to be accused of disloyalty?**
(The concluding clause — "Is Goodson a pinko?" — is a typical example of McCarthyism. Goodson had questioned the agency's judgment in a matter of internal security, opening him to the charge of disloyalty.)

Writing Assignments

1. Discuss the reasons that the entertainment industry became such a prominent target for the anti-Communist crusade.

2. How did economic considerations contribute to the reaction of the entertainment industry to blacklisting?

AMERICAN VOICES

Isaac Nelson: Atomic Witness (p. 809)

Document Discussion

1. **How did the testing of atomic bombs affect Nelson and his wife?**
(Nelson and his neighbors in Cedar, Nevada, were initially excited about the federal government's plans to test atomic weapons near their town. His wife and he sometimes went out to observe the detonations and often watched radioactive clouds pass overhead. Several years after the testing began, Nelson's wife became gravely ill with cancer. She eventually died from her ailment.)

2. **Why didn't Nelson's wife receive adequate treatment?**
(The citizens of Cedar and nearby communities were downwind from the site of the explosions. They did not understand, and the federal government probably did not fully comprehend either, the risks to which they were exposed. Due to the secrecy surrounding the testing, the government did not offer any assistance or information that might have helped to diagnose and treat the victims. The doctors who examined Nelson's wife did not recognize the cause of her sickness and provided little effective treatment.)

Writing Assignments

1. Why was Nelson initially pleased that atomic tests were going to be conducted near his home in Nevada? What does Nelson's attitude reveal about citizens' relationship to the nation-state in the post-World War II era?

2. What is the responsibility of the federal government in cases where its defense and security procedures harm citizens?

Skill-Building Map Exercises

Map 27.1:
Cold War in Europe, 1955 (p. 786)

1. **How would you account for the inclusion of Turkey and Greece in the North Atlantic Treaty Organization?**
   (Since the purpose of NATO was the containment of Soviet communism, the fact that Turkey shared a border with the Soviet Union gave it strategic importance. Both Turkey and Greece occupied important positions with regard to the Black Sea.)

2. **What does this map suggest about the reasons why the Soviet Union might have wanted to control the nations of Eastern Europe?**
   (Those nations formed a corridor that guarded the western border of the Soviet Union from attack by Western European nations.)

Map 27.2:
The Korean War, 1950–1953 (p. 793)

1. **Using the scale at the bottom of the map, calculate approximately how far the North Korean troops were driven back between September and November 1953.**
   (Between 350 and 400 miles.)

2. **What military strategy did MacArthur employ in September 1950?**
   (The Inchon landing outflanked the North Korean army and made it possible to drive the North Koreans quickly out of the South.)

Topic for Research

Truman and the Polls

The first Gallup polls appeared just before the 1936 election, and they have been a prominent aspect of political life ever since. For historians as well as politicians, polls offer a chance to sample a range of public opinion ("Americans believe . . . ") on a wide variety of issues. Yet polls have proved to be imperfect sources, especially in their early days.

The Truman administration offers many cases to test the usefulness of public opinion polls as sources. The most obvious example is the 1948 election, when polls widely predicted a Dewey victory. Also of interest are the dramatic fluctuations in Truman's popularity and the seeming contradiction between popular dissatisfaction with the Korean War and public support for General Douglas MacArthur. What can polls tell us about political events? How useful are they for forming assessments of the Truman presidency? How closely can you correlate a specific historical event with popular reaction? Conversely, can you show how public opinion shaped the course of a specific political event and history?

Gallup polls from the 1940s have been collected in three volumes in George Gallup, *The Gallup Poll: Public Opinion, 1935–1971* (1972). Alonzo Hamby, *Beyond the New Deal: Harry S. Truman and American Liberalism* (1973) is a good overview of the Truman administration. For the 1948 election, see Irwin Ross, *The Loneliest Campaign* (1968), and Jules Abels, *Out of the Jaws of Victory* (1959).

Suggested Themes

1. Examine the Gallup poll data for the 1948 presidential election compared with the actual outcome. Why did the polls incorrectly predict a Dewey victory?

2. Graph President Truman's popularity according to the polls, from the outbreak of the Korean War in 1950 to his departure from office in 1953. Discuss the correlation between political events and public opinion.

How to Use the Ancillaries Available with *America's History*

Refer to the Preface to *America's History* at the front of the book for descriptions of instructor resources, including the Instructor's Resource CD-ROM, Computerized Test Bank, transparencies, and *Using the Bedford Series in History and Culture in the U.S. History Survey*. Student resources, also described in the Preface, include the Online Study Guide and *Documents to Accompany* America's History, a primary-source reader.

For Instructors

Using the Bedford Series in History and Culture in the U.S. History Survey
This brief online guide by Scott Hovey provides practical suggestions for incorporating volumes from the highly regarded Bedford Series in History and Culture into your survey course. Titles that complement the material covered in Chapter 27 include *The Age of McCarthyism: A Brief History with Documents*, by Ellen Schrecker; *American Cold War Strategy: Interpreting NSC-68*, edited with an introduction by Ernest R. May; and *Brown v. Board of Education: A Brief History with Documents*, by Waldo E. Martin Jr. For descriptions of these titles and how you might use them in your course, visit **bedfordstmartins .com/usingseries.**

For Students

Online Study Guide at bedfordstmartins.com/henretta

Each of the activities listed below includes short-answer questions. After submitting their answers, students can compare them to the model answers provided.

Map Activity

The map activity presents Map 27.5: Atmospheric Nuclear Weapons Testing in the Pacific and at Home, 1945–1962 (p. 808), and asks students to analyze the environmental impact of atomic tests.

Visual Activity

The visual activity presents a photograph of postwar devastation in Germany (p. 784) and asks students to analyze the state of Europe after World War II.

Reading Historical Documents

The document activity provides a brief introduction to the documents Mark Goodson: Red Hunting on the Quiz Shows; or, What's My Party Line? (p. 802) and Isaac Nelson: Atomic Witness (p. 809) and asks students to analyze their content, thinking critically about the sources.

Documents to Accompany *America's History*

Each of the documents listed is introduced by a headnote, which places the document in context, and is followed by questions, which help students to analyze the piece.

Sources for Chapter 27 are

George F. Kennan, *Containment Policy* (1947)

Harry S. Truman, *Remembering the Truman Doctrine* (1947)

Arthur Vandenberg, *On NATO* (1949)

Robert A. Taft, *Against NATO* (1949)

NSC-68 (1950)

The Employment Act (1946)

Civil Rights and the National Party Platforms (1948)

Joseph R. McCarthy, *Communists in the U.S. Government* (1950)

Brown v. Board of Education of Topeka (1953)

Southern Declaration on Integration (1956)

Rosa Parks, *Describing My Arrest* (1955)

Lyndon B. Johnson, *The American West: America's Answer to Russia* (1950)

John Foster Dulles, *Cold War Foreign Policy* (1958)

Dwight D. Eisenhower, *Farewell Address* (1961)

The Affluent Society and the Liberal Consensus

1945–1965

Chapter Instructional Objectives

After you have taught this chapter, your students should be able to answer the following questions:

1. Explain the record of American prosperity during the two decades following World War II.

2. What were the changing roles of cities and suburbs in American society?

3. Assess the validity of the "fifties" as the historical norm of American life.

4. Evaluate President Kennedy's New Frontier platform.

5. How did President Johnson's Great Society program attempt to fulfill modern liberals' agenda for reform?

Chapter Summary

At the end of World War II, American economic hegemony abroad translated into affluence at home. The weakness of foreign competition enabled American businesses to exploit foreign markets when domestic markets were saturated or experiencing recessions. Millions of new jobs were created, consumer spending soared, and inflation was low; the nation entered a period of unprecedented affluence.

The middle class's postwar prosperity led to the development of a pervasive consumer culture. Advertising created images of the ideal middle-class family surrounded by the trappings of affluence. Television came to dominate the leisure hours of Americans, and its programming and commercials reinforced the values of middle-class consumerism.

Postwar family demographics changed from previous years: marriages were remarkably stable, there was a

drop in the average age at marriage, and the birthrate shot up. The baby boom prompted a major expansion in the nation's education system, and babies' consumer needs helped to fuel the economy. As parents of baby boomers, men were expected to conform to a masculine ideal that emphasized their role as responsible breadwinners. Women were encouraged to resume the traditional roles of wife and homemaker. Those who worked still bore full responsibility for child care and household management, allowing families and society to avoid facing the implications of women's new roles. A mass youth culture emerged, with its roots in the democratization of education, the growth of peer pressure, and the increasing purchasing power of teenagers.

With jobs and financial resources flowing to the suburbs, urban newcomers inherited a declining economy and a decaying environment — the "Other America." Internal migration from rural areas brought large numbers of people to the cities, especially African Americans. As affluent whites left the cities, urban tax revenues shrank, leading to the decay of services and infrastructure. Housing continued to be a crucial problem. In essence, two separate Americas emerged: a largely white society in suburbs and an inner city populated by blacks, Latinos, and other disadvantaged groups.

President Kennedy could not mobilize public or congressional support for his New Frontier agenda, and he was not as passionate about domestic reform as he was about foreign policy. However, Kennedy's youthful image, the trauma of his assassination, and the sense that Americans had been robbed of a promising leader contributed to a powerful mystique that continues today. Lyndon Johnson won the 1964 election in a landslide and used his energy and genius for compromise to develop many of Kennedy's stalled programs as well as many of his own.

A civil rights campaign known as Freedom Summer established freedom schools, conducted a voter registration drive, and organized the Mississippi Freedom Democratic Party. The reaction of white southerners to Freedom Summer was swift and violent. Fifteen civil rights workers were murdered, and only 1,200 black voters were registered. Johnson redoubled his efforts to get pending voting-rights legislation passed. The Voting Rights Act of 1965 suspended the literacy tests and other measures most southern states used to prevent blacks from registering to vote. The Twenty-fourth Amendment's outlawing of the federal poll tax, combined with the Voting Rights Act, allowed millions of blacks to register to vote for the first time.

Johnson used this mandate not only to promote the civil rights agenda but also to bring to fruition what he called "The Great Society." Great Society programs emphasized quality of life. The Johnson administration put issues of poverty, justice, and access at the center of national political life, and it expanded the federal government's role in protecting citizens' welfare.

Chapter Annotated Outline

I. The Affluent Society
  A. The Economic Record
    1. By the end of 1945, U.S. corporations and banking institutions so dominated the world economy that the period has been called the *Pax Americana*.
    2. American economic leadership translated into affluence at home; domestic prosperity benefited a wider segment of society than anyone had thought possible in the dark days of the Great Depression.
    3. The predominant thrust of modern corporate life was the consolidation of economic and financial resources by oligopolies — a few large producers that controlled the markets.
    4. Conglomerates were protected from instability in any one market by diversifying; therefore, they were more effective international competitors.
    5. The weakness of competition abroad enabled American businesses to enter foreign regions when domestic markets were saturated or experiencing recessions.
    6. A meeting in Bretton Woods, New Hampshire, resulted in the creation of two global institutions — the International Bank for Reconstruction and Development (World Bank) and the International Monetary Fund (IMF).
    7. The first General Agreement on Tariffs and Trade (GATT) led to the establishment of an international body to oversee trade rules and practices.
    8. The World Bank, the IMF, and GATT encouraged stable prices, the liberation of trade barriers and the reduction of tariffs, flexible domestic markets, and free trade based on fixed exchange rates.
    9. U.S. economic supremacy abroad helped to boost the domestic economy, creating millions of new jobs; the fastest growing sector was white-collar jobs.
    10. The AFL-CIO, created by the 1955 merger of the Congress of Industrial Organizations and the American Federation of Labor, represented over 90 percent of America's union members.
    11. In exchange for fewer strikes, corporate managers often cooperated with unions, agreeing to contracts that gave workers secure, predictable, and steadily rising incomes.
    12. Consumer spending soared, and inflation was low; yet the boon was marred by periodic bouts of recession and unemployment that particularly hurt low-income and nonwhite workers.
  B. The Suburban Explosion
    1. Americans began to leave older cities in the North and Midwest for newer ones in the South and West; there was also a major shift to the suburbs.
    2. Arthur Levitt applied mass-production techniques to home construction; other developers followed suit in subdivisions all over the country, hastening the exodus from farms and cities.
    3. New suburban homes, as well as the Federal Housing Administration and Veterans Administration loans to mortgage them with, were reserved mostly for whites.
    4. Although *Shelley v. Kraemer* (1948) ruled that restrictive covenants were illegal, the practice continued until the civil rights laws of the 1960s banned private discrimination.
    5. New growth patterns were most striking in the South and West, where inexpensive land, unorganized labor, low taxes, and warm climates beckoned; California grew most rapidly.
    6. Booming urban populations in the South and the West brought higher crime and poverty rates, and increasing demands for water in the Southwest resulted in environmental and health problems.
    7. Automobiles were essential to the growth of suburbs and to the development of the "Sun Belt"; the 1950s guzzlers became symbols of status and success.
    8. Highways were funded by federal government programs such as the National Interstate and Defense Highway Act of 1956; air pollution

and traffic jams soon became problems in cities.

9. As Americans began to drive to suburban shopping malls and supermarkets, downtown retail economy dried up, helping to precipitate the decay of the central cities.

C. American Life during the Baby Boom

1. The new prosperity of the 1950s was aided by a dramatic increase in consumer credit, which enabled families to stretch their incomes.

2. Aggressive advertising by corporations contributed to the massive increase in consumer spending.

3. Consumers had more free time in which to spend their money; millions took to the interstate highways, spurring dramatic growth in motel chains, restaurants, and fast-food eateries.

4. Television supplanted radio as the chief diffuser of popular culture; it portrayed American families as white, middle-class suburbanites, and nonwhite characters were usually servants.

5. The Federal Communications Commissioner called television "a vast wasteland"; however, its images of postwar family life and society fit with the expectations of many Americans.

6. After the depression, Americans yearned for security and a reaffirmation of traditional values; this yearning manifested itself in a renewed national emphasis on religion.

7. In 1954, the phrase "under God" was inserted into the Pledge of Allegiance, and in 1956 Congress added "In God We Trust" to all U.S. coins.

8. Norman Vincent Peale's *The Power of Positive Thinking* embodied the trend toward the therapeutic use of religion in order to assist Americans in coping with the stresses of modern life.

9. Evangelical religion experienced resurgence with the popular Reverend Billy Graham.

10. Postwar family demographics changed from previous years: marriages were remarkably stable, there was a drop in the average age at marriage, and the birthrate shot up.

11. The baby boom prompted a major expansion in the nation's education system, and babies' consumer needs helped to fuel the economy.

12. Coupled with national defense expenditures, family spending on consumer goods fueled unparalleled prosperity and economic growth in the 1950s and 1960s.

13. As parents of baby boomers, men were expected to conform to a masculine ideal that emphasized their role as responsible breadwinners.

14. Women were advised that their proper place was in the home; endorsing the "feminine mystique," psychologists pronounced motherhood the only "normal" female sex role.

15. Not all women chose to be housewives; an increase in the overall number of working women coincided with an increase in the number of older, married, middle-class working women.

16. Working women still bore full responsibility for child care and household management.

17. The emergence of a mass youth culture had its roots in the democratization of education, the growth of peer pressure, and the increasing purchasing power of teenagers.

18. America's youth were eager to escape suburban conformity, and they became a distinct new market that advertisers eagerly exploited.

19. The rock 'n' roll that teens were attracted to in the 1950s was seen by white adults as an invitation to race-mixing, sexual promiscuity, and juvenile delinquency.

20. In major cities, gay men and women founded gay rights organizations, but many gays were still perceived as a threat to mainstream sexual and cultural norms and therefore remained closeted.

21. Postwar artists, musicians, and writers expressed their alienation from mainstream society through intensely personal, introspective art forms; abstract expressionism captured the chaotic atmosphere of the nuclear age.

22. A similar trend developed in jazz, as black musicians originated a hard-driving improvisational style known as "bebop."

23. The rebellion of the Beats, although strictly cultural, inspired a new generation of rebels in the 1960s who championed both political and cultural change.

II. The Other America

A. Migration to Cities

1. With jobs and financial resources flowing to the suburbs, urban newcomers inherited a declining economy and a decaying environment — the "Other America."

2. The War Brides Act, the Displaced Persons Act, the McCarran-Walter Act, and the repeal of the Chinese Exclusion Act all helped to create an influx of immigrants into American cities.

3. The federal government welcomed Mexican labor under its *bracero* program but deported those who stayed illegally; 4 million Mexicans were deported during "Operation Wetback."

4. Residents of Puerto Rico had been American citizens since 1917, so they were not subject to

immigration laws; they became America's first group to immigrate by air.

5. Cuban refugees were the third largest group of Spanish-speaking immigrants; the Cuban refugee community turned Miami into a cosmopolitan, bilingual city almost overnight.

6. Internal migration from rural areas brought large numbers of people to the cities, especially African Americans, after the introduction of innovations like the mechanical cotton-picker, which reduced southern demand for labor.

7. By 1960, about half of the nation's black population was living outside the South, compared with only 23 percent before World War II.

8. After the 1953 "Termination" programs, many Indians settled together in poor urban neighborhoods alongside other nonwhite groups; many found it difficult to adjust to an urban environment and culture.

B. The Urban Crisis

1. Between 1950 and 1960, the nation's twelve largest cities lost 3.6 million whites and gained 4.5 million nonwhites.

2. As affluent whites left the cities, urban tax revenues shrank, leading to the decay of services and infrastructure; housing continued to be a crucial problem.

3. Urban renewal demolished about 400,000 buildings and displaced 1.4 million people between 1949 and 1967.

4. Postwar urban areas increasingly became places of last resort for America's poor; once there, they faced unemployment, racial hostilities, and institutional barriers to mobility.

5. Two separate Americas emerged: a largely white society in suburbs and an inner city populated by blacks, Latinos, and other disadvantaged groups.

III. John F. Kennedy and the Politics of Expectation

A. The New Politics

1. Democrat John F. Kennedy, with Lyndon B. Johnson as his running mate, won the 1960 presidential election over Republican Richard M. Nixon.

2. Kennedy called for civil rights legislation, health care for the elderly, aid to education, urban renewal, expanded military and space programs, and containment of communism abroad.

3. Kennedy practiced what became known as the "new politics," an approach that emphasized youthful charisma, style, and personality more than issues and platforms.

4. Television was a powerful medium for political life; voters who listened to the 1960 presiden-

tial debates on the radio concluded that Nixon had won, and those who watched it on TV felt that Kennedy had won.

5. Kennedy, a Catholic, successfully appealed to the diverse elements of the Democratic coalition; Johnson brought in the votes of southern white Democrats.

B. Activism Abroad

1. A resolute cold warrior, Kennedy proposed a new policy of flexible response measures designed to deter direct attacks by the Soviet Union; it greatly expanded the military-industrial complex.

2. Kennedy adopted a new military doctrine of counterinsurgency; soon the Green Berets of the U.S. Army's Special Forces were being trained to repel guerrilla warfare.

3. The Peace Corps, the Agency for International Development, and the Alliance for Progress provided food and other aid to Third World countries, bringing them into the American orbit and away from Communist influence.

4. Fidel Castro overthrew Cuban dictator Fulgencio Batista in 1959; Cuban relations with Washington deteriorated after Castro nationalized American-owned banks and industries and the United States declared an embargo on Cuban exports.

5. Isolated by the United States, Cuba turned to the Soviet Union for economic and military support.

6. In early 1961, Kennedy attempted to foment an anti-Castro uprising; the CIA-trained invaders were crushed by Castro's troops after landing at Cuba's Bay of Pigs on April 17.

7. U.S.-Soviet relations further deteriorated when the Soviets built the Berlin Wall in order to stop the exodus of East Germans; the Berlin Wall remained a symbol of the cold war until 1989.

8. In October 1962, American reconnaissance planes flying over Cuba photographed Soviet-built bases for intermediate-range ballistic missiles.

9. In a televised address, Kennedy confronted the Soviet Union and announced that the United States would impose a "quarantine on all offensive military equipment" intended for Cuba.

10. After a week of tense negotiations, both Kennedy and Khrushchev made concessions: the United States would not invade Cuba, and the Soviets would dismantle the missile bases.

11. In 1963 the United States, Great Britain, and the Soviet Union agreed to stop testing nuclear

weapons in the atmosphere, in space, and under water; underground testing would continue.

12. A new Washington-Moscow telecommunications "hot line" was established so that leaders could contact each other quickly during potential crises.

C. The New Frontier at Home

1. Kennedy could not mobilize public or congressional support for his New Frontier agenda; also, he was not as passionate about domestic reform as he was about foreign policy.

2. Funding for the National Aeronautics and Space Administration (NASA) and its Mercury program won support; on May 5, 1961, Alan Shepard became the first American in space.

3. After Kennedy's assassination, the Tax Reduction Act (the Kennedy-Johnson tax cut, 1964) marked a milestone in the use of fiscal policy to encourage economic growth.

4. Kennedy managed to push through legislation raising the minimum wage and expanding Social Security benefits, but he ran into congressional opposition on federal aid to education and medical insurance for the elderly.

D. New Tactics for the Civil Rights Movement

1. One of the gravest failures of the Kennedy administration was its reluctance to act on civil rights.

2. After the Woolworth's sit-in, the Southern Christian Leadership Conference helped to organize the Student Non-Violent Coordinating Committee in order to facilitate sit-ins by blacks demanding an end to segregation.

3. The Congress of Racial Equality organized freedom rides on bus lines in the South to call attention to segregation on public transportation; the activists were attacked by white mobs.

4. Most southern communities quietly acceded to the Interstate Commerce Commission's prohibition of segregated interstate vehicles and facilities.

5. Television cameras captured the severe mistreatment of civil rights activists during a protest in Birmingham, Alabama; American households viewed the spectacle on the evening news.

6. In what black leaders hailed as the "Second Emancipation Proclamation," Kennedy promised major legislation banning discrimination in public accommodations.

7. Medgar Evers, the president of the Mississippi chapter of the NAACP, was shot and killed the night of Kennedy's televised speech.

8. A massive civil rights march on Washington in 1963 culminated in a memorable speech by Martin Luther King Jr.; King won the Nobel Peace Prize in 1964 for his leadership.

9. Some civil rights activists were more radical than King; during the next few years, there were conflicts among the black activists over tactics and goals that were to transform the movement.

10. Southern senators blocked the civil rights legislation, and there was an outbreak of violence by white extremists; in Birmingham, four black Sunday school students were killed.

E. The Kennedy Assassination

1. On November 22, 1963, in Dallas, Texas, President Kennedy was assassinated by Lee Harvey Oswald; Lyndon Johnson was sworn in as president.

2. Kennedy's youthful image, the trauma of his assassination, and the sense that Americans had been robbed of a promising leader contributed to a powerful mystique that continues today.

IV. Lyndon B. Johnson and the Great Society

A. The Momentum for Civil Rights

1. Johnson won the 1964 election in a landslide and used his energy and genius for compromise to bring to fruition many of Kennedy's stalled programs as well as many of his own.

2. The Civil Rights Act passed in June 1964; Title VII outlawed discrimination in employment on the basis of race, religion, national origin, or sex.

3. The Civil Rights Act forced desegregation of public facilities throughout the South, yet obstacles to black voting remained.

4. A civil rights campaign known as Freedom Summer established freedom schools, conducted a voter registration drive, and organized the Mississippi Freedom Democratic Party.

5. The reaction of white southerners to Freedom Summer was swift and violent; fifteen civil rights workers were murdered, and only 1,200 black voters were registered.

6. Civil rights activists near Selma, Alabama, were seen on the news being attacked by white authorities; Johnson redoubled his efforts to get pending voting-rights legislation passed.

7. The Voting Rights Act of 1965 suspended the literacy tests and other measures most southern states used to prevent blacks from registering to vote.

8. The Twenty-fourth Amendment's outlawing of the federal poll tax, combined with the Voting Rights Act, allowed millions of blacks to register to vote for the first time.

B. Enacting the Liberal Agenda
  1. When Johnson beat out Republican senator Barry Goldwater for the presidency in 1964, he achieved one of the largest margins in history: 61.1 percent of the popular vote.
  2. Johnson used this mandate not only to promote the civil rights agenda but also to bring to fruition what he called "The Great Society."
  3. The Elementary and Secondary Education Act helped to benefit impoverished children; the Higher Education Act provided the first federal scholarships for college students.
  4. Federal health insurance legislation was enacted; the result was Medicare for the elderly and Medicaid for the poor.
  5. The National Endowment for the Arts and the National Endowment for the Humanities supported artists and historians in their efforts to understand and interpret the nation's cultural and historical heritage.
  6. At the insistence of his wife, Lady Bird, President Johnson promoted the Highway Beautification Act of 1965.
  7. Great Society programs emphasized quality of life: the problems of "vanishing beauty," "increasing ugliness," and shrinking open space and the effects of pollution, noise, and blight.
  8. Liberal Democrats brought about significant changes in immigration policy with the passage of the Immigration Act of 1965, which abandoned the quota system of the 1920s.
  9. The "War on Poverty" expanded long-established social insurance programs, welfare programs (like Aid to Families with Dependent Children and Food Stamps), and public works programs.
  10. The Office of Economic Opportunity created programs such as Head Start, the Job Corps, Upward Bound, Volunteers in Service to America, and the Community Action Program.
  11. The Johnson administration put issues of poverty, justice, and access at the center of national political life, and it expanded the federal government's role in protecting citizens' welfare.
  12. The political necessity of bowing to pressure from various interest groups hampered Great Society programs; another problem was limited funding.
  13. Democratic support for further governmental activism was hindered by a growing conservative backlash against the expansion of civil rights and social welfare programs.
  14. After 1965 the Vietnam War siphoned funding away from domestic programs; in 1966 the government spent $22 billion on the war and only $1.2 billion on the War on Poverty.

Lecture Strategies

1. Explain the conditions that contributed to the political and economic dominance of the United States in the postwar period. Consider that World War II was not fought on American soil, that war mobilization had restored the health of American industry, that years of depression and war made Americans ready to consume the domestic products of a converted war economy, and that technology advances during the war were put to use in peacetime industrial production. Compare and contrast America's situation in these terms with the nations of Europe and Asia. Consider how the United States may have used its position of relative economic and political advantage differently than it did.

2. The onset of the cold war after 1945 marked the first time in American peacetime history that the United States maintained its armed forces at a high level of readiness with relatively large numbers of troops, ships, planes, and weapons. Discuss how this affected American political and popular culture. Millions of Americans had served in uniform during World War II, and now millions more were being asked to serve in a confrontation that had no foreseeable end. Examine why Americans perceived Communist nations as such a threat that they agreed to support a large "peacetime" military establishment. Also, discuss how the increased share of the GNP devoted to military spending affected patterns of employment. Looking to the future, compare and contrast the "peace dividend" at the end of World War II with the end of the cold war in 1989 to 1990.

3. Students need to see what the shift in the economy from producing goods to providing services meant for the labor force and for organized labor in particular. What factors went into creating this shift? Note that women and ethnic minorities occupy the lowest rungs of the service economy. Describe the way in which high-wage blue-collar work was replaced by low-wage white-collar and service jobs, and why it drove more women into the workplace.

4. The impact of suburbanization on American cities needs to be analyzed. Students should see the ways in which federal financing of home mortgages and highway construction spurred the growth of suburbs at the expense of inner city renewal, often at a high cost to minorities. The example of the Levittown developments can help to illustrate this process.

5. Aspects of contemporary urban life can be more clearly understood if students can see the ways in

which the federal policies of the 1945 to 1965 period helped to create cities that were increasingly inhabited by the poor. The process of urban renewal and patterns of racial discrimination tended to force African Americans and other nonwhite ethnic minorities into dense and racially isolated sections of older cities.

6. Changes in U.S. immigration laws and shifts in patterns of external and internal migration began to change the demographic profile of the American population. Students should be made aware of the process by which an increasing number of Spanish-speaking groups came to reside in certain urban areas at the same time that the cities were experiencing a decline in services and infrastructure. Students should see how the loss of entry-level unskilled employment in the inner cities affected the prospects of the urban poor.

7. Students need to have a clear picture of the depth and breadth of racial segregation in the South before the civil rights movement. There should be a discussion of the impact of racial segregation on black self-esteem as well as its economic, political, and social effects. Daily annoyances involving terms of address, treatment in commercial establishments and at lunch counters, and the lack of "colored" toilet facilities should be pointed out. The implications of school segregation should be explored.

8. The middle class rode the tide of postwar prosperity and created a consumer culture that had a significant impact on all segments of the economy. Students should be instructed about the historical factors that led to the rapid increase in consumption (the psychological aftermath of depression and war, the expansion of consumer credit, and the ubiquity of advertising, among others).

9. The role of television in the 1950s should be explored so that students can see its importance in fostering the consumer culture and forming images of the "typical" American family. In analyzing the impact of TV, the elements of American life that were not visible on the screen, as well as the ones that were, must be noted. The implications of mass media as commercial enterprises need to be discussed. What did it mean when TV programming was described as "a vast wasteland"?

10. Much has been made of the baby boom that occurred in the period after World War II. What factors contributed to this development? How did this phenomenon change the childrearing practices of the period? What new or expanding occupations relied on this development? What were the implications of this demographic shift for the lives of women and adolescents?

11. The election of 1960 saw the advent of the "new politics," bringing about several changes in the way presidential campaigns were managed. Students should be shown the contrast in campaigning before and after television became the most important way to reach the public. What impact did the television debates between Kennedy and Nixon have on that campaign?

12. Kennedy's involvement with Cuba became an obsession in his administration. The failure of the Bay of Pigs invasion disillusioned some cold warriors in the CIA about Kennedy's promise of an activist foreign policy. The Cuban missile crisis, by contrast, portrayed him as a cool hand at the tiller of foreign policy. Students should understand the reasons for the missile crisis, the process of decision making in the administration, and the danger of a nuclear exchange in this confrontation. Much new information about the crisis has become available on film and in books since the breakup of the Soviet Union.

13. Students want to know who killed Kennedy. Tell them what we do know and what we definitely do not know. Various scenarios can be presented without coming to a conclusion. Why do so many people refuse to believe the Warren Commission report? Why does the assassination of a relatively ineffective president obsess some segments of the public? Perhaps a word should be said about the enhancement of the "Camelot" mystique after Kennedy's death.

14. An attempt should be made to give students a glimpse of the larger-than-life qualities of Lyndon Johnson. A survey of his political career will help students to understand the relish with which Johnson took command after Kennedy's death. Johnson's overbearing but effective personal style should be noted. The conflicts between his egomania and his genuine humanitarianism have to be understood to properly assess this complex politician.

15. The "War on Poverty" must be assessed for students. There is much disagreement among scholars about its potential and effectiveness. However, almost everyone agrees that it lost out economically to the war in Vietnam, but there is still much controversy about its potential for eliminating poverty or even reducing it significantly. To explore this issue, the instructor must evaluate the programs of the Office of Economic Opportunity that challenged the traditional federal structure of American politics. Never before had funds gone directly from the federal government to neighborhood associations, for example. The poor were to be empowered by the Community Action Program, a prospect that local politicians did not look upon with favor.

Class Discussion Starters

1. **What were some signs of the new affluence in American society after World War II?**

Possible answers:
   a. The GNP more than doubled between 1945 and 1960.
   b. The wages and benefits of blue-collar workers rose.
   c. Many people were able to build new homes in the suburbs.
   d. There was a rapid increase in consumer spending.
   e. More young people were able to attend college.
   f. Automobile ownership became a status symbol in popular culture.

2. **How did automobile ownership affect American culture after World War II?**

Possible answers:
   a. Automobiles were essential to suburban growth.
   b. Automobiles became symbols of status and wealth.
   c. Construction of highways expanded rapidly, notably the interstate highway system.
   d. The development of the Sun Belt states proceeded at a rapid pace as automobiles made travel and transportation of goods and services accessible.

3. **What important changes in the world of work began to appear in the 1950s?**

Possible answers:
   a. The labor force began to shift from blue-collar to white-collar employment.
   b. The economy began to shift from industrial to service oriented.
   c. The increasing availability of higher education led to the emergence of a new managerial class.
   d. Women and minorities were drawn into low-paying, dead-end service occupations.
   e. The rising productivity of agribusiness led to a decline in the number of agricultural workers.

4. **What factors contributed to the demographic changes that took place during the postwar years?**

Possible answers:
   a. The shift in the industrial economy from the Northeast and Midwest to the Sun Belt led to a similar shift in the population.
   b. Federal support for low-cost mortgages and highway construction led to the expansion of the suburbs.
   c. New patterns of external and internal migration increased the concentration of the poor in declining inner cities.
   d. Urban renewal in the older cities led to the isolation of nonwhite minorities.
   e. The rising birthrate and declining death rate caused a baby boom in the early 1950s.

5. **What was the relationship between the advent of television and the rise of consumer culture?**

Possible answers:
   a. By 1960 the majority of American families had television sets, so advertising on television helped to create a commonly shared mass-consumer market.
   b. The depictions of ideal family settings in television programming enticed viewers to purchase similar items and to behave in similar ways, so as to be like the characters on the screen.
   c. Glimpses of exotic domestic and foreign locations on the screen helped to alter the vacation patterns of the population, leading to increased spending on leisure.

6. **What impact did the baby boom have on the lives of women?**

Possible answers:
   a. The existence of a "feminine mystique" led many educated women to forsake careers in order to focus on motherhood.
   b. To afford the family lifestyle called for by the consumer culture, more middle-class women entered the labor force.
   c. Because more married women with children were employed, many of them found themselves with two full-time jobs: one in the workplace and one at home.
   d. Many poor and minority-group women found their lives further constricted by the demands of trying to maintain an adequate standard of living for their larger families.

7. **Why, during this time of unprecedented affluence, did so many Americans remain impoverished?**

Possible answers:
   a. Many agricultural workers of all races were displaced by the rise of agribusiness and often ended up in urban ghettos.
   b. The decline of blue-collar employment in the Northeast and Midwest left many workers unemployed.
   c. Long-existing pockets of rural poverty in Appalachia and the South were untouched by the affluence of the period.
   d. The movement of employment opportunities from the cities to the suburbs led to an increase in joblessness and poverty within cities.
   e. African Americans and other nonwhite minority groups continued to experience racial discrimination in housing and employment, which made it difficult to overcome poverty.
   f. Many people employed in the growing low-wage service sector of the economy were unable to earn enough to escape from poverty.

8. What were the results of Kennedy's foreign policy?

Possible answers:
  a. He was unable to dislodge Castro, but he forced the Soviets to remove their missiles from Cuba.
  b. The military policies of flexible response and counterinsurgency that were intended to make the United States more effective in the cold war would later fail in Vietnam.
  c. The Peace Corps and the Agency for International Development helped to build goodwill for the United States in portions of the Third World.
  d. Conflict with Khrushchev over the future of Berlin caused the Soviets and East Germans to build the Berlin Wall, heightening tensions in Western Europe.
  e. In the aftermath of the Cuban missile crisis, at Kennedy's urging, the United States, Britain, and the Soviet Union agreed to ban open-air nuclear tests.

9. What factors constrained Kennedy's effectiveness in domestic policy?

Possible answers:
  a. His slim margin of victory in 1960 left him without a mandate among the general population.
  b. Kennedy's need for southern Democratic support in the 1964 election inhibited him from taking decisive action on the most important domestic issue of the 1960s — civil rights.
  c. In general, he lacked interest in domestic affairs, except for the space race, and he failed to formulate persuasive policies.
  d. Conservative southern Democrats and Republicans were able to defeat most liberal reforms sent to Congress.

10. What developments in American society helped to make the racial revolution of the 1950s and 1960s possible?

Possible answers:
  a. Internal migration made race relations a national rather than a regional issue.
  b. Returning black veterans were determined to achieve the "Double V."
  c. A series of decisions by the Supreme Court led inexorably to *Brown v. Board of Education.*
  d. America's attempts to win the support of Third World nations in the cold war required that something be done about racial discrimination.
  e. An expanding economy benefited blacks without depriving whites.
  f. Televised broadcasts of racial violence accelerated calls for change.

11. Why did nonviolence prove to be a successful strategy for confronting segregation?

Possible answers:
  a. It allowed the civil rights movement to gain the moral high ground.
  b. It deflected whites' arguments about racial inferiority.
  c. It clearly demonstrated that whites needed to use violence in order to maintain segregation.
  d. The television pictures of white violence turned many viewers against the practice of segregation.
  e. It forced the federal government to intervene on behalf of citizens being violently abused.

12. What actions did the federal government undertake in support of racial change?

Possible answers:
  a. The Supreme Court continued to dismantle laws supporting racial discrimination.
  b. White violence forced Presidents Eisenhower and Kennedy to intervene in support of school desegregation.
  c. Freedom rides led the Justice Department to enforce the rulings of the Interstate Commerce Commission.
  d. Kennedy proposed a civil rights bill that was passed after his death.
  e. Congress passed the Twenty-fourth Amendment, which outlawed the poll tax in federal elections, and the Voting Rights Act of 1965, which outlawed literacy tests and other measures that prevented southern blacks from voting.

Chapter Writing Assignments

1. Describe the factors that contributed to the unprecedented prosperity of the two decades that followed World War II. Did the United States maximize this opportunity to establish international leadership?

2. Discuss the impact of the gradual shift of American workers from manufacturing to services. Include a consideration of the effect on labor unions, working women, and farmers in your answer.

3. How accurate was the image of 1950s suburbia portrayed in television sitcoms of, and since, that era?

4. Describe the changes in the population density, ethnic diversity, and residential patterns in American cities during that period.

5. Discuss the impact of the baby boom generation on the consumer culture of the 1950s and early 1960s. Do the "boomers" still play an important role in shaping culture and public policy in the new century?

6. Ask your mother or grandmother what it was like to raise children in that era. Was her experience similar to what is described in the text or very different?

What opportunities were there for working women? Was the situation of women in the 1950s appreciably different from prior and subsequent decades?

7. Describe the major successes and failures of the Kennedy administration. How can you account for Kennedy's enhanced reputation after his assassination?

8. In what ways did Lyndon Johnson use the skills honed as Senate majority leader to attempt to convince Congress to enact his social reform agenda?

9. What were the main elements of Johnson's War on Poverty? Analyze the effectiveness of the various programs in achieving their objectives.

Document Exercises

VOICES FROM ABROAD

Hanoch Bartov: Everyone Has a Car (p. 821)

Document Discussion

1. **What aspect of American society impressed Bartov and why?**
(Bartov marveled at how the automobile dictated the lives of Americans. He noticed that the layout of cities, the growth of suburbs, the notions of class, and even ordinary social interaction were determined by Americans' ownership of cars. He admitted that cars were alluring in many respects.)

2. **According to Bartov, why did Americans avoid public transportation?**
(Bartov explains that residents of Los Angeles did not partake of public transportation in large numbers because they were so fond of the convenience afforded by private automobiles. He has little positive to say about other transportation options. Bartov observes that the buses only traveled occasionally and only along fixed routes which were not convenient, and that most of the riders in any case were "eccentric types." He simply dismissed railroads, probably for the same kinds of reasons he frowned upon buses.)

Writing Assignments

1. How did Bartov believe automobiles had affected American society?

2. What aspects of automobile ownership and operation most disturbed Bartov?

AMERICAN VOICES

A Woman Encounters the Feminine Mystique (p. 824)

Document Discussion

1. **Why did "Sylvia" find her situation in the research department to be so difficult?**
(She was the only woman in the program at the time. Her male colleagues made derogatory statements toward her that reflected their bias about the role they expected women to play in society. Note that women also opposed "Sylvia's" career choice. Her mother, for instance, encouraged "Sylvia" to follow the traditional route of a middle-class woman — getting married and having a family.)

2. **How did "Sylvia" cope with the prejudice she faced?**
(She committed herself to persevere in the face of her uncomfortable surroundings. She ensured that she accomplished all of her work professionally so that men could make no reasonable objection to her accomplishments.)

Writing Assignments

1. Academic institutions enjoy a reputation for open-mindedness. Why did this woman encounter so much resistance toward her advancement in a research department?

2. What do the statements made by the men indicate about their motivation for opposing "Sylvia's" presence?

AMERICAN LIVES

Elvis Presley: Teen Idol of the 1950s (p. 826)

Document Discussion

1. **What changes in American society in the 1950s contributed to the success of the Presley phenomenon?**
(The population bulge known as the baby boom provided a larger audience of teenagers for his act. Not only the size of the audience but its relative affluence was critical for sales of records and concert tickets. Television provided wide exposure. The fact that Presley's music and performance style offended an older generation brought up in depression and war only made him more attractive to youth.)

2. **How can one account for the continuing mystique of Elvis and the cult of Graceland?**

(For those who were young in the 1950s, there is nostalgia for what they remember as a time when the world was a simpler and happier place. Elvis's early death has contributed an aura of tragedy to his memory. Many others simply enjoy Elvis's musical talent.)

Writing Assignments

1. What factors go into the creation of a teen idol? Compare the rise and career of Elvis Presley with those of a contemporary teen idol, and evaluate the process that generated their fame.

2. How and why does music serve as a cultural reflection of societal trends?

AMERICAN VOICES

Anne Moody: We Would Like to Be Served (p. 837)

Document Discussion

1. **Why did Moody and her friends stage a sit-in at the Woolworth lunch counter?**
(Moody was attempting to force the equitable treatment of blacks. She and her friends thought that by demanding service from the white section of a lunch counter they could make a statement regarding the poor treatment blacks received. By raising awareness of the unfair situation, they hoped change would come.)

2. **How did the whites react to Moody's actions?**
(Although several whites were sympathetic to Moody and her friends, most were hostile. A mob formed inside of the store and assaulted those participating in the sit-in as well as the few whites who supported Moody. The police and local officials provided only minimal protection for the protesters.)

Writing Assignments

1. Why did whites hold so strongly to their racist attitudes?

2. How decisive were actions like Moody's in breaking down racial stereotypes and discriminatory behaviors?

Skill-Building Map Exercises

Map 28.1: Metropolitan Growth, 1950–1980 (p. 819)

1. **What does this map indicate about the demographic impact of the changes taking place in the industrial economy in this period?**

(The population of the Sun Belt states increased significantly, whereas the Northeast and Midwest remained stagnant or decreased in population.)

2. **What factors led to the migration of Americans from the Northeast and Midwest to the South and West?**
(The interstate highway systems made these regions more accessible, better infrastructure and amenities, such as air-conditioning, were attractions; as new industries emerged in the South and West, they required a larger labor force, so jobs were more plentiful.)

Map 28.5: The United States and Cuba, 1961–1962 (p. 834)

1. **Why did Fidel Castro seek to place Soviet missiles in Cuba?**
(One reason that Castro sought Soviet arms was that by doing so he gained great stature in the region. With missiles in Cuba aimed at the United States, Castro also ensured that he would have some measure of leverage on the world stage. Castro could use his position in order to win political concessions or economic benefits that otherwise would have been difficult for a small island nation like Cuba to attain.)

2. **Why did President Kennedy react so sternly to the deployment of missiles in Cuba?**
(Placing Soviet missiles in Cuba would have directly undermined the ability of the United States to respond to an attack. The proximity of Cuba meant that American tracking stations would have barely minutes to identify the launch of missiles, to determine their targets, and to respond. Hence, the United States would have been placed at a severe disadvantage in any military confrontation with the Soviet Union.)

Topic for Research

Poverty in the Age of Affluence

In 1962, Michael Harrington published *The Other America*, which described the persistence of poverty in postwar America. Assume you have been asked to review this book for a newspaper in 1962. You suspect that most of your readers will be surprised to learn that more than one-quarter of the population lives in poverty and that the majority of the poor are white. Describe the findings of the book, and analyze how successful it is in presenting its argument. How can you reconcile Harrington's picture with the general view of the 1950s as a period of unbounded affluence? Reflect on why the poor are so invisible and why modern capitalist societies, even those with welfare states, have been unable (or unwilling) to address the persistence of poverty.

For general background, sources on the history of poverty and social welfare include Michael B. Katz, *In the Shadow of the Poorhouse* (1986); Frances Fox Piven and Richard A. Cloward, *Poor People's Movements* (1977) and *Regulating the Poor* (1971); James Patterson, *America's Struggle against Poverty, 1900–1980* (1981); and Oscar Lewis, *La Vida: A Puerto Rican Family in the Culture of Poverty* (1965). A classic text on the age of affluence in the 1950s is John Kenneth Galbraith, *The Affluent Society* (1958).

How to Use the Ancillaries Available with *America's History*

Refer to the Preface to *America's History* at the front of the book for descriptions of instructor resources, including the Instructor's Resource CD-ROM, Computerized Test Bank, transparencies, *Using the Bedford Series in History and Culture in the U.S. History Survey*. Student resources, also described in the Preface, include the Online Study Guide and *Documents to Accompany* America's History, a primary-source reader.

For Instructors

Using the Bedford Series in History and Culture in the U.S. History Survey
This brief online guide by Scott Hovey provides practical suggestions for incorporating volumes from the highly regarded Bedford Series in History and Culture into your survey course. Titles that complement the material covered in Chapter 28 include *American Social Classes in the 1950s: Selections from Vance Packard's* The Status Seekers, edited with an introduction by Daniel Horowitz; *Lyndon B. Johnson and American Liberalism: A Brief Biography with Documents*, by Bruce J. Schulman; *Postwar Immigrant America: A Social History*, by Reed Ueda; and *Women's Magazines, 1940–1960: Gender Roles and the Popular Press*, by Nancy A. Walker. For descriptions of these titles and how you might use them in your course, visit **bedfordstmartins.com/usingseries**.

For Students

Online Study Guide at bedfordstmartins.com/henretta
Each of the activities listed below includes short-answer questions. After submitting their answers, students can compare them to the model answers provided.

Map Activity
The map activity presents Map 28.4: Decolonization and the Third World, 1943–1990 (p. 832), and asks students to analyze the process of decolonization and the impact this had on global politics.

Reading Historical Documents
The document activity provides a brief introduction to the documents Hanoch Bartov: Everybody Has a Car (p. 821) and A Woman Encounters the Feminine Mystique (p. 824) and asks students to analyze their content, thinking critically about the sources.

Documents to Accompany *America's History*
Each of the documents listed is introduced by a headnote, which places the document in context, and is followed by questions, which help students to analyze the piece.

Sources for Chapter 28 are
David Potter, *The Nature of American Abundance* (1954)
Advertisement for Green Acres, a Planned Residential Community (1950)
Neil Morgan, *The Footloose Migration* (1961)
George M. Humphrey, *The Interstate Highway System* (1955)
Help Wanted — Women (1957)
Herbert Gans, *Boston's West Enders* (1962)
Visual Document: *What Does Chicago's Renewal Program Mean?* (1963)
Michael Harrington, *The Other America* (1962)
Theodore H. White, *The Television Debates* (1960)
John F. Kennedy, *Inaugural Address* (1961)
Martin Luther King Jr., *Letter from Birmingham Jail* (1963)
Barry Goldwater, *Acceptance Speech at the Republican National Convention* (1964)
Lyndon Johnson, *Address at the University of Michigan* (1964)
The Wilderness Act (1964)

CHAPTER 29

War Abroad and at Home: The Vietnam Era

1961–1975

Chapter Instructional Objectives

After you have taught this chapter, your students should be able to answer the following questions:

1. How and why did America enter the war in Vietnam?

2. What was the relationship between American domestic affairs and the conduct of the Vietnam War?

3. Discuss and analyze the origins, methods, and ambitions of the student movement of the 1960s, and assess its effect on American political, intellectual, and social institutions.

4. Why did racial and civil unrest turn violent during the late 1960s?

5. What did the election of President Nixon and the end of the Vietnam War signal about the nature of American politics in the early 1970s?

Chapter Summary

Beginning in the 1940s, the United States became interested in supporting an anti-Communist government in Vietnam. U.S. policymakers feared that the loss of any pro-Western government would prompt a chain reaction of losses in the region, termed the "domino effect."

President Kennedy increased American involvement in the region, but after his assassination, top U.S. advisors argued that a full-scale deployment was needed in order to prevent the defeat of the South Vietnamese. President Johnson moved toward the Americanization of the war with Operation Rolling Thunder, a protracted bombing campaign that failed to incapacitate the North Vietnamese. A week after the launch of Operation Rolling Thunder, the United States sent its first ground troops into combat. By 1968, more than 536,000 American soldiers were stationed in Vietnam. Hoping to win a war of attrition, the Johnson administration assumed American superiority in personnel and weaponry would ultimately triumph.

Approximately 2.8 million Americans served in Vietnam, at an average age of only nineteen. Until the draft was repealed in 1973, many young American men were conscripted to fight a war they did not support. Black and white sons of the poor and the working class shouldered a disproportionate amount of the fighting. Young men from more affluent backgrounds were more likely to avoid combat through student deferments, medical exemptions, and appointments to the National Guard.

Forced conscription, the length of the conflict, and a lack of clarity about strategy and tactics in Vietnam strengthened the growing antiwar movement at home, which took shape in the form of large-scale protests like "Stop the Draft Week" and the "siege on the Pentagon." Many criticized the government for fighting for democracy abroad while refusing to heed its own constituents at home. Sit-ins and teach-ins to protest of the war became popular on college campuses.

While many citizens mobilized trying to make the government more democratic, a very different movement was taking shape: the counterculture. The "hippie" symbolized this new movement, which glorified the rejection of political, social, and cultural norms. Instead of trying to reinvigorate politics and reform society, the counterculture rejected these outright, preferring to "drop out" instead. Drugs and sex intertwined with music as crucial elements of this rebellion. Ironically, while average, middle-class Americans were horrified by what they viewed as the moral laxity of the counterculture, many came to feel the same sort of disillusionment with the government.

Meanwhile, violent white reaction to racial change and the difficulty of breaking down discriminatory patterns in the North led to an increase in militancy on the part of many young black activists. The frustration and despair of many inner-city blacks led to episodes of racial violence in urban ghettos in the mid-1960s. The black liberation movement proved contagious as Mexican Americans, Native Americans, and homosexuals, among others, organized themselves to pursue legal equality.

A renewed struggle for gender equality also emerged from the protests of the 1960s and 1970s. Energized by the publication of Betty Friedan's *Feminine Mystique* in 1963, the women's rights movement tried to bring women into the mainstream of American economic and political life.

The events of 1968, both foreign and domestic, led to the final collapse of the Roosevelt Democratic coalition. Unable to resolve either the domestic troubles or foreign conflict, Johnson withdrew from the presidential race. Richard Nixon was elected with the support of the "silent majority" and set out to negotiate "peace with honor" in Vietnam. After being reelected in 1972, Nixon brought American involvement in Vietnam to an end. The war had cost the United States more than lives and money. The spirit of the American people had been damaged by the conflict, and American society was at war with itself.

Chapter Annotated Outline

I.   Into the Quagmire, 1945–1968
  A. America in Vietnam: From Truman to Kennedy
    1. Vietnam was once a part of a French colony but was occupied by Japan during Word War II; after the Japanese surrendered in 1945, Ho Chi Minh and the Vietminh proclaimed Vietnam an independent nation.
    2. In 1950, Soviet and Chinese leaders recognized Ho Chi Minh's republic in Vietnam; because France was a NATO ally, the United States and Great Britain recognized the French-installed government of Bao Dai.
    3. Truman and Eisenhower provided military support to the French in Vietnam; Eisenhower argued that aid was necessary in order to prevent non-Communist governments from collapsing in a domino effect.
    4. The 1954 Geneva accords partitioned Vietnam temporarily at the seventeenth parallel and committed France to withdraw its forces from the area north of that line.
    5. To prevent a Communist victory in Vietnam's election, Eisenhower saw to it that a pro-American government took power in South Vietnam under the leadership of Ngo Dinh Diem.
    6. Realizing that the popular Ho Chi Minh would easily win in both the North and South, Diem called off the reunification elections that had been scheduled for 1956, a move the United States supported.
    7. Eisenhower and subsequent U.S. presidents viewed Vietnam as a part of the cold war struggle to contain the Communist threat to the free world; America replaced France as the dominant foreign power in the region.
    8. President Kennedy saw Vietnam as an ideal testing ground for the counterinsurgency techniques that formed the centerpiece of his military policy.
    9. North Vietnam organized opponents in South Vietnam into the National Liberation Front (NLF); Kennedy increased the number of American military advisors but sent no line troops.
    10. American economic aid did little good in South Vietnam, and the NLF's guerrilla forces (Viet Cong) made considerable headway against Diem's regime.
    11. Anti-Diem sentiment flourished among Buddhists who charged the government with religious persecution; as opposition to Diem deepened, Kennedy decided the leader would have to be removed.
    12. Diem was driven from office and assassinated by South Vietnamese officers; America's role in the coup reinforced links between the United States and the new regime in South Vietnam.
  B. Escalation: The Johnson Years
    1. After Kennedy's assassination, top U.S. advisors argued that a full-scale deployment was needed to prevent the defeat of the South Vietnamese.
    2. Johnson knew that he needed congressional support or a declaration of war to commit U.S. troops to an offensive strategy, so he used a deceptive method to secure the Tonkin resolution.
    3. The Johnson administration moved toward the Americanization of the war with Operation Rolling Thunder, a protracted bombing campaign that used three times as many bombs as had fallen in World War II.
    4. The flow of North Vietnamese troops and supplies continued to the south unabated as the Communists quickly rebuilt roads and bridges, moved munitions underground, and built networks of tunnels and shelters.
    5. A week after the launch of Operation Rolling Thunder, the United States sent its first ground troops into combat; by 1968, more than

536,000 American soldiers were stationed in Vietnam.

6. Vietnam's countryside was threatened with destruction; the massive bombardment plus a defoliation campaign seriously damaged agricultural production and thus the economy.

7. Hoping to win a war of attrition, the Johnson administration assumed that American superiority in personnel and weaponry would ultimately triumph.

C. American Soldiers' Perspectives on the War

1. Approximately 2.8 million Americans served in Vietnam, at an average age of only nineteen; some were volunteers, including 7,000 women enlistees.

2. Until 1973 the draft stood as a concrete reminder of the government's impact on the lives of ordinary Americans.

3. Blacks were drafted and died roughly in the same proportion to their share of the draft-age population; black and white sons of the poor and the working class shouldered a disproportionate amount of the fighting.

4. Young men from more affluent backgrounds were more likely to avoid combat through student deferments, medical exemptions, and appointments to the National Guard.

5. Rarely were there large-scale battles, only skirmishes; rather than front lines and conquered territory, there were only daytime operations in the areas the Viet Cong controlled at night.

6. Racism was a fact of everyday life; many soldiers lumped the South Vietnamese and the Viet Cong together in the term *gook*.

7. Fighting and surviving under such harsh conditions took its toll; cynicism and bitterness were common.

8. As Women's Army Corps members (WACs), nurses, and civilians serving with organizations such as the United Service Organizations (USO), women volunteers witnessed death and mutilation on a massive scale.

II. The Cold War Consensus Unravels

A. Public Opinion on Vietnam

1. By the late 1960s, public opinion began to turn against the war in Vietnam; television had much to do with these attitudes.

2. Despite glowing statements made on television, by 1967, many administration officials privately reached a more pessimistic conclusion regarding the war.

3. The administration was accused of suffering from a "credibility gap"; 1966 televised hearings by the Senate Foreign Relations Committee raised further questions about U.S. policy.

4. Economic developments put Johnson and his advisors even more on the defensive; the costs of the war became evident as the growing federal deficit nudged the inflation rate upward.

5. Between 1963 and 1965, peace activists staged periodic protests, vigils, and petition- and letter-writing campaigns against U.S. involvement in the war.

6. Some Americans argued that the war was antithetical to American ideals; that American involvement would not help the Vietnamese; and that the goal of an independent, anti-Communist South Vietnam was unattainable.

B. Student Activism

1. The Students for a Democratic Society (SDS), disillusioned with the consumer culture and the gulf between the prosperous and the poor, also rejected cold war ideology and foreign policy.

2. The founders of SDS referred to themselves as the "New Left" to distinguish themselves from the "Old Left" of Communists and Socialists of the 1930s and 1940s.

3. At the University of California at Berkeley, the Free Speech Movement organized a sit-in in response to administrators' attempts to ban political activity on campus.

4. When Johnson escalated the war in 1965, University of Michigan students organized a teach-in, abandoning their classes and debating the aspects of the nation's involvement in the war.

5. The Selective Service abolished student deferment in 1966; in public demonstrations, opponents of the war burned their draft cards and closed down induction centers.

6. Much of the universities' research budget came from Defense Department contracts; students demanded that the Reserve Officer Training Corps be removed from college campuses.

7. The Johnson administration had to face the reality of large-scale opposition with protests like "Stop the Draft Week" and the "siege on the Pentagon."

C. The Rise of the Counterculture

1. The "hippie" symbolized the new counterculture, a youthful movement that glorified liberation from traditional social strictures.

2. Popular music by Pete Seeger, Joan Baez, and Bob Dylan expressed political idealism, protest, and loss of patience with the war and was an important part of the counterculture.

3. Beatlemania helped to deepen generational divides, and the Rolling Stones' songs addressed

sexual openness and made fun of the consumer culture.

4. Drugs and sex intertwined with music as a crucial element of the youth culture; the Woodstock Music and Art Fair was heralded as the birth of the "Woodstock nation" in August 1969.

5. Many young people stayed out of the counterculture and the antiwar movement, yet to adults, it seemed that all of American youth were rejecting political, social, and cultural norms.

D. The Widening Struggle for Civil Rights

1. Once the system of legal segregation had fallen, the civil rights movement turned to the difficult task of eliminating *de facto* segregation, especially in the South.

2. Desegregation of schools in the South began two decades before federal judges extended it to schools in the rest of the country.

3. Black separatism was revived by a religious group known as the Black Muslims, an organization that stressed black pride, unity, and self-help and was hostile to whites.

4. The Black Muslims' most charismatic figure, Malcolm X, advocated militant protest and separatism, although he condoned the use of violence only for self-defense.

5. Malcolm X eventually broke with the Nation of Islam and was assassinated by three Black Muslims while delivering a speech in Harlem in 1965.

6. A more secular black nationalist movement calling for "Black Power" emerged in 1966; the Black Panthers organization was founded to protect blacks from police violence.

7. Many young blacks insisted on usage of Afro-American rather than Negro, and they wore African clothing and hairstyles to awaken interest in black history, art, and literature.

8. White Americans became wary when blacks began demanding immediate access to higher-paying jobs, housing, and education, along with increased political power.

9. Racial riots over police brutality against blacks caused death, destruction of property, and looting in cities across the United States beginning in 1964.

10. The National Advisory Commission on Civil Disorders released a report on the riots and warned that the nation was moving toward two separate and unequal societies: one black, one white.

11. Martin Luther King Jr. was assassinated in Memphis, Tennessee, by James Earl Ray, setting

off another explosion of urban rioting in more than 100 cities.

E. The Legacy of the Civil Rights Movement

1. Segregation was overturned in the 1960s; federal legislation ensured protection of black Americans' civil rights; southern blacks were enfranchised; and black candidates were allowed to enter the political arena.

2. In 1986, Martin Luther King Jr.'s birthday became a national holiday.

3. African Americans' struggle toward civil rights provided a fresh and innovative model for other groups seeking to expand their rights.

4. The situation of Mexican Americans changed when the Mexican American Political Association (MAPA) mobilized support for Kennedy, who in return appointed Mexican American leaders to posts in Washington.

5. Younger Mexican Americans coined the term "Chicano" and organized a new political party, *La Raza Unida* (The United Race), to promote Chicano political interests.

6. Chicano strategists also pursued economic objectives; César Chávez organized the United Farm Workers (UFW), the first union to represent migrant workers successfully.

7. The National Council of American Indians lobbied for improvement of social conditions for Native Americans; Native Americans suffered from high levels of unemployment, poverty, inadequate housing, and inadequate education.

8. As a method of protest, Native Americans seized and occupied Alcatraz for over a year. Later, protesters occupied the Federal Bureau of Indian Affairs in Washington.

9. Native American activism by the leaders of the American Indian Movement (AIM) at Wounded Knee helped to alienate many whites, but it spurred government action on tribal issues.

10. The civil rights movement also sparked a new awareness among some predominantly white groups: the elderly, people of various ethnic backgrounds, and homosexuals.

11. After the 1969 "Stonewall riot," gay activists formed advocacy groups, newspapers, and political organizations in order to challenge discrimination and to offer emotional support for gays who "came out."

F. The Revival of Feminism

1. The black struggle became an inspiration for young feminists in the 1960s, but social and demographic changes also led to the revival of feminism.

2. By 1970, 42.6 percent of women were working, and 40 percent of working women were married.

3. During the baby boom, many women dropped out of college to marry and raise families; by 1970, 41 percent of college students were female.

4. The birth control pill and the intrauterine device (IUD) helped women to control their fertility, and more liberal divorce laws witnessed the increase of divorce rates.

5. As a result of these changes, traditional gender expectations were dramatically altered; the changing social realities created a major constituency for the emerging women's movement of the 1960s.

6. A report by the Presidential Commission on the Status of Women in 1963 documented the discrimination women faced in employment and education.

7. Betty Friedan's *Feminine Mystique* gave women a vocabulary with which to express their dissatisfaction and promoted women's self-realization.

8. The Civil Rights Act of 1964 had as great an impact on women as it did on blacks; its Title VII eventually became a powerful tool against sex discrimination.

9. Dissatisfied with the Equal Employment Opportunity Commission's (EEOC) reluctance to defend women's rights, Friedan and others founded the National Organization for Women (NOW) in 1966.

10. The women's liberationists came to the women's movement through their civil rights work; male leaders' lack of respect for women radicals caused them to see the need for their own movement.

11. Women's lib encouraged women to throw away all symbols of female oppression: hair curlers, girdles, bras, etc. "The personal is political" became their slogan.

12. By 1970, a growing convergence of interests began to blur the distinction between women's rights and women's liberation.

III. The Long Road Home, 1968–1975
  A. 1968: A Year of Shocks
    1. The Johnson administration's hopes for Vietnam evaporated when the Viet Cong unleashed a massive assault, known as the Tet offensive, on major urban areas in South Vietnam.
    2. The attack made a mockery of official pronouncements that the United States was winning the war and swung public opinion more strongly against the conflict.

3. Antiwar Senator Eugene J. McCarthy's strong showing in the presidential primaries reflected profound public dissatisfaction with the course of the war.

4. On March 31, 1968, Johnson stunned the nation by announcing that he would not seek reelection; he vowed to devote his remaining months in office to the search for peace, and peace talks began in May 1968.

5. That year, the nation suffered through the assassination of Martin Luther King Jr., the ensuing riots, student unrest, and the assassination of Robert Kennedy.

6. The Democratic Party never fully recovered from Johnson's withdrawal and Robert Kennedy's assassination.

7. At the Democratic convention, "yippies" diverted attention from the more serious and more numerous antiwar activists who came to Chicago as delegates or volunteers.

8. In what was later described as a "police riot," patrolmen attacked protestors at the convention with Mace, teargas, and clubs as demonstrators chanted "The whole world is watching!"

9. Democrats dispiritedly nominated Hubert H. Humphrey and approved a platform that endorsed continued fighting in Vietnam while diplomatic means to an end were explored.

10. The turmoil surrounding the New Left and the antiwar movement strengthened support for "law and order"; many Americans were fed up with protest and dissent.

11. George Wallace, a third-party candidate, skillfully combined attacks on liberal intellectuals and government elites with denunciations of school segregation and forced busing.

12. Richard Nixon tapped the increasingly conservative mood of the electorate and made an amazing political comeback, winning the 1968 Republican presidential nomination.

13. On October 31, 1968, Johnson announced a complete halt to the bombing of North Vietnam; Nixon countered by intimating that he had a plan for the end of the war, although he did not.

14. The closeness of the 1968 election suggested how polarized American society had become, and Nixon appealed to the "silent majority."

  B. Nixon's War
    1. When intensified bombing in Cambodia (unknown to the American public) failed to end the war, Nixon and Henry Kissinger adopted a policy of Vietnamization.

2. Antiwar demonstrators denounced the new policy, which protected American lives at the expense of the Vietnamese.

3. Nixon insisted that he would not be swayed by mounting protests; during the march on Washington, he barricaded himself in the White House and watched football.

4. An American incursion into Cambodia to destroy enemy havens was only a short-term setback for the North Vietnamese but helped to destabilize the country, exposing it to takeover by the Khmer Rouge later in the 1970s.

5. After the Kent State slayings and the killings at Jackson State College, Americans polled said that campus unrest was the issue that troubled them most.

6. In June 1970 the Senate expressed its disapproval for the war by repealing the Tonkin resolution and cutting off funding for operations in Cambodia.

7. The antiwar movement declined due to internal divisions and because Nixon's Vietnamization policy reduced the number of soldiers in combat.

C. Withdrawal from Vietnam and Détente

1. Nixon's policy of détente was to seek peaceful coexistence with the communist Soviet Union and China and to link these overtures of friendship with a plan to end the Vietnam War.

2. Nixon traveled to China in 1972 in a symbolic visit that set the stage for the establishment of formal diplomatic relations.

3. He then traveled to Moscow to sign the first Strategic Arms Limitation Treaty (SALT) between the United States and the Soviet Union.

4. The treaty signified that the United States could no longer afford massive military spending to regain the nuclear and military superiority it had enjoyed after World War II.

5. In late 1971, as American troops withdrew, Communist forces stepped up their attacks on Laos, Cambodia, and South Vietnam.

6. After yet another North Vietnamese offensive against South Vietnam, Nixon ordered B-52 bombings against North Vietnam and the mining of North Vietnamese ports.

7. With the help of a cease-fire agreement, Nixon won a resounding victory in the 1972 elections; however, the peace initiative stalled when South Vietnam rejected a provision concerning North Vietnamese troop positions.

8. Nixon stepped up the military actions with the "Christmas bombings"; the Paris Peace accords were signed on January 27, 1973.

9. The accords did not fulfill Nixon's promise of "peace with honor," but they did call for the withdrawal of American troops, and for most Americans, that was enough.

10. The South Vietnamese government soon fell to Communist forces; horrified Americans watched as American embassy personnel and Vietnamese citizens struggled to board helicopters leaving Saigon before North Vietnamese troops entered the city.

D. The Legacy of Vietnam

1. The Vietnam War occupied American administrations for nearly thirty years; U.S. troops fought the war for over eleven years, from 1961 to 1973.

2. Some 58,000 U.S. troops died in Vietnam, and another 300,000 were wounded.

3. In Southeast Asia the war claimed an estimated 1.5 million Vietnamese lives and devastated the country's physical and economic structure.

4. More than 30,000 Amerasians arrived in the United States in the 1990s.

5. The defeat in Vietnam prompted Americans to think differently about foreign affairs and to acknowledge the limits of U.S. power abroad.

6. The war shattered the liberal consensus that had supported the Democratic coalition.

7. The deception regarding American successes in Vietnam bred a deep distrust of government among American citizens and paved the way for a conservative mood and the resurgence of the Republican Party.

Lecture Strategies

1. Students should understand how the cold war policy of containment created the conditions that led to the Vietnam War. The Vietnamese struggle for independence against the Japanese and then the French provides the backdrop for increasing U.S. involvement in Indochina. The implications of establishing an independent non-Communist South Vietnam, whose safety would be guaranteed by American power, need to be pointed out. The failures of successive South Vietnamese governments to win the allegiance of the people meant that the United States had to supply more force to overcome resistance in the countryside. Explore the reasons that Johnson sharply escalated the war after his election to a full term as president in 1964.

2. Examine how the student movement emerged in the 1960s out of the "silent generation." Note the influence of the civil rights movement from which some student leaders emerged. Which developments in the Vietnam War energized the protest movement on

campuses? Why did a segment of the student movement turn to violence in order to achieve its goals?

3. Students often confuse activist movements of the 1960s with the counterculture that emerged during this period. Evaluate the ethos of the counterculture and show how distinct it was from movements such as the Students for a Democratic Society. Demonstrate how one movement embraced political action while the other rejected it outright.

4. Identify the sources of the backlash against the reform movements of the 1960s and 1970s. Note the way the "black power" slogan alienated some white supporters of civil rights. Violence in the antiwar movement, however slight, fostered militant suppression of that movement (at the 1968 Democratic convention in Chicago, for example). Note how the successes of feminism drew a sharp reaction from supporters of the traditional patriarchal structure of society.

5. What gave rise to the urban riots of the mid-1960s? Why did they occur so soon after the federal government had passed civil rights and voting rights acts? Note that the major riots were triggered by real or perceived episodes of police brutality. Mention the role of civil and military authorities in suppressing the uprisings. What did the Commission on Civil Disorders conclude about the direction of race relations in urban America? Why did the rioters burn down their own neighborhoods?

6. Compare and contrast the women's rights and women's liberation movements. Note the shared goals and different methods. Identify the major sources of the two movements. What role did the civil rights movement play in generating the notion that "the personal is political"? Identify the achievements of the feminist movement of the 1960s and 1970s.

7. Why was 1968 a critical year in American history? Students should be led through the decisive events of that year — the Tet offensive, the assassinations of Martin Luther King Jr. and Robert Kennedy, the Democratic convention in Chicago — and shown the impact they had on domestic and foreign policy.

8. The method by which Nixon got the United States out of the Vietnam War should be explained. Note that "Vietnamization" allowed American troops to be withdrawn without acknowledging defeat. But the expansion of the bombing and the raids on Cambodia spurred antiwar activity and led to the killings at Kent State. After his reelection in 1972, Nixon pursued the peace talks, and after the "Christmas bombings" of 1972, he arranged for a cease-fire and the

total withdrawal of U.S. troops in exchange for the return of prisoners of war. Left undefended, South Vietnam was soon overrun by the North, and the country was united under Communist rule. By that time, however, the United States was so relieved to get out of the war that few people complained.

Class Discussion Starters

1. **What factors contributed to the rise of black militancy?**

Possible answers:
   a. The assassinations of Malcolm X and Martin Luther King Jr. elicited rage in the African American community.
   b. The continuation of violent activities against civil rights activists.
   c. The difficulty of breaking down patterns of racial discrimination outside the South.
   d. The rise of a new generation of black activists who adopted the black power slogan and organized groups such as the Black Panthers.
   e. Real and perceived episodes of police brutality in both the North and South.

2. **Compare and contrast the women's rights movement and the women's liberation movement.**

Possible answers:
   a. The women's liberation movement attracted young social activists; whereas women's rights activists tended to be professional women.
   b. Women's liberation focused on consciousness raising; whereas the women's rights movement fought for equality in public and commercial life.
   c. Women's liberation activists tended to be more antimale than were advocates of women's rights.
   d. Both groups had gender equality as a goal.
   e. Both groups supported programs for adequate day care facilities, awareness of female health issues, and reproductive freedom.

3. **What changes in American society were achieved by the social reform movements of the 1960s and 1970s?**

Possible answers:
   a. *De jure* racial segregation ended, and *de facto* segregation was challenged.
   b. The inaction of the "silent generation" of college students gave way to widespread student activism that changed the rules at colleges and helped to end American participation in the Vietnam War.
   c. The counterculture led to new forms of popular music, alterations in sexual behavior, and a relaxation of clothing styles.
   d. Feminism began to challenge patterns of patri-

archy, and women began to play a more important role in education, business, and politics.

e. Many oppressed groups (Mexican Americans, Native Americans, and homosexuals, for example) became organized in the process of challenging their status in American society.

4. **What impact did the Vietnam War have on the political career of Lyndon Johnson?**

Possible answers:

a. It destroyed the liberal consensus that had supported Johnson's Great Society programs.

b. Antiwar activists vigorously condemned Johnson's war policy; he reacted by strengthening those policies and holding to them more steadfastly.

c. Leading members of Johnson's own party in Congress began to question his policies, reducing his congressional mandate.

d. His alliance with civil rights leaders collapsed when they began to oppose his war policies.

e. Johnson decided that he had enough and withdrew from the 1968 presidential race after attempting to set a peace process in motion.

5. **What accounts for the emergence of student activism in the 1960s?**

Possible answers:

a. A feeling of alienation from the cold war policies of the federal government.

b. The increasingly bureaucratic nature of the large "multiversities" they attended.

c. The lack of participatory democracy in managing the affairs of the nation.

d. Their growing awareness of the possibility of social change exemplified by the civil rights movement.

e. Opposition to the draft and the escalation of the Vietnam War.

6. **How did the counterculture manifest itself?**

Possible answers:

a. Hippies dressed in unconventional styles and let their hair grow.

b. Traditional folk music developed into psychedelic rock.

c. Hallucinogenic drugs were widely used to expand people's consciousness.

d. Many in the counterculture "dropped out" of middle-class society by forming rural and urban communes.

e. A sexual revolution took place in which young people challenged middle-class morality.

7. **What was the impact of the 1968 Tet offensive on the American war effort?**

Possible answers:

a. It showed that the U.S. military leadership in Vietnam had not been accurate in its predictions of imminent victory.

b. It showed that the North Vietnamese and Viet Cong were able to launch an offensive throughout South Vietnam despite the presence of 500,000 American troops, leading U.S. generals to call for reinforcements.

c. The disillusionment of Americans at this development began to shift public opinion against continuing the war.

d. Even though the offensive was broken and the North Vietnamese and Viet Cong forces were driven back, the suddenness and ferocity of the attack weakened American morale.

e. The request for more troops in the aftermath of the offensive finally made it clear to President Johnson that the war was unwinnable and that he had to rethink his Southeast Asia policy.

8. **What factors contributed to the election of Richard Nixon in 1968?**

Possible answers:

a. The dissension spurred in the Democratic Party by the violence at the nominating convention.

b. Disillusionment with the Democratic war policy and the potential of Nixon's "secret plan" to win the war.

c. Backlash against the social reforms of activists allied with the Democrats.

d. Appeals to the "silent majority."

e. The "southern strategy" of the Nixon campaign, which was designed to break the hold of the Democrats on the South.

f. The loss of Lyndon Johnson and Robert Kennedy as leaders of the Democratic Party.

9. **What policies were adopted by the Nixon administration in order to extricate the United States from the Vietnam War?**

Possible answers:

a. "Vietnamization" called for the gradual withdrawal of American troops, leaving the fighting to be done by the army of South Vietnam.

b. An increase in bombing during the withdrawal period.

c. The "secret war" in Cambodia was expanded without Congress or the public being informed.

d. The "Christmas bombing" of 1972 was ordered to shore up the regime in South Vietnam and prompt resumption of peace talks.

e. A cease-fire was signed in January 1973, calling for the removal of all U.S. troops in exchange for the release of American prisoners of war by the North Vietnamese.

Chapter Writing Assignments

1. Why did the United States get involved in the Vietnam War? How was America's involvement in Vietnam tied to the cold war?

2. What factors contributed to the rise of antiwar sentiment among the American public during the Johnson administration? What factors affected different segments of the American people?

3. Explain the reasons for student protests in the 1960s and early 1970s. What impact did student activism have on university programs, popular culture, and Vietnam War policy?

4. Discuss the long-range influence of elements of the counterculture on American life. Consider issues of style, music, dress, morals, and so forth.

5. What were the critical events of 1968 that have caused historians to refer to it as a "watershed year"? Evaluate the changes in the mood of the American people that ensued.

6. Explore how American servicemen and women viewed the war. What was the "Vietnam syndrome," and how did it come to exist? How were veterans received when they returned home, and did the response of the American public to the war affect veterans' perspectives of their experiences?

7. Outline the main strategies pursued by the civil rights movement (legal challenges, legislative reform, nonviolent protests, and so on). What were the principal accomplishments of each strategy? Why did the civil rights movement stall in the 1970s?

8. Was the women's rights or women's liberation movement more successful? Explain.

Document Exercises

AMERICAN VOICES

Dave Cline: A Vietnam Vet Remembers (p. 855)

Document Discussion

1. **How did Cline's stateside experiences differ from what he experienced in Vietnam?**
(During his initial military training in the United States, Cline had been told that America's mission in Vietnam was noble. The United States was committed to assisting the people of South Vietnam in their fight against Communist aggression. Once in Viet-

nam, however, Cline was told that all of the Vietnamese were contemptible. Cline observed the difficult social, political, and economic conditions of Southeast Asia first-hand and realized America was involved in a complex war.)

2. **How significant is the fact that the impression Cline was given at Fort Dix differed greatly from what he actually experienced in Vietnam?**
(To a certain extent, formalized training of soldiers in the United States prior to being committed to combat has always contained a measure of political rhetoric and a sanitized, institutional view of the situation. Soldiers in the combat zone, moreover, frequently adopt a very hard-nosed pragmatism that emphasizes individual and small-unit perseverance and survival. Cline's experience also points to the inherent complexity and ambiguities surrounding counterinsurgency wars such as the one in Vietnam.)

Writing Assignments

1. How did Cline react to the firefight with the enemy in which he killed a young North Vietnamese soldier?

2. What obligations does American society have to soldiers like Cline who have served and killed on behalf of the nation?

VOICES FROM ABROAD

Che Guevara: Vietnam and the World Freedom Struggle (p. 859)

Document Discussion

1. **What "strategic goal" did Guevara seek?**
(Guevara asserts that America is an imperialist power, systematically exploiting other nations for its own benefit. He accuses America of forcing its will on Vietnam, not liberating its people. Guevara's goal is a "real liberation" of the world's people, self-determination that can only come through armed struggle.)

2. **How did Guevara describe the responsibilities of the peoples of the developing world?**
(Guevara asserts that the "oppressed peoples" must eliminate "the bases sustaining imperialism." Thus it is up to the people to organize and overthrow oppression. Guevara also says that socialist revolution is the best means for achieving this.)

Writing Assignments

1. Why did Guevara's predictions of Marxist Revolution fail to come true?

2. What solutions did Guevara provide to resolve the conflicts he describes?

AMERICAN VOICES

Mary Crow Dog: The Trail of Broken Treaties (p. 864)

Document Discussion

1. **What tactic did Native Americans borrow from the student protest movement?**
    (The occupation of the Bureau of Indian Affairs headquarters and the presentation of demands proceeded in a manner similar to other student protests. Crow Dog indicates that her colleagues conducted very little planning but nonetheless shared a conviction that their actions would somehow result in positive results for their movement.)

2. **What is the value of a "moral victory" such as the one described by Mary Crow Dog?**
    (According to Crow Dog's testimony, the Indians failed to win any concrete demands but considered their campaign victorious because they had confronted federal power and had not backed down. This kind of victory can enhance the self-esteem of protesters and raise public consciousness of the cause.)

Writing Assignments

1. What did Crow Dog's protest seek to achieve? Were other avenues available to better meet Native Americans' objectives?

2. What policies does the federal government have today for dealing with its relationship with Native Americans, both on and off reservations?

AMERICAN LIVES

John Paul Vann: Dissident Patriot (p. 874)

Document Discussion

1. **How did Vann and American journalists in Vietnam interact?**
    (Vann leaked studies critical of military operations to journalists, and they provided him with an anonymous outlet for his views. In doing this, Vann furthered his policies, which contradicted the official position of the American government. Journalists sought to advance their professional standing by publishing coveted news and information.)

2. **What did Vann think was preventing the United States from winning the war?**
    (He felt that the bombing of South Vietnam was keeping the peasants from rallying to the American side and that continued corruption in the Saigon government denied it legitimacy among the people of South Vietnam.)

Writing Assignments

1. Describe the ways in which Vann's experiences in Vietnam reflected the contradictions in American military policy.

2. To what degree was the conduct of the war in Vietnam the responsibility of General Westmoreland versus civilian policymakers and political leaders?

Skill-Building Map Exercises

Map 29.1: The Vietnam War, 1954–1975 (p. 851)

1. **What does this map tell you about the difficulty of defending Saigon against North Vietnamese forces?**
    (The North Vietnamese army infiltrated far into the South along the Ho Chi Minh Trail and could strike at Saigon easily from within Cambodia.)

2. **What is significant about the location of the Ho Chi Minh Trail?**
    (The trail runs through Laos and Cambodia, not Vietnam. This meant that the North Vietnamese could use the trail with greater freedom from American firepower. The United States attacked the trail, but because it was not within the borders of Vietnam, American ability to intervene was limited.)

Map 29.2: Racial Unrest in America's Cities, 1965–1968 (p. 862)

1. **Why did most riots break out in cities?**
    (American cities contained concentrations of minority residents. They could organize themselves and unite for concerted action near their homes and workplaces where they regularly met to discuss their situations. They knew, as well, that they could attract the most media attention in the larger cities.)

2. **Why does the map show a big part of the central United States as being largely without riots?**
    (African Americans led and comprised the largest ethnic group who participated in the riots. Hence, the riots occurred in areas containing higher percentages of African Americans. Fewer African Ameri-

cans lived in the northern plains and mountain regions of the United States.)

Topic for Research

The Vietnam War

In many ways, Vietnam became an American war, fought for American aims. You have read about the war from the perspective of policymakers caught up in the cold war and trying to maintain American credibility and from the perspective of the American soldiers sent to "Nam." Yet those with the largest stake in the contest were the Vietnamese people themselves. How does the war look from the Vietnamese perspective(s)? Who supported the insurgents, and who supported the American-backed governments? What roles did religion and agriculture have in shaping loyalties? What is the relation between the kind of nationalistic communism practiced by Ho Chi Minh and Soviet (or Chinese) communism? What meaning would American democracy, however defined, have in a country such as Vietnam?

Several books concentrate on the Vietnamese. An excellent introduction is Frances Fitzgerald, *Fire in the Lake: The Vietnamese and the Americans in Vietnam* (1972), especially Part I. The writings of French journalist Bernard Fall are also insightful, including *The Two Vietnams* (1963), *Vietnam Witness, 1953–1966* (1966), and *Last Reflections on a War* (1967). Phillip B. Davidson, *Vietnam at War* (1988), offers a comprehensive examination of the conflict. Marilyn Young, *The Vietnam Wars, 1945–1990* (1991), treats the Vietnamese and American sides with equal weight. Jeffrey P. Kimball, *To Reason Why: The Debate about the Causes of U.S. Involvement in the Vietnam War* (1990), is a collection of speeches and essays on the reasons for U.S. involvement. Eric Bergerud, *Red Thunder, Tropic Lightning* (1993) presents a history of the war from the perspective of the soldiers of the army's 25th Infantry Division.

How to Use the Ancillaries Available with *America's History*

Refer to the Preface to *America's History* at the front of the book for descriptions of instructor resources, including the Instructor's Resource CD-ROM, Computerized Test Bank, transparencies, and *Using the Bedford Series in History and Culture in the U.S. History Survey*. Student resources, also described in the Preface, include the Online Study Guide and *Documents to Accompany* America's History, a primary-source reader.

For Instructors

Using the Bedford Series in History and Culture in the U.S. History Survey
This brief online guide by Scott Hovey provides practical suggestions for incorporating volumes from the highly regarded Bedford Series in History and Culture into your survey course. Titles that complement the material covered in Chapter 29 include *Lyndon B. Johnson and American Liberalism: A Brief Biography with Documents*, by Bruce J. Schulman; *My Lai: A Brief History with Documents*, by James S. Olson and Randy Roberts; *Postwar Immigrant America: A Social History*, by Reed Ueda; and *Women's Magazines, 1940–1960: Gender Roles and the Popular Press*, by Nancy A. Walker. For descriptions of these titles and how you might use them in your course, visit **bedfordstmartins.com/usingseries.**

For Students

Online Study Guide at bedfordstmartins.com/henretta
Each of the activities listed below includes short-answer questions. After submitting their answers, students can compare them to the model answers provided.

Map Activity
The map activity presents Map 29.2: Racial Unrest in America's Cities, 1965–1968 (p. 862), and asks students to analyze the widespread riots that erupted during the "long hot summers" of the 1960s.

Visual Activity
The visual activity presents a photograph of John Paul Vann (p. 875) and asks students to analyze the importance of photography during the Vietnam War.

Reading Historical Documents
The document activity provides a brief introduction to the documents Dave Cline: A Vietnam Vet Remembers (p. 855) and Mary Crow Dog: The Trail of Broken Treaties (p. 864) and asks students to analyze their content, thinking critically about the sources.

Documents to Accompany *America's History*
Each of the documents listed is introduced by a headnote, which places the document in context, and is followed by questions, which help students to analyze the piece.

Sources for Chapter 29 are
The Gulf of Tonkin Resolution (1964)
Lyndon Johnson, *Peace without Conquest* (1965)
Philip Caputo, *The Splendid Little War* (1965)
Students for a Democratic Society, *The Port Huron Statement* (1962)

Martin Luther King Jr., *Joining the Antiwar Movement* (1967)

Malcolm X and Yusef Iman, *Black Nationalism* (1964)

Inés Hernández, *Para Teresa*

DRUMS Committee of the Menominee, *The Consequences of Termination for the Menominee of Wisconsin* (1971)

National Organization for Women, *Statement of Purpose* (1966)

Richard Nixon, *Vietnamization and the Nixon Doctrine* (1969)

Richard Nixon, *The Invasion of Cambodia* (1970)

Lynda Van Devanter, *Coming Home* (1983)

Eleanor Wimbish, *A Mother Remembers Her Son at "The Wall"* (1984)

CHAPTER 30

The Lean Years
1969–1980

Chapter Instructional Objectives

After you have taught this chapter, your students should be able to answer the following questions:

1. How and why did America experience a severe economic crisis in the 1970s?

2. What effect did Nixon's presidency have on domestic politics?

3. How did expanding social activism lead to a conservative reaction at the end of the decade?

4. Why did President Carter fail to develop an effective style of leadership? How did foreign affairs affect his administration?

Chapter Summary

President Nixon, elected with the support of the "silent majority," adopted policies that heralded a long-term Republican effort to trim back the Great Society. He easily won reelection in 1972 with 61 percent of the popular vote, although Democrats maintained control of both houses of Congress.

The Watergate scandal was a direct result of Nixon's ruthless political tactics, his secretive style of governing, and his obsession with the antiwar movement. On August 9, 1974, facing certain conviction in a Senate trial, Nixon became the first U.S. president to resign. Vice President Gerald Ford was sworn in as president; a month later, he granted a full pardon to Nixon. The most significant legacy of Watergate was the wave of cynicism that swept the country in its wake.

After twenty-five years of world leadership, the economic dominance of the United States had begun to fade. The decline was exemplified by an energy crisis brought

on by the Organization of Petroleum Exporting Countries (OPEC) oil embargo. Due to a steadily growing federal deficit and spiraling inflation — coupled with a reduced demand for American goods — the United States posted its first trade deficit in almost a century. As the nation experienced deindustrialization, tens of thousands of workers became unemployed, and the standard of living declined.

After 1970, many baby boomers left the counterculture behind and settled down to pursue careers and material goods. The "Me Decade" saw an emphasis on physical fitness and personal enrichment. Despite the growing self-absorption, some were still committed to social and political change. Gender issues such as the Equal Rights Amendment (ERA) and abortion energized the women's movement. Although the civil rights movement was in disarray by the late 1960s, minority group protests over the next decade continued to win social and economic gains. Native Americans realized some of the most significant changes with the 1971 Alaska Native Claims Act and the Indian Self-Determination Act of 1974. The court-mandated busing of children in order to achieve school desegregation proved to be the most disruptive social issue of the 1970s. Affirmative action, which had expanded opportunities for African Americans and Latinos, also proved divisive. Activists for the various causes were part of a "rights revolution," a movement in the 1960s and 1970s to bring the issues of social justice and welfare to the forefront of public policy.

Vocal opposition to abortion, busing, affirmative action, gay rights ordinances, and the ERA, constituted a broad backlash against the social changes rooted in previous decade. The economic changes of the 1970s further fueled the "politics of resentment," a grassroots revolt against special-interest groups and the growing expenditures on social welfare. The rising popularity of evangelical religion also fueled the conservative resurgence of the 1970s. The extensive media and fund-raising networks of the Christian right became the organizational base for a larger conservative movement known as the "New Right," which wanted to limit the power of the federal government and a reverse declining social morality.

The Ford presidency passed largely without incident except for the recession of 1975, brought on by Federal Reserve actions to control soaring inflation. President Carter was unable to halt inflation, typifying the ineffectiveness of his administration. Although Carter's foreign-policy goals were promising, his achievements were limited to establishing peace between Egypt and Israel and the Panama Canal treaty. Carter's failure to resolve the Iranian hostage crisis convinced the American public of his ineffectiveness, which cost him the 1980 election. Ronald Reagan, his successor, won a decisive victory by promising to make America the dominant world power it had been at the peak of the cold war.

Chapter Annotated Outline

I.   The Nixon Years
A. The Republican Domestic Agenda
1. Nixon's policies heralded a long-term Republican effort to trim back the Great Society and shift some federal responsibilities back to the states.
2. The 1972 revenue-sharing program distributed a portion of federal tax revenues back to the states as block grants.
3. Nixon reduced funding for most War on Poverty programs and dismantled the Office of Economic Opportunity in 1971.
4. He impounded billions of dollars appropriated by Congress for urban renewal, pollution control, and other environmental issues.
5. Nixon agreed to the growth of major entitlement programs such as Medicare, Medicaid, and Social Security.
6. In 1970, Nixon signed a bill establishing the Environmental Protection Agency (EPA), and in 1972, he approved legislation creating the Occupational Safety and Health Administration (OSHA).
7. Nixon demonstrated his commitment to conservative social values most clearly with his appointments to the Supreme Court.
8. The Court appointees sometimes handed down decisions of which Nixon did not approve, such as court-ordered busing and restrictions on the implementation of capital punishment.
9. *Roe v. Wade* (1973) struck down laws prohibiting abortion in Texas and Georgia.

B. The 1972 Election
1. Disarray within the Democratic Party over Vietnam and civil rights gave Nixon's campaign a decisive edge.
2. Nixon's opponent, Senator George McGovern, ran a poorly orchestrated campaign and was far too liberal for many traditional Democrats.
3. Nixon took advantage of his national position; his policy of Vietnamization had virtually eliminated American combat deaths by 1972.
4. An improving economy also favored the Republican Party; Nixon easily won reelection with 61 percent of the popular vote, although Democrats maintained control of both houses of Congress.
C. Watergate
1. Watergate was a direct result of Nixon's ruthless political tactics, his secretive style of governing, and his obsession with the antiwar movement.
2. The *Pentagon Papers* was a classified study of American involvement in Vietnam that detailed many American blunders and misjudgments; it was given to the media by Daniel Ellsberg.
3. In an effort to discredit Ellsberg, a former Defense Department analyst, White House underlings broke into his psychiatrist's office to look for damaging information.
4. The White House established a clandestine intelligence group known as the "plumbers" to plug government information leaks.
5. The "plumbers" used government agencies to harass opponents of the administration; their actions were illegally funded by Nixon's Committee to Re-Elect the President (CREEP).
6. In June 1972, five men were arrested for breaking into the headquarters of the Democratic National Committee at the Watergate apartment complex in Washington.
7. The White House denied any involvement in the break-in, but investigations revealed that Nixon ordered his chief of staff to instruct the CIA to tell the FBI not to probe too deeply into connections between the White House and the burglars.
8. When the burglars were convicted in January 1973, Nixon approved of offering them money in return for their continued silence and possibly even pardons.
9. The Senate voted to establish a select committee to investigate the scandal after one of the burglars began to "talk."
10. In April, Nixon accepted the resignations of several of his closest advisors, and he fired

White House Council John Dean after he offered testimony in exchange for immunity.

11. In May, the Senate Watergate committee began nationally televised hearings; an aide revealed the existence of a secret taping system in the Oval Office.

12. Nixon eventually released heavily edited transcripts of the tapes; there was a suspicious eighteen-minute gap in the tape of a crucial meeting of Nixon, Haldeman, and Ehrlichman on June 20, 1972, three days after the break-in.

13. On June 30, 1974, the House of Representatives voted on three articles of impeachment against Nixon: obstruction of justice, abuse of power, and subverting the Constitution.

14. Nixon released the unexpurgated tapes, which contained evidence that he ordered a cover-up; facing certain conviction in a Senate trial, Nixon became the first U.S. president to resign, on August 9, 1974.

15. Vice President Gerald Ford was sworn in as president; a month later, he granted a full pardon to Nixon.

16. In 1974, a strengthened Freedom of Information Act gave citizens greater access to files that federal government agencies had amassed on them.

17. The Fair Campaign Practices Act of 1974 limited campaign contributions and provided for stricter accountability and public financing of presidential campaigns; unfortunately, it left a loophole for contributions from political action committees (PACs).

18. The most significant legacy of Watergate was the wave of cynicism that swept the country in its wake.

II. An Economy of Diminished Expectations
   A. Energy Crisis
      1. After twenty-five years of world leadership, the economic dominance of the United States had begun to fade.
      2. By the late 1960s the United States was buying more and more oil on the world market to keep up with shrinking domestic reserves and growing demand.
      3. The imported oil came primarily from the Middle East; four Middle Eastern states along with Venezuela were the source of more than 80 percent of the world's crude oil exports.
      4. Between 1973 and 1975, OPEC raised the price of a barrel of oil from $3 to $12; by the end of the decade the price was at $34 a barrel.
      5. In 1973, OPEC instituted an oil embargo against the United States, Western Europe, and Japan in retaliation for their aid to Israel during the Yom Kippur War.
      6. The embargo lasted until 1974 and forced Americans to curtail their driving or spend hours in line at the pumps.
      7. As Americans turned to more fuel-efficient foreign-made cars, the domestic auto industry slumped, profoundly affecting the American economy and the American psyche.
   B. Economic Woes
      1. Due to a steadily growing federal deficit and spiraling inflation — coupled with a reduced demand for American goods — in 1971 the dollar fell to its lowest level on the world market since 1949, and the United States posted its first trade deficit in almost a century.
      2. Nixon suspended the 1944 Bretton Woods system, which meant the dollar would fluctuate in relation to the price of an ounce of gold.
      3. Wage and price controls were instituted to curb inflation, and $11 billion in deficit spending was offered to boost the sluggish economy.
      4. Stagnating wages and rising unemployment produced a noticeable decline in most Americans' standard of living.
      5. "Stagflation," the combination of inflation and unemployment, bedeviled presidential administrations from Nixon to Reagan.
      6. American economic woes were most acute in the industrial sector, which entered a prolonged period of decline, or deindustrialization.
      7. By the end of the 1970s, the hundred largest multinational corporations and banks were earning more than a third of their overall profits abroad.
      8. In the Rust Belt, huge factories were fast becoming relics; many workers moved to the Sun Belt, where dramatic growth that began after World War II continued.
      9. As foreign competition cut into corporate profits, industry became less willing to bargain, some companies moved their operations abroad, and the labor movement's power declined.

III. Reform and Reaction in the 1970s
   A. The New Activism: Environmental and Consumer Movements
      1. After 1970, many baby boomers left the counterculture behind and settled down to pursue careers and material goods.
      2. In the "Me Decade," many Americans demanded an even higher standard of living that included healthy lifestyles, spiritual support, and a healthy environment.
      3. few baby boomers still pursued the unfinished social and political agendas of the 1960s, continuing their activism on a grassroots level.

4. The birth of America's modern environmental movement can be traced to Rachel Carson's 1962 publication *Silent Spring*, an analysis of the impact of pesticides on the food chain.

5. The Alaskan pipeline and Love Canal situations deepened public awareness of the culpability of businesses in generating environmental hazards.

6. Nuclear energy became a subject of citizen action in the 1970s; public fears were confirmed in 1979 when a nuclear plant at Three Mile Island came critically close to a meltdown.

7. In 1969, Congress passed the National Environmental Policy Act, and in 1970, Nixon established the EPA and signed the Clean Air Act; the insecticide DDT was banned in 1972.

8. The Endangered Species Act expanded the Endangered Animals Act of 1964, granting endangered species protected status.

9. In a time of rising unemployment and reindustrialization, activists clashed head-on with proponents of economic development, full employment, and global competitiveness.

10. The rise of environmentalism was paralleled by a growing consumer protection movement to eliminate harmful consumer products and to curb dangerous practices by American corporations.

11. Ralph Nader's Public Interest Research Group became the model for other groups that later emerged to combat the health hazards of smoking, unethical insurance and credit practices, and other consumer problems.

12. With the establishment of the federal Consumer Products Safety Commission in 1972, Congress acknowledged the growing need for consumer protection.

B. Challenges to Tradition: The Women's Movement and Gay Rights

1. Feminism was the most enduring movement to emerge from the 1960s; as the women's movement grew, it generated an array of women-oriented services and organizations.

2. Gloria Steinem's *Ms.* magazine was the first aimed at the feminist market; formerly all-male bastions such as Yale admitted women for the first time.

3. Women's political mobilization with the National Organization for Women (NOW) and the National Women's Political Caucus resulted in significant legislative and administrative gains.

4. Title IX of the Educational Amendments Act of 1972 prohibited colleges and universities that received federal funds from discriminating on the basis of sex.

5. Affirmative action was extended to women in 1967; in 1972, Congress authorized child-care deductions for working parents; in 1974, the Equal Credit Opportunity Act improved women's access to credit.

6. The Supreme Court gave women more control over their reproductive lives by reading the right of privacy into the Ninth and Fourteenth Amendments' concepts of personal liberty.

7. *Griswold v. Connecticut* (1965) overturned state laws against the sale of contraceptive devices to married adults; this was later extended to single adults.

8. The *Roe v. Wade* (1973) decision prevented states from outlawing abortions performed during the first trimester and fueled the development of a powerful antiabortion movement.

9. The battlefront for the women's movement was the proposed Equal Rights Amendment; not enough states ratified the amendment, and by 1982 it was dead.

10. Nonwhite and working-class women saw the feminist movement as catering to self-seeking white career women; the movement also faced growing social conservatism among Americans.

11. More women joined the workforce, many delayed getting married and having children, and the divorce rate went up; by 1980, women accounted for 66 percent of adults living below the poverty line.

12. The gay liberation movement achieved greater visibility in the 1970s as gay communities gave rise to hundreds of new gay and lesbian clubs, churches, businesses, and political organizations.

13. Some cities passed laws barring discrimination on the basis of sexual preference.

14. Gay rights came under attack from conservatives who believed that protecting gay people's rights would encourage immoral behavior; antigay campaigns sprang up around the country.

C. Racial Minorities

1. Although the civil rights movement was in disarray by the late 1960s, minority group protests over the next decade continued to win social and economic gains.

2. Native Americans realized some of the most significant changes with the 1971 Alaska Native Claims Act and the Indian Self-Determination Act of 1974.

3. The court-mandated busing of children to achieve school desegregation proved to be the most disruptive social issue of the 1970s.

4. The Supreme Court decisions of *Brown v. Board of Education* (1954) and *Milliken v. Bradley* (1974) sparked intense, sometimes violent, opposition such as that in Boston in 1974 to 1975.

5. Threatened by court-ordered busing, many white parents transferred their children to private schools; the resulting "white flight" increased the racial imbalance busing was intended to redress.

6. Affirmative action, which had expanded opportunities for African Americans and Latinos, also proved divisive.

7. *Bakke v. University of California* (1978) was a setback for proponents of affirmative action and prepared the way for subsequent efforts to eliminate those programs.

8. Activists for the various causes were part of a "rights revolution," a movement in the 1960s and 1970s to bring the issues of social justice and welfare to the forefront of public policy.

D. The Politics of Resentment
1. Vocal opposition to abortion, busing, affirmative action, gay rights ordinances, and the Equal Rights Amendment constituted a broad backlash against the social changes of the previous decade.

2. The economic changes of the 1970s further fueled the "politics of resentment," a grassroots revolt against special-interest groups and the growing expenditures on social welfare.

3. Resentment manifested itself in a wave of taxpayers' revolts such as California's Proposition 13, which undercut the local government's ability to maintain schools and other services.

4. The rising popularity of evangelical religion also fueled the conservative resurgence of the 1970s; many of the evangelicals spoke out on a broad range of controversial issues.

5. The extensive media and fund-raising networks of the Christian right became the organizational base for a larger conservative movement known as the "New Right."

6. The New Right's diverse constituents, such as the "neoconservatives," shared hostility toward a powerful federal government and a fear of declining social morality.

7. New Right political groups mobilized thousands of followers and millions of dollars to support conservative candidates and causes.

IV. Politics in the Wake of Watergate
A. Ford's Caretaker Presidency
1. During the two years Gerald Ford was president, he failed to establish his legitimacy; his pardon of Nixon damaged his credibility. Yet Ford's biggest challenge was the reeling economy.

2. Inflation soared to 12 percent in 1974, and the economy took its deepest downturn since the Great Depression; Ford's failure to take more vigorous action made him appear timid and powerless.

3. In foreign policy, Ford maintained Nixon's détente initiatives, increased support to the shah of Iran, and made little progress toward an arms limitation treaty with the Soviets.

B. Jimmy Carter: The Outsider as President
1. During the 1976 presidential election, Jimmy Carter shared the Democratic ticket with Walter Mondale, who had ties to the Democratic constituencies of labor, liberals, blacks, and big-city machines.

2. Playing up his role as a Washington outsider and pledging to restore morality to government, Jimmy Carter won with 50 percent of the popular vote.

3. Carter shied away from established Democratic leaders, turning instead to advisors and friends who had no national experience.

4. Inflation was Carter's major domestic challenge; to counter inflation, interest rates were raised repeatedly, and they topped 20 percent in 1980.

5. Carter enlarged the cabinet by creating the Departments of Energy and Education and approved environmental protection measures such as a "Superfund" to clean up chemical pollution.

6. Carter reformed the civil service system, and he deregulated the airline, trucking, and railroad industries.

7. Carter failed in his efforts to decontrol oil and natural gas prices and failed to provide leadership during the energy crisis.

8. In foreign affairs, Carter made human rights the centerpiece of his policy: he criticized the suppression of dissent in the Soviet Union, withdrew economic aid from countries that violated human rights, and established the Office of Human Rights in the State Department.

9. In 1977, Carter signed a treaty that turned over control of the Panama Canal to Panama effective December 31, 1999.

10. Carter curtailed grain sales to the Soviet Union and boycotted the 1980 Olympics in Moscow in retaliation for the Soviet Union's invasion of Afghanistan.

11. Carter — and later Reagan — provided covert assistance to an Afghan group of "holy warriors"; the CIA helped these radical Islamic

fundamentalists, thereby helping to establish the now infamous Taliban.

12. Carter brokered a "framework for peace" between Israel and Egypt that included Egypt's recognition of Israel's right to exist and Israel's return of the Sinai Peninsula.

13. In 1979 the shah of Iran's government was overthrown by fundamentalist government leader Ayatollah Ruhollah Khomeini; the Carter administration admitted the deposed shah to the United States for medical treatments.

14. In response to allowing the shah into the United States, Iranian fundamentalists seized the U.S. embassy in Tehran and took American hostages in November 1979.

15. A failed military rescue reinforced the public's view of Carter as being ineffective, and the crisis paralyzed his presidency for the next fourteen months.

C. The Reagan Revolution

1. For the 1980 presidential election, Republicans nominated former California governor Ronald Reagan; Reagan chose George Bush as his running mate.

2. Reagan won the election with 51 percent of the popular vote; Republicans won control of the Senate for the first time since 1954.

3. The core of the Republican Party remained upper-middle-class whites who supported balanced budgets and a strong national defense, disliked government activism, and feared crime and communism.

4. New groups gravitated toward the Republican vision: southern whites, urban ethnics, blue-collar workers, westerners, and young voters.

5. A significant constituency in the Republican Party was the New Right, whose emphasis on traditional values and fundamentalist Christian morality fit well with Republican ideology.

6. When Carter turned the presidency over to Ronald Reagan on January 20, 1981, the Iranian government released the American hostages.

Lecture Strategies

1. The impact of the Nixon administration on domestic policy should be explored. Nixon's "new federalism" called for revenue sharing that provided the states with funds to use as they saw fit. The importance of this development was not realized until the Reagan administration ended the program, leaving states and cities starved for funds. The establishment of the Environmental Protection Agency and the Occupa-

tional Safety and Health Administration benefited a variety of communities and individual workers. A bold proposal for welfare reform fell victim to attacks from both the left and the right. Perhaps the most ironic development occurred in the Supreme Court, where Nixon had been able to appoint four new justices. That Court ruled in favor of forced busing in order to achieve racial balance and ended the states' ban on abortion.

2. The Watergate scandal must be described and analyzed. "Dirty tricks," White House "plumbers," taping in the Oval Office — these dramatic revelations from the Watergate hearings should be discussed. It is important for students to understand the importance of the struggles between the president and the special prosecutors and the implication of those struggles for constitutional government. Note the impeachment hearings and the discovery of the "smoking-gun" tape. Consider the effect of Nixon's resignation on politics through the rest of the decade and on Clinton's impeachment hearings in the late 1990s.

3. The expansion of environmentalism should be traced. Beginning with *Silent Spring* (1962), awareness of the threat of chemical and radioactive pollution energized a grassroots movement. Issues such as oil spills, the Alaska pipeline, ozone depletion, and toxic waste disposal precipitated the establishment of government standards and procedures for the reduction of air, water, and ground pollution. The tension between ecological soundness and maintenance of economic growth needs to be considered.

4. The impact of the Supreme Court's decision in *Roe v. Wade* should be explored. How did the Court come to accept the notion that there is a constitutional right to privacy? What does the decision actually call for? Did the Court actually allow for "abortion on demand," as is claimed by the antiabortion movement? How did opposition to the decision become so well organized? The continuing importance of abortion in the national political debate requires that students understand how the issue originally evolved.

5. The controversial adoption of affirmative action policies should be examined. The extent to which affirmative action caused "reverse discrimination," as was alleged in the *Bakke* case, should be discussed. Students need to consider whether affirmative action is an appropriate remedy for discrimination. How and when should it be applied? What about "quotas"? Is there a level playing field? How can a society establish equality of opportunity?

6. The Iranian hostage crisis seemed to be a fitting end to the decade. The loss of American prestige in the world community was symbolized by the ineffective-

ness of the Carter administration in resolving the crisis. Students should consider alternative courses that Carter might have pursued. What might have worked? The national focus on this problem, led by a critical media, only emphasized Carter's inability to act decisively.

7. The popularity of Ronald Reagan should be explored. Many Americans welcomed his optimism after a decade of "stagflation" and the "misery index." Consider the voters who populated the Republican Party in the early 1980s and how general resentment of the many failed social reform policies of the 1960s and 1970s contributed to Republican resurgence. Discuss the role played by southern whites, urban ethnics, blue-collar workers, westerners, and young voters as well as middle-class whites in the New Right.

Class Discussion Starters

1. **What were some significant revelations of malfeasance in the Watergate affair?**

Possible answers:
   a. The illegal collection of campaign funds before the election of 1972 by the Committee to Re-Elect the President.
   b. Illegal wiretaps by the White House "plumbers" to find the source of leaks to the press.
   c. The burglary of the headquarters of the Democratic National Committee for reasons that are still not clear.
   d. The payment of hush money to the Watergate burglars.
   e. The "smoking-gun" tape in which Nixon ordered a cover-up of the Watergate break-in.
   f. The order not to investigate connections between the break-in and the White House.
   g. Nixon's reluctance to turn over the Oval Office Tapes.

2. **What was the impact of the energy crisis?**

Possible answers:
   a. The OPEC oil embargo led to shortages of gasoline and a sharp increase in gas prices.
   b. The search for domestic oil supplies led to the opening of the vast Alaskan oil field, threatening environmental damage.
   c. Nuclear power generators were built in spite of questions of safety and the problem of the disposal of nuclear waste.
   d. The public began to buy more fuel-efficient foreign cars, causing a crisis in the American automobile industry.
   e. President Carter tried unsuccessfully to mobilize the nation with an energy conservation program ("the moral equivalent of war").

3. **What were the characteristics of the "Me Decade"?**

Possible answers:
   a. The fitness craze.
   b. The emergence of the health-food industry.
   c. The expansion of the human-potential movement.
   d. The emergence of many new religious movements such as Hare Krishna, the Church of Scientology, and the Unification Church ("Moonies").
   e. A revival of evangelical Protestantism with its emphasis on being "born again."

4. **What were the main effects of the Carter administration's foreign policy?**

Possible answers:
   a. Human rights considerations came to play a larger role in foreign-policy decisions.
   b. Peace was established between Israel and Egypt.
   c. The Panama Canal treaty was ratified, establishing Panama's eventual control over the canal.
   d. Relations with the Soviet Union deteriorated after the invasion of Afghanistan.
   e. Failure to resolve the Iranian hostage crisis contributed to Carter's defeat in the election of 1980.

5. **What were the major factors in the apparent decline of American prestige during this period?**

Possible answers:
   a. The revelations of Watergate and the exposure of widespread illegality in the executive branch of government.
   b. The defeat of American forces in Vietnam and its subsequent unification under Communist control.
   c. The OPEC oil embargo, which indicated that the United States was not self-sufficient in energy resources.
   d. The declining American share of world trade brought about by the rise of Germany and Japan as commercial rivals.
   e. The failure of the United States to maintain its industrial base, leading to widespread unemployment and a decline in the standard of living for many Americans.

Chapter Writing Assignments

1. Discuss and evaluate the foreign-policy accomplishments of the Nixon administration.

2. Describe the gradual unfolding of the events collectively known as Watergate. For which misdeeds was President Nixon finally threatened with removal from office?

3. What events in the 1970s forced Americans to become more energy conscious? Evaluate efforts by the

federal government to adopt policies requiring energy conservation.

4. What factors contributed to the deindustrialization of the 1970s? Describe the impact of this development on the workforce.

5. For what reasons is the Carter presidency generally considered a failure? Do you agree with this evaluation? Explain your answer.

6. Explain why Ronald Reagan was elected president in 1980.

Document Exercises

AMERICAN LIVES

Lois Marie Gibbs: Environmental Activist (p. 890)

Document Discussion

1. **Why were toxic wastes "dumped" in the United States?**
(Some American businesses use chemical and industrial processes that generate dangerous waste materials. A lack of regulation before the 1970s allowed industries to expel wastes anywhere — in the air, ground, and water. The result was excessive environmental pollution, as was the case in Love Canal that harmed the residents of Gibbs's neighborhood. America now enjoys far stricter environmental standards than other industrialized and developing nations, in large measure due to activists like Gibbs.)

2. **Who should have the responsibility for cleaning up environmental pollution?**
(Federal, state, and local governments have taken on some of the responsibility, and that means that the taxpayers pay for the cleanup. Industry is now subject to some regulations requiring it to reduce environmental pollution. But there is still considerable controversy about the best and most cost-effective methods for cleaning up the air, ground, and water.)

Writing Assignments

1. What processes are involved in cleaning up a toxic waste site such as the Love Canal? What role do environmental activists play?

2. Do politicians bear greater responsibility to businesses or to individual citizens in matters concerning environmental protection? Cite evidence to support your answer.

AMERICAN VOICES

David Kopay: The Real Score: A Gay Athlete Comes Out (p. 895)

Document Discussion

1. **What happened to Kopay when the article identifying him as homosexual appeared in the *Washington Star*?**
(Kopay recounts that personally he did not suffer too much, although he never was able to secure a coaching position. The primary consequence of the article was a voluminous backlash directed at the media outlets that published Kopay's story. People objected not to Kopay as an individual but more generally to the public discussion of homosexuality. Many considered it an inappropriate topic.)

2. **What is Kopay's general attitude about his status as a gay athlete?**
(Kopay seems resigned to the fact that many people are not in favor of his "coming out." He does not promote or defend his choice to publish his story beyond stating that he needed to do so for himself irrespective of how others viewed him.)

Writing Assignments

1. How have the various legal and social policy solutions proposed by interest groups affected homosexuals?

2. Why is the issue of homosexual behavior so divisive? Assess the roles of social custom, religion, science, and history in your answer.

AMERICAN VOICES

Phyllis Ellison: Busing in Boston (p. 897)

Document Discussion

1. **To what extent did South Boston High School desegregate?**
(Only in the most limited sense. Students kept themselves racially separate, and their interaction was mainly limited to fighting.)

2. **How did whites react to the presence of black students in school?**
(Whites resented the black students' presence. Police escorts were required to safeguard the black students as they traveled to school, and teachers found keeping the peace in the classroom to be difficult. After the stabbing of Michael Faith, the fragile advance toward equality erupted in violence.)

Writing Assignments

1. Why did school desegregation in Boston lead to so much acrimony?

2. What were the goals of desegregation? Were they achieved?

VOICES FROM ABROAD

Fei Xiaotong:
America's Crisis of Faith (p. 900)

Document Discussion

1. **How does Xiaotong describe America's "loss of faith"?**
   (Xiaotong claims that Americans have lost faith in a social system that has become unhinged from the "forces of production." Xiaotong maintains that while the ruling class can deal with "the endless series of crises," the masses of people cannot. Not only are minorities suffering — even the "well-off families in gardenlike suburban residences" spend their time worrying.)

2. **Why does Xiaotong declare that America in the future will go on to contribute to the betterment of mankind?**
   (As with his criticism of the United States, Xiaotong offers scant substantive information to support his confidence in America. Xiaotong merely offers the trite note that as history unfolds, America will move forward.)

Writing Assignments

1. What do Xiaotong's comments suggest about the public and international perception of President Jimmy Carter's leadership?

Skill-Building Map Exercises

Map 30.2: States Ratifying the Equal Rights Amendment, 1972–1977 (p. 893)

1. **Why are the states that refused to ratify the ERA concentrated in the South and West?**
   (Those regions of the country typically express conservative views regarding the roles of men and women in society.)

2. **Why did so many men and women object to the ERA?**
   (Some opponents of the ERA feared that it would undermine gender-specific protections that labor

laws provided women. Others protested that the ERA would only improve the status of elite white women, while offering few advantages for other women.)

Map 30.3:
American Indian Reservations (p. 896)

1. **Why are there so few Indian Reservations east of the Mississippi River?**
   (The density of white settlement in eastern lands early in American history meant that Indians were pushed farther westward. As long as open areas remained, the Indians were forced there. Only when the "frontier" closed were Indians able to consolidate their land holdings in relatively stable locations.)

2. **Why does Kansas possess so few reservations, while neighboring Oklahoma contains so many?**
   (White settlement in Kansas, aided initially by travel up the Missouri River and then by the Oregon and Santa Fe Trails, and eventually by the railroads, was constant after the 1830s. This meant that Indians were pushed elsewhere. Oklahoma, on the other hand, was held open for Indians until near the end of the century. For decades, whites considered the land there to be undesirable. Many Indians remained even after the arrival of whites, who acquired much of the land.)

Topic for Research

The Alaskan Pipeline
and the Environment

In 1968, an "elephant" was found near Prudhoe Bay, on the Arctic coast of Alaska, that was twice as large as any oil field in North America. In 1977, completion of the 800-mile Trans-Alaska pipeline linked Prudhoe Bay to the port of Valdez at a cost of $7.7 billion. The delay in construction of the pipeline was due to extensive litigation that pitted oil companies against environmentalists. Environmental concerns included the impact of the pipeline on Alaskan wildlife and the risk of oil tanker accidents at Valdez in Prince William Sound.

Research the pros and cons of building the pipeline. What were the arguments on both sides? What strategies were pursued? What finally tipped the balance? In light of the Exxon Valdez accident in 1989 (which, as environmentalists had feared, saturated Prince William Sound with oil), were the earlier predictions of environmentalists accurate? Why had they failed to get their message across?

The best introduction to oil issues is Daniel Yergin, *The Prize* (1991). The public debate can be traced through newspapers and magazines in the 1970s as well as the government hearings on the issue. Other sources include Potter Wickware, *Crazy Money: Nine Months on the Trans-Alaska Pipeline* (1979); Ed McGarth, *Inside the Alaska Pipeline* (1977); Robert Douglas Mead, *Journeys Down the Line: Building the Trans-Alaska Pipeline* (1978); and Mim Dixon, *What Happened to Fairbanks? The Effects of the Trans-Alaska Pipeline on the Community of Fairbanks* (1978).

How to Use the Ancillaries Available with *America's History*

Refer to the Preface to *America's History* at the front of the book for descriptions of instructor resources, including the Instructor's Resource CD-ROM, Computerized Test Bank, transparencies, and *Using the Bedford Series in History and Culture in the U.S. History Survey*. Student resources, also described in the Preface, include the Online Study Guide and *Documents to Accompany* America's History, a primary-source reader.

For Students

Online Study Guide at bedfordstmartins.com/henretta
Each of the activities listed below includes short-answer questions. After submitting their answers, students can compare them to the model answers provided.

Map Activity
The map activity presents Map 30.3: American Indian Reservations (p. 896) and asks students to analyze the dispersement of lands controlled by Native Americans throughout the country.

Reading Historical Documents
The document activity provides a brief introduction to the documents David Kopay: The Real Score: A Gay Athlete Comes Out (p. 895) and Phyllis Ellison: Busing in Boston (p. 897) and asks students to analyze their content, thinking critically about the sources.

Documents to Accompany *America's History*
Each of the documents listed is introduced by a headnote, which places the document in context, and is followed by questions, which help students to analyze the piece.

Sources for Chapter 30 are
Daniel Patrick Moynihan, *Memorandum on Benign Neglect* (1970)
Watergate: Taped White House Conversations (1972)
Visual Document: *Gallup Polls, National Problems, 1950–1999*
William Serrin, *Homestead* (1970s)
Rachel Carson, *And No Birds Sing* (1962)
Gloria Steinem, *Statement in Support of the Equal Rights Amendment* (1970)
Phyllis Schlafly, *The Power of the Positive Woman* (1977)
Democratic and Republican National Platform Planks on the Equal Rights Amendment and Abortion (1976, 1980)
Jimmy Carter, *The National Crisis of Confidence* (1979)
Ronald Reagan, *Acceptance Speech, Republican National Convention* (1980)

CHAPTER 31

A New Domestic and World Order

1981–2001

Chapter Instructional Objectives

After you have taught this chapter, your students should be able to answer the following questions:

1. Explain how the domestic policies of Presidents Reagan and Bush reflected the rise of conservatism.

2. How and why did the cold war conclude with an American victory in 1991?

3. How did the end of the cold war precipitate the reemergence of regional, ethnic, and religious conflicts in Eastern Europe?

4. How effective was the Clinton presidency at home and abroad?

5. How has the administration of President George Bush confronted international security challenges?

Chapter Summary

The presidencies of Ronald Reagan and George Bush advocated decreasing the size and influence of the federal government, rolling back a half century of federal activism. Reagan's economic plan, dubbed Reaganomics, aimed to cut tax rates so that corporations could reinvest and invigorate the economy. As part of his policy to unleash the private sector, Reagan reduced government regulation of business and tried to weaken the power of organized labor. The net result of his policies was a widening of the income gap.

Reagan's feel-good campaign won him a landslide victory in the election of 1984, but his second administration was plagued by a mounting deficit and the Iran-Contra affair. His greatest foreign policy triumph came as a result of changes in Soviet policy brought about by Mikhail Gorbachev. The heads of the two superpowers were able to begin an arms reduction program that led to an easing of international tensions.

Vice President George Bush followed Reagan into the presidency in 1988 and continued to uphold many of his predecessor's policies. In foreign affairs the Bush administration took credit for ending the cold war when the Soviet Union dissolved as a result of Gorbachev's reforms. Bush's success in driving Iraq out of Kuwait during the Gulf War caused his popularity to soar, but his apparent lack of leadership in domestic affairs undermined his chance for reelection.

The 1980s and 1990s witnessed America's economy and society in transition. The income disparity between the richest and poorest Americans widened. At the same time, American society became increasingly pluralistic and was forced to confront issues such as affirmative action and multiculturalism. Exciting new technology gave Americans hope and changed the way they lived, worked, and communicated.

The Democratic presidential campaign of 1992 focused on social and economic issues and President Bush lost to Bill Clinton, the youthful governor of Arkansas. The first two years of the Clinton administration saw the adoption of several trade policies, the North American Free Trade Agreement (NAFTA) and the General Agreement on Tariffs and Trade (GATT), and a failure to enact health-care reform. The election of 1994 was a major setback for the administration, with Republicans gaining control of both houses of Congress. The conservative "revolution," however, was unable to maintain its momentum, and Clinton blocked any significant revisions to the federal budget. The Republican takeover united the usually fractious Democrats behind Bill Clinton, who won a second term in the 1996 election.

In foreign affairs, President Clinton committed military forces several times with limited effectiveness. In late 1998, America led a four-day bombing campaign against Iraq in order to curb that nation's ability to produce weapons of mass destruction. In March 1999, NATO, strongly influenced by the Clinton administration, conducted a three-month bombing campaign to protect ethnic Albanians in Kosovo. Neither action resulted in a long-term solution.

The major political issue in America during the late 1990s surrounded allegations of sexual misconduct and a cover-up by President Clinton. In December 1998 the House of Representatives approved two articles of impeachment against the president; one for perjury and a second for obstruction of justice. After a five-week trial in the Senate, President Clinton was acquitted, but the entire scandal limited his effectiveness to lead and further deepened public cynicism about politics.

The presidential election of 2000, between the Democratic vice president Al Gore and Texas governor George W. Bush, proved highly contentious. The race between these two moderate candidates was extraordinarily tight, and in Florida, alleged irregularities in the voting and counting processes threw the state's outcome into the courts for resolution. After five weeks of argument, the U.S. Supreme Court ruled in favor of George W. Bush; he thus won the state and became the forty-third president. The international landscape was profoundly altered on September 11, 2001, when Al Queda terrorists hijacked four airplanes and flew two of them into the World Trade Center and one into the Pentagon; the fourth crashed in Pennsylvania.

Chapter Annotated Outline

I. The Reagan-Bush Years, 1981–1993
   A. Reaganomics
      1. Distrustful of big government, both Ronald Reagan and George Bush turned away from the federal government as a source of solutions for America's social problems.
      2. The economic and tax policies that emerged under Reagan, dubbed "Reaganomics," were based on supply-side economics theory.
      3. The Economic Recovery Act of 1981 reduced income tax rates by 25 percent over three years.
      4. Overall, Reaganomics widened the income gap by making the rich richer without addressing the economic needs of the poor.
      5. The administration moved to abolish or reduce federal regulation in the workplace, in health care, in consumer protection, and in the environment.
      6. The money saved by these cuts was put into a five-year $1.2 trillion defense buildup; Rea-

gan's most controversial weapons plan was the Strategic Defense Initiative ("Star Wars").
      7. In the early 1980s the inflation rate dropped from 12.4 to just 4 percent; the Federal Reserve's tightening of the money supply also brought on the "Reagan recession" of 1981 to 1982.
      8. With inflation low, the Reagan administration presided over the longest peacetime prosperity expansion in American history.
   B. Reagan's Second Term
      1. Reagan won a landslide victory over Democrat Walter Mondale and his running mate, Geraldine Ferraro, the first woman to run on a major-party ticket.
      2. The Iran-Contra affair marred Reagan's second term; Congress investigated, but White House officials testified that the president knew nothing about the diversion of profits from arms sales.
      3. Reagan reordered the federal government's priorities, but he failed to reduce its size or scope.
      4. Reagan's spending cuts and antigovernment rhetoric shaped the terms of political debate for the rest of the century.
      5. One of Reagan's most significant legacies was his conservative judicial appointments; Sandra Day O'Connor was the first woman ever to serve on the Supreme Court.
      6. The national debt tripled during Reagan's tenure from the combined effects of increased military spending, tax reductions for high-income taxpayers, and Congress's refusal to approve deep cuts in domestic programs.
      7. Budget and trade deficits contributed to the U.S. shift in 1985 from a creditor to a debtor nation.
   C. The Bush Presidency
      1. Promising "no new taxes," George Bush with running mate Dan Quayle defeated Democrat Michael Dukakis in the 1988 election by winning 53.4 percent of the popular vote.
      2. Some significant domestic trends of the Bush era were determined by the judiciary branch: *Webster v. Reproductive Health Services* (1989) gave states more latitude in restricting abortions.
      3. In the wake of the Clarence Thomas hearings, national polls confirmed the pervasiveness of sexual harassment of working women.
      4. Although Bush promised no new taxes, when faced with the prospect of a layoff of thousands of government employees, he and Congress resorted to spending cuts and one of the largest tax increases in history.

5. Reagan's decision to shift the cost of federal programs to state and local governments caused problems for Bush; in 1990, a recession began to erode state and local tax revenues.

6. Unemployment rose to 7 percent in 1991, and state and local governments laid off workers even as the demand for social services climbed.

7. Another drag on the economy was the collapse of the savings and loan industry, which was deregulated during the Reagan administration; it took the Resolution Trust Corporation six years to clean up the mess, at a cost of $150 billion to taxpayers.

II. Foreign Relations under Reagan and Bush
   A. Interventions in Developing Countries
      1. Airplane hijackings and countless terrorist incidents in the Middle East led Reagan to order airstrikes against terrorist chief of state Muammar al-Qaddafi of Libya.
      2. Reagan's top priority was to overthrow the Communist-led Sandinista government in Nicaragua; in 1981, Congress passed a bill suspending aid from the United States to Nicaragua.
      3. The CIA began to provide extensive covert support to Nicaragua's opposition forces, known as the "Contras"; this situation precipitated the Iran-Contra affair.
      4. Reagan's second term brought a reduction in tensions with the Soviet Union; in 1987, Reagan and Gorbachev agreed to eliminate intermediate-range missiles in Europe.
   B. The End of the Cold War
      1. In 1989 the grip of communism on Eastern Europe eroded in a series of mostly nonviolent revolutions that climaxed with the destruction of the Berlin Wall.
      2. A failed coup to oust Gorbachev broke the Communist Party's dominance over the Soviet Union.
   C. War in the Persian Gulf, 1990–1991
      1. On August 2, 1990, Iraq invaded and quickly conquered neighboring Kuwait.
      2. Bush sponsored a series of resolutions in the United Nations Security Council condemning Iraq, calling for its withdrawal, and imposing an embargo and trade sanctions.
      3. When Saddam Hussein showed no signs of complying with the resolutions, Bush prompted the United Nations to create the legal framework for an international military offensive.
      4. The forty-two-day war was a resounding success for the UN's coalition forces, which were predominantly American, yet Hussein remained in power.

5. The euphoria produced at home by the success of Operation Desert Storm quickly subsided when a new recession showed that the country had serious economic problems.

III. Uncertain Times: Economic and Social Trends, 1980–2000
   A. The Economy
      1. The two most salient economic trends in the 1980s and 1990s were the slow growth in productivity and the growing inequality in income distribution.
      2. From 1945 to 1973, productivity had grown 2.8 percent annually, in the next quarter century, that figure had dropped to less than 1 percent annually.
      3. By 1996 the United States was the most economically stratified industrial nation in the world.
      4. Changes in the job market led to diminished expectations among workers; the number of minimum-wage jobs grew, but the number of union-protected manufacturing jobs shrank.
      5. Major corporations trimmed management positions.
      6. In 1994, 58.8 percent of women were in the labor force; one out of five women held a clerical or secretarial job, and their pay lagged behind that of men.
      7. The labor movement continued to decline; in 1998, unions represented only 13.9 percent of the labor force.
      8. To compete internationally, American firms adopted new technologies; by the late 1990s the United States led the world in information technology and expanded productivity in manufacturing.
      9. A booming stock market, energized by a flow of funds into the high-tech sector and the emergence of e-commerce, seemed to reach new highs daily.
      10. By 2000 the nagging deficit was wiped out and the budget for the next ten years was projected to be an astonishing $4.6 trillion surplus.
      11. Many stock market analysts feared that a steep drop in the stock market might cause a recession; others feared that consumer spending and economic growth was linked to debt.
   B. Popular Culture and Popular Technology
      1. Music Television (MTV) had a strong influence on popular culture with its creative choreography, flashy colors, and rapid cuts.
      2. *USA Today*, which debuted in 1982, adopted the "MTV style" with eye-catching graphics, color photographs, and short, easy-to-read articles; other newspapers followed suit.

3. Satellite transmission and live "minicam" broadcasting reshaped the television industry; soon cable access and satellite dishes were commonplace.

4. The 1980s saw the introduction of videocassette recorders (VCRs), compact disc (CD) players, cellular phones, and inexpensive fax machines.

5. The personal computer revolutionized both the home and office; by 2000, 77 percent of American households had at least one personal computer.

6. The computer created the modern electronic office, and the very concept of the office changed as a new class of telecommuters worked at home via computer, fax, and e-mail.

7. By 2000, almost 300 million people used the Internet; the debut of the World Wide Web in 1991 enhanced the commercial possibilities of the Internet.

8. Programs to wire public schools and libraries have increased access to new technology; in 2000, 63 percent of public classrooms were connected to the Internet.

C. An Increasingly Pluralistic Society

1. Between 1981 and 1996, 13.5 million immigrants entered the United States, most of them Latinos and Asians.

2. These immigrants have had a tremendous impact on America's social, economic, and cultural landscape, producing thriving ethnic communities, ethnic restaurants, and specialized periodicals.

3. Many Americans celebrated the nation's ethnic pluralism, while others viewed immigrants as scapegoats for all that was wrong with the United States.

4. In the 1980s, California absorbed more immigrants than any other state; more than a third of its population growth in that decade came from foreign immigration.

5. Opponents challenged the constitutionality of California's Proposition 187, but anti-immigrant sentiments soon spread to other parts of the country.

6. In the cities, African Americans and the new immigrants were forced by economic necessity and segregation patterns to compete for space in decaying, crime-ridden ghettos.

7. The 1992 Los Angeles race riots were multiracial, which showed that the cleavages in urban neighborhoods went beyond a simple matter of black indignation and were class-based protests against the failure of the American system to address the needs of all poor people.

8. In 1995 the University of California voted to end affirmative action, and the backlash against racial preferences was intensified by Proposition 209, which banned all preference based on race or gender.

9. Lumping affirmative action together with multiculturalism, critics warned that all this counting by race, gender, sexual preference, and age would fragment American society.

D. Backlash against Women's and Gay Rights

1. Conservative critics targeted the women's movement and held it responsible for every ill affecting modern women, although polls showed strong support for feminist demands.

2. The deep divide over abortion, one of the main issues associated with feminism, continued to polarize the country.

3. Although only a fraction of antiabortionists supported violent acts, disruptive confrontational tactics escalating to murder and bombings made practicing their legal right dangerous for women.

4. Conservatives insisted that gay rights threatened America's traditional family values; across the nation, "gay bashing" and other forms of violence against homosexuals continued.

E. The AIDS Epidemic

1. The gay men's struggle was made a matter of life and death by acquired immune deficiency syndrome (AIDS), first recognized by physicians in 1981 in the gay male population.

2. AIDS cases began to increase among heterosexuals and bisexuals as early as the mid-1980s.

3. New drug treatments offer some hope, but they are very expensive; to date, more Americans have died from AIDS than were killed in the Korean and Vietnam Wars combined.

4. Even though AIDS deaths have declined in developed countries, approximately 95 percent of HIV-infected people live in the developing world.

F. The Environmental Movement at Twenty-five

1. By the twenty-fifth anniversary of Earth Day, the nations waterways were cleaner; air pollution had been reduced; and lead emissions from fuel had been cut by 98 percent.

2. In 1987, thirty-four nations agreed to phase out chlorofluorocarbons (CFCs); in 1992, 170 countries adopted a treaty on global warming; and in 1994, the United States and sixty-three other countries banned the export of hazardous wastes from industrialized to developing countries.

3. The Kyoto Treaty was never ratified because Congress feared that the United States would be hurt economically.

4. By the late 1990s, Americans still used too much energy and lived in areas with smog, and many poor people lived near toxic waste dumps — but changes were made to address these ills.

IV. Restructuring the Domestic Order: Public Life, 1992–2001

A. Clinton's First Term

1. In the 1992 election campaign, Bill Clinton and Al Gore were the first baby boomers to occupy the national ticket.

2. The narrowness of Bill Clinton's victory over George Bush and Ross Perot and the public's perception that he did not stand for anything did not augur well for his ability to lead the country.

3. Clinton signed a Family and Medical Leave Act but backed off on the issue of gays in the military, offering a compromise policy of "Don't ask, don't tell, don't pursue."

4. With Clinton's support, the North American Free Trade Agreement was passed in 1993.

5. Clinton chose his wife, Hillary Rodham Clinton, to head a task force in order to draft legislation for universal health care; by 1994 the health-care reform initiative was dead.

6. Clinton appeared to the American public to be vacillating, indecisive, and lacking in vision, especially in his handling of foreign affairs.

7. President Clinton helped to facilitate a peace accord in 1995 that would, at least temporarily, end the fighting in Bosnia.

8. The United States established diplomatic relations with Hanoi in July 1995, two decades after the fall of Saigon.

B. "The Era of Big Government Is Over"

1. In the House of Representatives, the centerpiece of the new Republican majority was the "contract with America."

2. Clinton, bowing to political reality, declared that the "era of big government is over."

3. The budget that Clinton signed in April 1996 left Medicare and Social Security intact, and it met the Republican's goal of cutting $23 billion from discretionary spending.

4. Clinton, who had campaigned on a promise of welfare reform, signed the Personal Responsibility and Work Opportunity Act, a historic overhaul of federal entitlements.

5. The Republican takeover of Congress united the Democrats behind the president; unopposed in the 1996 primaries, Clinton was able

to burnish his image as a moderate "New Democrat."

6. In the 1996 elections, Republican Bob Dole made a 15 percent across-the-board tax cut the centerpiece of his campaign, while Clinton emphasized an improved economy.

7. A key factor in Clinton's second term would be the necessity of pursuing bipartisan policies or be left facing a stalemate.

C. Second-Term Stalemates

1. Bill Clinton's ability to pursue his domestic agenda was compromised by two international crises and by a scandal that would eventually lead to his impeachment trial.

2. The first crisis emerged in 1997, when Saddam Hussein ejected American members of a UN inspection team that was searching Iraqi sites for hidden "weapons of mass destruction."

3. With limited international support, the United States began a military buildup in the Persian Gulf, and in 1998, the same issues led to an intense four-day joint United States-British bombing campaign, called "Desert Fox."

4. The second international crisis began in March 1999 in Kosovo; there NATO, strongly influenced by the United States, intervened to protect ethnic Albanians from Serbians determined to drive them out of the region.

5. These two incidents showed that the United States was limited in its ability to achieve its foreign-policy aims.

6. Three months of bombing forced the Serbians to remove their troops from Kosovo and to accept the presence of a multinational peace-keeping force, but no long-term solutions were achieved.

7. In 1998, allegations emerged of an affair between Clinton and former White House intern Monica Lewinsky; Kenneth Starr widened his Whitewater investigation to include this scandal.

8. On December 20, 1998, the House of Representatives narrowly approved two articles of impeachment against Clinton: one for perjury and a second for obstruction of justice.

9. Clinton's approval rating remained high throughout the trial in the Senate; Americans approved of his presidential performance even if they disapproved of his personal morality.

10. Clinton was acquitted on both charges by the Senate, but the scandal and the trial limited his ability to be an effective president.

D. An Unprecedented Election

1. In the 2000 presidential election, Democratic vice president Al Gore and Senator Joseph

Leiberman ran against Republicans George W. Bush and Dick Cheney.

2. It was an extremely close election: Gore won 20 states and Bush prevailed in 29, but allegations of voting irregularities in Florida tied up the final 25 electoral votes each candidate needed to win the presidency.

3. Butterfly ballots and undervotes, as well as dimpled, pregnant, and hanging chads became a hotly debated issue.

4. In December the U.S. Supreme Court cited provisions of the Fourteenth Amendment to determine that George W. Bush was the legitimate winner of Florida's votes and hence the new president.

E. George W. Bush's Early Presidency

1. In the last hours of his administration, Clinton granted a series of dubious pardons, further tarnishing his reputation and deepening American cynicism.

2. In his first seven months in office, Bush banned the use of foreign-aid funds for family-planning programs abroad, appointed Colin Powell as the first black Secretary of State, and made good on his promise to cut taxes.

3. The stock market sank only months after Bush's inauguration, and economic growth slowed, leading to fears of a recession.

4. As gasoline prices rose and power shortages occurred on the West Coast, Bush resisted calls for federal price controls and emphasized the need for power plants and oil drilling.

5. Moderate Jim Jeffers left the Republican Party to become an independent; the Republicans lost their majority status in the Senate.

6. Bush's major initiatives called for maintaining UN sanctions against Iraq and for increased efforts to destabilize Saddam Hussein's regime.

7. On September 11, 2001, terrorists of Osama bin Laden's Al Queda network hijacked four airplanes and flew two of them into the World Trade Center and one into the Pentagon; the fourth crashed in Pennsylvania.

Lecture Strategies

1. How did Ronald Reagan become president? Reagan's background as a movie actor and ad spokesman provided excellent training for politics in the television age. His political career should be traced from the 1964 Republican convention through the governorship of California to the White House.

2. The impact of Reaganomics on the national economy needs to be traced. Supply-side economic theory called for a tax cut. How might tax cuts stimulate economic growth? How might they limit social welfare programs? Reaganomics also called for a sharp reduction in domestic spending, but Reagan actually increased spending during his presidency. Where did deregulation fit in? How was the federal deficit affected by these policies?

3. Students need to understand why the Iran-Contra affair brought the Reagan administration into disrepute. This requires a discussion of several disparate issues: relations with Iran, the arming and training of the Nicaraguan Contras, the functions of the National Security Council, and the authority for and nature of covert intelligence activities. The illegality of the support for the Contras and the selling of arms to Iran should be stressed.

4. Students should ponder the lessons of the American victory in the Persian Gulf War of 1990 to 1991. This might be a good time to discuss with students the extent to which the president and Congress each have the constitutional authority to prosecute military intervention overseas. Denial of media access to military action in the Persian Gulf became a controversial issue. Was the Pentagon's restriction of the press a result of the media's role in Vietnam? Was there a "Vietnam syndrome" to be overcome? Why was the United States so successful militarily? How did American and coalition forces achieve the dramatic, quick, and relatively casualty-free (for U.S. forces) military victory? What effects did the war have on the states of the Middle East?

5. Examine the AIDS epidemic. Because AIDS was first seen as a gay disease, public-health authorities ignored its spread, but the AIDS-related deaths of prominent celebrities and the media-friendliness of AIDS activists focused public attention on the illness.

6. Clinton's failure to enact health-care, Social Security, or Medicare reform provides a good backdrop for examining his administration. Link these failures with the Republican "revolution" of 1994. How did the Republicans' "contract with America" undermine Clinton's social reforms.

7. Is there a "new world order"? If so, what is America's place in it? Students should consider the effects of the end of the cold war on American foreign and domestic policy. With the collapse of the bipolar world, will American influence be reduced? How can students be led to see that the post–World War II world no longer exists and that the nation now faces a post-cold war world?

8. President Clinton was only the second president to be impeached by the House of Representatives. Discuss the significance of Clinton's impeachment with students. How does the process of putting the presi-

dent on trial affect the nation's political system? Explain the role of the House and Senate in the impeachment process. What happens to the nation's foreign policy when political leaders are consumed with a legal defense?

9. Debate the legal, ethical, and constitutional issues surrounding the presidential election of 2000, especially the subject of the contested votes in the state of Florida. Examine how Americans treat elections and how elections relate to American popular culture. Explain the electoral college, and assess the future of elections with and without the electoral college.

10. Examine the post-September 11, 2001 security environment confronting U.S. policymakers. American citizens are familiar with a view of the international community that supposes a state is either at "war" or at "peace." But other nations and groups do not share this bifurcated view. How must the United States react to this challenge? How should America deploy military, diplomatic, and economic tools in order to defeat external threats? Why have terrorists targeted the United States? Do they object to American power, ideals, or both? Is the "war against terror" a battle of ideas? If so, what ideas are at stake?

Class Discussion Starters

1. **What were some of the important elements in Reagan's domestic policy?**

Possible answers:
   a. A tax cut to stimulate economic growth.
   b. A sharp cut in spending for social welfare programs.
   c. A sharp increase in defense spending to ensure American superiority over the Soviet "evil empire."
   d. Deregulation of business.
   e. Weakening the influence of organized labor.

2. **What was the long-range impact of the Reagan presidency?**

Possible answers:
   a. The appointment of conservative justices shifted the balance away from the Supreme Court.
   b. A vast increase in the national debt resulted from budget and trade deficits.
   c. Agreements on arms control with Gorbachev led to a reduction of cold war tensions.
   d. An upward redistribution of income occurred, making the rich richer while the economic status of the rest of the people stagnated or declined.

3. **What economic problems beset the Bush administration in the early 1990s?**

Possible answers:
   a. The need to increase government revenues to address the mounting deficit, leading the president to break his "no new taxes" pledge.
   b. State and local governments were overburdened with debt as a result of the withdrawal of federal revenues.
   c. A serious recession began in 1990, causing a rise in unemployment and an increase in the number of people living in poverty.
   d. A sharp increase in business bankruptcies and mortgage defaults.

4. **What important developments occurred in black America during the Reagan-Bush years?**

Possible answers:
   a. Increased educational opportunity and lessened discrimination allowed more blacks to move in to the middle class.
   b. African Americans in the inner cities faced heightened levels of crime, poor schools, and high unemployment.
   c. Urban blacks had to compete with new immigrants for scarce jobs.
   d. Persistent police brutality led to the Los Angeles riots of 1992, a reaction to the Rodney King verdict.

5. **What was the health-care "crisis" of the late 1980s and early 1990s, and why did reform fail?**

Possible answers:
   a. Rising medical costs and insurance premiums caused Americans to spend more for health care.
   b. About 40 million Americans were without health insurance in 1995.
   c. Hillary Clinton's proposals for health-care reform were vehemently opposed by the pharmaceutical and insurance industries.

6. **What has been the impact of the computer revolution on American society?**

Possible answers:
   a. Firms have been able to cut back on white-collar employment.
   b. Communication has become more rapid and efficient.
   c. The shape of American industry has been reconfigured by the rapid and successful growth of the computer industry.
   d. Business operations have been transformed by computer-controlled transactions.

7. **In what ways did America's position of power and influence change during the Reagan-Bush years?**

Possible answers:

a. The end of the cold war made the non-Communist world less dependent on American military power.

b. The rise of Japan and Germany as industrial powers contributed to an American trade imbalance and a weak dollar.

c. The rise of regional conflicts caused other nations to look to the United States for leadership.

d. The growing strength of American military power enhanced the power and prestige of the United States.

8. Why did the Senate fail to convict President Clinton on the articles of impeachment?

Possible answers:

a. Senators were intimidated by the president's high public approval ratings.

b. The Democrats united, and enough Republicans joined them to acquit the president.

c. Some senators did not want to subject the nation to the political perils of a presidential trial.

d. Democratic senators did not want to convict a president from their own party.

Chapter Writing Assignments

1. What policies constituted the "Reagan Revolution"? Evaluate the impact of the Reagan presidency on the United States.

2. How did the Bush administration react to the foreign-policy crises of the late 1980s and early 1990s? Include an evaluation of American military actions and the collapse of Soviet communism.

3. What economic developments during the Bush administration contributed to the president's decline in popularity and defeat in the election of 1992?

4. What factors contributed to the widening income gap in the 1980s?

5. What impact did immigration and demographic trends among racial and ethnic minorities in the 1980s and 1990s have on urban areas in the United States? What effect did federal policies have on those developments?

6. Evaluate the Clinton presidency. Contrast Clinton's successes and failures with those of other modern presidents.

7. How has the rise of international terrorism affected America's security needs? How can the United States defend itself and its allies from the threat posed by weapons of mass destruction?

8. What balance should the United States seek between security, individual liberty, and economic prosperity at home and abroad?

Document Exercises

VOICES FROM ABROAD

Saddam Hussein: Calling for a Holy War against the United States (p. 915)

Document Discussion

1. **How and why does Hussein justify war against the United States?**
(Hussein calls for war against the United States on the basis of his religious convictions. In his interpretation, God (Allah) had chosen the Arabs, and in particular the Iraqis, to lead a fight to preserve His teachings. In Hussein's eyes, the United States is influenced by Satan and poses a threat to those teachings. Only the destruction of American forces in the Middle East would eliminate the threat to God's order and holy shrines.)

2. **Leaders have long invoked moral arguments in order to justify their actions. Despite his rhetoric, what were some of the concrete reasons behind his decision to invade Kuwait? How do his actions contradict his call for Arab unity?**
(Hussein frames the conflict between the United States and Iraq in completely moral terms without outlining any of the pragmatic reasons for his attack on Kuwait. His forces invaded Kuwait to gain control of its lucrative oil fields, not to wage holy war on the United States. Likewise, Iraqi aggression threatened neighboring countries like Saudi Arabia; his calls for Arab nationalism surely rang false.)

Writing Assignments

1. How did Hussein seek to enlist the help of other Middle Eastern nations?

2. On what basis does Hussein seek to gain the support of non-Islamic states for resistance to the United States?

NEW TECHNOLOGY

The Biotech Revolution (p. 918)

Document Discussion

1. **What promises does biotechnology hold for the future?**
(Fields such as health care, criminal justice, and reproductive science are among those that will likely see rapid change because of the ability to isolate and understand genes. Alongside this capability will arise

an increasingly complex series of ethical questions. Humans will have to devise novel solutions to biotechnology, just as they have done in earlier scientific and technological revolutions.)

2. **What is the foundation of the biotech revolution?**
(The essence of biotechnology is exploiting genes, a process revolutionized by the 1953 discovery of deoxyribonucleic acid [DNA]. Like fingerprints, no two people have the same genetic characteristics. Once DNA's structure was understood, it became theoretically possible to isolate the genetic codes that control everything from a person's hair color to height to inherited diseases. Laboratory advances in the 1980s made it possible to copy DNA.)

Writing Assignments

1. Once discovered, can technological processes or knowledge ever be suppressed? If not, who or what is responsible to safeguard society from the ill-use of technology?

2. What are some possible dilemmas posed by advances in biotechnology? What are some possible solutions to these dilemmas?

AMERICAN LIVES

Bill Gates: Microsoft's Leader in the Computer Revolution (p. 922)

Document Discussion

1. **What accounts for Gates's early success in the computer business?**
(Gates's keen business sense, ambition, and technical know-how made him a success. He and Paul Allen conceived and built Microsoft through commercial acumen and hard work.)

2. **What accounts for Microsoft's domination of the computer market?**
(The most important factor in Microsoft's success has been marketing. Experts claim that Microsoft's domination is a result not of elegant technology — many believe that Macintosh is superior — but of the ability to get computer manufacturers to use its operating systems. The hype that accompanied the release of each operating system is an example of Microsoft's marketing approach.)

Writing Assignments

1. Compare and contrast Microsoft with other major corporations that influenced the nation's economy in the past, for instance Standard Oil, Union Pacific, or

Ford. Do such business giants appear in every era? Have they been "good" or "bad" for America?

2. How important are technology companies like Microsoft to America's economy today? Does the "high-tech" industry contribute to America's international influence in any way?

AMERICAN VOICES

Laurie Ouellette: A Third-Wave Feminist (p. 926)

Document Discussion

1. **Why, at first, did Ouellette fail to identify with feminism?**
(Like many women of her generation, Ouellette felt she had inherited a world that had already been enlightened by the feminist struggle. She didn't face any obvious legal barriers to education and political participation, but as she entered the work-place, she began to perceive more subtle forms of sexual discrimination. Ouellette observes that there are many women — the poor, minorities, the elderly — that have yet to fully benefit from the feminist pioneers of earlier generations.)

2. **How does Ouellette accommodate her sister's career choices with the ethos of feminism?**
(Ouellette interprets the new wave of feminism as empowering women to make their own decisions and providing them with appropriate opportunities to live full and balanced lives.)

Writing Assignments

1. Examine the advances gained by feminists after World War II, and contrast those achievements with what feminists won during the last several decades. What are the accomplishments made by each generation? How have men participated in the feminist agenda?

2. Can feminism best be understood as a comprehensive ideology applicable only to women, or is it an expression of the ideals outlined in the Declaration of Independence? Explain.

AMERICAN VOICES

John Lewis: We Marched to Be Counted (p. 935)

Document Discussion

1. **Lewis makes a number of allegations about the suppression of black voters. Why, does he argue, is**

the right to vote so important for African Americans?

(Lewis reminds us of the incredible struggles blacks waged in order to secure voting rights. Literacy tests and poll taxes disenfranchised blacks long after the Fifteenth Amendment was ratified.)

2. **What positive result does Lewis mention that may occur because of the Florida vote furor?**
(He states that many Americans may be more interested in the process of voting and electing politicians because of the situation in Florida. This could serve to reinvigorate Americans' vigilance regarding civil rights.)

Writing Assignments

1. Lewis's allegations regarding the voting processes in Florida are disputed by many Americans. Explain how Lewis and those who disagree with him come to their different perspectives.

2. Lewis talks about African Americans and the right to vote. How do other ethnic minorities in Florida and elsewhere perceive the process of voting in America?

Skill-Building Map Exercises

Map 31.2: The Collapse of Communism in Eastern Europe and the Soviet Union, 1989–1991 (p. 914)

1. **How did the collapse of communism affect the map of Europe?**
(The collapse of the Soviet empire meant that the states of Eastern Europe that had formerly been satellites within the Warsaw Pact were now freely sovereign. Some states adjusted their borders by uniting, such as East and West Germany. Others split apart like Slovakia and the Czech Republic. A number of the Soviet Republics declared their independence as new states.)

2. **Why did the collapse of the Soviet Union surprise so many observers?**
(Most people believed that the economic and political strains within the Soviet empire would cause at least a significant retraction eventually. However, its rapid and generally peaceful implosion was a surprise. The Soviets had been able to mask many of the ongoing tensions, and accurate assessment by American leaders of Eastern Europeans' desires to be rid of Soviet control was lacking.)

Map 31.3: U. S. Involvement in the Middle East, 1980–2002 (p. 916)

1. **Why does the United States consider the Middle East to be of strategic importance?**
(The Middle East is a highly visible concern of American policymakers for several reasons. The region contains the world's largest deposits of oil, upon which the industrial world depends. It is the scene of ongoing military tension between states, some of which produce powerful military weapons that could threaten Europe. And many Americans value a Judeo-Christian heritage that deems the state of Israel and the holy sites of the Middle East to be important.)

2. **Why has the United States conducted so many military operations in the Middle East since 1980?**
(For the reasons stated above, political leaders consider the Middle East to be vital to American interests and have remained engaged in the region. The presence of American businesses, diplomats, and military contacts has aroused the hostility of Islamic fundamentalists and some rulers of Middle Eastern states who consider the United States to be imposing its will. The result has often been violent confrontation.)

Topic for Research

Feminism in the 1980s

In a widely read 1991 book, journalist Susan Faludi described a powerful backlash against the gains American women had won in the 1960s and 1970s. The media consistently held the women's movement responsible for every ill afflicting modern women — from infertility to eating disorders to rising divorce rates to the "man shortage." According to Faludi, the message that the women's movement was women's own worst enemy and that women were unhappy precisely because they had achieved equality was a myth. Instead, Faludi traced many of American women's problems to the fact that they do not have enough equality.

Use Faludi's thesis as a starting point for an assessment of the women's movement and women's lives in the 1980s and 1990s. Is there a backlash against women? How are women portrayed in the media and popular culture, especially in television, film, popular music, and advertising? Why is feminism often unappealing to younger women? Have we moved into a postfeminist era? What do current debates about reproductive rights, sexual harassment, pay equity, the "glass ceiling," and the "mommy track" tell us about how much equality American women have actually achieved?

In addition to Susan Faludi, *Backlash: The Unde-clared War against American Women* (1991), see Naomi Wolf, *The Beauty Myth* (1991), and Marilyn French, *The War against Women* (1992). Arlie Hochschild, *The Second Shift* (1989), challenges the notion that women can "do it all." Gloria Steinem's revealing memoir, *Revolution from Within* (1992), identifies self-esteem as the key to personal and political change.

How to Use the Ancillaries Available with *America's History*

Refer to the Preface to *America's History* at the front of the book for descriptions of instructor resources, including the Instructor's Resource CD-ROM, Computerized Test Bank, transparencies, and *Using the Bedford Series in History and Culture in the U.S. History Survey*. Student resources, also described in the Preface, include the Online Study Guide and *Documents to Accompany* America's History, a primary-source reader.

For Students

Online Study Guide at bedfordstmartins.com/henretta
Each of the activities listed below includes short-answer questions. After submitting their answers, students can compare them to the model answers provided.

Map Activity
The map activity presents Map 31.6: Ethnic Conflict in the Balkans: The Breakup of Yugoslavia, 1991–1992 (p. 932), and asks students to analyze this complex conflict.

Reading Historical Documents
The document activity provides a brief introduction to the documents Saddam Hussein: Calling for a Holy War against the United States (p. 915) and John Lewis: We Marched to Be Counted (p. 935) and asks students to analyze their content, thinking critically about the sources.

Documents to Accompany *America's History*
Each of the documents listed is introduced by a headnote, which places the document in context, and is followed by questions, which help students to analyze the piece.

Sources for Chapter 31 are
William Greider, *The Education of David Stockman* (1981)
Donald T. Regan, *For the Record* (1988)
George Bush, *Iraqi Aggression in Kuwait* (1990)
David Maraniss, *University Students Reflect on the Gulf War* (1991)
George Gilder, *Wealth and Poverty* (1981)
Jonathan Kozol, *Rachel and Her Children* (1988)
Bill Gates, *Friction-Free Capitalism* (1995)
Proposition 187 (1994)
Peter Applebome, *Anger of the '60s Takes Root in the Violent Right* (1995)
The Contract with America (1994)
Bill Clinton, *State of the Union Address* (1996)
George W. Bush, et al., Petitioners v. Albert Gore, Jr., et al. (2000)
National Security Strategy of the United States of America (2002)

Epilogue: Thinking about Contemporary History (p. 939)

Discussion Questions

1. What are some of the important international and domestic implications of the September 11, 2001, terrorist attacks?

2. How does the war on terrorism differ from more conventional wars the United States has fought in the past? How do wars tend to expand federal power and threaten civil liberties? Give contemporary and historic examples.

3. What are some of the implications of waging war against Iraq? Do you support or oppose the Bush administration's push for war? Why?

4. Discuss the recent crises in the economy, and analyze how they have impacted average Americans.

5. What is America's role in the world today? How has it changed over time? What factors shape the role we play in the international arena?